THE

REPUBLICAN

ESTABLISHMENT

For Vic Gold —

The best thing that ever
happened to the Republican party
and those of us who cover it.

With friendship and admiration,

David S. Broder

Jan. 5, 1968
Washington, D.C.

THE
REPUBLICAN
ESTABLISHMENT

The Present and Future of the G.O.P.

By Stephen Hess *and* David S. Broder

Harper & Row, Publishers
New York, Evanston, and London

FOR OUR PARENTS

at whose dinner tables we first discovered
the fascination of American politics:
Florence Morse Hess and the late Charles Hess
Nina Salzer Broder and Dr. A. I. Broder

FIRST EDITION

LIBRARY OF CONGRESS CATALOG CARD NUMBER: 67-22499

Contents

INTRODUCTION:

THE LUXURY OF CHOICE

"WHAT 1966 has given us," commented Washington's Governor Daniel Jackson Evans at the close of that year, "is the luxury of choice."

Suddenly, a party that had been bereft of leadership appeared to have a wealth of candidates from which to select its 1968 presidential nominee. Its affluence was the direct by-product of the 1966 elections—the victory of Charles H. Percy as Senator from Illinois; the sweeping Republican gain that Governor George Romney paced in Michigan; the election of Ronald Reagan as Governor of California; the renewal of Nelson A. Rockefeller's credentials as Governor of New York; and, not least, the re-emergence of Richard M. Nixon, not only as the busiest Republican campaigner of 1966, but also as the man who most accurately forecast the results.

Dan Evans made his observation at the Broadmoor Hotel at the foot of Cheyenne Mountain in Colorado Springs, where the Republican governors had come in December, 1966, to bask in the glow of their newly-won success.

Two years earlier, a smaller band of G.O.P. Governors had gathered eighty miles north, in Denver, for an appraisal of the 1964 election results. Though close in time and space, politically speaking the Colorado Springs and Denver meetings were aeons apart. In the euphoria of Colorado Springs, it was hard to remember that only twenty-four months before Robert E. Smylie of Idaho, chairman of the Republican Governors Association, had opened the Denver meeting with the words "We are a defeated party with a defeated leadership. We have suffered a defeat as severe in quality and quantity as any that the Republican party has ever sustained."

As Smylie spoke, the dimensions of that disaster were familiar to every Republican. Barry M. Goldwater, the party's nominee, had lost to Lyndon B. Johnson in the greatest popular-vote landslide in American history, 43,128,958 to 27,176,873, carrying only 6 of the 50 states. Republicans also lost 38 seats in the House of Representatives, leaving them with a smaller number—140—than at any time since 1936. In the Senate, the G.O.P. lost 2 seats and was left with only 32, a 24-year low.

The losses multiplied at the lower levels of the ticket. Some 493 seats were washed out in state legislatures across the land; Republicans emerged in control of only 7 of the 50 legislatures. Ravages among the county courthouse and local offices were comparable. The Republican party had almost been pulled up by the grass roots and tossed aside.

Bitterly divided by the quarrels that preceded the Goldwater nomination and that continued unabated after his defeat, the party faced what Robert J. Donovan, the nonalarmist Washington bureau chief of the Los Angeles *Times,* called "one of the worst crises in its entire history."

Smylie, in his talk to the Governors, quoted John Adams' warning: "Once the erosion of power begins, it develops a momentum of its own. Voters generally show a disposition to abandon a sinking politician or a defeated party." The Idahoan, a lover of words, concluded solemnly that rebuilding from the wreckage of 1964 "must seem a desperate task of heroic proportions."

But one midterm election later, to the astonishment of almost everyone in American politics, the "desperate task," or at least much of it, had been accomplished, and the victorious Republican Governors, grown in numbers from 17 to 25, gathered in Colorado Springs in an atmosphere of barely-restrained jubilation. (Smylie was there to preside for the last time as their chairman; ironically, he had been defeated for renomination in July, 1966, to what would have been a record-breaking fourth term, by a Goldwater conservative, Don Samuelson, who was elected in November.) Of the 15 Republican governorships at stake in November, 1966, the party had held all but 2—Maine and Kansas. (Two other G.O.P. Governors were in the midst of their four-year terms.) In addition, they had captured 10 states from the Democrats. Republicans now controlled half of the statehouses, including those in 7 of the 10 most populous states.

Looking to the future, it was not without significance that, with 270 electoral votes needed to win the presidency, the 25 Republican Governors represented states with that number and 23 votes to spare.

The men who gathered at Colorado Springs were attractive, articulate, and of many different types. Nevada's Governor-elect Paul Laxalt was the son of Basque immigrants; the parents of Spiro (Ted)

'DOWN BY THE OLD MAINSTREAM...!'

Crockett, Washington Star, Nov. 10, 1966

Agnew, Governor-elect of Maryland, had come from Greece; Minnesota Governor-elect Harold LeVander's father emigrated from Sweden.

Pennsylvania's Raymond Shafer had been a World War II PT-boat commander with eighty combat missions in the South Pacific. Rhode Island's John Chafee waded ashore with the First Marine Division in the initial landing at Guadalcanal and served again in a front-line rifle company during the Korean war. Both Jack Williams of Arizona and Tom McCall of Oregon had been popular news broadcasters; Winthrop and Nelson Rockefeller, the first "brothers act" since 1851, were the richest men to run for public office in American history. Alaska's first elected Republican Governor, Walter J. Hickel, arrived in Seward in 1940 with thirty-seven cents and proceeded to build a multimillion-dollar construction business. Next to Chafee, the biggest Republican gubernatorial victory (62.6 percent of the vote) was won by John A. Volpe of Massachusetts, whose parents came from the Abruzzi province in Italy, and who once had been a journeyman plasterer.

But the results of 1966 were deeper than top-of-the-ticket victories. The Republicans added forty-seven seats in the U.S. House of Representatives, nearly tripled the number of state legislatures they controlled, captured the legislatures for the first time since statehood in Arizona and Alaska, and won the major contested race in every one of the ten largest states—California, New York, Pennsylvania, Illinois, Ohio, Texas, Michigan, New Jersey, Florida and Massachusetts.

And there was impressive variety to the victories. In Democratic-Caucasian-Catholic Massachusetts, the Republican-Negro-Protestant candidate for the U.S. Senate was elected. In Democratic-Protestant-nativistic Oklahoma, the successful Republican gubernatorial nominee was an outsider from Ohio, a Princeton graduate and a Catholic. The G.O.P. elected a Lieutenant Governor in Arkansas for the first time since the job was created in 1926. He was Maurice (Footsie) Britt, a one-armed Medal of Honor winner and former professional football player for the Detroit Lions.

Nor were the victòries sectional. In the Middle West, where the ravages of 1964 had been heaviest, there were major recoveries in Ohio, Michigan, Iowa, Wisconsin, Nebraska and Minnesota. Volpe and Chafee paced the party in New England, an area of long Republican decline. Southern Republicans won the governorship of Florida for the first time since Reconstruction and made Howard Baker, Jr., the first of his party to be elected by popular vote to the U.S. Senate from Tennessee.

To top it off, perhaps, President Johnson's home state of Texas re-elected its first Republican Senator since 1875, while the voters of Minnesota, where Vice President Humphrey campaigned hard among his neighbors, retired its incumbent Democratic Governor.

Even in the cities—the areas about which National Chairman Ray C. Bliss had been most concerned—Republicans scored impressively. In the 1965 municipal voting, the party elected a Mayor in New York and a District Attorney in Philadelphia, and tallied other gains in smaller communities. In 1966, Baltimore, which had gone Democratic by 63,804 votes in the 1962 Governor's race, turned in a 29,910-vote plurality for the Republicans; Boston, where the 1962 Democratic candidate for Governor built up a 52,289 lead, gave the Republican a 10,063-vote edge in 1966; Romney reduced his Detroit deficit from 207,834 votes in 1962 to 68,382 in 1966; and in Los Angeles, Pat Brown's margin was shaved from 157,076 in 1962 to 54,243 votes in 1966.

While liberal Nelson Rockefeller was winning a third term in New York, conservative Ronald Reagan was returning the California state capitol to the G.O.P. Both the American Conservative Union and the Ripon Society, a liberal Republican group, hailed the midterm election's outcome. Liberal Hugh Scott announced that the 1966 returns gave "new strength to the centrist tradition of our party," and *Human Events,* the right-wing newsletter, wrote of the same results that they revealed "a sharp rise in conservative sentiment around the country."

An off-year election is almost always a collection of localisms that defy pat generalizations. Moreover, it is usually a time to vote against, whether it is against high prices, or against war, or against the President's style. In 1966 the G.O.P. did not give the voters something to be for, but it did give them someone, namely, a set of intelligent and appealing candidates. By and large they were young and good-looking. Michigan, for example, elected Republicans to five additional seats in the U.S. House of Representatives, and the average age of the new Congressmen was thirty-six. After watching the Republicans—Percy, Hatfield, Rockefeller, Romney, Reagan—troop across the TV screen on election night, Mike Royko of the Chicago *Daily News* concluded, "The modern Republican party is probably the handsomest political party in American history."

Yet the election outcome was more than skin deep. For 1966 was pre-eminently a party victory. The best evidence of this came in the finding of a post-election study ordered by the Republican National Chairman from Opinion Research Corporation. It showed that after twenty years of rather steady decline the basic strength of the Republican party, measured by the percentage of voters who identify themselves as supporters of the G.O.P. had turned upward. The gain was modest, from 25 percent to 29 percent, but the trend reversal was almost revolutionary.

As the *nouveau riche* G.O.P. turned its sights on the presidency, it became clear that political prosperity had produced no unanimity on the choice of the 1968 nominee. Romney was the front runner in the public opinion polls, but Nixon was the favorite of the Republican organization men, those who would be the convention delegates. Reagan, Percy and Rockefeller were still on the fringes of the presidential picture as 1967 began.

At the first post-election meetings, the Republican politicians did what politicians always do in an uncertain situation: they retreated into caution, talked vaguely of favorite sons and refused to make any commitments.

The situation was further complicated by the competing ambitions and expectations of those who felt they deserved the second spot on the ticket. In this expanding category of dark-horse, favorite-son, vice-presidential contenders were, at least:

—Governor *James A. Rhodes* of Ohio, the tough-talking, independent apostle of economic development, who led a second-term landslide in 1966 that was even more awesome than his old antagonist Romney's sweep in neighboring Michigan.

—*Warren P. Knowles*, Governor of Wisconsin, a handsome, grayhaired moderate, who also won a second term in 1966 and was moving quietly toward the center of power among the Governors.

—Representative *Gerald R. Ford* of Michigan, the House Republican leader, who survived a shaky first term in that post in the 89th Congress and who was greatly strengthened both in confidence and power by the 1966 gain of forty-seven seats. Ford, though limited by the presidential ambitions of home-state Governor Romney, did nothing to discourage talk that he would take second place on a ticket with Nixon or someone else, as he stumped ceaselessly for Republican candidates around the country.

—Cincinnati's *Robert Taft, Jr.*, the fourth-generation Republican who lost a Senate bid in the 1964 Goldwater débacle but regained his political footing by taking the most-publicized congressional contest of 1966, a hard-fought and narrow victory over freshman Democrat John J. Gilligan.

—Tall, handsome *John A. Love* of Colorado, a second-term Governor, who succeeded Smylie as head of the Republican Governors Association in 1967 and proceeded to use the position to enhance his national prestige in the party.

—Kentucky gentleman *Thruston B. Morton,* long prominent in party affairs as a former national chairman, who surprised old friends in 1967 by suddenly stirring himself as the leader of the growing band of moderate Republicans challenging Minority Leader Everett McKinley Dirksen for control of G.O.P. policy in the Senate.

—Mayor *John V. Lindsay* of New York, the glamorous liberal who gave the G.O.P. its first big win after the 1964 disaster. By 1967, Lindsay was beginning to emerge from the rigors of his struggle with metropolitis and was creeping back into Republican conversations as a candidate with magic appeal to youth, to minorities, and to big-city voters.

—Another New Yorker, Senator *Jacob K. Javits,* the probable "favorite son" of the biggest convention delegation, a brainy, hardworking and controversial figure, deadly serious about gaining the distinction of being the first Jewish Vice President.

—The three-term Governor of the Commonwealth of Massachusetts, *John A. Volpe,* a hard-headed businessman, ambitious to assemble a bloc of New England votes which could make him a logical running mate for a Midwestern or Western presidential nominee.

—*Edward W. Brooke* of Massachusetts, elected in 1966 as the first Negro U.S. Senator since Reconstruction. A smooth, plausible, progressive Republican whose nomination for Vice President would demonstrate the inclusiveness of the new Republican appeal.

—The new Senator from Oregon, *Mark O. Hatfield*, a former two-term Governor and the 1964 convention keynoter. The blacksmith's son who became a college professor offered the ticket fixers a bundle of attractive traits—youth and experience, liberalism and party loyalty.

—From the Lone Star State, Senator *John G. Tower*, the "little giant" of Lyndon Johnson country and G.O.P. favorite-son candidate of Texas and other Southern states for Vice President. Tower was an all-the-way Goldwater man in 1964, but his successful re-election campaign in 1966 showed him a skilled, pragmatic politician who was able to subdue ideology to necessity, a task he appeared willing to undertake again in 1968 if someone invited him onto the ticket in a bid for Southern support.

—The Republican Governor of the most Democratic state in the North, *John H. Chafee* of Rhode Island, a third termer whose quiet

Basset, Washington **Daily News,** Nov. 9, 1966

charm, Yankee honesty and efficient administration could serve as a model for a party that had to make converts to succeed.

—*Daniel J. Evans* of Washington, the author of the "luxury of choice" phrase and himself an example of its meaning, a civil engineer and legislator who, in 1964 at the age of thirty-nine, became the youngest Governor in his state's history, on a nonideological "blueprint of progress" platform. As much as any Republican in the country, Evans represented the problem-solving philosophy that was the common bond among the new G.O.P. leaders.

The list of Republican hopefuls was another example of the party's embarrassment of riches. Its political proliferation had produced two names each from Ohio, Michigan and Massachusetts and three from New York—not counting Richard M. Nixon, who slept there but did his political work elsewhere. Each of them may well have had in the back of his mind the knowledge that James K. Polk went to the 1844 Democratic convention seeking the vice-presidential nomination, and, after the three serious candidates had killed one another off, emerged as his party's standard-bearer.

Aside from the wealth of candidates, the most striking fact about the Republicans as they prepared for the 1968 campaign was their widespread expectation of victory. Their 1966 successes had persuaded party members at all levels that the presidency could be won.

Republicans knew as well as anyone that only twice in this century had the American voters turned out an incumbent President seeking another term. But they listened, too, when Theodore C. Sorensen, President Kennedy's alter ego and a ranking Democratic intellectual, pointed out that most Presidents who come to office in midterm, as Lyndon Johnson had, did not seek election in their own right more than once.

If President Johnson was going to defy this tradition and try his luck again, as every sign indicated in 1967, the Republicans were ready for him. They had read the fever charts—the midterm election returns and the continuing public-opinion polls—and most of them were convinced that politically the President could not recover.

He was conducting an unpopular, indecisive war in Vietnam, a conflict which had begun long before he became Chief Executive but which was identified in the public mind as essentially a Johnson enterprise.

The growing financial drain of Vietnam was choking his domestic programs and straining the economy, whose steady growth for six years had been the Democrats' greatest achievement and their strongest political asset. In 1966, the Republicans benefited from public resentment of a long-delayed but painfully-experienced period of inflation and high interest rates. In 1967, there was worry about recession, then worry about a massive budget deficit.

The President's habit of shielding all his decisions from public scrutiny and his frequent efforts to disguise what everyone knew to be unpleasant truths had made the "credibility gap" a nationally-understood phrase.

Suddenly it seemed the elements of the "Roosevelt coalition" that had made the Democrats the majority party for most of four decades were in conflict with each other. The promise of rapid strides toward a social Utopia, which seemed to be offered by the "Great Society" legislative program of 1965-66, had not yet been redeemed. In the rank ghettos of the big cities frustration grew, and was vented, in part, by the increasingly independent voting of Negroes, who had been for thirty years the Democrats' most reliable source of support. On the other hand, in the Polish and Irish working-class wards and in the white suburbs, resentment against the President's advocacy of open housing and school integration measures put Democratic candidates in a crossfire of criticism.

The "Solid South" was anything but solid. Chunks of it had broken off in 1960 and 1964. A nominal Democrat, George Wallace, the former Governor of Alabama, was cranking up a third-party presidential campaign for 1968 that promised to be far more disruptive than his abortive 1964 foray into the presidential primaries. Though Wallace almost certainly would cost the Republicans votes in the South, he might damage the Democrats in the vital industrial states of the North.

Many of the intellectuals to whom the Democratic party had been a haven since the New Deal were now leading the criticism of a Democratic President, chiefly because they disagreed with his policy on Vietnam. Among many young people who had savored the special grace of John F. Kennedy, the middle-aged cornponealia of Lyndon B. Johnson was regarded as an unfunny joke. The leaders of organized labor were still solidly in the President's camp, but there was increasing evidence that they were out of touch with their own rank-and-file members, who, now prosperous, were acquiring the same racial and economic attitudes as their suburban neighbors.

Factional squabbling between Democratic Senator Robert F. Kennedy and his adherents and the supporters of President Johnson had become more public and more bitter, as New York's junior Senator joined the Vietnam critics in early 1967. The same factionalism could be found in almost all the major states from New York and Pennsylvania through Ohio and Michigan to California and Texas, and in the great cities like Philadelphia, Cleveland and Los Angeles, where Democratic Presidents normally find their victory margins.

The national party machinery was allowed by the President to rust from disuse for more than two years after his 1964 victory until he finally heeded the danger signals and ordered the Democratic National Committee to step up its efforts in 1967. But by that time the rejuvenated Republicans were ahead in campaign funds, in organization, and, most of all, in the bright new faces that attracted support in an increasingly-youthful electorate.

The many points of the President's vulnerability, no less than the multiplicity of available Republican candidates, made the choice of a G.O.P. strategy and a G.O.P. ticket for 1968 far more complicated than is usually the case for an opposition party. Republicans could, and did, argue far into the night about whether the winning margin for 1968 could most likely be pried out of the once-Solid South or out of the Negro ghettos in the North; out of the ethnic blocs of New England or the open spaces of the West; by an avowed conservative or an avowed liberal or someone who defied any categorization; by a new face or a man of experience; by emphasizing Vietnam or by emphasizing domestic issues. Whether the Republicans' confidence was justified was, in one sense, irrelevant; the mere expectation of victory in itself altered the whole psychological climate of internal Republican politics from what it had been going into the 1964 election. The 1968 nomination was not one to be thrown away, by neglect or by bitter intraparty warfare. The Republicans were looking for a winner.

I

The Power Centers

1 OFFICE HOLDERS, PAST AND PRESENT

NO TWO presidential campaigns are ever the same. The cast of characters changes; so do the circumstances and the issues. But, just as every presidential election is a stop-action photograph of a nation at a moment of history, so does each contest for a party's nomination lay bare the network of forces within the party.

Frequently, this underlying pattern is obscured by the oratory and drama of the battle, by the trail of presidential primaries leading to the last climactic call of the roll. But, when the final shred of confetti has been swept away, the victor cheered and the vanquished consoled, what endure are the same power centers that were there before. Only their relationships will be altered; some will have gained influence and some will have lost.

These power centers form the candidates' constituency as the choice for President is narrowed from two hundred million to two. Only after they have acted will the vote of every American truly become of equal weight. For, until the nomination, there are men of power and position who are "more equal" than others. Some of these weighty men are office holders, past or present: titular leaders, Governors, Senators, Representatives, party officials. To the public mind, their speeches and acts also give the parties a point of view, a record, an image. Some are more shadowy figures who never command headlines: financiers and operators, intellectuals and promoters. They feed the money, ideas and technical skills into the body politic. These groups, the front men and the backstage figures, are the holders of power which will be translated into the nominations. So, although this constituency is small, perhaps no more than five thousand, it must be carefully courted and cultivated by the candidates until such times as the conventions' permanent chairmen announce the identity of the men who will be their parties' national tickets.

The last time the Republican party faced a real battle for its presidential nomination in a year when the winner might well become President was in 1952, when Dwight D. Eisenhower and Robert A. Taft were the main contenders. Let us begin, then, by comparing the alignment of power centers within the party in 1952 and 1968.

The Titular Leader. The Sage of Baltimore, H. L. Mencken, once proposed "that all unsuccessful candidates for the presidency be quietly hanged, lest the sight of their grief have a very evil effect upon the young." But instead of instant dispatch the American people chose for Thomas E. Dewey after 1948 and Barry M. Goldwater after 1964 what some would call a crueler fate—the protracted political purgatory that is known as the titular leadership.*

Dewey had lost twice for President and was barred from further consideration as a candidate; even worse, his second defeat, in 1948, came in a campaign that most Republicans believed he should have won. His repudiation by the Taft conservatives who seized control of the national chairmanship after the election was complete. Yet Dewey in 1951 and 1952 was able to take charge of the Draft-Eisenhower movement and push it through to victory. This feat was possible because he retained a base of political power—the governorship of the nation's largest state, New York, to which he was re-elected in 1950. He also commanded the most effective political force in the G.O.P., that combination of big money, mass-media influence and organizational skill in nominating conventions that is called the "Eastern Establishment."

* There has never been even the suggestion of a place in the party's power structure for the defeated vice-presidential nominee—"the most forgettable role in American public life," in the opinion of New York *Times* reporter Warren Weaver, Jr. After the 1964 loss, William E. Miller returned to a corporate law practice in Buffalo, New York. "I was going to retire from politics anyway," he recalls, "and I just did it a little more prominently than I had planned." His place in the political hierarchy of his home state was perhaps best illustrated when he announced his endorsement of Nelson Rockefeller's re-election in 1966. This prompted Jackie Robinson, the former baseball player, to say that if the Governor accepted Miller's support "there's no room for me." Rockefeller called a news conference to announce that he was choosing the Negro athlete over the defeated Republican vice-presidential nominee.

In some ways, Goldwater's position now is stronger than Dewey's was after 1948. He has been defeated only once for the presidency, and that in a year when most Republicans concede defeat was almost inevitable. He was, many would say, more victim than aggressor in the savage intraparty warfare that marked his campaign. Positions for which he was ridiculed—a step-up in the Vietnam war, a concentrated attack on "crime in the streets"—have become part of the

'Now, Dasher! Now, Dancer! Now, Prancer and Nixon!
On, Comet! On Cupid! On, Donner and Blitzen!'

Fawcett, Providence **Evening Bulletin**, Dec. 15, 1966

policy of the man who defeated him. To many Republicans, Goldwater seems a martyr whose unjust defeat cries out for vengeance.

But for a variety of reasons, Goldwater's personal influence on the outcome of the 1968 nomination struggle is likely to be minor. Whatever the causes, he led a "defeat in depth" that struck the professionals in his party most cruelly. On June 17, 1964, fifty-four Republican Congressmen signed a manifesto stating, "We are convinced that the nomination of Senator Barry Goldwater will result in substantial increases in Republican members in both houses of Congress." One-third of those optimists were pulled down in the November undertow. Almost five hundred state legislators were defeated. There was hardly a flaming liberal among them. Goldwater's conduct of the campaign came in for serious criticism, even from people who had been on his side. F. Clifton White and Stephen Shadegg, professional political organizers and staunch Goldwater men, both published books faulting his strategy and tactics.* In their hearts the Republican professionals may have known who was right, but his kind of rightness was a luxury they could not afford.

Second, when Goldwater was forced into retreat, it was not, as with Dewey, to a powerful industrial state governorship, but to the role of a private citizen in far-off Phoenix, Arizona. Goldwater retained a newspaper column, but complained himself of its limited readership. He maintained some contact with others in the party, attending meetings of the Republican Coordinating Committee in Washington and engaging in a busy correspondence from his home. Yet there were few requests for his help in the campaign of 1966. Even Ronald Reagan, regarded by many as his disciple, asked him to stay out of California, which Goldwater did. In Mississippi, where he was asked in, party leaders found his comments on integration more of an embarrassment than a help.

Third, Goldwater's own interests centered increasingly on his home state of Arizona. Soon after his presidential defeat, he made it clear that his chief political goal was to return to the place in the Senate he yielded in 1964 when he ran against Lyndon Johnson. He announced plans to oppose aged Democratic Senator Carl Hayden in 1968. Hayden had gone to Washington as Arizona's first Congressman while William Howard Taft was in the White House. His precarious health required Goldwater to be ready for a special election at any time. (Arizona law forbids the Governor to appoint a Senator if a vacancy occurs.) So he concentrated his time on Arizona politics, helping the Republicans win a major victory there in 1966 but also probably further diminishing his impact on national party affairs.

Fourth, Goldwater, even had he been ambitious for national influence, would have been forced to share his role as titular leader with two other men. On the symbolic level, there was the Republicans' last presidential winner, Dwight D. Eisenhower, a benevolent

---

* See F. Clifton White, *Suite 3505: The Story of the Draft Goldwater Movement* (New Rochelle, N.Y.: Arlington House, 1967); Stephen Shadegg, *What Happened to Goldwater?* (New York: Holt, Rinehart & Winston, 1965).

if somewhat erratic father figure. The old general was hard to gauge as a political force and even harder to predict. In 1964, when he was badly whipsawed by friends and opponents of Goldwater, he ended as a study in futility, blessing a candidate the best evidence indicates he never wanted to see win. In declining health, Eisenhower seems likely to have an even more marginal role in 1968, though all prospective candidates for the nomination paid regular courtesy calls on him, hoping for an endorsement that is still a prize worth coveting.*

On the operational level, Richard M. Nixon has functioned as the surrogate Goldwater. It was he who bore the brunt of the national campaigning for Republican candidates in 1966, he who made the response for the party to President Johnson's only partisan appeal of the campaign. More than any other politician, Nixon always has had two distinct roles—the public one (Congressman, Senator, Vice President) and the semiprivate one (Republican spokesman). When election defeats ended the influence that flowed from public position, he seemed to intensify his self-imposed party duties—giving himself a sort of permanent *ex officio* titularity, as well as keeping open an avenue to power and publicity.

Goldwater's remaining possibility of exercising substantial influence at the 1968 convention lies in "the foot troops," as Robert D. Novak called them, who in 1964 "swarmed into precinct meetings from Seattle to Atlanta to take over the Republican party."† He was their symbol and their hope in 1964, but he was not their organizer.

---

* President Eisenhower's relations with the party and its key leaders are unofficially handled by Bryce N. Harlow, fifty-two, Washington representative for Procter & Gamble. The diminutive, soft-spoken Harlow is one of the most influential and least-known figures in the G.O.P. He came to Washington in the late thirties from Oklahoma to work for his home-town Congressman and stayed on to become a chief congressional lobbyist for the Army during World War II and the staff director of the House Armed Services Committee after the war. With the advent of the Eisenhower Administration he joined the White House staff as a speechwriter and congressional liaison officer, eventually heading the President's congressional-relations section. In the course of three decades in the capital, Harlow has become the trusted confidant of virtually every Republican who is now in a position of responsibility. So besides his role as Eisenhower's spokesman, he is constantly on call to offer words of advice to party leaders and is regularly invited to take part in such top meetings as those of the Republican Coordinating Committee and the Joint Senate-House Leadership.

† See Robert D. Novak, *The Agony of the G.O.P. 1964* (New York: Macmillan, 1965), p. 468.

F. Clifton White, who made them an effective political force, is still active in Republican politics, but he remained uncommitted on his 1968 presidential preference long after Goldwater endorsed Nixon. White himself is not certain what has happened to the Goldwater foot troops or how many of them would respond to another call to arms. There is a higher rate of turnover among convention delegates than most people realize. Goldwater said in March, 1967, that about 60 percent of the 1968 delegates would be "the same guys" who favored him in 1964. Republicans for Progress, an organization which operates on the non-Goldwater flank of the party, agreed with this estimate in its April, 1967, newsletter. Yet from 1944 through 1964, there was no G.O.P. convention in which as many as one-fourth of the delegates and alternates were either delegates or alternates at the previous convention. In 1968, if normal patterns hold, the number of "repeaters" from Goldwater's year will be between 21 and 24 percent.

The Senate Leadership. If the power of the party's titular leader is a chancy affair, dependent on his personality, his home base and the circumstances of his defeat, that of the out party's congressional leaders is almost guaranteed to endure, having been institutionalized through long evolution. The history of the Republican party can almost be described adequately in the recurring collisions between its conservative congressional wing and its more progressive Governors.

Superficially, the 1968 lineup between Nixon, with his close ties to the congressional wing, and Romney, the most prominent of the Governors, has the earmarks of the same battle that pitted the pro-Eisenhower Dewey forces against Senator Taft in 1952. But there are important differences within the congressional leadership that need to be noted.

First, in the Senate, the most obvious difference is one of numbers. Going into 1952, Republicans had forty-seven Senators, two short of a majority; on the eve of 1968, they have just thirty-six. Also in 1952, the power of the Senate was concentrated behind one of its own—crusty, intellectual Robert A. Taft, who had become Mr. Republican to millions, not only because of his role as the pre-eminent arbiter of party policy but because of his smashing re-election victory over organized labor's opposition in 1950. Arrayed with him were such other senatorial powers as New Hampshire's Styles Bridges, Colorado's Eugene Millikin and Wisconsin's Joseph R. McCarthy.

Going into 1968, the Senate leadership lacked both a candidate from its own ranks and the kind of muscle that could make him a formidable contender. Minority Leader Dirksen's prestige in the party generally is probably second only to General Eisenhower's,

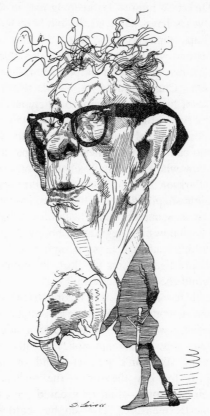

SENATOR EVERETT McKINLEY DIRKSEN

Levine, Washington **Post,** Jan. 4, 1966

but age, illness and the scars of a variegated career have removed him from the area of presidential contention. "That boat," he mellifluously intones, "left the dock a long time ago."

Everett McKinley Dirksen, now seventy-one, has come a long way from the 1952 convention, when a startled television audience watched him point to Governor Dewey and say, "Tom, you led us

to defeat in 1948, don't lead us down the road to defeat again."
Part of the difference is that his elevation to Senate leadership in
1959 gave Dirksen the stage, the scope and the prominence to develop
his unique style of political leadership. It is a style that sometimes
serves his party's interest, sometimes serves his nation's interest, but
always serves Dirksen's interest by keeping him in the spotlight.

The passing years have removed the binds of ambition for higher
office and perhaps replaced them with a sense of history—or at
least of how history will remember him. Also, the contrast with a
younger, housebroken generation of politicians has underscored the
charm of Dirksen's Chautauqua style, a style that resists being cloy-
ing only because of his ability to wink publicly at himself. Indeed, as
Washington observer Milton Viorst has pointed out, Dirksen has
"mastered the technique of translating style into power." He is the
only Senator who can pack the galleries for a speech on the marigold
and one of the few who can actually change votes with a speech. To
his colleagues, Dirksen is more than an entertainer and more than
the kind and gentle shepherd he is. Dirksen is also one of the hardest-
working Republican Senators, a man who *always* has done his homework, who *always* knows the legislative booby traps camouflaged in
the harmless-looking language in paragraph 2 a (1). As a result of
his position, his prestige and his intellect, Dirksen's influence in the
Senate goes beyond the Republican ranks.

It is the use he has made of this incomparable influence that has
made him almost as controversial as he is popular. He has arranged
a unique relationship with the last two Democratic Presidents, supporting them generally on foreign policy (unlike Taft, who fought
many of President Truman's policies) and on notable occasions
mustering support for key measures—the nuclear test-ban treaty,
the UN bonds, for example—that they could not put through themselves. On domestic measures, Dirksen has battled the Democrats
often, balked them sometimes (as with the repeal of Taft-Hartley
Section 14b), and sometimes yielded gracefully and eloquently (as
with the Civil Rights Act of 1964) after sufficient courtship and
concession.

But Dirksen's course is chartable only by Dirksen, and the vagaries
of his positions have left some Republicans disillusioned. He has
made a personal crusade of reversing the Supreme Court decisions
on prayer in public schools and one-man, one-vote apportionment of

legislatures. Younger Republicans have found themselves uncertain from day to day whether Dirksen will be animated by his notion of the national interest, the party interest or the home-state interest, or will simply want to be amusing for the television camera focused on his rumpled visage. In 1967, Senator Thruston B. Morton of Kentucky, hitherto a loyal Dirksen lieutenant, organized support among young moderates for a deliberate campaign to reduce Dirksen's dominance of the Senate—and, not incidentally, the likelihood that he will influence another convention choice, as he did in 1964 when he agreed to nominate Barry Goldwater. What role Dirksen will play in 1968 is uncertain, but he is up for re-election himself and that, more than anything Morton might contrive, may inhibit him from exercising his full potential influence at the convention.

Nor are the men around Dirksen as intellectually formidable as Millikin, as shrewd in the manipulation of power as Bridges or as politically potent as McCarthy, in 1952 at the height of his power. John Tower of Texas and John Williams of Delaware are conservatives with brains and tenacity. But many of Dirksen's troops are men of ponderous mentality and a remarkable lack of political charm.

Even in Taft's day, there were divisions among the Senate Republicans, but the liberal forces, led by Henry Cabot Lodge, who managed the Eisenhower nomination, were even more submerged than they are going into 1968. The 1968 liberals—men like Thomas H. Kuchel of California and Hugh Scott of Pennsylvania—may not have been more blessed with parliamentary skill or courage, but they represent a larger slice of the group, perhaps as many as fifteen of thirty-six, and, more important, can claim that the political trend is moving their way.

For the greatest difference between the Senate Republicans of 1952 and those of 1968 is in the character of the new members, the latest to gain admission to the club. In 1951, the Senate added eight new Republicans, of whom six, Nixon, Dirksen, Francis Case of South Dakota, Wallace Bennett of Utah, John Marshall Butler of Maryland and Herman Welker of Idaho, were conservatives; and two, Frank Carlson of Kansas and James H. Duff of Pennsylvania (both ex-Governors, non-coincidentally), were on the liberal side.

In 1967, by contrast, five new Republicans came to the Senate; two of them are from the liberal edge of the party, Mark Hatfield of

Oregon and Edward W. Brooke of Massachusetts; one is a Southern moderate, Howard Baker, Jr., of Tennessee; one is a classic Western conservative, Clifford P. Hansen of Wyoming. And one is the only real presidential contender in the chamber, Senator Charles H. Percy of Illinois, who claims the title of progressive.

The House Leadership: As to the House of Representatives, the Republicans' numerical strength going into 1968 was far more nearly on a par with 1952 than was the case in the Senate. Thanks to the sweeping midterm comeback in 1966, House Republicans held 187 seats, only 12 less than they had in 1952. Moreover, the House contingent had considerably more cohesiveness and self-consciousness as a political force than it had sixteen years earlier.

The Republican minority leader in 1952 was the venerable Joseph W. Martin, Jr., of Massachusetts, already sixty-eight years old. He would be the neutral chairman of the convention, although he was suspected of being a Taft man (at least his alternate, Cape Cod publisher Basil Brewer, voted for Taft while the heavy majority of Massachusetts delegates went to Eisenhower). The other two principal figures in the House Republican leadership were whip Leslie C. Arends of Illinois and Assistant Minority Leader Charles A. Halleck of Indiana. Arends was an inconspicuous member of his state's pro-Taft delegation. Halleck, an Eisenhower supporter, held so fragile a position that the Taft men who controlled Indiana denied him membership in the convention delegation.

Thus the role of the House Republicans in 1952 was not overly impressive. In a battle between the Governors' candidate and the Senate's, they stood on uncomfortable middle ground. Halleck and another Representative, Walter Judd, were on the list of possible vice-presidential nominees, but in the end Eisenhower chose Senator Nixon for the post.

The 1968 Republican leadership in the House is like that of 1952 in one respect: there is no single commanding figure. Arends alone has survived the successive waves of revolution, his white hair, leathery face and lean, long figure still familiar. But his politics are, if anything, more constricted than ever. He has his cronies and he has his pet issues and, as he proved more than once, he has the ability to survive.

Yet the leadership and initiative have moved elsewhere, specifically to a group of activists, in their forties or early fifties, who in a series of coups between 1959 and 1965, ousted first Martin and then Halleck from the minority leadership. When the shuffling was finished, Gerald R. Ford, Jr., of Grand Rapids, Michigan, was the Minority Leader and Melvin R. Laird of Marshfield, Wisconsin, was in the number-two job, chairman of the Republican Conference. Aligned with them, in varying degrees of closeness were Charles E. Goodell of New York, John J. Rhodes of Arizona, and Arends.

The principal figures in the group, Ford and Laird, were as conservative as Midwestern Republicans are traditionally supposed to be. But they were also young men of boundless ambition and energy, dissatisfied with Martin's feebleness and later with Halleck's acerbic negativism toward all Democratic proposals.

The revolution that put them in power was not a revolution of ideas but one of generations, reflecting the fact that when the toll was counted after the heavy Republican losses of 1958 and 1964, only 89 of the 187 Republicans in the 90th Congress (1967-68) had started their service before 1962. Ford had come in 1949 and Laird in 1953, but their ambitions pointed them in the same direction and, for a time at least, made them allies.

The House Minority Leader was born Junior King in Omaha. His parents were divorced when he was two and his mother took him to Grand Rapids, where she married a highly respected paint manufacturer (and Republican county chairman), Gerald Rudolph Ford, who adopted the boy and gave him his name. Young Jerry was never a great student, but he was an Eagle Scout, a football hero, and a ruggedly handsome, reddish-blond six-footer. (Lyndon Johnson, who detests Ford, has been known to refer to him privately as "the pretty boy.") He played center on the University of Michigan championship teams of 1932 and 1933, and was voted most valuable player in 1934, when the squad won only one game while scoring 21 points all season. Ford turned down pro offers from the Green Bay Packers and the Detroit Lions to enter Yale Law School, earning his way as junior varsity football coach and freshman boxing coach.* After forty-seven months on active naval duty during World War II, Ford

---

* He also was a classmate of Sargent Shriver, Senator Peter Dominick (R., Colo.), Governor Raymond P. Shafer (R., Pa.), Representative Peter Frelinghuysen (R., N.J.), and Supreme Court Justices Potter Stewart and Byron White.

and—to the extent practicable—tries to enforce party positions on specific items of legislation that come before the House.

Fourth and youngest of the quartet is forty-one-year-old, cigar-smoking Charles E. Goodell of Jamestown, New York, in the southwestern corner of the state. Goodell, a Phi Beta Kappa from Williams College and, like Ford, a Yale Law School graduate, did not come to the House until the spring of 1959, when he won a special election to fill a vacant seat. He joined Bob Griffin on the Education and Labor Committee, where he has made an expert reputation on manpower training and antipoverty legislation, and very quickly became part of the inner circle steering Ford toward the leadership. Though he is as conservative as his leader, his lack of seniority and the accident that his district is in New York still make him somewhat suspect to the rank-and-file of older Midwest conservatives.*

Relationships among the House Republican leaders are tinged with jealousies and tensions. After his own election as leader, in a close fight with Halleck, Ford tried to replace Arends as whip, but failed. He would have preferred Goodell to Rhodes as Policy Committee chairman, but was unable to swing that post either, and was forced to create a new title—chairman of the House Republican Committee on Planning and Research—to give Goodell leadership status. For most of his first two years as leader, Ford was forced to keep looking over his shoulder at Laird, who frequently behaved as if he, not Ford, were calling signals for the minority. But since the 1966 election strengthened the ranks of House Republicans so dramatically, Ford

---

* A fifth member of the House G.O.P. leadership is Representative Bob Wilson of San Diego, fifty-one, chairman since 1961 of the National Republican Congressional Committee, an organization—now in in its 101st year—which maintains a staff of forty in the Congressional Hotel across the street from the offices of the House of Representatives. In election years the committee spends some $2 million, partly for direct contributions to G.O.P. candidates, partly for a wide variety of campaign services. Its highly professional staff can provide a Congressional candidate with designs for brochures and letterheads, the voting record of a Democratic incumbent, a speech kit on the issues of the day, or a photographic record of a visit to Washington.

On the other hand, the G.O.P.'s campaign organization in the Senate, the National Republican Senatorial Committee, has always preferred to distribute its funds directly to the candidates rather than to provide elaborate services. Therefore it operates with a skeleton staff under the chairmanship of freshman California Senator George Murphy, sixty-four, who proved his mettle as a national politician by outmaneuvering Hugh Scott for the job in January, 1967.

majority that this accusation would be thrown at them. And it was when, in May, 1967, the House handed Johnson his first major setback of the year by voting to cut off funds for the rent-supplements program. Predictably, the Democratic National Committee rushed out a press release attacking those "who voted to let our cities drown in their present ills." But a week before the vote, Ford moved to blunt the attack by announcing a political strategy that was the very opposite of the "conservative coalition" tactics of the 1940's and 1950's. At the start of the session he had said in a major speech, "By definition, a coalition requires advance consultation and ultimate compromise of conviction to win a legislative victory. Republicans will make no such deals." At Bowling Green University in May, he went a step further and outlined what he called "my Southern strategy":

> The strategy is to drive Southern Democrats in the House into the arms of the Administration—where they belong—on votes that will hurt them in their home congressional districts. This strategy runs exactly counter to the old pattern of a Southern Democrat-Republican coalition that often prevailed over Administration forces in the House in years past. But I think it is far better to lose a few legislative battles and win the next election.

When Ford talks about winning the next election, his chief goal is gaining the majority that would make him Speaker of the House. But neither he nor Laird is unmindful that the record they write will also be of vital importance to the 1968 presidential candidate. As activists, Ford and Laird depart from the traditional view of House leaders of both parties that nothing outside that chamber compares in power, pleasure or rewards to the prizes that lie within. Both men turn naturally to the arena of nominating-convention politics. It was typical of the differences in their makeup that Ford in 1960 and 1964 went to the conventions seeking the vice presidency and failed, while Laird, choosing the platform committee as his arena, sought power and gained it.

Both Nixon and Goldwater had Ford on their lists of "eligible young men," and the Michigan Congressman was armed in both Chicago and San Francisco with a lawyer's opinion that he could accept the vice-presidential nomination without giving up his candidacy for a safe seat in the House. But in 1960 and 1964 he had no cause to take the legal ruling out of his wallet.

On the other hand, Laird was named vice chairman of the 1960 platform committee at Nixon's request. When a battle erupted in Chicago after the secret Nixon-Rockefeller meeting, platform committee chairman Charles H. Percy panicked. A dilettante in politics at that point, Percy was powerless to stem the revolt against the "Compact of Fifth Avenue," and it was left to Laird to assuage the conservative committee, while getting it to accept Nixon's demands.

Always inventive of institutional arrangements that suit his political needs, Laird moved from his impressive performance in Chicago to the chairmanship of a committee of G.O.P. House and Senate members that drafted a "statement of Republican principles" for the 1962 campaign. That job, in turn, made him an obvious choice to head the 1964 platform committee, a post to which Republican National Chairman William E. Miller was only too glad to appoint him. Laird's exploitation of these opportunities is significant only because it shows how the thrust of the activist young House Republicans, when ably directed, can carry them to a central power position in convention politics. No House member had been head of the platform committee in the twentieth century. But Laird wanted to be there and he knew the way.

Laird and Ford are also prepared to make the House group's influence felt in 1968—in the selection of a ticket and in the drafting of a platform. Both have certain home-state political problems, but they do not appear to be insurmountable.

With Wisconsin looming as a likely presidential primary battleground among Nixon, Romney, Reagan and perhaps Percy, Laird must remain on good enough terms with all the contenders to insure that whoever wins will accept him as a member of the delegation. Ford's problem is that his state has in Romney a serious presidential contender and Ford therefore is restricted in his own freedom of political movement. He finessed one embarrassing moment in May, 1967, when the entire Michigan congressional delegation endorsed Romney for President; Ford issued a separate statement praising the Governor but asserting that he must remain neutral in presidential politics because of his role as leader of "all the Republicans" in the House.

Actually, there is every reason to think that Ford, while recognizing the priority that Michigan Republicans attach to Romney's presidential bid, still maintains a lively interest in the vice-presidential nomination for himself. As a result of hs speechmaking for House Republican candidates across the country—166 speeches in 42 states in 1965; 182 speeches in 37 states in 1966; 54 speeches in 20 states in the first half of 1967—his standing and his popularity in the party have grown significantly.

Personal ambitions, philosophical bents and long private association all make it easy for Ford and Laird to favor Nixon for the nomination. Both men have worked closely with him in past campaigns and they are fellow members of the Chowder and Marching Club, a fraternal organzation of present and past House Republicans. They share his hard-line anti-Communism and general domestic conservatism. Moreover, they know that Nixon could do one thing for them which Romney could not: Nixon could reach into Michigan and take Ford as his vice-presidential candidate, thus elevating him and leaving Laird the top Republican in the House.

But Ford and Laird and the House Republicans they represent are also practical men; the opportunities for all of them (and even the chances of political survival for the newer, less secure members) will be greater with a Republican President, so they, too, are making no lasting commitments. But, more unified, more numerous and more ambitious than their Senate colleagues, they look to the 1968 convention as an arena in which they can exert more influence than ever before.

The Governors. The outcome of the 1952 convention was decided, for all practical purposes, when Thomas Dewey went to the National Governors' Conference in Houston on June 29, a week ahead of the convention, and persuaded eighteen of the twenty-three Republican Governors there to endorse the "fair-play" amendment that disqualified the challenged Taft delegates from voting on the test roll calls in the convention. Taft, in his memo analyzing his own defeat, referred time and again to the "pressure of the governors" on the delegates from their states as being one of the decisive factors.

Ever since 1952, the memory of Houston has inspired or haunted the Republican party, depending on which side of the fight you were on.

In 1964, those who had been seeking revenge for twelve years finally had their chance. Another Governors' Conference, this one in Cleveland, saw an attempted power play by the Governors to block the nomination of Goldwater collapse in a tragicomedy of conflicting ambitions, inept communication and bad politics. This humiliation of the Governors was an accurate foretaste of the humiliation their leading members—Romney, Scranton and Rockefeller—received from the booing delegates in San Francisco.

Nonetheless, the Governors survived 1964 better than any other element in the G.O.P. and it was the Governors who took the lead in the dump-Dean Burch movement that broke Goldwater's grip on the party machinery. It was the Governors, too, who scored the major breakthrough in 1966, adding eight new capitols to come back to their 1952 strength of twenty-five. And, finally, it was the Governors who furnished, in the former maverick of the auto industry, George Romney, the early favorite for the 1968 nomination. Were they ready in fact, or just in appearance, to replay an old script? The parallels between 1952 and what 1968 could be expected to yield were striking, on the surface. Sixteen of the twenty-five states with Republican Governors were the same. In both periods, the Governors of New York (Thomas Dewey and Nelson Rockefeller), disqualified from further serious presidential consideration themselves, moved to align the Governors behind the candidates of the progressive wing (Eisenhower and Romney), and counted as potential allies the liberal Republican Governors of such states as Colorado (Dan Thornton and John Love), Maryland (Theodore R. McKeldin and Spiro T. Agnew), Oregon (Douglas McKay and Tom McCall), Pennsylvania (John Fine and Raymond Shafer), Wisconsin (Walter Kohler and Warren Knowles) and Washington (Arthur Langlie and Daniel Evans). In both 1952 and 1968, California's Governors (Earl Warren and Ronald Reagan) were favorite sons and a little more than that, dark-horse prospects in case of a deadlock.

Thus far the parallels, and thus strongly the auguries for another power play by the Republican Governors. But there are important differences, too, that tend to negate such prospects or at least make them more difficult of achievement.

No less than eight of the 1952 Governors were Eastern progressives—Dewey, McKeldin, Fine, John Lodge of Connecticut, Fred Payne of Maine, Sherman Adams of New Hampshire, Alfred Driscoll of New Jersey and Lee Emerson of Vermont. The three Pacific Coast Governors, Warren, McKay and Langlie, were also of that stripe. In 1968, only five of the Republican Governors are Easterners: Rockefeller, Shafer, Agnew, John Volpe of Massachusetts and John Chafee of Rhode Island. Instead of a solid lineup of progressives on the Pacific shore, there are Evans and McCall, who are far outweighed in political influence by the conservative Reagan. Also weighting the Governors to the conservative side is the addition in 1968 of Republicans from two Southern states, Florida and Arkansas, and a border state, Oklahoma, where the basic political climate sets a limit on political liberalism.

Within the Governors' ranks, there is evidence of some reluctance to let the liberal Easterners take command. The Republican Governors Association was reconstituted in 1963, with Robert Smylie of Idaho, a progressive Westerner, as its chairman. Smylie stayed in control for over three years and in all that time insisted on running the association from Boise, rather than staffing a Washington headquarters with men who might come under the sway of the closer-at-hand Eastern Governors.*

When Smylie lost his renomination fight in Idaho in 1966, an open contest developed for the chairmanship of the association. The winner at Colorado Springs in December was John Love of Colorado. The best the Easterners could manage was to make Chafee of Rhode Island vice chairman and the designated successor to Love in 1968.

Not only were the Westerners, particularly the conservatives like Don Samuelson of Idaho, Tim Babcock of Montana and Stanley Hathaway of Wyoming, wary of Eastern control, the Easterners themselves were not blessed with the political savvy that Dewey and his allies brought to the task of running the Republican Governors in 1952. Romney was inhibited by his own presidential candidacy. Rockefeller, despite a personal fortune and a political machine that could have made him the dominant figure in the group, was still suspected by some of playing a presidential game of his own; in any case, his political instincts were nowhere near as sure as those of Dewey. It was hard to imagine him maneuvering eighteen of twenty-three Governors into a decisive bloc as Dewey did on the eve of the 1952 convention.

* On April 28, 1967, the Republican Governors Association finally announced the opening of a Washington office in the same building that houses the Republican National Committee. Run by two experienced New Englanders, Executive Director Richard T. Fleming, thirty-five, an assistant to Elliot L. Richardson when he was Lieutenant Governor of Massachusetts, and Press Secretary James J. Marshall, thirty-seven, a former seminarian who spent five years on the Providence *Journal-Bulletin* before joining Governor Chafee's staff, the association's Washington office received $90,000 from Republican National Committee for its 1967 operations.

An added complication was the presence of Ohio's Governor James A. Rhodes, a complete lone wolf, too big to be ignored but too independent to be anything but a divisive force among the Governors.

So the outline of the struggle, holding it up to the most useful model of the past, looks like this: Titular leader Goldwater in 1968

`FANCY MEETING YOU HERE!'

Crockett, Washington **Star,** May 25, 1966

commands less convention power through normal channels than titular leader Dewey did in 1952. Goldwater endorses Nixon and opposes Rockefeller and Romney, yet his opinions, at least with the professionals, have only minimal political impact. The Senate is still controlled by conservatives, but they now lack depth, both intellectually and politically, while the Senate liberals, greatly increased in numbers over 1952, are inexperienced, or, as in the case of Republican whip Thomas Kuchel, vulnerable at home. The House leaders are shrewd and ambitious, conservative but pragmatic, a force that could go either direction, yet historically of only modest significance in presidential nominating politics. The Republican Governors, representing half the states and seven of the ten most populous, have immense potential, at least one candidate from their own ranks, and several secondary figures of ability. But still, other factors point to the conclusion that they will not exert convention leadership as decisively as they did in 1952.

The biggest difference in the G.O.P. of 1952 and 1968, however, is the two sets of front runners—Eisenhower and Taft, Romney and Nixon. Held up to the nonideological, pragmatic yardstick, Romney is compared to Eisenhower because he is a "winner," his supporters say, a candidate of the minority party who appeals across party lines to Democrats and independents. Like Eisenhower, he is above politics—in part, because his reputation was also founded outside of the political arena. The case for Eisenhower was very strong, and probably decisive. For Romney it is more fuzzy. After all, Ike led a victorious army; Romney's claim to nonpolitical distinction is that he convinced the nation to buy compact cars.

On the ideological, progressive-conservative spectrum, Nixon-Taft and Romney-Eisenhower are equally shaky equations. Nixon was Eisenhower's Vice President for eight years, and, in his Cabinet, sided with the liberal minority—James P. Mitchell (Labor), Arthur S. Flemming (Health, Education and Welfare) and William P. Rogers (Attorney General). On the other hand, Romney runs a progressive state administration, while, at the same time, delivering speeches that mirror the classical economics of Henry C. Simons and Garet Garrett. The prime contenders have their own collections of assets and liabilities, but their basic philosophies may not be so far apart as many of their supporters like to suppose.

In 1968 the Republican party may replay 1952. But there is no Eisenhower. And there is no Taft.

2 THE VIEW FROM 1625 EYE STREET

THE modest wood-paneled office on the second floor of the Cafritz Building at 1625 Eye Street, in downtown Washington, is occupied by a florid-faced, intensely nervous man, who chain-smokes so rapidly that he rarely takes more than three or four puffs from any cigarette before lighting another.

He neither looks nor sounds like a person who has devoted his entire adult life to the manipulation of political power. His natural shyness is heightened by eye trouble that forces him to wear bottle-thick glasses. He can be nearly blinded by television lights or the spotlights that beam down on the head table at a testimonial dinner. His speech has a slight tendency to lisp. He pads around his office in bedroom slippers to ease the excruciating pain of gout. Yet he pushes himself through day after day of sixteen-hour labor, fretting and fussing endlessly over the smallest detail of his job.

This is Ray C. Bliss, fifty-nine, probably the most thin-skinned, excitable operator ever to rise to the top of the political heap. He is chairman of the Republican National Committee.

Considering that his tenure in office coincides with a dizzying rise in G.O.P. fortunes, to the party faithful his surname must have a Restoration Comedy aptness. While under our fragmented system of government no individual is unmistakably the leader of the opposition party, in the period 1965-67, Bliss's share of the burden of leadership was larger than anyone else's.

What makes this surprising is that legally the Republican National Committee, like its Democratic counterpart housed in another anonymous office building a few blocks away, has few responsibilities. Only half kidding, two political scientists said in a scholarly study that "a major purpose of the national committee is to survive"—to provide a measure of continuity so that every presidential campaign does not have to begin completely from scratch.*

It is the national committee that issues the call for the presidential nominating convention, sets its time and place, and apportions the delegate strength among the states. The committee also has the duty to provide whatever degree of interim organization, vitality and leadership its officers can furnish and its contributors can be persuaded to finance.

In fact, it is the chairman and his staff who must seize the reins of power, for the committee in its corporate sense is a creature of intrinsic weakness. There are two members—a man and a woman— from each state, territory and the District of Columbia, elected normally for four-year terms and more frequently chosen from the ranks of the elder statesmen or big contributors than from the state's current political leadership. Republicans also offer bonus seats on the national committee to state chairmen who show their prowess by electing a Governor or Senator or carrying the state for the presidential candidate. But, even with the infusion of practicality that the state chairmen bring, the national committee, with its infrequent meetings (normally only twice a year, for two days at a time), and its cumbersome size, is virtually impotent.†

* Cornelius P. Cotter and Bernard C. Hennessy, *Politics Without Power* (New York: Atherton, 1964), p. 8.

† Former Republican National Chairman Leonard W. Hall has written: "Generally speaking, the chairmanship of the Republican Party is what the person holding the office wants to make of it. The National Committee itself has lost most of the power it once had." Hall cites two reasons for the decline of the committee: (1) the national committeemen have been replaced by the state chairmen as "the dominant political power" within the states; and (2) the national committeemen have lost control of federal patronage to the Congressmen, which, in Hall's opinion, creates the "ridiculous situation" where the only powerful members of the national committee are those from states that never elect Republicans. See James M. Cannon, editor, *Politics, U.S.A.* (Garden City, N.Y.: Doubleday, 1960), p. 117.

Malcolm Moos, an academic political scientist who has also served as Baltimore G.O.P. chairman, adds: "The National Committee, made up of a man and woman from each state, is designed to be separate, but equal, from the real mainstream of the party. It need not be separate, and it's never been equal. By setting a National Committeeman and woman alongside the state hierarchy—Chairman and Vice Chairman—the parties have asked for trouble. If the National Committee representatives go their separate way, they

Nonetheless, although the committee has lost its power, the chairman's job is a post of potential influence and therefore a prize worth fighting for. The pressures that resulted in Bliss's election in early 1965 lay bare much of the internal power structure of the Republican party.

"O. K., YOU'VE HAD YOUR FLING, NOW COME ON HOME!"

Sanders, Kansas City *Star*, Nov. 6, 1964

---

naturally cause friction in the state organization and possibly a useless schism. On the other hand, if they are just puppets of the state chairman or governor, they serve no useful purpose (except to carry a proxy to Washington)." Moos proposes turning the national committee into a "state chairmen's committtee of the whole." See "The President and the Constitution," *Kentucky Law Journal,* Fall, 1959, p. 118.

The story begins in July, 1964, when Barry Goldwater, fresh from his nomination victory, designated a young Arizona attorney named Dean Burch, who had been his administrative assistant in the Senate and later the executive officer of his preconvention campaign, as his choice for national chairman. Burch was chosen to succeed Representative William E. Miller, the vice-presidential candidate, for a very special reason. Next to winning the presidency, the chief goal of Goldwater and his cadre of conservative advisers was to secure control of the party mechanism.

Karl Hess, a member of the Goldwater high command, has written in his account of the campaign that a major factor in Goldwater's decision to run for President was that "if Goldwater could win the candidacy, he would also win control of the Republican National Committee and that this, for the future of the party, would be secondary in meaningfulness only to an electoral victory."*

A second Goldwater aide, Stephen Shadegg, has written that Goldwater was urged by Richard Kleindienst, another campaign lieutenant, to name Bliss as national chairman because "Bliss is the only man who can appeal to the Scranton people, the Rockefeller people, the Lodge people and unite the party." Shadegg says, "Goldwater was deaf to Kleindienst's argument. He believed that Bliss had opposed his nomination and could not be trusted."†

No sooner was Burch installed as chairman by a national committee willing to grant the nominee the traditional prerogative of putting his own man in charge of the campaign than he drastically reshaped the executive committee, dropping progressive Republicans from New York, Michigan, Idaho and other states, and substituting conservatives from Mississippi, Louisiana and Arizona. The Goldwater men dug in for the long pull, ready to resist the ouster attempts they knew would come if Goldwater lost.

Lose he did, more lopsidedly than any of them had thought possible, and the reaction was not long coming. Pennsylvania's Senator Hugh Scott, a progressive, who had been ousted as national chairman himself in the wake of Thomas E. Dewey's 1948 defeat, led the cry for Burch's scalp. The demand was powerfully reinforced in Decem-

---

* *In a Cause That Will Triumph* (Garden City, N.Y.: Doubleday, 1967), p. 135.
† *What Happened to Goldwater?* (New York: Holt, Rinehart and Winston, 1965), p. 172.

ber, 1964, when the Republican Governors met in Denver and called for new leadership that would practice "a policy of inclusion, rather than exclusion."

In their statement, the Governors—led by George Romney of Michigan, Nelson Rockefeller of New York and William Scranton of Pennsylvania, all of whom explicitly demanded Burch's ouster—set themselves flatly against the Goldwater leadership. Their strength was rooted in the so-called "Eastern Establishment," but they had valuable allies among progressively-inclined Governors of several of the smaller Western states, including John Love of Colorado, Robert Smylie of Idaho, Mark Hatfield of Oregon and Daniel Evans of Washington, whose presence in their camp took some of the curse of regionalism off the drive against Burch.

Arrayed against them were Goldwater himself, John Grenier of Alabama, most brilliant exponent of the so-called "Southern strategy," and most of the leaders of the emergent Southern Republican party, who had just proved that it was possible to organize and finance a Republican presidential campaign—if not to win it—without the participation and help of the Eastern Establishment.

The balance of power between these two warring armies was held by three groups: the congressional Republicans and their allies in their home states and districts; the Midwestern party leaders; and Richard M. Nixon.

The congressional Republicans—represented at the Denver Governors' meeting by the chairmen of their semi-autonomous campaign committees, Senator Thruston B. Morton of Kentucky and Representative Bob Wilson of California—first counseled caution against any move to dump Burch.

The two men were typical of the congressional power bloc. Wilson, an advertising man from San Diego and a complete political pragmatist, had gone along joyfully with the Goldwater nomination, believing the Senator would bring in dozens of new Republican congressmen, particularly in the South, whether or not he defeated President Johnson. Morton, a man of wealth and charm, who in 1952 had been an Eisenhower leader in the Taft stronghold of Kentucky, was skeptical at first of his good friend Goldwater's candidacy. But on this issue, as on a good many others, Morton finally took the path of least resistance and followed his leader, Senator Dirksen, into the Goldwater camp.

Now both Wilson and Morton came to counsel against the dump-Burch movement, not so much because they were eager to save Burch as because of their fear of letting the Governors succeed too easily. Wilson and Morton could see all too plainly that if the Governors could remove Burch they could also name his successor—and thus seize control of the party. Wilson and Morton, like the colleagues they represented, were not prepared to yield to anyone the formulation of opposition party policy that traditionally resides with the congressional leadership. So, pleading the need for unity, they threw their diminished weight into the fray.

Nixon, for reasons of his own, took the same go-slow stand in phone calls to Governors in Denver. The former Vice President's motives were clouded, but a reasonable assumption is that he too, like Morton, Wilson and the congressional party generally, feared a complete power coup by the Governors.

But the decisive weight against Burch came from a surprising source: the very conservative heartland of the Republican party, which had at first been so enthusiastic about Goldwater's candidacy. It came, specifically, from Nebraska and from one of the least-known but most influential "insiders" in the party, National Committeeman Donald R. Ross. A man who can make himself inconspicuous in a crowd of three, Ross is one of those Midwest Republicans who are instinctively conservative in their politics but have a healthy desire to win. He had gone along with his state's support of Goldwater, led by Senator Carl Curtis, but was appalled at the conduct of the Arizonan's campaign and at the results. The Middle West was the chief victim of Goldwater's failure. Half of the Republicans' thirty-eight-seat loss in the House came from this region, and seventeen of the nineteen lost seats had been held by conservatives. Here it was no question of ideology; simple political survival required that the Goldwater experiment be liquidated. Thus Ross, joined by Republican leaders from Minnesota, Iowa, Wisconsin, Kansas and Ohio, gave the dump-Burch move the essential conservative base that neither the Eastern Establishment nor the Governors could provide. The Midwesterners also gave it something else: the substitute candidate. Ray Bliss had always been high on the list of likely successors to Burch, but his choice was made inevitable by the vital role his fellow Midwestern conservatives took in tipping the scales against Goldwater's man.

The final acts of the drama were swift and sure. Goldwater tried one last approach, a face-to-face meeting with Bliss at the Senator's Washington apartment, where he attempted to bluff the Ohio chairman out of the race by exploiting his well-known abhorrence of controversy. Goldwater told Bliss he could not win if the fight went to a roll-call vote in the national committee and that Burch would not pull out. Contrary to Goldwater's expectations, Bliss did not buckle; he said he had made a commitment to Ross to let his name go in, and it would stay in.

Then Nixon and others moved to ease Goldwater's predicament. Nixon floated news stories saying the new chairman, if there was to be one, would have to be acceptable to Goldwater. The final face-saving details were worked out by Bliss, Burch and Goldwater at the latter's Phoenix home—Bliss would be elected unanimously at the national committee meeting in January but Burch would not have to move out until April. The Phoenix session was held in a something-less-than-spontaneous atmosphere of good will.

On January 22, 1965, the national committee met in windswept Chicago to perform the necessary rites.

In sum, Bliss's election was a defeat, albeit a disguised one, for the Goldwater cadre's hope for long-term control of the party organization. But it was not a clear-cut victory for any other faction of the party. All the new chairman had was a license to walk the tightrope among conflicting rivalries while trying to rebuild the shattered hulk of the Grand Old Party.

In a curious way, Ray Bliss was uniquely fitted for the task. The circumstances of his election as national chairman paralleled, to a surprising degree, those that surrounded his selection as Ohio Republican chairman sixteen years earlier, in 1949. Harry Truman had carried Ohio over Thomas E. Dewey, and the Republicans lost every statewide race and control of the legislature in 1948. So Senator Robert A. Taft, facing a 1950 campaign that was vital to his future presidential hopes, turned to Bliss, the Summit County (Akron) Republican chairman, to direct the rebuilding job.

Bliss had then been in politics almost half his forty-one years. Starting as a volunteer worker in a mayoral campaign in his home city of Akron while still a student at the University of Akron, he moved slowly up the political ladder from precinct to ward to city to county chairman, while building an insurance business that still provides him an independent income.

The state committee he took over was, he recalls, about as debilitated a political vehicle as could be imagined. "The first package that came in here after I became chairman," he once remarked, "arrived C.O.D. They were going to take out the phones unless I guaranteed the bills myself."

Despite these inauspicious beginnings, Bliss achieved a remarkable record. By the time he yielded the reins as state chairman in 1965, the Ohio Republicans had outscored the Democrats 51 to 20 on statewide races (including three of four presidential elections), 125 to 59 in Congressional battles, 694 to 403 in assembly races and 140 to 87 in state senate contests. And Bliss's record was compiled despite an unhappy adventure with the right-to-work issue in 1958, despite an unbeatable conservative Democrat, Frank Lausche (former Governor and now Senator), and despite Goldwater.

Had it not been for Bliss's personal attributes—the nervousness of manner, prickly personality, low boiling point, and a fear of public controversy that is rare in one so long in politics—he would probably have been national chairman long before 1965. Eisenhower and Nixon both held him in high esteem and Nixon more than once tried to persuade him to take over the job. (So, incidentally, did Barry Goldwater, two years before he rejected him in 1964.) The proposal once was serious enough that Bliss canvassed the leading Republicans whose support he thought essential for success in the job. Governor Rockefeller, then still on the political rise, told Bliss that if he wanted to be chairman he should simply announce his interest. Deeply offended at what he took to be a suggestion that he was acting out of personal ambition, the Ohio leader withdrew his name from consideration and the job went to William Miller, much to Rockefeller's chagrin.

It was not the only time, however, that Bliss had shown himself too proud to fight. In 1958, the leaders of his Ohio Republican finance committee decided somehow that the time had come to have a state right-to-work law. Although himself a Taft conservative, pragmatist Bliss remonstrated and pleaded that a right-to-work initiative on the November ballot would bring a massive turnout by organized labor and sink the whole Republican ticket. The showdown came in the quiet splendor of Cincinnati's Queen City Club, and the money men were adamant. Bliss, true to his personal code, shut his mouth in public and that fall, while the voters were rejecting the right-to-work proposal, the Republican party lost a Governor, a Senator, three Congressmen, and its majority in the legislature.

Again, in 1964, though Bliss opposed Goldwater's nomination, he agreed with Dick Kleindienst, Goldwater's man, to keep hands off the makeup of the Ohio delegation and to take no sides in the national fight for the nomination; in return, Goldwater was to stay out of the Ohio presidential primary. Bliss's goal was to spare his own state organization the agony of a public battle between Goldwater and anti-Goldwater forces. His hope was that the Senator, whose deadly effect on the ticket he well envisaged, would be blocked from the nomination somewhere else.

The strategy collapsed, however, when Governor James A. Rhodes, whose 1962 nomination Bliss had accepted reluctantly rather than risk another internal fight, released his favorite-son delegation to Goldwater on the eve of the San Francisco convention, without a word of notice to the Ohio chairman.

Among other things, the Rhodes action put Bliss's carefully-nurtured senatorial candidate, Robert Taft, Jr., in a spot where he had to vote for Goldwater in San Francisco. In the ensuing campaign, Rhodes, who was not on the ballot himself in 1964, took a complete walkout on Goldwater, shunning him whenever he came into the state. But Taft stuck grimly to the man he had been forced to endorse, and lost the Senate race to the Democratic incumbent, Stephen M. Young, by sixteen thousand votes, while Goldwater was losing Ohio by over one million.

What Rhodes's power play against Taft and Bliss cost Bliss in internal suffering can only be guessed, but once again he raised no voice of public protest and instead tried to salvage what could be salvaged from the wreckage.

The penchant for secrecy and the willingness to keep his word, no matter what the cost, are the qualities that make Bliss a favorite with other organization men. But the fear of public controversy, combined with his intense nervousness, also make Bliss ill equipped to handle the pressures attendant on the national chairmanship. Even before he took the job, one of his close friends remarked, "I'm afraid his enemies will nibble him to death with petty criticism. They'll make him a nervous wreck."

Actually, Bliss's introduction to the job was even rougher than that. The committee staff he inherited from Burch included holdovers from the Goldwater campaign. The tension between them and Bliss's new crew was evident.* Suspicions were not eased when, barely two months after Bliss's formal takeover, Goldwater and Denison Kitchel, his 1964 campaign manager, announced they were forming the Free Society Association, a mass-membership group designed to perpetuate the conservative cause. To Bliss and to many others, it sounded as though a rival Republican organization was being set up under his nose, and, in a rare burst of public anger, he denounced it.

As it happened, virtually the only person left in the finance division of Republican National Committee headquarters was one Frank Kovac, a professional fund raiser who had climbed to prominence and some power by way of the Draft Goldwater movement. Rumors circulated that Kovac or someone was spiriting away to the Free Society Association the committee's list of 1964 contributors.

On the night of June 18, 1965, William Cody Kelly, a wealthy Cincinnatian whom Bliss had brought with him as his executive director, was caught breaking into Kovac's desk. Bliss fired Kelly, who promptly told reporters he had only been following orders. The whole thing would have been ludicrous, had it not been for the fact that it seriously jeopardized Bliss's initial efforts to establish some degree of authority over the chaotic situation he inherited. Only after the laughter had subsided and Kovac had finally left for other pursuits (finance man for William Buckley's New York mayoralty campaign), was Bliss able to begin the kind of rebuilding job he had undertaken in Ohio.

The first step, unsurprisingly, was to secure the party's financial base. As state chairman, he had disciplined Ohio business to believe that its best investment in what he was pleased to call "good government" came not in financing individual candidates on a hit-or-miss

* However, Bliss, like every Republican national chairman since 1949, has had the stabilizing counsel of Albert B. (Ab) Hermann, now fifty-nine, who, at various times, has held such titles as executive director, campaign director, special assistant to the chairman and nationalities director. Hermann has also managed nine successful statewide contests for the U.S. Senate in his native New Jersey and was once an infielder with the old Boston Braves baseball team. Men like Hermann and the late Victor Johnston of Wisconsin, for many years the executive director of the Republican Senatorial Campaign Committee, provide much needed continuity in organizations that usually shed their chairmen at least once every four years.

basis, but in underwriting the G.O.P. Buckeye organization. A separate finance committee, professionally staffed, conducted annual fund-raising drives for the *party,* starting with the "Early Birds," a select circle of big givers who annually underwrote much of the basic operating budget, and extending down through business, community and civic channels in a Community Chest–style appeal that exerted just the right degree of conformist pressure on junior executives and allied professionals to match, on their own scale, what the big boys were doing.

In return, Bliss gave his Ohio financial committee an audited account of where the money went and an annual businesslike budget. He paid out of the $3 million or more collected each year not only the expenses of his own committee, but those of county committees as well. He also provided most of the money for the campaigns of statewide candidates and legislators. That his role as the chief source and allocator of campaign cash gave Bliss remarkable influence on the party went without saying; but over the years he built a reputation with the finance men for successful political investment, and with the candidates for fair-mindedness, that allowed him to preserve and even to expand this power.

Now Bliss set out to duplicate his system at the national level. Burch had left him with a small cash balance (thanks to an election eve surge of contributions to Goldwater that could not be spent) and a more valuable asset in the roster of small contributors. The Republican National Committee had begun a "sustaining member" drive for $10-a-year donors, using purchased mailing lists, in 1962. Goldwater's personal appeal vastly expanded the list of contributors, and, by the time Bliss took over, the Republican National Committee was receiving the bulk of its funds in gifts of $10 or less—the first time this had happened in American party history.

That was about the only useful inheritance Bliss found. Ralph Cordiner, the retired General Electric executive who had been Goldwater's finance chairman, had quit immediately after the election. Kovac was guarding his lists and no money was being raised.

Bliss's first task—and a vital one in his eyes—was to find a new finance chairman whose name and prestige would in itself assure the confidence of the nation's business leadership. He found his man in General Lucius D. Clay, the Berlin airlift commander, who, since his military retirement, had lent his illustrious name to an impressive list of corporate boards. Clay took over the Republican treasury in June. The results were almost immediate. In 1965, the first partial year for the Bliss-Clay team, the Republican National Finance Committee raised $4 million. In 1966, the take was $7.1 million, a record for a midterm election year. And in 1967 Bliss and Clay set their sights on $6.7 million, more than 50 percent above the previous comparable year of 1965.

Bliss has had less success in centralizing his control over the distribution of funds. The semi-autonomous Congressional and Senatorial Campaign Committees, jealous of their own prerogatives and suspicious of control from "downtown," held independent fund-raising dinners in each of Bliss's first three years as chairman and guarded their own authority in distributing the proceeds. Yet Bliss was able to co-opt, at least partially, the most original and most important of the Congressional Campaign Committee's fund-raising devices, the $1,000-per-member Boosters Club, which Bob Wilson started in 1965 as an answer to the Democrats' equally high-priced President's Club.

In its first two years, the Boosters Club raised $1.2 million, all of which was allocated to support nonincumbent Republican candidates for the House. Moreover, the money was on hand early, most of it pledged or paid by March, 1966, when the first primaries began. Using as targets for their efforts fewer than one hundred districts, Wilson and Jack Mills, his executive director, were able to promise real financial support—$15,000 or $20,000 per man—to top-flight prospects if they would run. They were also, in many instances, able to use their financial club to ease the best candidate's way through a primary fight and to jog the local organization into providing extra support. The effectiveness of the device was seen in the fifty-two seats, almost all of them beneficiaries of Boosters Club funds, that switched from the Democrats to the Republicans in 1966.

The best Bliss was able to do was to persuade Wilson to let the man handling the Boosters Club fund raising, political aristocrat C. Langhorne Washburn,* serve also as General Clay's top aide, working out of Bliss's headquarters. But, even though he did not control it, the Boosters operation fulfilled a major criterion of Bliss's finance

---

* Washburn's grandfather was a millionaire Minnesota flour miller and U.S. Senator, whose brothers served as Governors of Maine and Wisconsin, and as U.S. Ambassadors to France and Paraguay.

program: big money was raised early and given to politicians to dispense without regard to their liberalism or conservatism but solely on the basis of where the investment might pay the greatest return.

Bliss's second front was organization, and it was here that he was

'Cool It, Boy—Don't Start Chasing Your Tail'

Hesse in the St. Louis **Globe-Democrat**, Nov. 16, 1966

most at home. As the party's senior state chairman, he had been asked by Senator Morton, then national chairman, to make a post-1960 survey of Republican organizations in the big cities and metropolitan areas, where Richard M. Nixon lost his presidential bid. The Bliss Big City Task Force plowed through the returns, visited several key areas and produced a report whose verdict on the status of big-city Republican organizations boiled down to one word: "Pitiful." Nixon had lost and Republicans would continue losing because the structure that was needed to produce votes was simply not there.

Over and over, Bliss hammered the same theme: "There are no pushbutton methods for victory. . . . The Republican party is out-manned, out-organized, out-spent and outworked. We need more full-time staff people at all levels. We need more precinct workers. We need to realize on all levels that politics is a full-time job and not a three-month fling."

From 1962 to 1965, the Bliss report gathered dust on the shelves of the national committee. So the problems were there waiting for him when he arrived, magnified by the shattering difference between Nixon's hairbreadth loss and the landslide defeat of Goldwater.

He attacked them in the dullest, most prosaic way possible, the only way that could possibly work, by holding workshops. He started with the state chairmen; went on to the county chairmen; then the big-city chairmen; then the small-city chairmen; then the suburban chairmen. In all, some twenty thousand party workers participated in the seminars. At each, Bliss hammered away at the same funda-mentals: recruit qualified candidates; develop programs that are meaningful to your constituency; strengthen the women's organiza-tion; broaden your financial base; make a special drive for young voters; establish contact with Republican professors and teachers; expand supplemental groups to reach the aged, ethnic groups, minori-ties; bear down on registration; set realistic vote quotas and insist that your precinct captains meet them; work with, not independent of, elected Republicans.

It was obvious, "nuts and bolts" (Bliss's favorite expression). Yet suddenly—after years of part-time, speechifying chairmen; after years of nothing but ideological bickering—Ray Bliss's hackneyed phrases were becoming the basis for a fresh stream of action.

The chairman tried to set an example in the areas where the na-tional committee could help. Special seminars on technique were organized for Republican researchers, public-relations men and cam-paign managers—three categories where trained personnel are always in short supply. Bliss reactivated the national committee's minorities division, whose last director had been under indictment in New Jersey for his part in the Goldwater group's effort to organize a last-minute drive to deflect Negro votes from Lyndon Johnson by urging a write-in for Martin Luther King. Bliss's new minorities aide, Clarence Lee Townes, Jr., a well-to-do Negro insurance executive from Virginia, quietly assembled a small staff and worked in nineteen states, including several in the South.

The Young Republicans, controlled nationally by a group of over-age conservatives who loved to dabble in an organization designed for easy absentee control, were a continuing headache to Bliss. He delayed overlong in cracking down on them, in the view of many in the party, but finally in the fall of 1966 bypassed them with a brand-new effort designed to involve campus leaders directly with the Republican party, rather than with the YR's. The campus program—called "Opportunities Unlimited"—reached students at 200 schools in 12 regional meetings during the 1966-67 year. It was a project of the committee's arts and sciences division, headed by John M. Hunger, a thirty-three-year-old professor with a Ph.D. in political science from Indiana University, who joined Bliss's staff on a full-time basis in mid-1966. Working with him was Howard Phillips, twenty-six, a Harvard graduate who had served as the salaried Republican chairman in Boston. Their other main project was to re-establish ties with college teachers across the country, many of whom had severed their Republican affiliations during the Goldwater campaign. By 1967, they were sending newsletters and other Republican research material to a mailing list of some eleven thousand "Republican-oriented" professors.

As national chairman, Bliss also did what he could to persuade or nudge able candidates to try for key jobs. Soon after taking office, he met Congressman John V. Lindsay at a Washington dinner party and took him aside for a few moments of earnest conversation about the political and psychological importance of a victory in the New York mayoral race. When primary opposition threatened to block Edward W. Brooke's bid for the Senate in Massachusetts, Bliss had the word passed to the other aspirants that if the first Negro since Reconstruction with a serious prospect of winning a Senate seat had to be beaten, it would be far better for the G.O.P. to let a Democrat do it.

The matter of issues and ideology was the most difficult for Bliss. Priding himself on his prowess as a technician of politics, he had remarked in Ohio, "If I wanted to make policy, I should go out and run for office and make speeches." In Washington he continued to shun policy talk. Always reticent at his infrequent news conferences,

Bliss would clam up completely if someone asked a question about Vietnam, the budget or President Johnson. A year after taking office, most reporters had learned the chairman's whims. At a mid-1966 press conference, however, he peered through the television lights trying to make out who had broached one of the forbidden topics. Giving it up as futile, Bliss said, "You must be new here, or you'd know I don't answer questions like that."

But, whatever the chairman's preferences, the Republican party itself could not stand mute; not after an election like that of 1964, when its nominee was depicted as a nuclear bomber, a defender of extremism and an enemy of civil rights; not after a campaign in which Republican leaders in state after state had risen to dissent from the platform their own party had adopted.

The vehicle of Bliss's deliverance was at hand, in the form of the Republican Coordinating Committee, first proposed by Melvin Laird and sanctioned by the same national committee meeting that elected Bliss. Laird's plan was, in effect, a countermove to the Governors' call for a special convention to rewrite the 1964 platform, and the makeup of the Coordinating Committee reflected his desire to keep the congressional voice strongest in policy making.

Its membership included General Eisenhower, five members of the Senate leadership, seven of the House, only five Governors, Nixon, Goldwater, Dewey and Alf M. Landon (the four surviving unsuccessful presidential candidates), five members of the 'national committee and a single state legislator.

The eighteen position papers churned out by the Coordinating Committee in 1965 and 1966 were exactly the sort of bland documents so large and diverse a committee might be expected to approve. What little punch they contained was due chiefly to Dewey's skill with words. But, for the most part, they were designed to compose differences rather than kindle new fires of enthusiasm.

In a few areas, they nudged the Republican party gently away from some of the more contentious positions it had taken in 1964:

Civil Rights. For more than 100 years, the Republican party has fought to protect the rights of every minority group and we urge all citizens to join us in this cause. We urgently favor Federal action to assure all citizens of the United States their constitutional rights without discrimination on account of race or color. . . . At the state and local levels of government, we urge enactment of laws designed to protect Constitutional guarantees and a vigorous implementation of such laws. We also urge private action at the local level to insure equal opportunity for all in the fields of education, housing, employment and public accommodations.

Extremism. The Republican Coordinating Committee endorses the position of Republican National Chairman Ray C. Bliss that all Republicans should reject membership in any radical or extremist organization including any which attempts to use the Republican party for its own ends or any which seeks to undermine the basic principles of American freedom and constitutional government.*

Vietnam (December 13, 1965). We Republicans believe that the people of South Vietnam should have an opportunity to live their lives in peace under a government of their own choice free of Communist aggression. We believe that our national objective should be not the unconditional surrender of North Vietnam, but unconditional freedom for the people of South Vietnam and support of their struggle against aggression. . . .

Under our present policy in Vietnam, there is a growing danger that the United States is becoming involved in an endless Korean-type jungle war. A land war in Southeast Asia would be to the advantage of the Communists.

. . . Our first objective should be to impose a Kennedy-type quarantine on North Vietnam. . . . We also recommend the maximum use of American conventional air and sea power against significant military targets. Our purpose is and must be, once again to repel Communist aggression, to minimize American and Vietnamese casualties, and to bring about a swift and secure peace.

The only issue with any real cutting edge that the Coordinating Committee developed and that Bliss pushed hard through the national committee's publicity arm was inflation. Bliss spotted it as early as mid-1965 and he never wavered from his belief that there were more Republican votes in inflation than in any other midterm issue. Post-election surveys indicated that his judgment proved right.

But the more important effect of the awkward Coordinating Committee was to bank the fires of ideology that almost consumed the Republican party in 1964. Goldwater was not a major figure in the

* The committee also endorsed a statement Bliss had made tagging Robert Welch, the founder of the John Birch Society, as an "irresponsible radical" because of his criticism of General Eisenhower. Despite this, John Rousselot, public spokesman for the Birchers, said, "It was wise of the Republican party to make it clear it doesn't seem to be influenced by extremist groups."

committee's closed-door debates, but the very fact that he was in the meetings and subscribed to the statements kept his conservative followers from bolting the G.O.P. The Free Society Association, launched with such publicity, settled quickly into being another tract-writing outfit, and Goldwater himself appeared to lose interest in it as his own campaign to return to the Senate from Arizona in 1968 drew nearer.

On the other side of the party spectrum, the liberals like Scranton and Rockefeller felt they had a voice in party councils again and were no longer victims of Burch's "exclusionary" tactics. The congressional leadership was happy; their numbers were sufficient to keep the Coordinating Committee from becoming a thorn in their side, as Paul Butler's Democratic Advisory Committee had been to his party's Congressmen during the 1950's.*

Gradually, an atmosphere of live-and-let-live spread through the party. This mood of tolerance, combined with Bliss's steady prodding for organization effort, plus the flow of cash from the Boosters Club and other sources, plus the appearance, both spontaneous and induced, of dozens of bright new candidates to replace the veterans who were retired by the Goldwater landslide—all these factors, plus the liabilities of the incumbent Democrats, went into the Republican comeback of 1966.

The size of the victory exceeded the predictions even of those pundits who believed that Republicans were fated to bounce back to some extent in the midterm election. How "automatic" that recovery was is subject to debate; in 1962, the last previous off-year election, the out-of-office Republicans gained only two seats in the House and lost four in the Senate.

---

* Members of the Republican Coordinating Committee in 1967 were: National Chairman Ray C. Bliss; past presidential candidates Dwight D. Eisenhower, Barry Goldwater, Richard M. Nixon, Thomas E. Dewey, Alf M. Landon; Senators Everett M. Dirksen, Thomas H. Kuchel, Bourke B. Hickenlooper, Margaret Chase Smith, George Murphy, Thruston B. Morton, Milton R. Young, Hugh Scott; House members Gerald R. Ford, Leslie C. Arends, Melvin R. Laird, John J. Rhodes, Bob Wilson, H. Allen Smith, Richard H. Poff, William C. Cramer; Governors John A. Love, John A. Volpe, George Romney, Nelson A. Rockefeller, Raymond P. Shafer, John H. Chafee, Nils A. Boe, Daniel J. Evans; Mrs. C. Wayland Brooks, assistant chairman of the Republican National Committee; National Committee vice chairmen Mrs. Collis P. Moore, Donald R. Ross, Mrs. J. Willard Marriott, J. Drake Edens, Jr.; and F. F. Montgomery, speaker of the Oregon House of Representatives and president of the G.O.P. State Legislators Association.

Chairman Bliss knew that the 1966 recovery guaranteed no victory in 1968. Republicans had scored even more impressive gains in 1938 and 1946, then lost the succeeding presidential elections. But, from a psychological viewpoint, it was exactly the sort of victory Bliss would have ordered if he could, a "victory in depth," he called it, spanning all the ideological and geographical sections of the G.O.P.

In Chicago in January, 1965, Bliss told the national committee members who had just elected him chairman, "I am no modern miracle man, but I will work hard and try to do a job for you." To friends he added that same day, "Our party has been sliding downhill for twenty-four years, and for anybody to think we're going to reverse it in one, two or three years is unrealistic. What I am hoping for is an improvement, but it's going to be no picnic."

Less than two years later, at 1:25 on the morning after the 1966 election, Bliss sat at his desk munching a hot dog, watching the television screen. "I'd say we're on our way, Thrus," he called over to Senator Morton, who was sprawled in a chair nearby.

"You damn betcha we are," replied the Kentucky Yale man. "It's a new ball game and it's a long time coming."

The improvement that registered in the 1966 election, Bliss told reporters that day, "exceeded my fondest expectations." His broad face wreathed in smiles, Bliss enjoyed the triumph to which he had made so significant a contribution. He was too realistic to think that the party's future course would be smooth, but he told the press that he did not expect to be asked, as he had been at his first news conference, "if the Republican party can survive."

"It's a very live elephant now," he said.

3 FAT CATS
AND KINGMAKERS

AFTER the Republicans nominated William McKinley on the first ballot in 1896, *Life* magazine wrote: "When the Prince of Wales won the Derby the other day with Persimmon he led his horse off to the unsaddling enclosure amid a stupendous expression of the enthusiasm of the spectators. It would have been a great sight to see Mr. Hanna lead Major McKinley off to be weighed after the vote of Ohio was cast at St. Louis, but unfortunately they don't do it that way at political conventions." The man who inspired this comment, of course, was Marcus Alonzo Hanna, the Cleveland industrialist who almost single-handedly engineered and financed the nomination of the man who would be the twenty-fifth President of the United States. Politics has changed remarkably little since the days of McKinley, and yet today he would need no Hanna. For one of the most profound of the recent national political developments has been the diffusion of managerial and financial talent.

No longer in either party is there a single man or even a "group of willful men" with a monopoly on the funds and the finesse needed to nominate a President. Instead, there are clusters of such "fat cats" and "kingmakers" across the country, for whom the lure of power, of profit, or even the chance to put their ideas into practice is all the inducement a candidate need offer them. Indeed, in the Republican party in 1964, the money men and managers came seeking the candidate who eventually was nominated.

No myth has been more persistent in and about the Republican party than that of its control by a handful of Eastern bankers and investment men and their allies in government and the press. The classic statement of this view is given in Phyllis Schlafly's volume, *A Choice, Not an Echo,* distributed wholesale by the Goldwater forces in advance of the 1964 convention.

"From 1936 through 1960," she writes, "the Republican presidential nominee was selected by a small group of secret kingmakers who are the most powerful opinion makers in the world. They dictated the choice of the Republican presidential nominee just as completely as the Paris dressmakers control the length of women's skirts."*

The kingmakers, in Mrs. Schlafly's opinion, come from the top ranks of Eastern business and banking. In 1936, when a small group of them met "in a royal suite on the 21st floor of the Waldorf-Astoria Hotel in New York . . . the presiding genius of this secret gathering . . . was Thomas Lamont, senior partner in the J. P. Morgan and Company. . . . Lamont was flanked on the right and left by Thomas Cochran, also of the Morgan firm, and by Alfred P. Sloan of General Motors. Five other prominent financiers and industrialists were also present." It was they, she says, who picked Alf Landon in 1936, knowing he could not win, and they who foisted off Wendell Willkie, a public utilities lawyer and registered Democrat, as the 1940 Republican nominee. "The Willkie boom," she asserts, "was engineered by top advertising executives from Madison Avenue

* If, instead of savoring a good conspiracy theory, Mrs. Schlafly had merely sought to confirm that there have been powerful "fat cats" in politics, she would have been on firmer historical grounds. Back in 1851, Delaware politician John M. Clayton wrote the Attorney General, "Now, my dear Crittenden, these Duponts have spent a fortune for the Whig party, and have never received a favor for it, for they never desired any." (Clayton told his friend to fortify himself with a bottle of whiskey and then ask President Fillmore to appoint a Du Pont to a minor naval post.) Major Republican contributors of the nineteenth century included banker Jay Cooke, department store moguls A. T. Stewart and John Wanamaker, the Vanderbilts and Astors. The Democrats, in the same era, were heavily endowed by August Belmont, American representative for the Rothschild interests; traction magnate William C. Whitney; Marcus Daly, owner of the fabulous Anaconda mines; and publisher William Randolph Hearst. During the 1896 McKinley-Bryan campaign, Republican National Chairman Mark Hanna, himself a multimillionaire, actually levied an "unofficial taxation" on the financial community—in the case of the banks it was one quarter of one percent of their capital. See Jasper B. Shannon, *Money and Politics* (New York: Random House, 1959); Stephen Hess, "The Making of the President, 1896," *The Nineties* (New York: American Heritage, 1967).

public relations firms," working hand-in-glove with such publishers as the New York *Herald Tribune's* Ogden Reid.

"The kingmakers sought to influence delegates by having the mortgage holders and bankers to whom they owed money call them in behalf of Willkie," continues Mrs. Schlafly. "Powerful economic interests brought pressures on state delegations to force officeholders into line if they wanted to keep their jobs."

Lest Mrs. Schlafly's views be dismissed as the somewhat exaggerated rantings of an aroused right winger, consider the memorandum Senator Taft wrote analyzing his 1952 defeat by General Eisenhower.

"I don't want my supporters to feel that there were any serious mistakes of omission and that some striking move would have solved the whole problem," Taft wrote. "The result of the convention came far more from underlying causes which had operated steadily for eight months and continued to operate in Chicago. First, it was the power of the New York financial interests and a large number of businessmen subject to New York influence, who had selected General Eisenhower as their candidate at least a year ago."*

The merit of the Schlafly contentions and Senator Taft's more restrained rendering of the same judgment may be debated. What cannot be doubted is that the monopoly power of the big Eastern contributors and their allies in the G.O.P. has been sharply diminished.

The evidence of the change is everywhere. The *Herald Tribune,* pre-eminent organ for Establishment views, disappeared into the short-lived *World-Journal-Tribune.* The New York *Times* was Democratic in its presidential endorsements in 1960 and 1964, while the *Wall Street Journal,* the only other national newspaper that might conceivably be responsive to the banking-industrial community, is far more akin to the Taft-Goldwater conservatism in its editorial views

---

* For the full text of the Taft memorandum see p. 556 of *The Politics of National Party Conventions* by Paul T. David, Ralph M. Goldman and Richard C. Baine (Washington: Brookings, 1960). There is fine dissection of the breakdown of the Eastern Establishment on pp. 90-94 of George F. Gilder and Bruce K. Chapman, *The Party That Lost Its Head* (New York: Knopf, 1966). Richard H. Rovere, in a tongue-in-cheek essay, lays down the rule—or rather quotes approvingly Margaret Creal's rule—that "When an Establishment man is nominated for the Presidency by either party, the Vice-Presidential candidate must be drawn from outside the Establishment. When, as has occasionally happened, the Establishment is denied the Presidential nomination it must be given the Vice-Presidential nomination." Both parties ignored the rule in 1964—with wildly differing results. See Rovere's *The American Establishment* (New York: Harcourt, Brace & World, 1962), p.20.

than to the liberal Republicanism of the financial commuity it supposedly represents.

More basically, the influence of Wall Street and the big corporations has been reduced by the growth of such vast independent financial and industrial centers as Detroit, Chicago and, even more important, Texas and California. The dispersal of financial power is reflected directly in internal Republican politics, perhaps most dra-

Turned tiger

Fawcett, Providence **Evening Bulletin**, Nov. 29, 1966

matically in the inability of Nelson Rockefeller, symbolic bugaboo of Eastern financial-political power, to gain the presidential nomination in 1964.

Rockefeller, according to the best estimates, spent over $3 million, almost all of it his own and his family's money, on his futile pursuit of the nomination. The last-minute effort for Governor Scranton, who then took over as the liberal Republicans' hope, cost another $827,000. But the Eastern candidates were outspent by the Goldwater supporters, who raised over $5.5 million to finance the anti-Establishment campaign. This pre-convention total includes $2 million raised and spent in California for the decisive primary in that state.* Other large sources of Goldwater financial support were Texas, Ohio, Michigan—and New York, where conservative businessmen funneled large sums through broker J. William Middendorf and Jeremiah Milbank, Jr.

Again, in the general election, the Goldwater candidacy proved that despite the opposition of the Eastern financial interests (many of whose leaders swung over to support President Johnson) adequate money was available for the campaign. "There was little change from 1960 to 1964 in the number of large contributions," reports Herbert E. Alexander, director of the Citizens' Research Foundation, "though in geographic terms there were indications in 1964 of increased financial support in the South and Southwest and decreases in parts of the North and the East."†

But the real financial revolution in American politics, and one of particularly historic import for the Republican party, was brought into being by a man whose name has seldom appeared in the newspapers and who well may have been unaware of the significance of his own inventiveness.

He is William S. Warner, a member of the political party bureaucracy, who joined the staff of the Republican Congressional Campaign Committee as a young man, and, in 1951, having as his main attributes a pleasant personality and long seniority, was elevated to the top staff post of executive director. Bill Warner was neither an in-

* Nineteen-sixty-four figures come from Herbert E. Alexander, *Financing the 1964 Election* (Princeton, N.J.: Citizens' Research Foundation, 1966). Also see Alexander Heard, *The Costs of Democracy* (Chapel Hill: University of North Carolina Press, 1960) and Walter Pincus, "The Fight Over Money," *The Atlantic,* April, 1966.

† There is another source of party funds, although not as substantial in the G.O.P., which controls few of the big city machines: namely, contributions from political office holders. These have a time-honored place in American politics. An 1882 form letter to Pennsylvania employees reads, "Two per cent of your salary is ———. Please remit promptly. At the close of the campaign we shall place a list of those who have not paid in the hands of the head of the department you are in." See Albert Bigelow Paine, *Th. Nast, His Period and His Pictures* (New York: Harper, 1904), p. 459.

At a closed-door meeting of Republican city chairmen in Washington, January 25, 1966, former Louisville Mayor William O. Cowger (now a Congressman) revealed how his city administration collected "voluntary" contributions from non-civil-service employees of 2 percent of their monthly salaries. Cowger commented that he raised "so much money that I find it difficult to intelligently spend it all [in a campaign]." One use for the "extra" money, he said, was to throw a big victory celebration party.

tellectual nor an operator; he was a good administrator, who could keep track of the money going out and coming in. So in 1961, when William E. Miller, the Congressional Committee chairman, was shifted to the chairmanship of the Republican National Committee, he took Warner along with him.

When they arrived at Eye Street, Miller and Warner discovered that they had inherited some $750,000 in debts left over from the 1960 presidential election and had about $25,000 in the bank. For the rest of the year they tried to get by with the old "quota system" for raising funds. But it was apparent that the states were not meeting their assigned obligations with the alacrity necessary to make the party solvent. It was at this point, in February, 1962, that Warner convinced Miller to persuade the Republican National Committee's executive committee to try an experiment. Would the committee, Miller-Warner wanted to know, choose a three-state test market— New Jersey, Montana, Missouri—and, using its "house lists," conduct a direct mail campaign for ten-dollar contributions? The committee, accustomed to getting its money in fairly large doses from a fairly small circle of friends, showed little enthusiasm for the proposed innovation, but finally agreed to send out twenty thousand letters. The result was a return of 3 percent. Since everything above 1 percent was profit, the mailing was viewed as a firm success.

Now Warner's "sustaining member" program, with success as its mandate, started to buy commercial mailing lists—at $15 to $30 per thousand names. It purchased lists of Carte Blanche credit card holders (for $10,000); Disabled American Veterans (one of the most successful); Standard & Poor, McGraw-Hill business publications and *Wall Street Journal* subscribers; mail-order buyers of Richard M. Nixon's book, *Six Crises;* clients of investment houses. In all, the national committee probably has used one hundred lists. It has found that the biggest, most broad-based ones bring the least satisfactory returns, barely paying the costs. On the other hand, one of the most successful solicitations has come from the clients of a man in Batavia, New York, who sells car-polishing cloths. There also have been good responses from people who have answered advertisements for courses in bookkeeping and in how to succeed in business.

In the program's second year, 1963, it raised $700,000; in 1964, over $1 million was brought in before the presidential convention;

more than 3 million letters were sent in 1965, resulting in contributions of $1.7 million. This technique was adopted for the Goldwater campaign, which drew pre-convention support from 300,000 givers and general election support from 650,000.

By comparison, in the 1952 Eisenhower campaign, the Republican National Committee had only 17,500 contributors and the Citizens for Eisenhower-Nixon about 20,000. In 1964, only 28 percent of the Republican money came from gifts of over $500; in 1952, it was 88 percent. Almost half of the 1964 money came in response either to televised appeals or direct mail requests for small gifts.

While the large individual contributor is still important in the pre-convention campaign (much more so than in the general election), clearly there is no small group of "secret kingmakers," in Mrs. Schlafly's phrase, with sufficient monopoly power over the sources of Republican funds to dictate the choice of a nominee. To the contrary, there is every reason to think that any serious presidential aspirant, from any wing of the party, can secure adequate financial backing for his pre-nomination campaign. Such backing appears available to Romney, Nixon, Reagan and Percy—to say nothing of Rockefeller—in 1968.

The Republican party itself has been liberated from whatever degree of control the small group of financial angels imposed, so far as financing of the presidential campaign is concerned. The continued increase in numbers of small contributions in response to direct mail solicitations and the success of the televised appeals during presidential campaigns frees the party from any veto power over a nominee by a specific number of its principal contributors.

Whatever form the 1968 struggle takes, there is no reason to suppose that its outcome will be decided by access to money.

The same diffusion principle that has altered the Republican financial base has affected its supply of managerial talent. If it was true—as most historians of the event suggest—that the Eisenhower victory over Taft was, at least in part, the product of superior management, then the conservatives showed in 1964 that they could, in turn, outorganize and outguess their liberal intraparty rivals. Just as there is no longer a monopoly on money sources for Republican campaigns, so there is no monopoly in any section or any segment of the party on talent to manage nomination campaigns.

Two interlocking processes underlie the diffusion of managerial talent in the Republican party. One is the rise of professional political management specialists, available for hire to the highest bidder. The phenomenon had its start and its early success in California in the late 1930's, when the proliferation of referendum questions and the absence of effective party organizations created a demand for someone who could organize public relations, volunteer workers, research, finances and all the other elements of an issue- or office-campaign.*

The pioneers in the field were Sacramento newspaperman Clem Whitaker, a Baptist minister's son, and red-haired Leone Baxter, manager of the Redding, California, Chamber of Commerce, who was to become Mrs. Whitaker in 1938. Their business partnership, begun in 1930, was credited thirteen years later with "teaching Earl Warren to smile." In the 1942 gubernatorial campaign, years before a women's magazine coined "togetherness," Whitaker and Baxter presented District Attorney Warren, until then chiefly known for putting people in jail, as the happy head of a household of healthy daughters.

Although Robert Smalley, a Whitaker and Baxter partner, ran Robert Griffin's successful 1966 Senate campaign in Michigan, the firm, now under second-generation management, has been easing itself out of campaigning for individual candidates into the more lucrative representation of such giant utilities as Pacific Gas and Electric and Pacific Tel. and Tel. However, its place has been quickly filled by new faces like Harry Lerner, a sometimes San Francisco political reporter, who works for Democratic candidates, notably Pat Brown; Cross, Roberts & Rocky, one of the few firms that handles both Republican and Democratic accounts (it has been associated with Republican Thomas Kuchel and Democrat Alan Cranston); a small-time Los Angeles operator named Hal Evry, who believes he can elect anyone who will keep his mouth shut; and the two current California leaders, Baus & Ross and Spencer-Roberts.†

From California, the process spread eastward across the major industrial states. Demands for the specialists grew with the growing role of mass media in political campaigns. While anyone may flatter

---

* Useful guides to this phenomenon are Stanley Kelley, Jr., *Professional Public Relations and Political Power* (Baltimore: Johns Hopkins Press, 1956) and William L. Worden, "Tales of the Kingmakers," *Saturday Evening Post,* May 23, 1959.

† See pp. 262-63 for the role of Spencer-Roberts in Ronald Reagan's 1966 gubernatorial campaign.

himself that he can write a campaign speech or organize a precinct, the purchase and production of political television programs and the measurement of the public opinion they are supposed to influence are obviously not work for an amateur. Increasingly, candidates at all levels turned to advertising agencies, commercial survey firms, professional fund raisers and political organizers, or companies offering all of these services in a package.

One of the newest and most successful of these "packagers" is Campaign Consultants Incorporated (C.C.I.) of Boston, founded in January, 1966, by David B. Goldberg, thirty-six, a Harvard-trained attorney, who was part of the quartet that masterminded the surprising write-in victory of Henry Cabot Lodge in the 1964 New Hampshire primary, and Dr. Douglas L. Bailey, thirty-three, issues consultant to the Wednesday Club, a group of twenty moderate Republican Congressmen. (In January, 1967, they added a third partner, thirty-three-year-old John Deardourff, director of research for the New York Republican State Committee and a veteran of the Rockefeller and Lindsay campaigns.)

In its first year, C.C.I. participated, at roughly $200 per man per day, in Republican campaigns in ten states, from Oregon to Michigan, Kansas to New Hampshire. The young operators could not salvage their biggest client, wealthy but unknown insurance executive Clayton Gengras, who wanted to be Governor of Connecticut; though they point with pride to the fact that Gengras got about 45 percent of the vote only six weeks after the polls showed him with a mere 17 percent. However, they claim to have given winning advice to at least two major candidates. Edward Brooke called them in when mid-October polls showed that he might be seriously hurt by a "white backlash." They told the Negro senatorial candidate that he must hit the civil rights issue head-on. It was then that the Massachusetts Republican opened his attack on the "extremists of black power and white power," condemning both Stokely Carmichael and Lester Maddox. In Maryland, the campaign manager for the G.O.P. gubernatorial nominee Spiro T. Agnew sent out an S.O.S. for C.C.I. two weeks before the election. Goldberg, Bailey, Robert Ellsworth, a Kansas Representative who worked closely with them on several projects; a Boston pollster, John F. Becker; and Cliff Brown, a statistician, answered the call for a day-long session in Baltimore. They carefully examined the polls, advertising copy and proposed speeches. Then they announced that Agnew's dignified campaign, designed to show his depth on issues and suitability to be Governor, was all wrong. The only issue, they felt, was George Mahoney, the Democratic candidate, whose slogan, "Your Home Is Your Castle, Protect It," had not very subtle racist overtones. Agnew did change tactics, began attacking his know-nothing opponent, and won a smashing victory.

The second and related reason for the diffusion of G.O.P. managerial talent is the increasing professionalization of the party organization itself.

In the postwar years, despite the temporary relief provided by Eisenhower's presidential victories, Republicans increasingly confronted a superior Democratic organization in the key states and, even more significant, a steadily more professional operation run by the labor unions. Genuinely alarmed, Republicans began studying the COPE (AFL-CIO Committee on Political Education) handbooks and copying their techniques. Corporations and Chambers of Commerce began recruiting businessmen, especially junior executives, for "political training" and "citizenship" classes. The theme: power goes to those who learn how to get it.

Increasingly, the G.O.P. operated year-round, full-time, professionally-staffed headquarters on the state, county and city levels. Republicans in Washington State gave $16,000 a year to their chairman, C. Montgomery ("Gummie") Johnson, a former Weyerhaeuser lumber lobbyist; William J. Devlin, an ex-schoolteacher, presided over a Philadelphia G.O.P. committee with a $150,000 annual operating budget; and on January 3, 1966, the Fifth District Republican Committee of Michigan (Grand Rapids and environs) presented a thirty-nine-page itemized budget that even projected estimates for 1967 and 1968. Its eight full-time employees were able to predict that in Kent County in 1968 they would raise $5,250 in contributions of $1 to $24 and to report that 7 percent of the funds raised in Ionia County in 1965 came from "new contributors." More than ever before, the Republican party was being run as a business.

Supplementing the party's rising professionalism was the growth of suburbia and the spread of industry into rural areas, particularly in the South, in the post–World War II period. The new suburbs challenged the political techniques of both parties, but at the same time provided, in the form of the suburban housewife, the largest available supply of volunteer manpower either party had ever seen.

A new generation of political operatives developed, skilled principally in organizing volunteer workers.

The spread of industry into the South and into rural areas brought with it a spread of two-party competition. It was a two-edged sword. As Iowa, for example, changed from a rural to an urban state, the traditional Republicanism of the state faced increasing challenge. In the 1940's Iowa Republicans hardly needed an organization to win; by the 1960's, they needed every bit of organizational talent they could muster. In politics, as in everything else, necessity bred invention.

In the South, by contrast, the infusion of managerial talent, frequently Republican in its politics, from the Eastern and Northern home offices of newly arrived corporations ended the long social stigma of Republicanism in Dixie. These Southern Republicans were fascinated by the organizational aspects of politics. Coming from a business background, deprived as newcomers of social prestige or control of mass media as their techniques of persuasion, they turned automatically to organization and fell to the task with a fury few of their peers in older Republican parties could match. The first computerized precinct organization in the Republican party was established in Dallas; effective volunteer organizations sprang into being in most of the metropolitan areas of the Southern states.

As a result, the Republican party today has not a single dominant set of political organizers but clusters of independent organizing talents. Increasingly, the tendency is for men of talent to move from full-time work for the party to the status of independent contractors, available for hire. Stewart Spencer and Bill Roberts, whose firm engineered the Ronald Reagan campaign in 1966, started in California Young Republican politics. F. Clifton White, a product of the late years of the Dewey organization, skillfully directed the Goldwater pre-convention campaign in 1964, and now works as an independent operator out of a small office near New York's Grand Central Station. Travis Cross, former press secretary to Mark Hatfield and now a Romney aide, runs his own outfit from Salem, Oregon.

Beyond such full-time professional managers—of whom there are perhaps two dozen in the country—there are many experienced lawyer-politicians who give all or a large part of their time to campaign management in presidential election years. In this category are such prominent Republicans as Leonard W. Hall, Robert J. Mc-

Intosh, Charles K. McWhorter and Robert F. Ellsworth. Typical, perhaps, of the younger generation of lawyer-politicians is Sherman Unger, forty, a partner in the prestigious Cincinnati firm of Frost & Jacobs. Introduced to national politics as an advance man for Nixon in 1960, Unger returned to Washington in 1964 to try his hand at the thankless task of organizing the big cities for Goldwater. Like most volunteer "kingmakers," Unger plays politics partly for its ideological content, partly for the profit that may accrue from the high-level friendships he makes, but chiefly for the sheer fun of the game. Unger and many others like him were on the fringes of the Republican National Committee meeting in New Orleans in January, 1967, watching the action and sizing up the opportunities and problems for potential contenders.

They follow in an honorable tradition. One of the greatest, New York's Thurlow Weed, perfected the hero candidate, and was responsible for the nomination of two, Generals William Henry Harrison and Zachary Taylor. Both times, in 1840 and 1848, the main opposition came from Henry Clay. Weed claimed to be "warmly attached" to the Kentucky Senator. It was just that he did not think he could win. Clay, so went Weed's argument, had been too partisan for too long and had too many enemies. Perhaps some contemporary operator will borrow Weed's line.

But, at any rate, the availability of so many potential "kingmakers" indicates that the aspirants for the 1968 Republican presidential nomination will not lack for managerial skill any more than they will lack for money.

4 INTELLECTUALS, RIGHT AND LEFT

THE Governors, the money men, the congressional leaders, the operators all have certain ideological predispositions, and all have pressures working on them that tend to make them liberal or conservative on certain issues. But if none are philosophically neuter, neither can they afford to be so rigidly consistent in their ideology as to jeopardize their basic purpose as politicians—gaining or sustaining power.

Ideology, in this context, means a body of doctrine and a plan for putting it into operation; it is a scheme of politics which shapes decisions on specific issues and tactics and, at points of conflict, may even override "political" considerations of advantage or expediency. But there is a limit to how much ideological freight a party can take aboard without injuring itself.

This is chiefly because an ideological view of politics does not accord with the reality of American life. In their classic study, *The American Voter,* the University of Michigan Survey Research Center scholars noted that on even the most visible specific political "issue," only about one-fourth of the voters will recognize the issue exists, have an opinion about it and know that their opinion is shared by one or the other of the parties. When it comes to a consistent, overall view of public policy—a "liberal" or "conservative" position on social welfare, for example—only about 2 percent of the voters are classifiable as having an "ideological" viewpoint. Disillusioning as it may be for the theory of democracy, the survey authors conclude that elections are less concerned with *what* the government shall do than with *who* shall do the governing.*

* See Angus Campbell, Philip E. Converse, Warren E. Miller, Donald E. Stokes, *The American Voter* (New York: John Wiley, 1960), especially chapter 9.

There is a perceptible difference, however, between the public and the "elite" groups—political activists and the journalists who write about them, for example. The activists are inclined to be far more "ideologically aware" than the general public; and the danger for a political party lies precisely in the possibility that the ideological activists may take control and steer the party in a direction the public is not prepared to move. Thus, the politican's rule of thumb becomes: always have idea men (intellectuals) in a campaign, but never (as happened with Goldwater) in control of the campaign.

Around the fringes of a political party, certain purely ideological groups come into existence, whose purpose is twofold: to pull the party, and its members, toward their part of the political spectrum, and to serve as a communications center and rallying place for the scattered adherents of their point of view.

On the larboard, or liberal side, of the Republican party, there are two major ideological organizations—the Ripon Society and Republicans for Progress. Both had their origins in the period of Goldwater ascendancy, and were formed largely as a response to its conservative tug.

The Ripon Society, named after the Wisconsin town that claims to be the birthplace of the G.O.P., was founded in December, 1962, by seventeen young men, primarily graduate students at Harvard and the Massachusetts Institute of Technology, who chose to pattern themselves after the highly successful Bow Group, which, about ten years earlier, had brought Cambridge and Oxford students together to do research for the British Conservative party.

Its leading figure has been Dr. John Saloma III, thirty-three, an assistant professor of political science at MIT, who had attended meetings of the Bow Group and interviewed its leaders while on a Fulbright scholarship at the London School of Economics during 1959-60.*

There are now four chapters of the Ripon Society: the initial one in Cambridge, Massachusetts, which has operated out of a drab two-room office above the Harvard Square Theatre and has about

* Jack Saloma served as president of the Ripon Society from its inception until March, 1967, when he was succeeded by Lee W. Huebner, a teaching fellow in history at Harvard. The other key figure in the organization is executive director Thomas E. Petri of Wisconsin, a graduate of the Harvard Law School, who was editor of the Ripon Society's most ambitious publication, *From Disaster to Distinction* (New York: Pocket Books, 1966).

150 members; another branch in Los Angeles with some 40 members; and, thanks to mergers with existing groups at Yale and Columbia, units in New Haven and New York City.

The organization has been in a constant financial bind. In 1965 it sent out seven direct-mail solicitations, on which it expended $2,782 in order to gross $3,997. Eighteen hundred letters to contributors of $1,000 or more to the 1960 Nixon-Lodge campaign or the 1964 Scranton campaign brought in just twenty-one gifts, netting $720. Another mailing, to subscribers of the defunct *Advance* maga-

'IT HAD TOO MANY HEADS AND KEPT WALKING IN CIRCLES...'

ELEPHANTUS REPUBLICANUM-EXTINCT

Oliphant, Denver **Post**, Jan. 24, 1967, © 1967, The Los Angeles Times Syndicate

zine, actually lost $333. In fact, the group's only successful direct-mail solicitation was when Walter N. Thayer, president of the New York *Herald Tribune,* sent letters on his personal stationery to seventeen friends and received five responses for $2,800. The Ripon Society had expenses of $4,270.35 in 1964, $19,928.41 in 1965, and $32,000 in 1966.

Although small and hard-pressed, even its severest critics agree that the Ripon Society is having an impact far beyond its numbers and expenditures. Each week a Washington service forwards over one hundred newspaper clippings to the Cambridge headquarters. This notoriety obviously is galling to the conservatives. In a speech on the floor of the House of Representatives, John Ashbrook (R.,

Ohio), who doubles as chairman of the American Conservative Union, said, "Ever since 1963, when the Ripon Society came into existence, news coverage of their activities has far outstripped their reputations within the G.O.P. For this reason, I felt that an exposé of the methods of this little group, which seeks to take over and make over my party, was in order." Representative Ashbrook's twenty-six-page "exposé," prepared by the ACU staff, was primarily a summary of Ripon policy papers. However, to explain the Cambridge group's extensive press coverage it concocted a near-conspiracy theory about a "ubiquitous" public relations man, one Frederick H. Sontag, "who will boast that he and Nelson Rockefeller have adjoining summer houses at Seal Harbor."

The Ripon Society's influence may in part, of course, be a product of good public relations. Nonetheless, it has risen mainly because, as the ACU report states, "there is no doubt that the members of the Ripon Society are brilliant, conscientious, and even clever." Indeed, it is the quality of the Ripon Society papers, both its critiques of Republican party trends and its discussions of such issues as tax sharing and the draft, that has given the group its reputation as spokesman for the party's responsible left. The society has developed a close but informal working relationship with the more liberal Republican Governors, and, to a lesser extent, with the younger, more liberal members of the House and Senate. Ripon Society members also held important posts in a number of key 1966 campaigns, including those of Edward Brooke, Charles Percy, Robert Griffin, Robert Taft, Jr., and Robert Finch.

Like all the splinter groups, left and right, the Ripon Society has worked out its own demonology. It regularly attacks such expectable targets as Barry Goldwater and Ronald Reagan, but, surprisingly, also directs its fire at Republican National Chairman Ray Bliss, who has irritated the self-styled "flaming moderates" of Cambridge by his aloofness to ideological debate, and whose emphasis on party unity, they feel, will utimately be of greater comfort to the conservatives in the 1968 pre-convention jockeying.

By G.O.P. standards, Ripon members are sort of button-down Mario Savios. In four pages of the Ripon publication *From Disaster to Distinction,* they write of "an exciting new era of politics," "a new Republican party," "a new generation" (twice), "the new politics" (twice), "a new and yet untried political force," "a new and powerful factor in party politics," "this new breed," "ever newer and younger faces," "broad new support," "the new America," "new ideas," "a new order" (twice) and "new faces." Underlying these new clichés is a strong identification with their own age group, a generation that looked to John F. Kennedy as a model, yet distrusts those over thirty.

Clearly the Ripon Society's favorite Republican politician is New York City's John V. Lindsay. But, recognizing that 1968 is not his year, its members will undoubtedly go for the most left-leaning of the serious contenders. While steeling themselves to take Romney, they complain of "the generational gap between Romney and the young Republican lights, men like John Chafee of Rhode Island and Daniel Evans of Washington" (*Ripon Forum,* July, 1966), and one of their leaders privately called the Michigan Governor "middle-aged and middle-class."

If the Ripon Society represents youth, the second major organization of the G.O.P. left represents the older order. Republicans for Progress is the outgrowth of another group, the Committee to Support Moderate Republicans, which was set up during the 1964 campaign in order to funnel money to such anti-Goldwater Republicans as Lindsay and Senators Kenneth Keating and Hugh Scott.

Its principal sponsor has been Charles P. Taft, the former Mayor of Cincinnati, whose career has reflected neither his brother Bob's conservatism nor his statewide popularity in Ohio. Taft's board of directors reads like an Eisenhower Administration alumni association: Arthur S. Flemming (Secretary of Health, Education and Welfare), Walter Williams (Under Secretary of Commerce), W. Randolph Burgess (Under Secretary of the Treasury), Mary P. Lord (U.S. delegate to the UN General Assembly), James C. Worthy (Assistant Secretary of Commerce), John J. Gilhooley (Assistant Secretary of Labor), and ex–White House assistants Malcolm Moos, Maxwell Rabb, and Philip Areeda. The executive director of Republicans for Progress is Albert E. Abrahams, forty-three, who arrived in Washington in 1949 as a reporter for the Newhouse newspapers and later became a respected figure on Capitol Hill as legislative assistant to Senator Clifford Case.

Unlike the Ripon Society, RFP does not see its role as pamphleteer; it published only four newsletters during 1966. Rather, it attempts to serve as a fund-raising organization for liberal Republican candidates, as a research agency for Senators and Representatives to supplement the work of their own staffs, and as a liaison between progressive state leaders and like-minded Republicans in the capital.

During its first year of operation, 1965, RFP spent about $75,000. In 1966 its budget was $90,000, of which two-thirds was passed on to candidates. Some $25,000 was raised for the 1965 Lindsay mayoralty campaign, $5,000 was sent to Brooke in Massachusetts, and smaller sums went to men like Virginia senatorial candidate Lawrence Traylor and Oregon congressional candidate John R. Dellenback.

The G.O.P. left, like its counterpart on the right, weaves a fine spider's web of interlocking directorates, officers and organizations. During 1965-66, Republicans for Progress, for example, gave $18,000 to the Committee for Republican Research, whose function, in turn, is to underwrite a staff for the Wednesday Club.

The Wednesday Club, only representative of the liberal congressional viewpoint, was named for the day on which it holds its weekly meetings. Called the Wednesday *Group* by its members, it was founded in mid-1963 by six very junior Republican Congressmen: John V. Lindsay of New York, F. Bradford Morse of Massachusetts, Abner Sibal of Connecticut, Stanley Tupper of Maine, Robert F. Ellsworth of Kansas and Charles M. Mathias of Maryland. The group's membership has hovered around twenty, and, since Lindsay's departure, the House member with the most influence over its direction—if only because of his unending energy and enthusiasm—has been Brad Morse. Perhaps Morse best illustrates the reason for the organization. A pudgy forty-seven-year-old "swamp Yankee," who went through the Lowell public schools and Boston University Law School, the articulate and engaging Morse has a first-rate mind, the highly developed ambition of any good politician, and no place to go. Blocked from immediate advancement in his home state by a trio of firmly-entrenched Republicans—Governor John Volpe, Senator Edward Brooke, and Attorney General Elliot Richardson—Morse has keenly felt the need to improve his role in the House of Representatives. Lacking the seniority and conservatism that have generally been the keys to preferment in the House Republican hierarchy, the Massachusetts Congressman and his similarly-troubled colleagues felt they could increase their effectiveness if they created some mechanism which allowed them to swap information, both on issues before their committees and on political developments in their areas, and put out joint statements. Position papers prepared under the direction of the Wednesday Club, but always signed by the Congressmen as individuals, have covered a wide range of topics from foreign aid (suggesting that emphasis move from economic to political development) to the military draft to the application of systems management techniques in domestic programs.

Despite some attempts to paint the Wednesday Club as a group of flaming liberals, the membership carefully clears its statements with the House G.O.P. leadership and includes in its ranks several men of almost-conservative views while excluding several of the most left-leaning Republican Congressmen, for, like any limited-membership group, Wednesday Clubbers can be snobs.*

There are a number of other moderate Republican groups across the country that are loosely joined together in the Council of Republican Organizations. But, like the Oregon Council for Constructive Republicanism—1966 operating budget, $2,400—their titles are often longer than their bank accounts.

Pennsylvania's liberal Republican Senator, Hugh Scott, devised an "in" and "out" theory of G.O.P. splinter groups, described in a speech in 1965 before the California Republican League Convention:

The more moderate groups might be termed "in" groups while the activist right-wing groups might be termed "out" groups. "In" groups such as Republicans for Progress are actively working with and helping Republicans in Congress and elsewhere to evolve their own positions and to pose constructive alternatives to the Democratic programs and proposals. They are not attempting to create an alternative to the Republican party, but rather to strengthen the Republican party by bringing new support to the aid of the party.

The "out" groups, such as Denison Kitchel's Free Society Association,

---

* The following have been members of the Wednesday Club (* denotes no longer in Congress): Mark Andrews (North Dakota), the late John F. Baldwin* (California), Alphonzo Bell (California), William S. Broomfield (Michigan), William T. Cahill (New Jersey), Silvio O. Conte (Massachusetts), John R. Dellenback (Oregon), Robert F. Ellsworth* (Kansas), Marvin Esch (Michigan), Peter H. B. Frelinghuysen (New Jersey), Frank Horton (New York), John V. Lindsay* (New York), William S. Mailliard (California), Joseph M. McDade (Pennsylvania), Charles M. Mathias (Maryland), Chester L. Mize (Kansas), F. Bradford Morse (Massachusetts), Charles A. Mosher (Ohio), Ogden R. Reid (New York), Howard W. Robison (New York), Herman T. Schneebeli (Pennsylvania), Richard S. Schweiker (Pennsylvania), Fred Schwengel (Iowa), Garner E. Shriver (Kansas), Abner Sibal* (Connecticut), Robert T. Stafford (Vermont), William Stanton (Ohio), Robert Taft, Jr. (Ohio), Stanley Tupper* (Maine) and Charles W. Whalen, Jr. (Ohio).

are not only working outside the party, but seem to be heading by their own definition in the direction of a non-party. Some conclude that their beliefs tend to magnetize them toward the Buckleyite Conservative party. Certainly the "out" groups seem to be holding over the head of the [Republican] party, the threat of "Do it our way or we will ruin your candidates."

Despite the high political coloration of Scott's remarks, they do contain, with one exception, a real distinction between the ideological left and right. Of the four major conservative groups—Americans for Constitutional Action (ACA), American Conservative Union (ACU), Free Society Association (FSA), and Young Americans for Freedom (YAF)—only ACU calls itself a Republican organization. At a Washington banquet celebrating the fifth anniversary of YAF in May, 1966, Barry Goldwater, the former G.O.P. standard-bearer, told his youthful audience to avoid direct political action. "You are not a political party, not even a second cousin to a political party," he said of YAF. "You are conservative and there's nothing wrong about being conservative." (Great applause from the twelve hundred listeners.) Republican Goldwater was preceded by Democratic Senator Spessard L. Holland of Florida, who also reminded YAF, "Not all who love the Constitution and conservativism are in one party." Yet the right-wing is hardly as bipartisan as its manifestoes suggest. The proportion of Republicans to Democrats in both YAF and FSA is about that of gin to vermouth in a very dry martini— something around nine to one. And the ACA's ratings for the 89th Congress gave 100 percent approval to fifteen Representatives and Senators—eleven Republicans and four Southern Democrats. (On the other hand, all thirty-seven legislators who received a zero rating were Democrats.)

The oldest of the conservative political-ideological organizations is Americans for Constitutional Action, which was formed in 1959. It is probably also the most effective, although its operations are almost exclusively limited to congressional politics. Its staff director is Charles A. McManus, thirty-nine, whose astuteness is highly regarded by conservatives on Capitol Hill. ACA's chief sponsor is Admiral Ben Moreell, organizer of the Seabees and ex-President of Jones & Laughlin Steel. He presides over a board of trustees that is studded with retired military officers—Major General Thomas A. Lane, Brigadier General Bonner Fellers, Brigadier General Robert

W. Johnson. The group's unpaid finance chairman is Frank J. Kovac, the former Goldwater fund raiser.

After each session of Congress the ACA publishes an elaborate analysis of the voting record of every legislator, judged on a scale of "constitutional conservatism." A few blocks away from ACA headquarters on Capitol Hill, the rival Americans for Democratic Action puts out a similar tabulation based on "forward-looking social responsibility." From this right-left rating game comes a reliable index of a Congressman's political philosophy.

While ACA is best known for its widely reprinted scorecards, its major impact comes through subsidies to Congressmen, most of them Republicans. "We do not make direct financial contributions to any campaigns," says McManus, "but if an eligible candidate asks for help we supply clerical workers, speech writers, researchers, public-relations men, or organizers to help him." Such services are not commonly announced, but it is known that ACA hired a statewide organizer for Senator Karl Mundt (R., S.D.) and a public-relations man for congressional candidate Gene Snyder (R., Ky.) in 1966, and a full-time headquarters secretary for Representative Paul Findley (R., Ill.) in 1964. Also during the 1966 campaign, ACA gave its 225 "eligible" candidates a set of twelve speeches with such titles as "Shadow Over the White House" (i.e., President Johnson's "credibility gap"), written by former Goldwater aides Tony Smith and Karl Hess.

The ACA budget was $187,500 in 1964; in the political "off-year" of 1965 it collected $123,000 from about 4,800 contributors; and in 1966 the budget was $114,305 for "general expenditures" and $99,150 for "campaign assistance."

Two newer conservative organizations, the Free Society Association and the American Conservative Union, were set up following the ouster of Goldwater adherents from control of the Republican National Committee in 1965. FSA has Goldwater as its honorary chairman and his former campaign manager, Arizona attorney Denison Kitchel, as its president. Kitchel's plan was to turn FSA into a mass-membership organization with a very ambitious publications program, including a series of "new Federalist Papers," television productions, study groups, and a speakers' bureau. He figured that of the twenty-seven million Goldwater voters there were seven to eight million "hard-core Goldwater fans," eight to nine million "regular Republicans," who would vote for any G.O.P. candidate, and the rest were "convicted conservatives." With such a sizable field of potential FSA recruits, Kitchel told the San Diego *Union* in August, 1965, that he was "quite optimistic of our ability to obtain within a very short time a membership in the neighborhood of four or five hundred thousand. I would hope this would just be a starter. . . ."

For staff director, Kitchel hired Lynn Mote, a veteran Senate aide, who, since 1939, had worked for such G.O.P. stalwarts as Eugene Milliken (Colorado), and Hugh Butler and Carl Curtis (both Nebraska). With the assistance of a professional fund-raising organization, FSA took in $500,000 in its first eighteen months, and spent most of it on setting up an office and trying to attract members. But by 1967 Mote had left, FSA membership had leveled at 36,500 (with the largest number coming from California), and its hopeful plans had been trimmed to a modest program of monthly newsletters and occasional pamphlets put out by Charles Lichenstein, forty, a member of Goldwater's 1964 brain trust, and two female assistants.

While the Free Society Association ruled out direct political action from its start, the American Conservative Union described itself as a combined political-education and political-action group, "representative of the main trunk and roots of Republican thought." The organization, however, ran into serious financial problems almost immediately after it was launched in late 1964. It set a first-year goal of $400,000, raised only $218,000 from some ten thousand persons, and spent almost all of it on start-up expenses and the production of a few pamphlets. Before it weathered a year, ACU's chairman resigned. He was Donald C. Bruce, a former two-term Indiana Congressman. He was replaced by Ohio Representative John Ashbrook, whom William Buckley has called "by all odds the most exciting young man in the Republican party." In its second year ACU's operations cost $125,000. By 1967 Ashbrook was steering his anemic organization into close alliance with the most robust group on the political right, Young Americans for Freedom. David R. Jones, twenty-nine, the salaried executive director of YAF, assumed the ACU top staff position on a volunteer basis, while Mrs. Carol Bauman, a former editor of YAF's monthly magazine, took charge of ACU publications.

YAF was founded by about one hundred young people who met at William Buckley's ancestral estate in Sharon, Connecticut, over the weekend of September 9, 1960. By January of 1961 they had put together the first picket line ever organized *in favor of* the House Committee on Un-American Activities; by March of 1962 they had not only filled New York's Madison Square Garden to capacity—nineteen thousand—but turned away another ten thousand; in 1964 they cheered and cheered for Barry Goldwater—their presence at countless demonstrations confirming that right-wing girls are prettier than their left-wing counterparts; in 1965 they pressured the Firestone Tire and Rubber Company into abandoning plans to build a plant in Communist Rumania; in 1966 they held mammoth rallies to support "victory in Vietnam."

Today YAF's posh central office in one of Washington's most handsome skyscrapers on fashionable Massachusetts Avenue employs 18 full-time workers to service a membership of over 25,000. Executive Director Jones admits to an operating budget of $25,-000 a month, but this figure does not include the expenses of YAF's self-sufficient regional offices, its 192 college and 150 high school chapters, and such special activities as a leadership training conference it held in the summer of 1966 on the Franklin and Marshall College campus, Lancaster, Pennsylvania, at a cost of $20,000. Seventy-five percent of YAF's budget is raised through direct mail, a technique at which its young leaders have become highly sophisticated. Dave Jones can give a disquisition on why the "Kozak list" (buyers of a car-polishing cloth) will work for the Republican National Committee, but not for his organization. Some of YAF's best returns come from letters to "expires" (former subscribers) of conservative journals, such as *National Review* and *Human Events*—current subscription lists are not for sale—and from large contributors to certain political campaigns, whose names are on record at the office of the Clerk of the House of Representatives.

Judging from *The New Guard*, YAF's house organ, Ronald Reagan is the group's overwhelming favorite. During 1966 the former actor's picture appeared on the slick-paper cover of two of its eleven issues, and he was featured in articles, comments, ads ("100 books of Ronald Reagan stamps for $30.00," rent a 16 mm. black and white film of "Reagan 1964 Campaign Speech"), and even on a cut-out 33⅓ rpm plastic phonograph record. When the 175 YAF leaders at its 1966 summer conference were polled on their presidential preference, the results were Reagan 53 percent, Goldwater 30 percent, Nixon 15 percent, Romney 1 percent.

Certain names appear time after time on the letterheads of conservative organizations—William A. Rusher, Brent Bozell, Frank S. Meyer, John Chamberlain, Charles Edison, Gerhart Niemeyer. The example of Ralph de Toledano, syndicated newspaper columnist, is not untypical of the right-wing activist. The political writer is (1) Vice Chairman, American Conservative Union, (2) Member, Board of Trustees, Americans for Constitutional Action, (3) Member, National Advisory Board, Young Americans for Freedom, (4) listed as "Associate" on the *National Review* masthead, (5) Sponsor, Conservative Book Club, (6) recipient of a $2,000 fee from the Citizens for Goldwater-Miller Committee.

The conservatives, to a far greater degree than the Republican left (though probably not the Democratic left), form their own subsociety. They have their own magazines, most importantly *National Review* and *Human Events*, both with circulations of around 100,-000; their own book-publishing firms—Henry Regnery, Devin-Adair, Arlington House; their own book club; newspapers, particularly those owned by the Copleys and Eugene C. Pulliam, that give them sympathetic coverage and often provide personnel for their political campaigns; certain businessmen who always contribute to their causes and advertise in their journals, such as Walter Knott of Knott's Berry Farm and Ghost Town, Buena Park, California, and Patrick J. Frawley of Schick Safety Razor Company; even their own institution of higher education, the University of Plano, outside of Dallas, where the president is Robert Morris, former counsel for the U.S. Senate Internal Security Subcommittee, and the faculty includes the contemporary giant of classical economics, Ludwig von Mises, and the flamboyant Bella Dodd.

But by all odds the pre-eminent figure of the New Right is William F. Buckley, who has been called "a Yale version of Mort Sahl" (by Doris Fleeson), "the highest Camp" (by Norman Mailer), and the wittiest man ever to run for Mayor of New York (by almost everyone who lived through the Lindsay-Beame-Buckley campaign of 1965). When asked what he would do if he won, the Conservative party's candidate gave the now classic reply, "Demand a recount." He probably also is the only New York City mayoralty nominee to live in Connecticut and to have campaigned from a bright red Triumph 1200 convertible.

Buckley comes from a Kennedyesque background: son of a strong-willed Irish Catholic, self-made multimillionaire; sixth of ten

YOUNG MAN-ABOUT-TOWN

Scott Long, Minneapolis Tribune, Oct. 29, 1965

attractive, competitive, quick-witted children, the girls equal to their brothers; product of a semi-European secondary education and an Ivy League finish; an outdoor type, though tending to skiing and sailing, rather than touch football; with a beautiful wife. Not surprisingly, he has somewhat the same effect on young conservatives as Jack, Bobby, and Teddy have had on a wider cross-section of American youth.

In 1955 Buckley founded *National Review,* with himself as editor, his sister Priscilla as managing editor, another sister as a frequent contributor, brother-in-law Brent Bozell in various capacities, and a healthy infusion of family money to meet the magazine's yearly deficit. The Buckleys' journal occasionally suffers from fallen archness, and, for its secular audience, perhaps an overdose of Catholic debate (in response to Pope John XXIII's encyclical, *National Review* editorialized, *"Mater sí, Magistra no"*). But the writing is rarely dull—a review of a book of Brigitte Bardot nude photographs stated, "Her navel is totally undistinguished"—and for the first time Americans can get a steady stream of conservative comment coated with style and wit.

With his rococo vocabulary, waspish style and Oxbridge accent, Buckley has become a popular TV performer with his own show and a frequent lecturer on the college circuit. He also runs for public office and writes a syndicated newspaper column, a column for the *National Review,* and books, the most recent being *The Unmaking of a Mayor.*

As Buckley has become an institution, he has gathered disciples— "the *National Review* crowd"—who act as guardians and advisers for many of the groups that seek to influence the Republican party, notably the Young Americans for Freedom, the Young Republicans, the American Conservative Union, and the Intercollegiate Studies Institute (formerly the Intercollegiate Society of Individualists— same initials), which is the most academic—almost esoteric—of the rightist organizations. Only the Free Society Association, which is run by a personal Goldwater clique, seems to stay clear of the Buckley influence.

National Review's publisher, William A. Rusher, along with Representative Ashbrook of the ACU, F. Clifton White and Tennessee Representative William Brock have maintained an influential position in the National Young Republican Federation, an important party auxiliary group. Ashbrook once headed the organization and the Ashbrook-Rusher-White-Brock quartet provided tactical guidance for the so-called "Syndicate" faction that has controlled the YR's for most of the past decade. Though the paper membership of the Young Republicans is in the 400,000 range, the active leadership is small and has considerable overlap with the leadership of the Buckley-influenced YAF. Young Republicans are an important recruiting group for the party and provided much of the early impetus for the Goldwater movement, which eventually captured the senior party organization. At the biennial convention in Omaha in June, 1967, the "Syndicate" faction retained its control of the Young Republicans by electing Jack McDonald of Tennessee, a protégé of Brock's, to succeed state Senator Tom Van Sickle of Kansas, White's deputy in the Goldwater campaign, as chairman of the organization. The youthful delegates cheered Goldwater's advice that they fight to stay ideologically and organizationally independent of senior party control and acted on it by roundly rejecting a series of rules changes that would have curbed their freedom. They also cheered themselves hoarse for California Governor Ronald Reagan, the speaker at their final banquet and, quite obviously, their chosen successor to Goldwater as the Republican presidential nominee.

The other major volunteer group, the half-million-member National Federation of Republican Women, is also firmly in conservative control. Its Washington, D.C., convention in May, 1967, featured a bitter battle for the Federation presidency between an old-fashioned conservative, Mrs. Gladys O'Donnell of California, and the famous pamphleteer of the radical right, Mrs. Phyllis Schlafly of Illinois. The prize went to Mrs. O'Donnell by a vote of 1,910 to 1,494, with Mrs. Schlafly and her backers protesting before and after the tally that there had been fraud and bias in the credentials committee and in the actual voting.

Mrs. O'Donnell, a widow of sixty-three, has been, successively, a backer of Robert A. Taft, Richard M. Nixon and Barry Goldwater for the presidential nominations of 1952, 1960, and 1964. She said she would be delighted to support her Governor, Ronald Reagan, in 1968, if such a position did not violate the official neutrality expected of a federation president. Her rival, Mrs. Schlafly, is of course the author of *A Choice, Not an Echo,* the pro-Goldwater tract that blamed the problems of the Republican party on the insidious influence of the liberal Eastern kingmakers.

Faced with a choice between these two ladies, New York, Pennsylvania and Michigan and other "moderate" delegations supported Mrs. O'Donnell, but her victory can in no sense be described as a triumph of liberal Republicanism. She also had the support of most of the Arizona delegates and, significantly, of Mrs. Pat Hutar of Chicago, one of F. Clifton White's ablest protégés in Young Republican politics and the Draft Goldwater movement.

After the vote, Mrs. Schlafly threatened to form a rival Republican women's group of her own, but the emotional climate of her indignation meeting was effectively cooled by a speech from Reagan's daughter, Mrs. Maureen Reagan Sills, cautioning the dissident Schlafly supporters not to be hasty about abandoning the national federation. Though she had supported Mrs. Schlafly for president of the federation, Mrs. Sills' speech was viewed as a signal that her father wanted to retain his credentials with those who call themselves "responsible conservatives" rather than follow the fringe right-wingers as far as their emotions would carry them.

"The *National Review* crowd," which sets the tone for the responsible right, has been scrupulously careful to disassociate itself from extremists like the Birchers, the Minute Men, and the Kent Courtneys of New Orleans. The John Birch Society, according to its monthly maagzine, *American Opinion*, believes that 60 to 80 percent of the United States is under the influence of Communists, that "the principal object of medicare is to destroy the independence and integrity of American physicians," that "the whole racial agitation was designed and is directed by the international Communist conspiracy," that "the theory that the Warren [Supreme] Court is working for a domestic, as distinct from foreign, dictatorship becomes less tenable every day," and that "Communist domination of many of the departments of the Federal Government is too obvious to require much comment." All this, in the word of William F. Buckley, is "drivel."

In fact, Buckley was in advance of many national Republican leaders in his condemnation of Robert Welch's organization. While some top Republicans, such as Richard Nixon and Thomas Kuchel, had been after the Birchers since 1962, it was not until October 1, 1965, when Senator Thruston B. Morton, chairman of the Republican Senatorial Campaign Committee, announced "the time has come to give the John Birch Society a kick in the tail," that the G.O.P. declared open season on extremists.

Why did it take the party so long to come to grips with an organization that had called Dwight D. Eisenhower, the only Republican President in a generation, a Communist dupe? There were a variety of reasons, among them: politicians are inclusionists, they instinctively oppose reading voters *out* of their party; many did not see any danger in the Birchers, viewing them as simply misguided or silly; most did not feel threatened by them; and almost none thought there was any political sex appeal in attacking them.

The 1964 election and its aftermath proved that their reasons were wrong and the consequences possibly dangerous. The party had clearly been hurt by failing to repudiate the Birchers. Even Barry Goldwater saw this and called for Republicans to quit the Birch Society, while admitting that he had made a mistake in rejecting the anti-extremism resolution at the San Francisco convention. Moreover, the Birchers were becoming increasingly irksome within the party. John Tower, hardly a liberal, had to rush back to Texas to fight off a Birch attempt to take over the Harris County (Houston) Republican executive committee. On July 1, 1965, by a slim 95 to 80 vote, he and State Chairman Peter O'Donnell, Jr., managed to install an outspoken moderate, James Mayor, as county chairman. And that paragon of conservatism, Senator Karl Mundt, who had made his national reputation by ferreting out Communists, found himself challenged in a South Dakota primary by a thirty-six-year-old Bircher who ran a right-wing book and gift shop in Sioux Falls. When Mundt was accused of having voted "for the most socialistic school bill in history" and "being a UNESCO man from the very beginning," the national Republican leadership collectively gulped.

Back in mid-March, 1964, when the right wing captured control of the California Republican Assembly, a band of progressive state legislators founded the F.A.B. Society, whose initials, politely translated, stood for "Foil a Bircher." Eighteen months later virtually every major Republican, led by congressional leaders Dirksen and Ford, pinned the F.A.B. label to his lapel.

The result of the new G.O.P. unity on the extremism issue, as well as the reduced tug of civil rights as a party issue—not because it was either less important or solved, but rather because it had temporarily moved out of the national legislative arena, where the Republicans operated—removed the two most divisive domestic issues of 1964 from the intraparty debate. And what was left to debate illustrated how narrow really was the separation between the G.O.P. left and right.

While George Gilder and Bruce Chapman, the young liberal

activists, were writing, "The objective of the progressive Republican should be to transform the Republican party into a responsible conservative party," editor-columnist James J. Kilpatrick, the conservative activist, was saying in a speech sponsored by the Free Society Association, "I do not want to leave the impression that I stand before you blindly opposing a strong Federal Government—for I do not. . . . I do believe, pessimistically, that we are moving into the era of the megalopolis, a new age of the anthill, in which *of necessity* there must be vastly more government as a whole than we have known in the past." Indeed, Gilder-Chapman and Kilpatrick, and all who ideologically fell between them, were operating from the same set of four Republican touchstones—a written constitution, with its separation of powers among the three branches of government; the principle of federalism, most often meaning, in the present context, a shoring up of state and local government to restore the former balance; strong reliance on private enterprise, often as the means to roll back Federal programs; and an emphasis on the integrity of the individual man and a broadening of his opportunities.

In examining the literature of the G.O.P. left and right in the post-1964 election period, there are, of course, certain pet issues that each camp champions. The rightists, for example, have urged with vigor the Dirksen amendments—to open an avenue to overturn the Supreme Court rulings on reapportionment and school prayer—and the retention of Section 14(b) of the Taft-Hartley Act, allowing state right-to-work laws. The leftists generally have been on the other side. Some right-wingers still talk about the so-called "Liberty Amendment" to abolish the Federal income tax, but almost all of the responsible conservatives agree with the late Robert M. Schuchman, first national chairman of Young Americans for Freedom, who said, "It is merely another magic formula, another wistful short cut to success which, unfortunately, diverts conservatives from the arduous tasks of persuading and organizing the electorate. . . ." The questions of domestic Communism and internal security, which almost tore the party system, if not the country, apart in the late 1940's and early 1950's were rarely raised by either group. When Denison Kitchel announced in the summer of 1966 that "the entire structure of our internal security laws must be rebuilt," it was almost nostalgic, like the Charleston or the blackbottom.

Of more interest, perhaps because so few have pointed it out, are the surprising parallels between the supposedly opposing forces within the party.

Tax sharing, the proposal to return part of the Federal tax revenue to state and local governments, became a key plank in the Republican State of the Union Message as presented by House leader Gerald Ford at the beginning of the 90th Congress. It was an issue that the Ripon Society had been lobbying for since July, 1965, and in .which the young men of Cambridge felt an almost proprietary interest. Yet the record also showed that Melvin R. Laird, the liberals' *bête noire,* had introduced a tax-sharing bill in 1958, making him the first Congressman of either party to do so in modern times.

A volunteer army as an alternative to the draft system was another proposal pushed by both the Republican right and left, winning the approval of the Ripon Society and the Young Americans for Freedom, Barry Goldwater and the Wednesday Club. In fact, the case for abolishing the draft was made in *National Review* by Bruce Chapman!

Both left and right also spoke the same language—from the same sources—on urban renewal. To make the case that the program had been "a $5-billion fiasco," both referred to Martin Anderson's *The Federal Bulldozer: A Critical Analysis of Urban Renewal, 1949-1962;* for an alternative, each looked to see Jane Jacobs's design for diversity, restoration and mixed communities (residential, commercial and industrial), which she outlined in *The Death and Life of Great American Cities.*

Even the most "radical" proposal endorsed by the G.O.P. left— the negative income tax, a plan for giving direct cash payments from the Federal treasury to families whose income fell below a certain level—was, in fact, proposed five years earlier in *Capitalism and Freedom* by Milton Friedman, one of Barry Goldwater's economic advisers during the 1964 campaign.

Therefore, it was not so ironic to discover that George Romney and Ronald Reagan, often pictured as the opposite extremes of viable Republicanism, actually had the same philosophical mentor: Richard C. Cornuelle, forty, a former California foundation executive who looked more like a matinee idol than either of his famous disciples. It was Cornuelle's belief that most public problems—from juvenile crime to air and water pollution to racial segregation—could be solved by mobilizing what he called "the independent sector," the

network of voluntary associations that function outside the governmental and commercial arenas. To prove the point by example, he set
up a successful nonprofit corporation, United Students Aid Funds,
which competed with the existing Federal program for giving loans to
college students. Even before the publication of his popular tract,
Reclaiming the American Dream, Cornuelle was being called to Lansing to tutor the Michigan Governor in "independent sector" action.
And the same services were made available to Reagan during his 1966
campaign. In fact, Reagan's first program, established even before he
took office, was a Cornuelle-type operation to match unemployed
workers in disadvantaged areas, such as Watts, with available jobs
in California industry.

If there has been a marked absence of divisive issues on the
domestic front, the same cannot be said of foreign affairs. Here the
left and right have had decidedly different points of view and enough
live issues on which to sharpen their scalpels.

The position of the Republican right was stated by Professor
Gerhart Niemeyer of Notre Dame in a May, 1966, speech before a
Free Society Association regional meeting:

. . . the policy we [U.S. Government] are pursuing now is precisely
the wrong policy, because it really involves two separate policies toward
communism. We have made an official and unofficial distinction between
so-called "good" Communists in the Soviet Union and "bad" Communists
in Communist China. We are trying to accommodate the "good" Communists with test-ban treaties, all kinds of direct wires and communications, reassurances and exchanges, and also with massive efforts to ease
their economic difficulties and aid their industrialization programs—
which, of course, allow them to increase their military strength.

As long as we conduct ourselves like this toward the Soviet Union,
and in a totally different way toward the "bad" Communists in China,
we cannot possibly convince either the world or our own people that
the enemy is communism. . . .

So, unless we can restore a global policy toward communism, unless
we can persuade everyone that we are following a consistent principle
of reducing the power of communism, of stopping it where it wants to
advance and of blocking its aspiration to world conquest—unless we can
do that, we really have no leg to stand on. Therefore, we must halt the
programs that build up communism, particularly the trade programs.
And we must win in Vietnam—although all of us, most especially the
"hawks" among us, must understand that our victory there cannot be a
total victory.

The Ripon Society would probably consider Niemeyer a responsible representative of "The Doctrinaires," those who operate, according to a recent *Ripon Forum,* from a three-point set of abstractions: "1) Communism is our enemy; 2) Communism is everywhere; 3) all our activities should be guided by the need to oppose whatever looks like Communism."

But, say the Ripon men, "the simple lessons of the cold war— with its emphasis on military containment of monolithic communism —are becoming obsolete." The loosening of power blocs, they contend, makes it necessary to reach decisions on pragmatic rather than ideological grounds. Rather than by "The Doctrinaires," foreign policy must be determined by "The Problem-solvers," whom they describe as:

. . . tentative, pragmatic men who take their problems one by one and are skeptical of philosophies that purport to give all the answers. They are most useful when history is moving quickly and flexible responses are required. If they are now about to have their day in foreign policy debate, it is because the institutional solutions of the past twenty years are in need of appraisal. NATO, the UN, East-West relations, the structure of international finance and world trade, the administrative machinery of American diplomacy, intelligence and foreign aid—these are some of the problems that must be dealt with, and their existence means that the Problem-solvers must supplant the Doctrinaires as national spokesmen for the Republican Party on matters of foreign policy.

The first major test since the 1966 election of the relative strength of the two forces in the G.O.P. came on March 16, when the Senate passed the U.S.–Soviet Consular Treaty, providing for an exchange of consulates between the two countries. The 36 Republican senators split 23 to 13 for the treaty.* However, this was probably not a true picture of the philosophical division within the party because of the

* Republicans in favor of the Consular Treaty: Aiken (Vermont), Allott (Colorado), Baker (Tennessee), Bennett (Utah), Boggs (Delaware), Brooke (Massachusetts)—not voting, but paired for, Carlson (Kansas), Case (New Jersey), Cooper (Kentucky), Dirksen (Illinois), Dominick (Colorado), Fong (Hawaii), Griffin (Michigan), Hatfield (Oregon), Hickenlooper (Iowa), Javits (New York), Kuchel (California), Morton (Kentucky), Pearson (Kansas), Percy (Illinois), Prouty (Vermont), Scott (Pennsylvania), Smith (Maine). Republicans against the treaty: Cotton (New Hampshire), Curtis (Nebraska), Fannin (Arizona), Hansen (Wyoming), Hruska (Nebraska), Jordan (Idaho), Miller (Iowa), Mundt (South Dakota), Murphy (California), Thurmond (South Carolina), Tower (Texas), Williams (Delaware), Young (North Dakota).

brilliant maneuvering of Senator Morton in behalf of the treaty. If all political considerations could have been put aside, the Republicans would most likely have divided right down the middle.

However, even this sparring on foreign policy cannot disguise the fact that the two ideological wings of the party are closer together than they have been in years though it does not serve their short-term interests, particularly financial, to admit it.

What this has meant is that—like the Trotskyites and Stalinists of the 1930's—the sectarian groups on the fringe of the G.O.P. have spent more and more of their considerable energy battling each other.

The American Conservative Union, commenting on the groups that make up the Council of Republican Organizations, writes, "Taken together they provide the thinnest caliber of political leadership for the Republican Left since Harold Stassen." The *Ripon Forum* takes pot shots at *National Review, Human Events*, and YAF. YAF's *New Guard* devotes a page each month to a "Report on the Left." The ACU issues a report assailing the Wednesday Club members' voting records.

This, perhaps, is a way to convince themselves of their own importance. For, since they are sniped at, *ergo,* they must be important. Thus do they reinforce each other's egos.

Yet, outside of the party auxiliaries that have become ideologically-oriented, all the groups combined on the G.O.P. right probably spend less than $1 million a year and do not have as many as 100,000 members, while those on the G.O.P. left spend about $150,000 and may have as few as 1,000 members.

Neither size of membership nor annual expenditures are necessarily an accurate index of their political influence. Ideas, which are the commodities they deal in, do not have price tags and need not be backed by an army. The party's splinters, in fact, often perform useful jobs that would not be done without them. But the mood of the Republican party as it approaches 1968 is not receptive to even muted voices from its outer limits. Unlike that of 1964, the odds are that this nomination will be a battle of the professionals.

II | The Candidates

5 GEORGE ROMNEY:
The Traveling Salesman

IF A point in time must be fixed, Governor George Romney of Michigan began his presidential campaign in the third week of February, 1967. Re-elected to a third term the previous November as the pace setter of a sweep that also netted the Republicans a Senator and five new Representaives, blooded in the national forum of *Meet the Press*, leading President Johnson in both the Gallup and the Harris polls, Romney left Lansing on February 17 for a series of speeches to the Lincoln's Birthday fund-raising dinners that every Republican of any prominence is required to make each year. He was accompanied by his wife, Lenore, a staff of six and forty newsmen.

The first stop was Anchorage, Alaska, and the first day, a Saturday, was in the classic tradition of American political hokum. Arriving in a snowstorm, the Romneys doffed their topcoats and slipped into sealskin parkas, lent them by an enterprising local furrier. They "competed" against Alaska Governor Walter J. Hickel and his wife in a carefully-staged dog-sled race, which the Hickels somehow managed to lose. Romney threw snowballs in the air for the television cameras, took a sightseeing flight to Mt. McKinley (which turned out to be obscured by clouds), and, after his speech, dropped in on the "Miners and Trappers Ball," where he obligingly judged the beard-growing contest and rubbed noses, Eskimo style, with a series of pretty, costumed Alaska women.

On Sunday morning, reporters, awakened early by the Romney staff, rubbed the sleep from their eyes and noticed on the mimeographed schedule that the only event preceding the flight back to Seattle was listed as: *8 a.m. Alaska Standard Time. Governor and Mrs. Romney attend LDS Stake Priesthood Service.*

A few of them decided to skip church and enjoy an extra hour's

"Then You Haven't Decided Yet Whether You'll Run, Governor?"

© 1966, Herblock in the Washington **Post**

sleep before leaving for the airport. They made a mistake. For in that hour the churchgoing newsmen learned that, conventional as he might be in his acquiescence to the silly rituals of a political campaign, fundamentally George Romney was very different from anyone who had previously run for President.*

The church hall was a large, plain room, with pews in front, folding chairs in the back, filled to the far corners by 850 persons—one-fifth of the entire Alaska membership of the Church of Jesus Christ of Latter-day Saints.

The Romneys were escorted to the platform; the reporters, a bit self-conscious in the strange surroundings, to a front pew. The opening hymn was spirited; George and Lenore, a handsome couple, sang with gusto about the day "when all that was promised the Saints will be given."†

Orson P. Millet, the president of the stake (as the LDS Church calls its geographical subdivisions), introduced the guests. The previous morning, he had led a large Mormon delegation at the airport, carrying "Romney in '68" signs. Now, in the somewhat more restrained rhetoric fitting a church, he said, "We are proud that he is being considered for a position . . ." and added, in most matter-of-fact tones, "The reason that he is . . . is that he has been true to the Gospel of Jesus Christ. We look forward to his message, but first we would like to hear from Sister Romney."

Lenore stepped to the rostrum, slim, pretty and amazingly youthful-looking for a fifty-seven-year-old grandmother of nine, and said, with perfect assurance, "Good morning, dear brothers and sisters."

She spoke for only six minutes, but the reporters were left with mouths agape. This was no shy and stumbling candidate's wife, nor one who would confine herself to platitudes. She was a witty, dramatic and highly professional platform performer in her own right, as becomes one who had taken a flier at an acting career in Hollywood before her marriage. She was obviously to be reckoned into any calculation of Romney's assets for the presidential cam-

* Whatever it may prove, the odd fact is that the Republican party, trying to get back into the "mainstream" of American political life, has presidential contenders in 1968 of anything-but-ordinary religious background. Romney, a Mormon; Richard M. Nixon, a Quaker; and Senator Charles H. Percy, a Christian Scientist, all belong to religious groups that are relatively small in numbers and unusual in doctrine. Governor Ronald Reagan, the fourth prospect, had an Irish-Catholic father and a Protestant mother, and now belongs to the Christian Church.

† Romney, like most of his co-religionists, prefers the designation Saint to Mormon.

paign, and when she referred to the "four years *we* have been in state government," it was surely no slip of the tongue.

Her message was a simple one, that the basic tests for the American people were moral, not material. Quoting Scripture, Abraham Lincoln and Martin Luther King, she said, "We have had our industrial revolution, our scientific revolution, our intellectual revolution. But we will not be judged by our material or intellectual achievements. We will not be known by whether we can put a man on the moon first, or build a bigger intercontinental missile—but [pause] by how we treat each other." She spoke with compassion of the Negro mothers raising children in the slums, then slid smoothly into a discussion of the concern all parents feel "over changing moral standards." "I resent with all my heart those scientists and psychologists who would tell us how to live when we have been given a Supreme Law and a Supreme Authority to guide us." It was an intense, emotional talk, and then, just as she seemed about to lose herself in tears, she regained her composure with a quip. "I've always had a lot to say, but nobody seemed to care until George became Governor," thanked them, and sat down.

In the stunned silence, Romney began by making the only sensible remark possible on the occasion: "You have just heard," he said, "the one person who can beat me in Michigan."

He essayed a little joke, as feeble as most of his efforts at humor: "Lincoln said that the people of this country were almost a chosen people. Up here, we're among the frozen chosen."

Laboriously, with none of the quickness and brevity of his wife, he moved toward his subject; only the religious tone was the same as hers. When confronted with difficult questions, he said, "it has always semed to me that if God would reveal His truths to simpler ages, with simpler problems, certainly He would reveal them to ours. . . . One current problem where modern revelation has some pertinence is that of lawlessness and crime."

Like his wife, he spoke with obvious sincerity of the conditions that breed disregard for laws and social standards. "You have no idea," he told the all-white congregation in the state that lies closest to the frontier, "what life is like in the ghettos of the East. You have no idea what it means for a child to reach first grade with a vocabulary of twenty words. Racial discrimination is the greatest social injustice we face." But, he asked himself, can "the urgent need to correct social injustice justify defiance of the law? I believe personally that God has given a very clear statement on this point." He quoted (from the 58th Section of *The Doctrine and the Covenants*): "Let no man break the laws of the land. For he that keepeth the law of God hath no need to break the laws of the land."

"To me," said George Romney, "that is clear and precise. When men take the law in their own hands, whether to correct social injustice or for other reasons, they open the way to anarchy, mob rule and the loss of human liberty. We must deal with social injustice and with respect for law. We must do both. We must not sacrifice one for the other."

Reporters filed out, puzzled. Had they heard two sermons or two political speeches, they asked. How odd to go to church with a candidate who avowedly refuses to politick on Sundays and emerge with a crackling good story on a major domestic political question.

"I am completely the product of the Church of Jesus Christ of Latter-day Saints," Romney had said to New York *Times* reporter Wallace Turner in August, 1965.

What is this church that produced him? What is there in it that evokes the peculiar sort of energetic evangelism, the righteousness and self-righteousness that underlie Romney's unique political appeal and at the same time cause so many of his political problems?

"My religion," said Brigham Young, the great organizer, "must be with me from one Monday morning to the next, the year around, or it will not answer me." To insure that Saints are plugged in to life's meaning, the church has created an organization, which Richard T. Ely, a pioneer student of Mormonism, said in 1903, "is the most nearly perfect piece of social mechanism . . . excepting the German Army alone." And, over the years, the church hierarchy has devised a truly staggering variety of activities to occupy the time of its faithful—religious observances, socials, educational programs, charitable projects.

If Huey Long wished to make every man a king, it was Joseph Smith's inspiration to make every man a priest. The Mormons have no professional clergy. Starting at around twelve years, a Mormon boy enters the first order of priesthood. By college age he will probably serve a two-year hitch as a missionary. For a practicing Mormon like George Romney, religion can become an almost all-consuming way of life.

In order to bring Romney into focus it is necessary to keep in mind four facts about Mormonism.*

1. Mormonism is an American religion.

Calvin was a Frenchman, Luther a German, Wesley an Englishman, but Joseph Smith, Jr., was born in Sharon, Vermont, and grew up in Palmyra, New York.

The Book of Mormon, which young Smith claimed he received from the Angel Moroni in 1827, and on which he founded a religion, tells of the arrival of the Hebrews on the American continent before the Christian era. Zion to the Jews may have been Israel, but to the Mormons, so said Joseph Smith, "The whole of America is Zion itself. . . ." A close follower of the prophet even calculated that the Garden of Eden stood in Jackson County, Missouri.

More than being merely American, Mormon doctrine is patriotically American, reflecting a kind of romantic nationalism peculiar to the nineteenth century. "And this land shall be a land of liberty . . . and there shall be no kings upon the land. . . . And I will fortify this land against all other nations." (II Nephi 10:11-12.) As a devout Mormon, Romney firmly believes this and his political speeches bear witness. Both church and country have a Manifest Destiny. Addressing a 1966 Lincoln Day dinner in Boston, he said: "I believe that the Declaration of Independence and the Constitution are divinely-inspired documents, written by men especially raised up by their Creator for that purpose. I believe that God has made and presented to us a nation for a purpose—to bring freedom to all the people of the world." This is purest Mormon teaching (*Doctrine and Covenants,* 101:77,80), but exotic fare for the average Republican contributor, who has come to expect nothing more exalted with his roast beef than an attack on the Democrats and their evil works. Thus, a paradox in Romney turns out to be a paradox in Mormonism itself. These people, whose beliefs and practices are so idiosyncratic, and who actually took arms against

* Published works that are useful in studying the Latter-day Saints are: John Henry Evans, *Joseph Smith, An American Prophet* (New York: Macmillan, 1933); Thomas F. O'Dea, *The Mormons* (Chicago: University of Chicago Press, 1957); Wallace F. Bennett, *Why I am a Mormon* (Boston: Beacon, 1958); Wallace Turner, *The Mormon Establishment* (Boston: Houghton Mifflin, 1966); Robert Mullen, *The Latter-day Saints* (Garden City, N.Y.: Doubleday, 1966); Christopher Lasch, "Burned Over Utopia," *New York Review of Books,* January 26, 1967; Seymour Freedgood, "Mormonism: Rich, Vital, and Unique," *Fortune,* April, 1964.

the United States government, are also as hyper-American as a rodeo or county fair. It is what one scholar calls a "curious combination of typicality and peculiarity."

2. *Mormonism is rooted in the American West.*

Joseph Smith took his small band of believers to Ohio, then Missouri, then Illinois, where he was murdered by a mob. His successor, Brigham Young, starting in 1847, directed the church's migration to the Great Salt Lake Valley of Utah.

It was to Salt Lake City that the first Mormon Romney, George's great-grandfather, an English carpenter, took his family by oxcart in 1850, nine years after his arrival in the United States. With the exception of two decades at a polygamous colony in Mexico, the Romneys have been closely identified with the old Utah Territory. It was there that George Romney spent most of his boyhood.*

Partly because they had been a highly disciplined and persecuted minority, the Mormons brought a history of cooperative action to Utah. The tradition was further developed there by the need for communal water control. Thus they added to the existing image of the Western pioneer as an attractive, if somewhat contradictory, fellow: part rugged individualist, part communitarian; self-sufficient, yet quick to meet common problems with cooperative efforts. Sometimes the two strains did not quite mesh. In the Mormons, a social idealism seemed to be warring with a political-economic conservativism. During the depression of the 1930's, for example, their leaders could set up a most elaborate public welfare program while being, at the same time, pungently hostile to the New Deal.

Perhaps it is this Western-Mormon ambivalence that makes Romney's views so hard to pigeonhole. Nelson Rockefeller calls him a "progressive," while Barry Goldwater says he "makes as conservative a speech as I'll ever make in my life." Both, as we shall see, are right. And Romney, when asked to label himself, enigmati-

---

* In 1966, reporter Saul Friedman of the Detroit *Free Press* counted sixty-four Romneys in the Salt Lake City phone book. But, because the family was large and migrated around the West, Governor Romney found relatives almost everywhere he went on his speaking tour of the Mountain States in February, 1967. At Ricks College in Rexburg, Idaho, where he spoke, one of the main buildings is named for an uncle, also a George Romney, who was a former president of the college. In Phoenix, on the same trip, the *Arizona Republic* noted he had two uncles and twenty-three first cousins in the state—more than enough to fill the Arizona delegation to the G.O.P. convention by themselves.

cally replies, "I'm trying to be as conservative as the United States Constitution, as progressive as Theodore Roosevelt, and as liberal as Lincoln."

3. Mormonism believes in self-deification through effort.

A joke that made the rounds in Detroit in 1964 went: "Romney might make a pretty good President, but I hate to have anyone use the White House as a stepping-stone to higher office."

There is no record of whether Romney thought this funny. Columnist Joseph Alsop has correctly stated that the Governor "has a hearty laugh but a somewhat deficient sense of the ridiculous." More to the point, George Romney, as a thoughtful Mormon, probably would not find the joke's premise so ridiculous. For it is almost a proverb among Latter-day Saints that "as man is now, God once was; as God is now, man may become." Or as Professor Thomas O'Dea, the sympathetic chronicler of the Mormons, explains: "God is God because he has risen to 'Godhood' by his own labor." Man, too, can be raised to Godlike status through his accomplishments in this world. Unlike the fatalistic theory of predestination, the Mormon's "free agency" prods its adherents into a life of action and good works—a life like Romney's.

George Romney, in his wife's opinion, has "a fetish about wasting time." Once, when he could find nothing else to do, Mrs. Romney told reporter Earl Mazo, "George took down the draperies, then sat in the middle of the floor and proceeded to pull out the hems. Apparently . . . he recalled a chance remark of mine that I planned to send the draperies to the cleaners, but first the hems needed to be taken out."

Theology, probably more than glands, explains the amazing energy of this man, who was in his mid-fifties when he first ran for public office, and who has been compared to a "one-man earthquake, a tidal wave, an elemental force."

4. Mormonism encourages definite personality traits.

The Mormons are a homogeneous group of predominantly Anglo-Scandinavian ancestry. They neither smoke nor drink, not even tea or coffee. They tithe, that is, give 10 percent of their gross income to the church.

They do not curse. Romney says "gosh," "by golly," and an occasional "aw, nuts." When *Newsweek* in 1967 attributed to him the improbable quote, "I call my best friends sons of bitches,"

Romney fired off an anguished letter to the editor denying he had said any such thing. Carefully avoiding any repetition of the offensive "vulgarism," as he called it, he said, "The quotation is particularly repugnant to my character. . . . Use of such a phrase is contrary to my belief and my nature."

Physical fitness is as integral a part of their applied Christianity as moral purity, since Mormons believe that "the body is the temple of the spirit." Romney plays a sort of "compact golf" in the early mornings before going to work. By using four balls at the same time, he can play the equivalent of thirty-six holes in about one hour and fifteen minutes. "I play golf for exercise and humility," he says. "And on that basis I never lose, you see, because the more exercise, the more humility." (This is a set line and he always laughs after he has delivered it.)

Mormons, despite rigid convictions, are not a dour or antisocial people. They encouraged dancing, for instance, at a time when such frivolity was generally frowned upon in church circles. The Romneys have made some adaptations to the customs of the business and political world. At a party, they may hold a "consommé on the rocks" to assure that their drinking guests are not self-conscious. They began serving liquor in their home after learning, through sad experience, that guests confronting a dry evening often fortified themselves too well in advance.*

But Mormons are not conditioned to take a passive attitude toward the non-Mormon or "Gentile" world, as Saints call all outsiders. Instead, they are trained to feel that "theirs is still the task of carrying the option of redemption and salvation to all men," writes Robert Mullen, the author of a highly laudatory book on the Latter-day Saints. It is a proselytizing and a missionary church, in which Romney and most other men serve their two-year turns as missionaries.

This proselytizing urge may give Mormons a tendency to be argumentative and long-winded. A close political associate of Romney's observed that during the 1962 debates with Governor John Swainson it was almost impossible for Romney to keep his remarks within the allotted time segments. Reporter Julius Duscha wrote in

* As Governor, Romney refused to veto two bills permitting sale of liquor in state armories, thereby incurring the wrath of the Michigan Temperance Foundation.

the Washington *Post*, "He is the kind of man who can make a political cliché . . . sound like a sentence from the Sermon on the Mount." More succinctly, a one-time (and now disenchanted) adviser described Romney as a speaker in three words: "A dynamic bore."

The dangers of carrying a strong sense of one's own virtue and a missionary zeal into the political arena are many. The *Book of Mormon* can be read as a story of "good guys" and "bad guys." Romney has been accused by his critics of applying these same simple standards to politics and politicians.

Whether it is more of a handicap than a help may be argued. John F. Kennedy, who laughed off Richard M. Nixon's clumsy effort during their television debates to make a moral issue of President Truman's salty language, apparently did not take Romney's moralism as a joke. According to the late President's friend, Paul Fay, Kennedy once said, "The one fellow I don't want to run against [in 1964] is Romney. . . . No vice whatsoever, no smoking, no drinking. Imagine someone we know going off for 24 or 48 hours to fast and meditate, awaiting a message from the Lord on whether to run or not to run. Does that sound like one of the old gang?"

Kennedy was referring to Romney's much-publicized day-long fast before announcing his candidacy for Governor in 1962. Mrs. Romney once said that "fasting is basic to our worship, and prayer on appropriate occasions is to us like breathing." But to some the pre-announced fast was more sanctimonious than pious. Said August (Gus) Scholle, the president of the Michigan AFL-CIO, "The big clown. He thinks he has a private pipeline to God." Romney replied that "the same pipeline is available to Mr. Scholle, if he cares to take advantage of it."*

The equivocal standing of personal purity as an attribute of a

---

* The Romney-Scholle feud is one of the classics of current politics. The labor chief, who had great political influence in Michigan until Romney's first victory in 1962, finds it impossible to forgive or forget the man who keeps beating him at the polls. In 1966, Scholle and the Michigan AFL-CIO published and distributed wholesale a thirty-page booklet entitled *Who is the Real George Romney?* From the first sentence—"This documentation of acts and statements of Governor George Romney has been carefully assembled to convey the many conflicting statements of the man who now aspires to become the President of the United States"—to the last—"The above statements are made by a man who piously goes about telling other people about morality while he practices the kind of outrageous duplicity demonstrated in these pages"—the book is a masterpiece of political character assassination.

candidate was perhaps best expressed by John Fischer of *Harper's Magazine*, who wrote, "Romney is so clean-cut he makes your teeth ache." Certainly for Romney it has been a mixed blessing in his relations with other Republicans. It is recognized by some of them as a political asset to the party. Governor Hickel of Alaska, explaining why he thought Romney might be the strongest candidate for 1968, said Romney had, more than Richard Nixon, the "non-political image" needed to defeat President Johnson. "He is knowledgeable, competent but not too political," Hickel said, whereas Mr. Johnson has the reputation for being "strictly political" about everything.

But, whatever its appeal to the voters, Romney's conspicuous purity makes other Republicans squirm. Long before they had any differences over Republican policy and politics, Romney had irritated Barry Goldwater by a simple act of what Goldwater regarded as pure effrontery. As a matter of courtesy, Goldwater, then chairman of the Republican Senatorial Campaign Committee, sent an aide to see newly-elected Governor Romney in 1963 to inform him that the committee would be contacting Michigan Republicans to buy tickets to its $500-a-plate fund-raising dinner. In response, the novice Governor felt called upon to read Goldwater's man a lengthy lecture on the iniquity of big-money contributions and their corrupting effects on politics. Goldwater fumed when he got the report, and he has never really stopped fuming.

The same holier-than-thou attitude permeates the incredible letter Romney wrote Goldwater in December, 1964, explaining why he had refused to support Goldwater during the campaign. In all the twelve single-spaced pages, Romney never once concedes or even hints that there was an element of expediency—or even political necessity— in his decision to stay clear of the national ticket. Instead, he repeats the statement that Goldwater had already criticized: "I did not endorse you because I was not willing to compromise one iota the principles I fought for in San Francisco."

Nor is it just his intraparty opponents who have felt the wrath of Romney's always-confident moral judgment. A vitally important potential ally or opponent for 1968, Senator Charles H. Percy, was as "hurt" and "shocked" as Goldwater had ever been to discover on a visit to Detroit in early 1967 that Romney had called him an "opportunist" on the grounds that he had refused to support two 1964 Romney platform amendments which, on later recollection, Romney agreed had been voted on before Percy had received his plea for help.

The joke among unamused politicians at the time was that Romney, if nominated, would be the first presidential candidate without a running mate, because he could find nobody who was worthy of the honor.

But, if Romney's assurance of his own righteousness irritates some Republicans, it is also his armor for political combat. As Tennyson said of Sir Galahad, his "strength is as the strength of ten, because [his] heart is pure." Mormonism is an exceedingly difficult religion to live, and, just as in every other faith, there are many who consider themselves members of the church without abiding by all its prescriptions. Yet those who fully live it acquire an assurance that is awesome. It is almost certainly the literal truth to say that Romney would not be a presidential contender were it not for his religious faith; nothing else seems likely to have armed him with the burning sense of mission that has carried him this far in the battle.

As one who has seen the true light, he is determined that his view shall prevail. Abraham Lincoln, a Gentile, once observed, "In a dispute, it is fatal to be able to see the other fellow's point of view." Lenore Romney says of her husband, "He has always had tremendous confidence in himself," and an old friend remarks, "With George, it has never been a question whether he would be President. Just when."

In December, 1957, TV reporter Martin Agronsky asked John F. Kennedy to comment on "religious bias" as it affects presidential elections. The Senator from Massachusetts replied:

> I think there are evidences of a greater comprehension of the obligations which the citizens have, whatever their religious faith may be. I remember reading about the objection raised to the seating of Senator Smoot because he was a Mormon. Today that question never would come up. There has been an evolutionary development in the United States. . . .

The young man who cited end-of-the-century prejudice against a Mormon was himself to give the first proof that the American presidency was not "For Protestants Only." Caution is an occupational characteristic of the professional politician and Jack Kennedy, the Catholic, had to blast his way to the nomination. Even co-religionists, such as Pennsylvania's Governor David Lawrence, at first opposed him on the grounds that "a Catholic can't win." The Kennedy breakthrough now gives other minorities a powerful analogy to stand on.*

In political terms, however, the analogy has certain sharp limitations. If it is true to say that Kennedy's victory makes Romney's way easier, it is equally true to point out that Romney has in his fellow Mormons no such significant base of support as Kennedy had in the Catholic voters of the United States.

Post-election surveys in 1960 agreed on one main point. When all the clamor and shouting over the "religious issue" had died, Protestant voters supported Richard Nixon in almost exactly the same strength —63 or 64 percent—that they had supported Dwight D. Eisenhower in 1956. But there was a huge switch to Kennedy among Catholic voters; Nixon's share of the Catholic vote—19 to 22 percent—was much less than half of Eisenhower's.†

While Romney, if nominated, could certainly anticipate exceptionally strong Mormon support, its political value would be minimal compared to what Kennedy received from his fellow Catholics. There are almost 46 million Roman Catholics in this country, but just over 2 million Mormons (of a worldwide total of 2.5 million). Half the U.S. Mormons live in Utah. There also are sizable concentrations in eastern Idaho, western Wyoming, southern Nevada, the Phoenix-Mesa area of Arizona and in California's San Fernando Valley.

California Mormons, as a statewide political force, are swallowed up in a population of over 18 million and Barry Goldwater's opposition to Romney makes it questionable how much support Romney can expect from Arizona. By the most generous estimate, Mormon influence is a strong force in states with only 2 or 3 percent of the 1,333 delegates to the 1968 convention. Those states—Utah, Idaho,

---

* Reporting on a nationwide survey, pollster Louis Harris wrote on February 13, 1967: "A special test was made to see how much his [Romney's] Mormon religion might hurt him. On a national basis, 12 percent say it would matter to them if a Mormon were in the White House, far less than the 30 percent who were worried about John F. Kennedy's Catholic religion in 1960."

† Scholars differ in their interpretation of the figures. The University of Michigan Survey Research Center team, arguing, in effect, that 1956 was an abnormal base of comparison, concluded that the religious issue cost Kennedy a net loss of 1.5 million votes from what a theoretical average Democratic candidate would have received. Other scholars, notably Dr. William Prendergast, the respected elections analyst of the Republican National Committee, sharply disagreed. They noted that the gain for Kennedy among Catholics, and the concentration of Catholic voters in states with large blocs of electoral college votes, made the probable effect of the religious issue the reverse of what the Survey Research Center study indicated.

Wyoming, Arizona and Nevada—have only 19 of the 270 electoral votes needed to elect a President. Even adding in scattered pockets of Mormon influence, such as Southern California or the District of Columbia, where Romney might benefit from his religion in the convention or the election, the basic point remains that Mormons, as such, are an insignificant base of political support.

There is no assurance, of course, that Romney will even get all the Mormon votes. There is considerable conservative strength in these areas and Nixon has kept his fences mended in the Mountain States. There is much evidence to show that candidates and issues supported by the Mormon hierarchy fare no better than those not so favored. It was the "disgraceful" vote of Utah that repealed the prohibition amendment to the Constitution. Church spokesmen, in fact, point with pride to their lack of political clout.

However, though Mormons are not politically monolithic, they feel a justifiable sense of identification with one of their boys who is making good, as Romney found on his Mountain States tour in early 1967. A poll taken for the Republican State Central Committee of Utah in 1966 reported that Romney would receive 63 percent of the vote against President Johnson, while Nixon was about even with the President. State Republican Chairman Richard Richards has said the prospect of a Mormon at the head of the Republican ticket is so exhilarating that "we've got about 20 guys already who want to run for Governor next year. There's going to be the darnedest scramble to be on the ticket with him you've ever seen."

In Arizona, the Republican whip of the state House of Representatives, DeLoss Ellsworth, has urged his friend Barry Goldwater to "soft-pedal" his criticisms of Romney in the interest of his own relations with the state's eighty thousand Mormons. "They're kind of like the Catholics were in 1960," said Mormon Ellsworth. "It's the first time they've had a candidate of their own and they might take his [Goldwater's] criticism of Romney as a slap at themselves."

The three questions Romney is likeliest to face because of his church affiliation involve polygamy, the church's relations to the Negro and its attitude toward church-state relations.

When Alfred Henry Lewis wrote a series on the Latter-day Saints for *Cosmopolitan* in 1911, polygamy was still fresh enough in memory for the articles to be given such lurid titles as "The Viper on the Hearth" and "The Viper's Trail of Gold." It is remarkable that the

Mormons, in some ways so attuned to American sentiment, could have so misjudged it as to sanction "plural marriages"—the name they use. In 1890 the church leadership finally outlawed the practice. But public opinion was so riled that when monogamist Reed Smoot, a Mormon apostle, was elected to the United States Senate in 1902, it took over two years for that body to agree to seat him, despite Senator Penrose's classic defense: "Give me a Mormon who does not polyg rather than a non-Mormon who practices monogamy but does not monog."

Clearly those most embarrassed by the polygamous past are today's Mormons, so self-consciously middle-class. Romney, though often recounting his family's flight to Mexico, rarely makes it particularly plain that his grandfather was fleeing Federal authorities rather than abandon polygamy. If anything, today's Mormons have tried to out-American their Gentile compatriots because of the habits of their fathers. Yet there are some Mormons in Utah (and a famous colony in Short Creek, Arizona) who are still polygamists. When discovered, they are promptly excommunicated. But in 1968, with a prominent Mormon in the headlines, there surely will be a rash of stories on polygamy in those publications that specialize in graffiti.

A much more serious problem is the relationship of Negroes to the Mormon church, which now refuses them admittance to its priesthood. The theological basis for this bias, stated in one of Joseph Smith's revelations, "Pearl of Great Price," is that Negroes, even before birth, wear the mark of Cain and are descendants of the union between Ham, the son Noah cursed, and Egyptus, daughter of a Pharaoh. The doctrine holds out hope to Negroes that if they live good lives they will eventually earn God's grace, the curse will be lifted, and they will be eligible for equal status among the Saints. There is reportedly pressure on the church hierarchy for a change in doctrine on the Negroes.

But, in respect to the current practice, Wallace Turner argues that, since Mormon theology decrees that a male's opportunity for greater exaltation in the hereafter is largely based on his activities in the priesthood, "the ultimate effect of this aspect of LDS doctrine is as racist as anything asserted by the Theodore Bilbos and Robert Sheltons in the bigoted corners of the southern states." Romney disagrees. He insists there is a distinction between "a religious faith which deals with life before and after this one on earth and public policy and our rights as citizens." He attempted to make this distinction in a dramatic meeting with the interracial Salt Lake Ministerial Association (composed of non-Mormon ministers) during a 1967 visit to Salt Lake City. The interview, surely not Romney's last test of this sort, recalled Kennedy's 1960 confrontation with the Houston Ministerial Association.

Meeting in a Catholic mission hall, barely two miles from the Mormon temple, where no Negro may enter, Romney was asked by the Reverend Louis Williams, a Baptist, if he accepted the tenet of his church that bars Negroes from the priesthood.

His reply indicated the position he will take on this question in the campaign. "First of all," Romney said, "I don't think I'm required as a public official to discuss the doctrine of the LDS church. It would be wrong for me to do so. I'm not running—or considering running —as a member of my church, but on the basis of my personal beliefs and record. I'm entitled, as any other public official is, to be judged on my record.

"Second," he said, "there is no question of the LDS position on civil rights. It is on the record.* Third, we are not a faith where a vote of the members . . . is going to influence a question of doctrine.†

"Fourth," Romney continued, "there is nothing in my faith that has influenced me other than to believe that every human being is a child of God as I am . . . and that he should have every opportunity

---

* Romney referred to a statement in October, 1963, from President Hugh B. Brown, on behalf of the church council, which said in part: "We would like it to be known that there is in this Church no doctrine, belief or practice that is intended to deny the full civil rights by any person regardless of race, color or creed. . . . We believe that all men are the children of the same God and that it is a moral evil for any person or group of persons to deny to any human being the right to gainful employment, to full educational opportunity, and to every privilege of citizenship, just as it is a moral evil to deny him the right to worship according to the dictates of his own conscience. . . . We call upon all men everywhere, both within and outside the Church, to commit themselves to the establishment of full civil equality to all God's children. Anything less than this defeats our high ideal of the brotherhood of man."

† There are Mormons, however, who believe that doctrine is affected by politics, just as Mr. Dooley said "th' Supreme Coort follows th' iliction returns." Mormon Sterling McMurrin, a former U.S. commissioner of education and now provost of the University of Utah graduate school, told Saul Friedman of the Detroit *Free Press* in 1966 that church doctrine on Negroes was "a lot of damn nonsense" and said it could be changed easily—with a new revelation —adding that Romney's candidacy "might force a change."

I have. I have fought for twenty-five years to eliminate discrimination. I believe I am entitled to be judged on the basis of my actions—not someone's ideas of what may be the precepts of my church."

The Rev. Dr. Palmer S. Ross, Negro pastor of Trinity A.M.E. Church, was not satisfied. If Romney really felt that strongly, he said, why did he not repudiate the teachings of his church?

"If my church prevented me from working to eliminate social injustice and racial discrimination," Romney replied, measuring his words carefully as he fought to remain calm, "I would not belong to it—but that is not the case. You name me one other man in the Republican party who has gone as far as I did [in the cause of civil rights]."

With the exception of Nelson Rockefeller, it would be hard to do. Even after Rockefeller gave up, Romney was still trying to strengthen the civil rights section of the 1964 Republican platform, and he has always insisted that it was the "Southern, rural, white" character of the Goldwater campaign that made it impossible for him to support his party's ticket. Indeed, even before he entered political life, Romney's record on civil rights was exemplary. During World War II he worked with Victor Reuther to combat segregated housing in Detroit. While president of American Motors his company was the only major employer in Michigan to support publicly and lobby for a Fair Employment Practices Act on the state level. The new Michigan constitution, for which Romney was largely responsible, goes further than any other similar document to assure full civil rights. Under his administration as Governor a state Civil Rights Commission has been given real power. He has marched with Martin Luther King through the exclusive Grosse Pointe suburb of Detroit and he is on record in support of full-coverage Federal open-housing legislation. That the Negro in Michigan has responded favorably to Romney is written in polls and voting statistics: 1962, his first campaign, he received 18 percent of the Negro vote; 1964, his percentage rose to 25; 1966, 34 percent. At home, at least, performance has outweighed church doctrine.

The third issue of concern is the Mormon position on church-state relations. U.S. Senator Elbert D. Thomas, a Mormon and liberal Democrat who defeated Reed Smoot, a Mormon and conservative Republican, used to say that when Brigham Young was both head of the church and Governor of Utah, he would sit on one side of his desk in the morning to conduct state business and then switch to the other side for church work in the afternoon.

The story was meant to illustrate the Mormon's devotion to the concept of separation of church and state, but there are historians who assert the principle has not always been honored in practice. J. D. Williams of Salt Lake City, a Mormon bishop and professor of political science at the University of Utah, wrote: "The Mormon church, in trying to administer the kingdom of God on earth, was deeply immersed in the politics of the kingdom of men on earth." The church is the dominant factor in Utah politics. Before statehood, it controlled the territorial government through a one-party system; when pressure mounted to institute a two-party system as a precedent to statehood, church leaders simply divided their congregations in half and told some of them to be Republicans and some Democrats. When Joseph Smith, Jr., announced his candidacy for President before he was murdered by an anti-Mormon mob in 1844, his platform was the establishment of what he called "theo-democracy."

As recently as 1965, Church President David O. McKay wrote letters to the eleven Mormons in Congress urging them to vote against the move to repeal section 14(b) of the Taft-Hartley Act, which authorizes state right-to-work laws. At least five of the Congressmen are known to have replied politely that they would appreciate the church hierarchy's staying out their temporal business, and Romney has consistently opposed introduction of a right-to-work law in Michigan. While President McKay had clearly slipped out of his spiritual role in this instance, there are presently no pressing public issues—such as birth control or medical care—on which Mormons hold doctrinal beliefs.

Romney has said repeatedly that he believes "profoundly in the separation of church and state." In Michigan, he has signed into law three bills providing transportation and supplemental services, such as health care and remedial reading, for parochial school pupils and tuition aid for students at private and parochial colleges. He has been criticized for this action by the Protestants and Other Americans United for Separation of Church and State, but told a representative of the group that he did not feel such measures "subsidized religious education."

In the meeting with the Salt Lake Ministerial Association, he said the churches should encourage their members to take part in politics and should take positions on issues which have moral implications.

"But the church itself," he added, "should not become active or identified with a political party or candidate, nor should it become a special interest group seeking governmental funds."

Romney told the ministers he would never accept contributions from the Mormon church for his own campaigns and declined to join the criticism of the Supreme Court decisions barring prayers from public schools. He said some school boards were "going too far" in prohibiting "even spontaneous expressions of faith," but that in general "I'm not personally as concerned about increasing opportunities for prayers in schools as I am for increasing prayer in homes."

Because George Wilcken Romney* was born July 8, 1907, in the Mormon settlement of Colonia Dublan, Chihuahua, Mexico, some two hundred miles south of the border at El Paso, he has a special problem if he should aspire to the presidency of the United States. An eavesdropping cameraman for station WOOD-TV, Grand Rapids, overheard the Michigan Governor discuss this with Mrs. John Eisenhower during a Republican fund-raising dinner in April, 1966:

MRS. EISENHOWER: What a good dinner.
GOVERNOR ROMNEY: Yes, a good dinner.
MRS. E.: It isn't chicken.
GOV. R.: No, it isn't chicken.
MRS. E.: I like Midwesterners; they're so normal. You are from the Midwest, aren't you?
GOV. R.: No, I was born in Mexico. My grandparents moved there because they were practicing polygamy.
MRS. E.: Oh, really! Then your foreign birth prevents you from . . .
GOV. R. (interrupting): No, no. My parents were American. I'm a natural-born American, not a naturalized citizen.

Gov. R. and Mrs. E. were referring, of course, to Article 2, Section 1, Paragraph 4 of the U.S. Constitution: "No person except a natural born Citizen . . . shall be eligible to the Office of President."

* Romney's middle name was the family name of his maternal grandmother, who was born in Holstein, Germany. The Grand Rapids *Press* asked a cross-section of that city's leading citizens if they could recall their Governor's middle name. None could. The closest was Walter J. Russell, 5th Congressional District Republican Chairman, who said, "It's something like Micklin. I asked him once what the heck it was and he told me. He dismissed it rather quickly and I had a feeling he didn't like it." Mr. Russell probably is right. The Governor does not list a middle name in *Who's Who in America*. After working with such famous initials as FDR, JFK, and LBJ, headline writers might find special problems with a Romney administration.

Whether a man born out of the country of American parents is a
"natural born" citizen has never been tested in the courts. But the
most authoritative source, *The President: Office and Powers,* by
Princeton professor Edward S. Corwin, after citing conflicting
evidence, concludes: "At any rate, should the American people
ever choose for President a person born abroad of American parents,
it is highly improbable that any other constitutional agency would
venture to challenge their decision." (However, Stephen Shadegg, in
his book, *What Happened to Goldwater?,* implies that the Arizona
Senator ruled out Romney as a potential running mate because of his
Mexican birth.)

Being born in Mexico has had some political rewards, especially when campaigning for office in polyglot Detroit. Speaking
there to the Hellenic Republican Federation in October, 1966, immigrant Romney told his audience of their common bond: "There
are many of you here tonight and in the radio audience who are not
native-born Americans. I, too, was born in a foreign land, although
of American parents. My people came back to this country in much
the same circumstances that brought you or your parents or your
grandparents here—destitute and somewhat afraid of the future."

What brought the Romneys back to this country was the warring
between Pancho Villa's rebels and the Mexican government. Eventually the rebels gave the Mormon community forty-eight hours to get
out. The U.S. government rushed a train down from El Paso. And
George Romney, age five, was "literally a revolutionary refugee." His
father tried carpentry in Los Angeles, farming in Idaho, general
contracting in Salt Lake City. He grew poor growing potatoes and
growing wheat. George did stoop labor in the sugar-beet fields, dug
potatoes, canned tomatoes, worked as a carpenter's helper. On the
Romneys' Idaho farm in 1914 and 1915, George recalls, "We ate
potatoes for breakfast, lunch and dinner." Being poor was an experience that he was to have in common with his 1968 Republican
rivals, Nixon, Percy and Reagan. Yet none of them claim to have
had an unhappy childhood, although they all worked at an early
age. Today, Romney, Percy and Reagan are millionaires; Nixon,
who got a late start at money making, will be one too if he continues
as a Wall Street lawyer. Poverty may have prodded each man
equally, but it left different bench marks. Of the four, Romney is the
only one who sparks any empathy among underprivileged groups. As

William H. Hessler wrote when the auto magnate first ran for public office, "Not everybody can draw a salary of $150,000 a year, plus stock options and bonuses, and still look like an underdog."

"You know, I am not a college graduate," says Romney. He has had about two years of college: a year at the Latter-day Saints Junior College in Salt Lake City (1925-26) and a semester each at the University of Utah (1929) and George Washington University (1929-30). To some degree he has tried to make up for his lack of higher education by reading. His prepared speeches are mined with literary quotations. In one talk at Miami Beach in August, 1965, he called upon the wisdom of Carl Sandburg, Shakespeare, Robert Louis Stevenson, G. K. Chesterton, Goethe, Robert Frost, Victor Hugo, Edmund Burke and John F. Kennedy. If his speeches reflect his knowledge, they show that he has read widely but not well. He is full of instant history and such philosophy as "there is no difference between genuine conservatives and genuine liberals." The books he likes, such as Max Ways' *Beyond Survival* and Father Bruckberger's excellent *Image of America,* tend to reinforce notions he already holds, rather than challenge or broaden his thinking.

"The best training I ever had was my church training," says Romney. "I do not think there is any college training that is a substitute for my religious training." In 1926, having earned $630 for expenses, George Romney left for two years of missionary work in England and Scotland. As stump speaker for the Mormon Church he addressed passers-by from the Mound in Edinburgh and at London's Hyde Park. (He also learned the utility of having a heckler around to draw the crowd.) Just as Nixon, at about the same period in his life, was learning the indelible tricks of debating, so was Romney's oratorical style then shaped by his experiences as an evangelist. Perhaps because he learned on street corners, Romney is ill at ease with a prepared text. But even extemporaneously he is not a facile performer. His vocabulary is not large. He gropes for the right word, even when delivering his "boilerplate" speech. Yet his very lack of polish can be highly effective, like the stutterer that you want to help along. And his tone is earnest, his appearance commanding, his message filled with "fundamental principles," which gild the commonplace—"the principle of competition," "the principle of voluntary cooperation," "the principle of reward based on contribution," "the principle of equal opportunity," "the principle of limited government," "the principle of just administration of the law," "the principle of civilian supremacy"—his principles are endless. He gestures a great deal with his right hand (left hand in pocket), and employs vigorous fist and finger action. On a good day, standing above the crowd, this is George Romney at his best—missionary, salesman, inspirationalist. Watching Romney on such a day, Mary McGrory of the Washington *Star,* wrote, "The Republican women responded to him as the ladies of Florence to Savonarola."

When he returned from his European mission, Romney settled in Washington, D.C., not because of an abiding interest in government, but because it was the new home of his high school sweetheart, Lenore LaFount, whose father had been appointed by President Coolidge to the Federal Radio Commission, precursor of the Federal Communications Commission.

On his third day in the capital the ex-missionary answered a want ad in the Washington *Post* and was hired to do secretarial work in the office of Democratic Senator David Walsh of Massachusetts. Fortunately for young Romney his shorthand was so bad that his employer switched him to tariff research. He was twenty-two years old and sitting beside a powerful legislator on the floor of the Senate, handing him bits of information to use in debate. His work on the tariff bill also came to the attention of the Aluminum Company of America, which hired him, and, after a training period as a salesman in Los Angeles, sent him back to Washington as a lobbyist. "My responsibility really was to know where things were happening," Romney said years later, ". . . and to bring them to the attention of the appropriate people in the organization." In those days, said Richard L. Strout of the *Christian Science Monitor,* "he used to be around the National Press Club in Washington, where he was a hard-driving, aggressive Mormon business representative of conservative views." After nine years with Alcoa Romney joined the Automobile Manufacturers Association as manager of its Detroit office. When Pearl Harbor was attacked, Romney was the industry's choice to head the Automotive Council for War Production, and in that post served as the liaison man between the government and the auto companies in scheduling and expediting military production. The job kept him out of uniform in World War II, though Romney's recollection is that he never asked for a draft deferment or discussed his status in any way with his local board.

In 1948 the chairman of Nash-Kelvinator, George Mason, asked Romney to become his personal assistant. Six years later the company merged with Hudson to form American Motors, and, when Mason died in 1954, Romney was given the dubious honor of heading a firm that would lose $7 million in its first year. That Romney, "The Rambler Man," was to take American Motors to a peak annual profit of over $60 million within five years rates as one of the great corporate success stories. The basis of the success, of course, was the "compact car." Romney could not claim to be its originator. It was conceived by Meade Moore, American Motors' engineering vice president, and had long been the dream of George Mason. Romney's unique contribution was his ability to *sell* the concept to the American people. In part, he did this by turning himself into a sort of Detroit David opposing the three mighty Goliaths of the industry. Auto companies, points out sociologist E. Digby Baltzell, are "unusually addicted to ethnic homogeneity of management personnel." Yet here was a Mormon outsider, armed with a brilliant sense of promotion, storming the citadel. Moreover, he didn't always play by the rules of the game. As one auto company executive explained, "You plug your own product; you don't knock the other fellow's. He named names." While his purpose was to sell Ramblers, Romney also was selling Romney. American Motors bought full pages in newspapers and magazines to present the face, signature, and message of its boss. He personally delivered his company's commercials on *Disneyland,* a popular television program. George Romney was becoming both rich and famous.*

Romney's war on the auto giants was something special in the annals of American business. It was a holy war. Selling Ramblers

* It is difficult to judge precisely how rich Romney is. By picking up his American Motors stock options he became that company's biggest individual stockholder in 1958. He reported the sale of 10,000 shares of AMC in 1960 for about $900,000, or a gross profit of approximately $700,000 ($70,000 went to the Mormon church as his tithe). When Romney decided to run for Governor in 1962 he placed 104,000 shares of AMC in the hands of a bank trustee. At the then current market price this was worth about $1.8 million. The price of AMC shares has since dropped substantially, but it is known that the Romney trust has divested itself of some of this stock in order to diversify its financial portfolio. Commenting on stock options in 1960, Romney said, "It's the only way an individual can accumulate wealth. You certainly can't do it these days on salary alone." His peak salary was $250,000 in the fiscal year ending September 30, 1960. The next year, when he was devoting part time to public service projects, he was paid $140,211 by American Motors.

was not the end in itself; the end was converting people to economical cars. "St. George of the Compacts," *Fortune* magazine dubbed Romney. His clever campaign against the "gas-guzzling dinosaurs" also had obvious social overtones. "Suddenly," wrote Romney's biographer, Tom Mahoney, "big cars were being treated with ridicule rather than reverence." The Los Angeles County Medical Association asked doctors to take medical insignia off their Cadillacs!

This would have fascinating ramifications when Romney entered public life. For, by some sleight-of-hand syllogism, it made him a political liberal. No matter that his speeches on economics echoed the conservatism of a Ludwig von Mises. If he was against the Big Car, therefore he was for the Little Man. He was a celebrity in an age of the celebrity-candidate. The stage now was set for George Romney to become the first man to use the business world as a springboard into high elective politics since a "barefoot boy from Wall Street," Wendell Willkie, stepped out of the corporate offices of Commonwealth and Southern to capture the 1940 Republican presidential nomination.

Jackson, Michigan, claims to be the birthplace of the Republican party. And from the Reconstruction Era until the "Soapy" Williams Era, Michigan gave heart and vote to its home-grown party. For three terms at the beginning of the century the Democrats did not have even a single seat in the state legislature.

Then in 1948 G. Mennen Williams, heir to a toiletry fortune, a political unknown with an ebullient personality, a firm handshake, boundless energy, a green polka-dot bowtie, and the support of Walter Reuther, cracked this Republican bastion.

In the year that Williams became Governor, the state CIO Political Action Committee formally resolved that "to serve the best interests of Michigan labor is to join the Democratic party." If Michigan under Republican control had been "a company town," now, under the paternal political supervision of the United Automobile Workers, it would be more like "a closed shop."

But, while Williams was to win six consecutive two-year terms, through the magic of malapportionment the Republicans would continue to control the legislature. "Williams dealt with the legislature," wrote James Reichley in his authoritative *States in Crisis,* "as though setting out to whack the snout of a large and obstreperous hog." The culmination of the feud was Michigan's "payless pay day" in April,

1959. Williams went off to join the Kennedy Administration in Washington, but his successor, a legless World War II veteran named John Swainson, had no easier time with a hostile legislature. Moreover, the auto industry was experiencing a slump. Newsdealers in Cadillac Square pedaled copies of California job openings. A bitter-tasting joke of the period went:

Customer: I'll have the usual.
Bartender: One "Michigan on the rocks" coming up.

George Romney's entry into Michigan politics came in late 1956 when he became chairman of a citizens committee to conduct a two-year investigation of Detroit's educational needs. (His group made some two hundred recommendations, most of which were accepted by the city's board of education.) But he was not fully initiated until he formed Citizens for Michigan in 1959. The new group, Romney hoped, would be a third force that could resolve the stalemate between the Democratic Governor and the Republican legislature. CFM quickly concluded that the root problem was the state's antiquated constitution, written in 1850, somewhat revised in 1909, amended almost seventy times. A constitutional convention was called for October, 1961. Romney was chosen a "con-con" delegate, and, because it was a partisan election, he was "forced" (he said) to declare his allegiance to the Republican party.

"Con-con represented an invaluable opportunity for Romney to learn every facet of state government," says fellow delegate Richard C. Van Dusen, who roomed with him at Lansing's Jack Tar Hotel while the convention was meeting. "It gave him an opportunity to feel his way along and make some mistakes where the consequences were not horrendous, while he developed a rapport with Republicans from all over the state." For widely disparate reasons, the opposition to writing a significant document came from mossback Republicans and CIO Democrats. Romney's major contribution to con-con's success was his ability to resolve differences among the Republicans. The end result was a series of compromises on reapportionment, home rule and other issues. However, it was a great improvement over the unwieldy document which preceded it, and its ratification in April, 1963, by the narrow margin of 10,760 votes in a total vote of over 1,609,000 marked the beginning of a new era in Michigan government.

Midway through con-con, Romney announced his candidacy for

the Republican nomination for Governor in 1962. He had been close to declaring for the Senate two years earlier, when Michigan Republicans were seeking an opponent for Senator Philip A. Hart. (Richard Nixon, who began touting Romney as a political "comer" in the late 1950's, urged him to become a candidate in 1960 and 1962.) Romney went to a meeting of the board of directors of Citizens for Michigan in 1960 with a statement in his pocket announcing his resignation in order to run for the Senate. However, he completely reversed his plans, without consulting any of his major political advisers, when a woman member of the board told him his candidacy would break his pledge to keep CFM out of partisan politics.

In 1962, when he finally took the plunge, Republican party leaders, having run seven consecutive losers, hailed his decision. Had they lost only four or five elections, they might not have been quite so enthusiastic. For George Romney was the most ill-fitting Republican since Fiorello La Guardia.

An acquaintance remarked at the time to the *Wall Street Journal's* Alan L. Otten, "When he [Romney] meets with party professionals, it's like a Salvation Army girl in a burlesque house." In plain fact, Romney in 1961 had been a businessman for fourteen years. Before that, for nineteen years, he had been a congressional assistant, Washington lobbyist, and trade-association executive, all jobs in which it was his duty to know the operations of government's wheels within wheels and to know where to squirt the oil. But somehow Romney had come through the experience deeply distrustful of political parties, both Democratic and Republican. "They're not run by citizens any more—they're run by the special-interest groups." On the state level in 1960 he had said, "It is difficult now to accomplish anything on a partisan basis because both parties are responsible for the fundamental difficulties that face Michigan today." This was the reason he had set up the Citizens for Michigan organization. And he applied the same doctrine of "a plague on both your houses" to national politics. "Both parties are headed in exactly the same direction and will reach the same destination," he disapprovingly told a Miami audience on June 30, 1960. Later in the year he sent an "open letter" to presidential candidates Nixon and Kennedy in which he could not think of anything good to say about either. Nixon must have been particularly stung since Romney singled out the steel settlement for criticism. (The settlement was largely the result of patient efforts by Nixon and Eisenhower's secretary of Labor, James P. Mitchell.)

Nor did Romney make any concessions to the Republicans once he become their candidate. He maintained a separate headquarters in Detroit, unsullied by party label or pictures of other G.O.P. office seekers. His campaign literature did not indicate his party affiliation. He traveled the state alone and made no mention of his ticket-mates. When challenged on the record of the rural, reactionary Republican legislators, rather than attempt the almost impossible job of defending them, he simply argued that he could cajole better things out of them than could a Democratic Governor. The closest Romney came to acknowledging that he was a Republican at all was to say, when pressed, "I'm a citizen who is a Republican, not a Republican who is incidentally a citizen."

By a modest majority of 78,000 votes out of 2,760,000, George Romney was elected Governor. He was the only Republican to win statewide office.

There were a lot of reasons why he won: because many Michiganders were tired of the bickering between Democratic Governor and Republican legislature; because American voters believe in the football adage that whenever you're unhappy fire the coach; because his opponent was lackluster; because he gave Democrats an excuse to vote for him; because, with his Dick Tracy jaw, his blue-hazel eyes, his halo of silver hair, his well-proportioned build, he "looked like a Governor"; because he was exciting and a little larger than life; and because, said Professor John T. Dempsey, who ran the huge "Romney Volunteers" organization, he was "a better politician than his opponent."

Although it was still to be honed, the Romney style of campaigning was already distinctive. Its hallmark was a great explosion of energy that sought out and assaulted the voter. He did this on the run, moving at about the pace of a practiced half-miler. He would handshake his way through dense crowds, using a modified Australian crawl, left hand, right hand, left, right. When the situation called for open-field running he would snake his way through a newspaper composing room or the aisles of a supermarket like a single-wing back. In parades, he never rode in his assigned convertible, but loped a half block in front of the lead drum majorette, coatless, always coatless, French cuff rolled up to the right elbow for easier handshaking, while the kids ducked under police barricades to run along-side him. A sort of pied piper of politics, he had—thanks to those years of Rambler advertising—the instant recognition that every novice candidate dreams of and few achieve.

The strategy of the Romney campaign, and his own missionary zeal, sent him into heavily Democratic areas where no ordinary Republican ever campaigned. Uninvited, he burst into union halls. Early morning and late afternoon, he would take up a boxer's stance, feet wide apart, and wait to shake hands with the workers entering or leaving a factory. The union started sending crews to heckle him at the plant gates and to shout warnings to the workers, "Don't shake his hand; he's a company fink." Many workers shook off his hand and Romney would turn on them and shout, "That's what's wrong with this state! How can we ever work together on anything if you won't even shake my hand?" A few surprised workers turned back for the handshake and a few ended up voting for him—enough to provide the slim margin of victory.

Romney won in 1962 the only way he could win, by running away from his state party's label and its reputation. But even victory did not markedly improve his opinion of the G.O.P. Attending his first Governors' Conference in Miami Beach in 1963, the Michigan Governor, now dubbed "the lonesome end of politics," failed to attend his party's caucus. The reason, he said, was that it was held on a Sunday. Never one to neglect an opportunity for moral instruction, Romney issued a formal statement declaring that no conference business should be transacted on Sunday, a day, he said, that he, like most Americans, chose "to spend at church and with my families." Romney's press secretary later slipped into the press room and managed, amid general hilarity, to correct the unintended reference to plural marriage.

Nineteen sixty-four, both a presidential and a gubernatorial election year, presented special problems for Romney as a Republican. Committed early to seek re-election, he nonetheless hesitated to shut the door entirely on the chance for a presidential nomination. In May the professional feeling in the party was that if Rockefeller defeated Goldwater in the California primary it would show that the Arizona Senator did not have the kind of popular support necessary to win the nomination. On the other hand, the New York Governor's sole role was as dragon slayer. Neither his liberalism nor his personal life would be acceptable to the convention. With Rockefeller ahead in the early California polls, Romney—along with Nixon and Scranton —publicly declared that they would not be part of a stop-Goldwater movement. If they were to benefit when the front runner's balloon burst, it was necessary for them to keep their pins out of sight. But Goldwater won in California and thus clinched the nomination.

Now Romney had to face a problem as old as the party system. Back in 1884, when the Republicans nominated James G. Blaine, a Massachusetts politician named Henry Cabot Lodge, after much soul searching, decided he would stick with the G.O.P. convention's choice. His friend, William Lawrence, later to be an Episcopal bishop, wrote, "I had no use for Cabot politically for years after. I felt that he had traduced his cause, and that his personal ambition to go to Congress was mixed up with his action." It was the thirty-four-year-old Lodge's first race for Congress and he was defeated. Mugwumps like Lawrence may have damned him, but he had won the gratitude of the party pros and he would never lose another election.

Romney's dilemma was the same: Should he support Goldwater and face possible defeat himself or should he cut Goldwater and face the future hostility of the party's faithful?

"Reliable polls . . . well before the San Francisco convention," Romney later admitted, showed that Goldwater would take a drubbing in Michigan. Romney decided he could not support him. The first indication that he was publicly pulling away from Goldwater came at the Governors' Conference in June when he broke his rule against politicking on Sundays in order to issue a Sabbath blast at the Arizona Senator, implying that his nomination would "commence the suicidal destruction of the Republican Party." "I will devote all of the time I can," he announced, "to persuading Republicans generally and convention delegates to keep from committing themselves before the convention opens. . . ."

In the frantic three days that followed, Romney was pushed hard by Nixon and some moderate Republican Governors to get into the race himself. He wobbled visibly several times, but in the end his Michigan advisers prevailed and he recalled his pledge to seek a second term as Governor. When Scranton announced a week later that he would make the futile fight against Goldwater, Romney conspicuously withheld his endorsement of the effort.

Romney's behavior at the Republican convention in San Francisco is the subject of endless debate. He was nominated as the Michigan favorite-son candidate and received all but eight of its forty-eight votes. However his main efforts centered not on derailing Goldwater but on revising the platform. Romney, once again the lone wolf, stayed aloof from the Rockefeller–Scranton–Hugh Scott effort to line up support for a series of liberal amendments and, instead, after theirs had been defeated, offered his own revisions of the civil rights and extremism planks. Romney insists his purpose was to take the policy questions, which he described as "vital," out of the political context of the anti-Goldwater forces. Melvin Laird, the platform chairman, insists that Romney's suggestions could have been accepted had he offered them earlier, instead of saving them for a dramatic floor presentation, and strongly implies that Romney was looking for an excuse to repudiate Goldwater. Whatever the real motivation, the most charitable thing that can be said about Romney's performance was that it left almost everyone confused and many people, both allies and opponents, irritated. The consternation was complete when Romney, acting on impulse, leaped to his feet to second the motion that made Goldwater's nomination unanimous—a step that, in the view of his own advisers, undercut a long and careful effort to show Michigan voters that he was not a Goldwater man.

After the convention, Romney said he would "accept but not endorse" Goldwater. A University of Delaware professor of speech, D. Duane Angel, who had written a Ph.D. dissertation on "The Campaign Speaking of George Romney," analyzed the "accept-endorse" statement. "What does that mean?" he asked. "I don't know," he answered.

The excuse Romney gave for not endorsing the Republican candidate was that he had been unable to have a "conversation in depth" with the Senator to clarify Goldwater's views on civil rights and extremism. Yet in the year before the election they had two private meetings in Washington and two semiprivate meetings (Goldwater's session with the Michigan delegation in late June and the Hershey conference of Republican leaders in August). Commenting on Romney's oft-repeated phrase, "conversation in depth," a Goldwater assistant, Tony S. Smith, asked, "What does he mean—a ten-hour teach-in?" Another Goldwater aide, Edward K. Nellor, later recalled one of the Goldwater-Romney meetings he attended: "It reminded me of two retired Army sergeants, long parted but now rejoined to swap fibs and fairy tales about old times. It was as bloodless as a Girl Scout picnic, and about as useful politically. It lasted well over an hour and not a single word was spoken about politics or political differences. When it broke up everybody exchanged smiles, handshakes and boloney about how worthwhile it had all been."

In Michigan Romney was a bit more of a regular than in 1962. Some, but not all, of his literature and bumper strips included the word "Republican." He appeared with and plugged other candidates for state office. But the first time Goldwater came to Detroit, Romney gave him a polite, non-endorsing introduction at Cobo Hall, and during Goldwater's second appearance the Michigan Governor was in Massachusetts campaigning for Attorney General Edward Brooke.

The Democratic candidate for Governor in Michigan was Representative-at-Large Neil Staebler, a portly patrician from Ann Arbor, with a fondness for old-fashioned, double-breasted suits and baggy pants. His twelve years as state party chairman earned him a reputation as a brilliant backstage organizer. But in front of the footlights, with his hair parted down the middle, his little Teutonic mustache, and his high, squeaky voice, he was something less than a stellar performer. Romney was again blessed, as he had been in his first race, and would be in his third, with fine but miscast opponents. Staebler based his campaign on linking Romney to Goldwater. The connection escaped both Goldwater and the Michigan voters. In fact, it was clear that among Negroes and Jews Romney was gaining votes solely because he would not support Goldwater. Romney was re-elected by 382,913 votes while Goldwater was losing Michigan by 1,076,463. If the first law of politics is survival, Romney's strategy had been grandly successful, but there were some who would never forgive him his success.

The problems Romney faced in 1966 were of an entirely different order. No one doubted that he would win a third term. When all the big-name Democrats refused to become sacrificial lambs, state Democratic chairman Zolton Ferency was forced to nominate himself for lambdom. He was a peppery campaigner with a flashing wit, but so little known that President Johnson mispronounced his name during the traditional Labor Day festivities. "My good friend, Zolton [long pause] Fe-REN-cy," said the President. "Not often," commented the Detroit *Free Press,* "[do] you run across a man who has such good friends he's never heard of before." Although most politicians do not even mention their opponents' names, on the grounds that any free advertising is useful, FAIR'n-see took large newspaper ads to announce: "George Romney will be watching Zolton Ferency tonight at 7:00 on channel 4. So should you." Ferency's hope was to get Romney to lose his temper. ("Well, he does flare up at times," says Lenore Romney, who thinks people sometimes mistake her husband's "intensity" for anger.) At a joint appearance, Ferency charged, among many things, that the Governor was a "politician who couldn't care less if half the cities of the state burned down." Terrible-tempered George listened and smiled. As the campaign progressed, the Democratic contender said, "People used to ask *what* is Zolton Ferency. Now they're asking *who* is Zolton Ferency. So I've made progress."

The election for Romney had a significance far beyond the modest obstacle that Ferency presented. A candidate seeking the presidential nomination is not unlike Hercules performing his twelve labors. In 1966 Romney had two labors to perform. First, he had to "win big," in much the manner that Robert Taft in 1950 and John Kennedy in 1958 were elected over equally unknown opponents. Second, he had to carry into office with him U.S. Senator Robert Griffin and reclaim at least two or three of the four congressional seats that the party had lost in 1964.

For ten years Griffin had been a Congressman from Traverse City (1960 population: 18,432). His record in Washington bordered on the remarkable for a minority member with so little seniority. He had organized the coup that had won the House leadership for Gerald Ford, and had left his name and imprint on two major pieces of legislation, the Landrum-Griffin labor reform bill and the National Student Loan program. Following the death of Senator Patrick McNamara on April 30, 1966, Governor Romney appointed Griffin to the upper chamber. But the Democratic candidate would be that aging *enfant terrible* "Soapy" Williams. And Griffin, short, myopic, somewhat shy, carried himself with the presence of a certified public accountant. Romney's labor was cut out for him.

The Governor started the canvassing three weeks earlier than in 1964 and worked harder. He opened a joint headquarters in Detroit, an arrangement previously unheard of in a Romney campaign. On bus placards, billboards, brochures, and television, Romney and Griffin were paired as "The Action Team for the Action State." The

Governor's speeches actually seemed to gloss over his own accomplishments in order to dwell at length on the need to elect Griffin, "the ablest man Michigan has had in the Senate since Arthur Vandenberg." Team player Romney was equally generous with praise for state legislative and congressional candidates. He found time in the midst of the campaign to make flying trips to Indiana and Illinois to endorse two ancient Republican worthies, Charles Halleck and Leslie Arends, who had each served thirty-one years in Congress and were hardly in danger of being toppled. He even took to wearing a dark blue necktie with figures of a tiny elephant, symbol of the G.O.P. (In 1962, when he announced for Governor, his dark blue tie had the figure of a dinosaur.)

The victory, Romney rightly said, was "sensational," exceeding his "most optimistic expectations." The Governor's margin was 527,047 votes. He carried all but the largest and smallest counties, Wayne and Keweenaw, while gaining the second-greatest gubernatorial majority in Michigan history, topped only by the election of 1928. Griffin won by 294,146 votes to become the state's first elected Republican Senator in fourteen years. The party regained the state Senate and earned a tie in the House. Five marginal congressional seats were captured by the G.O.P. George Romney had performed his Herculean labors of 1966 and now was positioned for the assault on the presidency.*

As a front-running candidate for the 1968 Republican presidential nomination, George Romney's record is now in the process of being carefully dissected by friend and foe. Each can find what he is looking for. And, by the same token, each can find data that in no way fits into his preconceived notions. For rarely have the words and deeds of a public man run on such separate tracks.

Examining the words first, one finds that the candidate uses a limited inventory of rather simple economic and political principles collected in the course of his career and compiled rather than sys-

---

* Romney continued to demonstrate his coattail power in Michigan in 1967, helping his party's candidates win two special elections that gave the Republicans a 56-54 edge in the state House of Representatives. One of the victories was particularly significant: Romney's campaigning helped Anthony Licata, an obscure political novice, win in a traditionally Democratic Detroit district over James P. Hoffa, son of the jailed Teamster Union president, who had outside help from Vice President Hubert H. Humphrey and Senator Robert F. Kennedy.

tematized, into a philosophy of public affairs that could be called, as Robert Novak has, "Rambling Romneyism."

To columnist James Reston, Romney is "the anti-big candidate." The basis of his economic thought is the belief that the nation is endangered by the "enormous aggregations of power" in both business and unions. His solution is to (1) break up any company that controls 25 to 35 percent (using different yardsticks) of a basic industry, and (2) limit labor unions to not more than ten thousand members and prohibit industrywide collective bargaining.

Economic Romneyism probably is an amalgam of his LDS experience (where the church organization—wards and stakes—grows by addition and division), his experience with Alcoa, then a monopoly (where he was passed over for promotion because he lacked seniority), and his experience with American Motors (his scheme would break up General Motors and Ford). While Romney has been peddling these ideas for a decade he is still without any important disciples.

Political Romneyism, as we have seen, began as a sort of populist distrust of political parties combined with a romanticized view of the citizen-politician. In 1960, he proposed a "Citizens for America," based on his Citizens for Michigan experience, which he described as "a national organization [that] could hold a national convention and develop a national platform based on the issues far enough in advance of the two-party conventions to influence their platforms and their selection of candidates." CFA died of its propounder's success. For as Romney rose in his party's councils, less and less was heard of "nonpartisan" and "citizen"—his favorite words, circa 1958-62. R.I.P. 1966. (A sixty-two-line Romney interview with UPI in 1960 mentioned eleven "citizens," three "nonpartisans," and one "Republican"; his 1966 talk to the Federation of Republican Women in Washington included twenty-four "Republicans," but not a single "citizen" or "nonpartisan.") This is an example of his adaptive instincts.

As a former Michigan county Republican official, Charles A. Ferry, put it in an article in *The New Republic,* Romney has "an unshakeable conviction of the rightness of anything he undertakes, which permits him to rationalize personal inconsistency and contradiction."

Yet, except for some exotic economic ideas, an emphasis on the citizen in politics, and heavy doses of Mormon theology, Romney's public philosophy is not very different from the kind of small-town Republicanism that the late Senator Kenneth Wherry brought to Washington from Pawnee City, Nebraska. There is the suspicion of the Federal government ("an octopus-like creature"), the accent on action at the state level ("states give individuals greater opportunity for direct participation . . ."), and the call for voluntary cooperation ("That's what made America unique").

The Michigan Governor's world view is bounded by his rural roots, his business experience and the Mormon church. Broadly speaking, a Romney foreign policy would have these three goals for the world: feed it, trade with it, convert it.

"The United States should be the champion of plenty in the world," Romney told the Illinois Chamber of Commerce in 1965. "We should reshape our domestic agricultural policies from an approach of economic nationalism and artificial shortage to economic internationalism. We should press every available acre into the production of shippable, storable, high-protein foods. . . . And we should feed hungry peoples until they are able to feed themselves." A writer who asked Romney for specifics—such as how the U.S. would deal with wheat-rich Canada and Argentina if we dumped our surpluses on the world market—came away with the impression that he was long on goals and short on details.

Romney feels that "most American economic aid should be in the form of private investment, rather than governmental handouts." When he was still president of American Motors he proposed an "international bridge" approach to encourage world trade on a company-to-company and industry-to-industry basis. As an example, Romney says that the U.S. produces cars more cheaply than Canada while Canada produces aluminum more cheaply than the U.S. "Why should not we set up an international bridge to permit Canada to produce aluminum components for American automobiles and ourselves send back American automobiles in equal proportions without tariffs?" Our goal, he later wrote in *The Atlantic Community Quarterly,* "must be the freest practicable trade over the widest possible area."

As a former foreign missionary, Romney's talk about world affairs still has a strong undercurrent of *we* know what is right for *them.* Selig S. Harrison reported in *The New Republic* that when asked what he would do about countries that lean toward Communism, Romney answered, "Persuade them they're off the track, by precept and example!" But when this does not work, Romney adds, "we might just as well face the fact that we have to push them in the right direction."

While Romney has some first-hand knowledge of Europe and Latin America, geography is not his forte. At a 1966 news conference in Exeter, New Hampshire, he gave a disquisition on the British "blockade of Nigeria." (He was reminded that he meant Rhodesia.) When in Saigon in 1965 with a group of Governors, he told a news conference about the enemy in North Korea. (He was reminded that he meant North Vietnam). The Vietnam War has proved particularly puzzling to Romney. At various times these headlines have correctly stated his views:

ROMNEY BACKS VIET POLICY (Detroit *News,* July 29, 1965)
GOVERNOR [ROMNEY] CRITICIZES U.S. POLICY (Detroit *News,* July 30, 1965).
GOVERNOR [ROMNEY] OPPOSES ESCALATION (Lansing *State Journal,* January 30, 1966)
ROMNEY FAVORS WIDENING BOMBING OF NORTH VIETNAM (New York *Times,* June 13, 1966)

In the presence of the national press corps at the 1966 Governors' Conference, Romney provided one of the most damaging quotations ever inflicted by an American politician on himself:

Well, look . . . I . . . I think it should . . . the question is this—there's been a great deal of interest in the governors' position on Vietnam and would I give my views. This is not a simple situation. There are no simple answers. I've been there. I've seen the type of conflict that's going on. I know the conflict is far more than a military conflict, and we could still lose the struggle. . . . I think there are ample reasons to wonder whether or not the people of South Vietnam still want us there. . . . I'm concerned on that score, No. 1, and I'm not going to answer your questions completely, but No. 2, if this conflict involves the question of our stopping communism, the international Communist conspiracy, and stopping it in South Vietnam, if this conflict is really being supported by the Red Chinese and the Russians, and if this really is naked communism, international conspiracy, then I think we have to weigh the question of how much we can escalate without their continuing to escalate if we agree that's the real issue in Vietnam. If this conflict is what we seem to say at times it is, then we need to risk the ultimate because . . . I mean then that's in the hands of the enemy, not our hands. Now as a young boy I got kicked out of old Mexico. I was born down in old

Mexico. These people kicked us out because they envied the prosperity of my people. . . . I have refrained from taking a clear-cut position one way or the other, ah, I just . . . the President hasn't either. If he hasn't, I don't see why a governor should.

Romney promptly called on two young men from the Ripon Society to "clarify" his statement, but not before Thomas O'Neill of the Baltimore *Sunpapers* had summed up his performance: "Down deep he's shallow."

The contradiction and confusions of his Vietnam position continued to plague Romney, and to do serious damage to his presidential prospects, until April 7, 1967, when he finally gave a major speech on the subject in Hartford, Connecticut. The Governor ruled out as unrealistic both United States withdrawal from Vietnam and "massive military escalation" of the conflict. He endorsed the use of "military force as necessary to reduce or cut off the flow of men and supplies from North Vietnam, to knock out enemy main force units, and to provide a military shield for the South." He said that, once military victory was achieved, the pacification of South Vietnam was a task for the South Vietnamese and warned against "Americanizing that other war." He said the United States should seek a "peace with amnesty" for all combatants but should not permit a coalition government involving the National Liberation Front, political arm of the Viet Cong. Later he added a suggestion that the United States encourage direct peace talks between the South Vietnam government and the Viet Cong and called for de-escalation of U.S. bombings.

In main points, his position paralleled that of the Johnson Administration and the President expressed his "gratitude" for Romney's stand. But he was a bit disingenuous in doing so, for Romney also staked out ground for serious criticism of the President if Vietnam remains an issue in 1968. He said the President had bypassed Congress and excluded the public from the decisions to escalate the American commitment in Vietnam and thereby had provoked an unprecedented "rupture of trust" in the government. "A commitment of the character and massiveness of ours in a country the size of Vietnam has the inevitable result of turning it into an American dependency," the Governor said. "This is as unconscionable to our tradition as it is resented by other free countries. . . . We must avoid such future entrapments."

Romney's speech achieved what it was intended to achieve. It gave him a sensible position on the major issue of the day and it satisfied Republicans of as differing views as Jacob Javits and Karl Mundt, Clifford Case and John Tower. But the doubts that had been planted during his nine months of indecision on Vietnam did not disappear overnight. To bolster his understanding of foreign affairs, he scheduled trips overseas, including a return visit to Vietnam. "It's nice over there," said newspaper humorist Jack Wilson. "On a clear day you can see the White House."

Yet, until Romney entered the national arena, neither his policy views nor his convoluted syntax affected his rapid political ascent. The reason is that probably fewer people have voted for him because they agreed with him than because they admired him. As a political leader in Michigan, Romney has made his moral fervor an effective tool for focusing public attention on practical problems, without being excessively literal about putting his specific "philosophy" into practice. True, one can find evidences of "Romneyism" in Lansing. The Wednesday-morning open-door sessions he instituted to give anyone an opportunity to talk to his Governor for five minutes harked back to his belief in "citizen participation." And in line with "voluntary co-operation" he has convened a number of Governor's conferences on subjects like "Strengthening the Family" and "Community Concerns."

As Governor, Romney has been first rate, perhaps even superb, in the tradition of Earl Warren and Thomas E. Dewey, Herbert Lehman and Adlai E. Stevenson. He has done so well because he is (1) lucky, (2) a fine administrator, (3) a good judge of people, (4) attuned to the needs of his state, and unwilling, as he has said, to put money ahead of people as public priority. And perhaps also because he has never doubted that he has a mission to lead and lead well.

Almost as if by command, Michigan's economy picked up at the moment Romney became Governor. The state is highly sensitive to auto industry trends, which means, as University of Michigan economist William Haber has said, "When times are good we eat higher on the hog than anyone else. When times are bad, we get hungrier." It was the 1963 recovery in national auto sales, rather than any major Romney cost cutting in government, that was responsible for turning an $86-million state deficit (July, 1962) into a $167-million surplus (July, 1966).

The administrative pattern for a Romney operation is a wheel, not a pyramid. He has never been part of a military chain of command and does not like his information to be filtered up to the top. So he has no chief of staff or number-two man. But Romney is the hub, rather than the apex, and his staff might be diagramed as the spokes. It is a good staff and Romney has the rare gift of being able to inspire it to great effort. No doubt his young assistants are encouraged by his ability to involve them in his business. Even in the midst of an election campaign he has been known to call in the clerical workers to explain "grand strategy." He was delighted when one of the young secretaries in his office outguessed the "brain trust" on the size of his 1966 election margin. The Governor is also a good detail man, who, under the devoted prodding of Peg Little, his long-time personal secretary, seldom puts off matters that need his attention.

No doubt the gubernatorial years have matured Romney as a politician. Considering that the legislature during his first term was controlled by the oxcart wing of his party, and that the legislature during his second term was controlled by the Democratic party (for the first time since 1934), the Governor can be said to have gotten along reasonably well with his coequal branch of government. While each year raising the state budget, he remains on good terms with Michigan's businessmen, in part, because—in the manner of Lyndon B. Johnson and his electric lights—he has specialized in symbolic, visible economies (like driving an Ambassador instead of a Continental).

For a man who fled the Republican label in 1962, he has managed in only four years to rebuild and take firm control of most of the state party. He has done this by precept, example and a strong arm. Yet, despite his long and steady attacks on what he has called "purveyors of hate" and "parasites" attached to the party, extremists still control the 14th Congressional District Republican organization (including part of Detroit and all of Grosse Pointe) and portions of two other districts, thus assuring that four to six Michigan delegates to the 1968 G.O.P. presidential convention probably will not consider Romney their favorite son.

The Governor has turned over management of the Michigan Republican party to tall, heavy-set Elly Peterson, of whom he has rather inelegantly said, "She looks like a woman, thinks like a man, and works like a dog." The degree to which State Chairman Peterson knows her business can be judged from "Operation Accent," run by her "nationalities" assistant, Ilmar Heinaru, an Estonian who came to the United States after World War II. There are over 1.8 million Michiganders of foreign stock, one-fifth of the population, including some 255,000 Poles and over 100,000 Ukrainians. The Romney-Peterson-Heinaru team has created a Republican State Nationalities Council and 25 Republican nationalities clubs, including an Iraqi-American Republican Club of Michigan. Each week about 300 people become naturalized Americans in the state and each receives a handsome brochure, "Congratulations from George Romney [smiling picture of the Governor] to [the recipient's name in fancy script] on becoming a United States Citizen." Those who read on will learn that the state flower is the apple blossom, the state bird is the robin, and "The Republican Party was organized more than a century ago in a spontaneous revolt against the spread of slavery. Today, it remains the party of human freedom and equal justice." This mailer costs the G.O.P. twenty-two cents plus six cents in postage.

The program that has brought Romney successively enlarged majorities is called "Total Michigan Progress" (a slogan that will never rival "compact car" or even "The Great Society"). Despite this pretentious title, it is not a systematized approach to dealing with state problems, but just another honest and energetic attempt to meet needs as they rise to the surface, with as much cash as it is possible to raise. Yet Romney has taken risks: he fought for the new constitution, which narrowly was adopted; put through a complete administrative overhaul of the executive departments; and battled repeatedly for an income tax, finally achieved in 1967. And even the usual *ad hoc* way of doing business has produced an impressive list of "firsts":

—Scholarship programs to help needy students go to Michigan private or public colleges.

—Use of state funds to guarantee low-cost bank loans for college students.

—A work-release program for adult offenders, allowing them to leave prison to work during the day, thus easing their transition back into the community and helping them support their families.

—A day care center for retarded children.

—A day care center for emotionally disturbed children.

—A specially-constructed children's unit at a state mental hospital.

—Outpatient services for the retarded at state hospitals.

—A volunteer program for college students to help disadvantaged children by tutoring and personal attention.

Even this sampling shows that while the Governor has not pulled back from committing state funds he also has kept an eye out for programs that may cost little more than initiative and imagination. As New York *Times* editorial writer William V. Shannon has summed up the Romney administration in *Harpers' Magazine,* "In place of the myth of the fiscal miracle man bringing the magic of 'citizen participation' to government, there is, in fact, the story of a shrewd, hardheaded, reasonably pragmatic politician who very much wants to win and has demonstrated how Republicans can do it in a major industrial state."

The problem confronting the Romney boosters in early 1967 was how to persuade the people who go to Republican conventions that Shannon was right—that the Mormon preacher was also a powerhouse vote-getting politician and that the good citizen who had once scorned all political parties was really a Republican at heart. Political parties are something like big Elks clubs. Almost anyone can join, but one must make the effort. Romney had been making a modest effort for two years, picking up occasional G.O.P. fund-raising invitations, and traveling enough so that Democrats in the Michigan legislature posted a big signboard logging his time out of the state. But in 1967 his backers decided that one way to hasten Romney's acceptance in the Republican lodge would be to have him vouched for by a member in good standing. And there were few members who had longer, more loyal records of service in the club's inner circle than the man they turned to—Leonard Wood Hall. Even Republicans who had come to power in the last eight years and had never laid eyes on Len Hall knew his was a reputation to be reckoned with.

Romney's chief drumbeater was born into Republican politics, on October 2, 1900, at the Oyster Bay estate of vice-presidential candidate Theodore Roosevelt. He was the youngest of eight children of TR's coachman. Roosevelt wrote, "My little girl Ethel, who acted as its [sic] godmother, selected Leonard Wood for its name. This was done purely on her own account." (Nine-year-old Ethel was not pleased with the responsibilities of godmothership, but consented because in the Roosevelt family godparents were allowed to rest their elbows on the dinner table.) After working his way through Georgetown Law

School, Hall returned to Nassau County politics, where, starting in 1927, he was successively elected assemblyman, sheriff and congressman. In Congress (1939-52), the great laugh that explodes from deep within his 230 pounds, along with his habit of making few speeches and doing much committee work, made him a popular figure. His colleagues named him chairman of the Republican Congressional Campaign Committee. At the 1952 convention he wore a button, "I Like Everybody." Especially Ike, who reciprocated by making Hall the chairman of the Republican National Committee. If Hall did not make the creaky national committee exactly hum like Du Pont or General Motors, he still was its best chairman since a Cleveland industrialist named Marcus Alonzo Hanna. In 1955, acting solely on his own nerve and political instinct, he asserted that Eisenhower, then stricken with a heart attack, would surely run again in 1956. He thereby spared his party what could have been a year of divisive incipient candidacies. With equal coolness, he snuffed out the rebellion against the renomination of Richard Nixon.

For a gent who had been weaned on the cigar smoke of clubhouse politics, Hall was remarkably responsive to new techniques and became an early convert to the political value of television. Yet at heart he believed that the real work of politics could only be done by the pros, and, as national chairman, he made it his job to know who they were. He traveled the country, never forgetting a name or face, it has been said. He was the nearest thing to Jim Farley that the Republican party ever produced.

But politics began to turn sour for Hall in 1958. He thought he deserved the Republican nomination for Governor of New York: it went instead to a rich upstart, Nelson Rockefeller. In 1960 Richard Nixon made him, along with Robert Finch, co-manager of his campaign. Hall called Nixon "the best equipped candidate the party has ever had," and predicted that the Vice President "would have more to say about the operation of his campaign than any other candidate in my lifetime." Unfortunately for Campaign Manager Hall, Prophet Hall was right. Nixon did not need a Len Hall; in his opinion, he was his own Hall. The real Hall felt slighted. Once, after the secret Nixon-Rockefeller meeting on the platform, he almost quit. In early September, 1963, Nelson Rockefeller called Hall to his Tarrytown estate ("life-size marble statues, life-size bronze statues, fountains all over the place . . .") and asked his support for the presidency. Hall was not yet in a mood to feel charitable toward his old rival. He felt even less inclined after the New York Governor offered him "a handsome retainer." Hall prides himself on not being for sale. "Well, Nelson," he said, "I've been in the practice of law for forty years and I haven't had to do that yet." He then sat out the presidential nomination fight.

It is over a decade since Len Hall left the party chairmanship "with plaudits," said a Washington *Post* editorial at the time, "for one of the most remarkable performances in the annals of his party" (the re-election of Eisenhower by a 9.5-million-vote majority). In 1964, Hall is supposed to have told Clif White, Goldwater's strategist, to "see Harry Darby" about the Kansas delegation. But old Senator Darby didn't run Kansas any more. Nor did Hall's friend Mort Frayn have anything to say about Washington State—he was beaten in his own precinct. Politics is a profession of high mobility; the turnover in the past six years, because of the Goldwater revolution and counterrevolution, has been even greater than usual. Hall talked about resuscitating his "old team" for Romney. Thomas G. Judd, a Salt Lake City businessman and Republican official of the fifties, was asked to "scout" the Mountain States. Robert Carter, Hall's assistant at the national committee, opened a "public relations office" in Washington with a retainer from J. Willard Marriott, a close friend of Romney's. But Romney himself realized that, good as Hall's counsel and useful as his prestige might be, younger men were needed for the legwork of rounding up delegates.

Among those recruited for or reporting to Hall's Washington-based political operation were:

—Robert J. (Jack) McIntosh, forty-five, a World War II fighter pilot and one-term (1957-59) Congressman from Port Huron, Michigan, who served the Romney administration as a legislative lobbyist, public service commission chairman and director of the department of commerce, to be a traveling troubleshooter, liaison man with Congressmen and delegate-hunter.

—William G. Murphy of Pennsylvania, a Purple Heart veteran of the Korean war and formerly a top assistant to Senator Hugh Scott and Governor William W. Scranton of Pennsylvania, to oversee the Washington office operations.

—David Goldberg, the Boston-based veteran of the 1964 Lodge write-in campaign, and John Deardourff of New York, a Rockefeller organization man, to handle the New Hampshire primary and oversee New England.

—Carl Spad, fifty, a veteran of Young Republican politics who resigned as New York Republican chairman in May, 1967, with Rockefeller's blessing, to work in the Washington headquarters and handle the campaign in the mid-Atlantic states.

—Lawrence B. Lindemer, a youthful-looking Michigan attorney who was Republican state chairman from 1957 to 1961, a Midwest organizer in the 1964 Rockefeller-for-President campaign, to handle the Midwestern states.

—Richard H. Headlee, thirty-seven, a former president of the U.S. Junior Chamber of Commerce and a convert to Mormonism, who supervises volunteer groups and handles special projects from the Washington office.

—Thomas C. Stephens, sixty-four, the wry, spry political veteran from New York who was President Eisenhower's appointments secretary and who has been involved in every campaign in which Nelson Rockefeller has had an interest in the last eight years.

While political operations were starting up in Washington, in an office four blocks from the capitol in Lansing, a group of policy advisers set up shop as "Romney Associates." (The Lansing office was known to the local news corps as "Governor Romney's Office for Presidential Explorations," or simply, GROPE.) The Lansing staff, like that in Washington is a mixture of old and new. Its pivotal figure is Romney's "resident egghead" and special assistant, Walter B. De-Vries, who, like former presidential assistant Bill D. Moyers, is equally expert at the frug and at analyzing an opinion poll. The thirty-seven-year-old DeVries worked his way through Michigan State University as an assistant to the Speaker of the State House of Representatives, and did a Ph.D dissertation on "The Michigan Lobbyist: A Study in the Bases and Perceptions of Effectiveness." Apparently he found the lobbyists far too effective, because he later wrote a strict lobbying control provision into the new Michigan constitution. His work caught the attention of a fellow convention delegate, George Romney, who in 1963 prevailed upon DeVries to leave his position as assistant professor of political science at Calvin College, Grand Rapids, to join the Governor's staff. At the beginning of 1967 DeVries resigned his $20,000-a-year state job to devote himself full time to research for Romney's presidential drive.

His only associate, for a time, was Glen L. Bachelder, thirty-two, of Kalamazoo, who was working on his Ph.D. in political science at

Michigan State University when DeVries recruited him to help do research for Romney's 1964 campaign. But in mid-1967, Romney reached outside Michigan for additional aid in preparing himself on national and international issues.

To coordinate foreign policy research, he persuaded apple-cheeked, thirty-four-year-old Jonathan Moore to cut short his academic sabbatical at Harvard's Institute of Politics and come out to Lansing. Moore is the son of Romney's long-time friend and former neighbor, Charles Moore, retired vice president in charge of public relations for the Ford Motor Company. Young Moore is also well connected in Massachusetts politics, having been an assistant to former Senator Leverett Saltonstall and a key worker in Elliot Richardson's election as Attorney General in 1966. He also served under William Bundy in both the Pentagon and State Department. Assisting Moore in preparation of foreign policy position papers is James C. Kellogg, twenty-nine, formerly on the intelligence and planning staffs of the State and Defense Departments and the Arms Control and Disarmament Agency.

To direct research on domestic issues, Romney hired William B. Prendergast from his post as research coordinator for the House Republican Conference. Prendergast, fifty-one, a graduate of Notre Dame and the University of Chicago, won a reputation as one of the country's top political analysts as research director of the Republican National Committee from 1960 to 1964, but left the staff after Goldwater's nomination.

There has been a similar expansion of personnel on the speechwriting and press relations staffs in Lansing. Romney began 1967 with Charles Harmon, a thirty-four-year-old Michigan native, as his press secretary and Albert A. Applegate, a thirty-eight-year-old University of Michigan political science graduate, as his only full-time speech writer. S. John Byington, a thirty-year-old lawyer (who also is a licensed pharmacist), also worked part time on campaign publicity.

Several moves were made to bolster the staff. Jack C. Vandenberg, a former United Press International reporter from Michigan, left the staff of New Jersey Senator Clifford P. Case to help Harmon with press duties in Lansing, while Richard Milliman, Romney's press secretary and public relations adviser in his 1962 campaign for Governor, left his executive post with a chain of Michigan newspapers and radio stations to take over part of the speechwriting burden from Applegate. George F. Gilder and Bruce K. Chapman, who as members of the Harvard class of 1962 had founded the lively but short-lived journal of progressive Republican opinion, *Advance Magazine,* and later wrote an angry book about the 1964 campaign, *The Party That Lost Its Head,* were put on retainer for special writing projects. Finally, in midsummer, Romney obtained the services of Travis Cross, the former assistant to Oregon Governor and Senator Mark Hatfield, who is probably one of the half-dozen best political public relations men in the country. Cross, forty, who set up his own public relations firm in Salem, Oregon, after helping elect his old Stanford friend, Hatfield, to the Senate in 1966, has exactly the unflappable professionalism and long experience with the national press corps that was so conspicuously lacking in the Romney operation during the early part of 1967.

DeVries, a native of Holland, Michigan, is part of what has become known as Romney's "Dutch Mafia." The Governor's staff is peppered with names like Danhof and De Jonge. But the Mafia leader is not on the state payroll. He is Richard C. Van Dusen, perhaps the most astute Michigan politician in Romney's inner circle. Tall, balding, and a smoker of long, thin cigars, Van Dusen was a star football player at the University of Minnesota and a graduate of Harvard Law School before entering the Michigan legislature at the age of twenty-nine. Two years later, in 1956, he became the Republican candidate for state Attorney General, losing by eighty-thousand votes out of three million. So Van Dusen at thirty-seven was already a seasoned politician when the constitutional convention met. During its deliberations he carefully steered his fledgling roommate, George Romney, past some of the more dangerous political eddies. Following the 1962 election, Van Dusen served as the new governor's legal aide, and, along with L. William Seidman, a wealthy Grand Rapids accountant and Romney intimate, he drafted the proposed fiscal reform program. But after eight months in Lansing he returned to his partnership in the prestigious Detroit law firm of Dickinson, Wright, McKean and Cudlip, keeping himself available to Romney for major political chores, including representing Michigan on the 1964 platform committee and traveling to many high-level Republican meetings. As counselor and political operative, Van Dusen is expected to play a major role in the Romney drive.

So, too, is Michigan's Republican National Committeeman, white-haired John B. Martin of Grand Rapids, a man of tact as well as deeply-held convictions, who frequently travels with Romney, then doubles back to consolidate alliances in the states the Governor has visited.

The Governor's presidential campaign will not fail for lack of proper financing. American journalists of the late nineteenth century never wrote about money in politics without calling it "the sinews of war." And behind the Romney operation are three of the most sinewy men in today's Republican party—J. Willard Marriott, J. Clifford Folger and Max M. Fisher.

Marriott and Romney are fellow Mormons with long family connections. Mrs. Romney and Mrs. Marriott went to high school together; their mothers were friends before them; and Mrs. Marriott's widowed mother married Senator Reed Smoot after meeting him at the home of Mrs. Romney's parents. Marriott and Romney came to Washington at about the same time in the late 1920's. "As father is always saying," says J. Willard Marriott, Jr., "he owed $2,000 when he first came to Washington as a young man. Now he owes $20 million and that, he says, is progress." The elder Marriott exaggerates his indebtedness, but it is hard to overstate the success of his six-stool root-beer stand that grew into the Hot Shoppes restaurant and motel chain, which now grosses in the neighborhood of $150 million a year.

J. Clifford Folger is a kindly but wily Washington investment banker who holds membership in the best clubs (The Brook, Chevy Chase, Metropolitan, F Street) and seats on the bluest-chip boards of directors (Chesapeake and Potomac Telephone, Hilton Hotels International, Hiram Walker, Burlington Mills, International Business Machines). During the Eisenhower Administration he was the top national fund raiser in the Republican party. Eisenhower made him Ambassador to Belgium; he returned home after two years to raise funds for Nixon. Like many of the old-school G.O.P. money men, he is more amused by politics than by government, more interested in picking a winner than in ideology.

The third of Romney's financial big three is Max M. Fisher, son of immigrant Jews, who earned an engineering degree from Ohio State and a fortune from oil and real estate. On the wall of his handsome office in Detroit's towering Fisher Building (named for the "Body by . . ." Fishers, but owned by Max), there is prominently displayed an autographed picture of Richard M. Nixon, to whom he was a major contributor in 1960. Although only fiifty-nine, Fisher, who looks more like a scholar than a businessman, retired nearly a decade ago to devote his considerable energies to philanthropy. He now spends much of his time raising huge sums for Detroit charities, the United Jewish Appeal, and his good friend George Romney.

In the Catbird Seat

Green, Providence **Sunday Journal**, Nov. 13, 1966

In George Romney's campaign to become the first presidential nominee from Michigan since Lewis Cass in 1848, certain initial advantages and disadvantages are clear. He begins with the backing of two men who bled profusely in the 1964 struggle and of most others who share with them the overriding purpose of avoiding the political catastrophe of that year. Nelson Rockefeller and William Scranton have long memories and have had time to plumb their experiences for the lessons of that fateful year. The chief lesson is solidarity. Says the New York Governor, "I am determined not be used as an instrument to split the unity of progressive Republicans behind a candidate who can win in 1968." Says the former Pennsylvania Governor, "I have been preaching . . . [that] it is important to stick together. After my experience in 1964, I think I have a right to."

Equally hardened by his own experiences in 1964 is Barry Goldwater. Early declaring his own support for Richard Nixon, Goldwater displayed a consistent distaste for Romney. In December, 1964, he wrote Romney: "I don't claim for one moment that had you, Governor Smylie, Governor Rockefeller, Senator Keating, Senator Javits, etc., supported me, I would have won. But I can tell you that many rank-and-file Republicans got a bad taste in their mouths when they saw leaders of their own party failing to support a national ticket." Two years and three months later, he said, "I cannot forgive him." Asked about Romney's prospects in early 1967, Goldwater said, "It depends if he decides to come back to the Republican party. . . . We will have to wait and see what he stands for." In late 1966 conservative groups, like the United Republicans of America and Americans for Constitutional Action (to which Romney once contributed $100) launched bitter campaigns against the Governor for his walkout in 1964.

On the political level, Goldwater's hostility is tempered slightly by the fact that he will be running for the Senate in Arizona in 1968 on a ticket that, he recognizes, may be headed by Romney. He is pledged to support the nominee of his party, whoever he is. But on a personal level there is probably no way Romney can reconcile Goldwater and the irreconcilables. However, there is a way he can bring around the larger group of party-oriented conservatives who were vexed, but not fatally antagonized, by his 1964 defection, and at the same time unite behind him not only Rockefeller and Scranton but the young moderate Governors, Senators and Representatives who hung back from endorsing him in 1967 out of an abundance of caution.

That way is to convince them that he is a winner—by meeting and defeating all comers in a series of presidential primary contests. The primaries are strewn with dangers. Operating under differing rules, each offers a unique opportunity for disaster: the open field of contenders in Nebraska, Wisconsin and Oregon; the small and seemingly quixotic electorate of New Hampshire. Wendell Willkie was undone by the 1944 Wisconsin primary, Harold Stassen by Oregon's in 1948.

But the primaries are Romney's natural arena; his surest political talent is as a person-to-person campaigner. Held suspect by the professionals, his obvious tactic is to take his case to the people. In March, 1967, a year ahead of voting time, David Goldberg and John Deardourff, two talented young operatives, were retained by Hall to scout New Hampshire for Romney. Also on the likely Romney list: Wisconsin, Nebraska and Oregon.

Nineteen sixty-eight is Romney's last chance. Unlike others in the Republican field, Romney has no choice about avoiding a race with the incumbent. At the time of the 1968 election, he will be sixty-one—a year older than Johnson and older than all but seven Presidents in our history at the time they took office.

What would it be like—a Romney-Johnson contest? Romney's greatest assets would be his demonstrated ability to appeal to normally Democratic and independent voters and his image on the television screen. The President, despite the efforts of his tailors and his television advisers, looks like a weather-beaten ranch hand. The Governor looks like a President. The President, whatever the reality of his conduct, often appears sly and devious; the Governor looks like a middle-aged Eagle Scout: clean-cut, honest, sincere.

But Lyndon B. Johnson knows this country and the world as only a man who has stood at or near the center of power in Washington for more than three decades can know them. Romney, to put it charitably, is not his match in this regard.

The real question is: What do people look for in a President, or what will they be looking for in 1968? Johnson was greatly admired for the genius of his *performance* in his first two years in office, then came to be distrusted and disliked for his *personality*. Romney, with his evangelical fervor, is obviously not everybody's cup of tea. National political reporters, who are probably beyond his redemption, find his preachings irritating. "If Romney bores the press," hypothesized columnist Roscoe Drummond, "he may bore the nation."

Yet moralizing has an honored place in presidential campaigns. Eisenhower summoned us to a "great crusade" and Kennedy called on us for "sacrifice." In Michigan, the only place where Romney has really been tested, the people have responded to his message. As Judd Arnett of the Detroit *Free Press* writes, Michiganders "look upon him as a Good Man and vote accordingly."

Would they and their fellow Americans make the Good Man their President if they had a chance? Or would Lyndon Johnson be able to persuade the country that he is telling the truth when he says, "It's not hard to do the right thing when you are President. The hard thing is to *know* what is right." And, hearing them both, would the voters conclude that there is wisdom in Lyndon Johnson that neither Mormonism, motorcars nor Michigan has given George Romney?

That is Romney's—and the Republicans'—quandary.

6 RICHARD M. NIXON:

The Durable Man

EARLY in November of 1961 arid Southern California experienced a disastrous series of brush fires, which played an eerie game of leapfrog from house to house in the fashionable Bel-Air and Brentwood sections of Los Angeles. Richard M. Nixon, at the time, was renting a movie director's English Tudor house on North Bundy Drive. Across the street flames destroyed the residence of actor Joe E. Brown. And, as the first press photographer reached the scene, the former Vice President was hosing down a small fire. "He got a true action photo," a Nixon aide later commented. But, true to the code of the *paparazzi,* the photographer insisted that Nixon re-enter his house and pose at the door with a suitcase. The next day almost every newspaper in the country showed Nixon with suitcase instead of Nixon with hose. For the real Nixon looked posed and the posed Nixon looked real.

The search for "the real Nixon" now has been a popular pastime since 1948. He has been written off as finished, *kaput,* done for, washed up and all through in national politics more often by more people and more erroneously than anyone else in American life. In 1948, his closest friends thought he was signing his political death warrant by taking up Whittaker Chambers' charges against Alger Hiss. In 1952, when the "Nixon fund" story broke, Thomas Dewey and other top Eisenhower advisers told him bluntly to get off the national ticket. In 1960, having survived a minor challenge to his nomination, he proceeded to lose a presidential campaign which most Republican politicians thought he should have won, and by a margin so close that the second-guessers had a field day at his expense.

In 1962, incredibly even to himself, he lost the governorship of California to Democratic incumbent Edmund G. Brown. "And the morning after the election," as *Time* reported, "Nixon wrote his own political obituary" with his bitter attack on the press. "Barring a miracle," said the magazine on November 16, 1962, "his political career ended last week."

But he was alive again in 1964. Alive enough for his backers to run him in three of the presidential primaries; for Nixon himself to mount a last-minute drive for the nomination; and even, for a time, to consider a bid to be Vice President. All failed, and in January, 1966, Nixon told William Lawrence of ABC News, "As a practical political realist, I do not expect to be a nominee again."

And yet fourteen months later, in March, 1967, a group of reputable and well-financed Republican professionals announced the formation of a Nixon for President Committee, whose chairman asserted with confidence, "When the time is right, we will have a candidate." "The operation," as *Newsweek* wrote, "had all the spontaneity of a calculating machine," but no one doubted that Nixon would indeed be running again. Or thought that he had ever stopped.

It is hard, in fact, to picture Nixon standing still. There was the day in October, 1966, for instance, when he began his final two-week burst of campaigning for Republican congressional candidates. For two weeks before that, lawyer Nixon had lived, breathed, talked and thought sixteen hours a day about the case he was to argue, for the second time, before the Supreme Court. He flew down from New York to Washington on a Tuesday morning and spent the day in court. But Tuesday night, instead of having the case behind him, as he had hoped, he was reworking it again in his Washington hotel room, because he had been interrupted in mid-argument by the Court's self-imposed curfew.

So on Wednesday he arose early again, scrubbed and shaved and faced the Justices for another hour of questioning and argument. The airline held the plane at National Airport for fifteen minutes so he would not miss his connection in Chicago. In his few minutes at O'Hare Field, he made phone calls to three Chicago friends to check the progress of Charles H. Percy's campaign for the Senate. Then he flew on to San Francisco, arriving with his day already twelve hours old and a full schedule of campaigning still ahead.

There were three television crews waiting at the San Francisco airport, and that took fifteen minutes. He was driven to the St. Francis

Hotel, where he shaved again and then faced another thirty-five-minute press conference. Back upstairs, he had sandwiches and coffee while dictating to his secretary.

Then he drove across the bay to Oakland and spoke for fifty minutes, imbuing a soon-to-be-forgotten Republican congressional candidate with virtues his own wife never suspected he possessed, talking of Vietnam, of Lyndon Johnson, of the future of the two-party system, with only his eyes showing the fatigue he felt.

After the speech, after twenty minutes of handshaking and autographing, he drove an hour south to Palo Alto, where he talked for fifteen more minutes in the midnight chill outside his motel with the two University of California law students who had volunteered as chauffeurs for him and his party. His day was now twenty-one hours old and he had traveled three thousand miles from the Supreme Court to his resting place, but he was not done. He took his former campaign manager, Robert Finch, in tow and discussed for two more hours Finch's campaign for Lieutenant Governor of California. Then for three hours Richard Nixon slept. The phone rang to awaken him for the television interview program which preceded a Finch fund-raising breakfast, a flight to Bakersfield, a press conference, a rally for candidate (now Congressman) Bob Mathias, a flight to Burbank, another press conference, a television taping, a flight to Ontario, California, a rally for candidate (now Congressman) Jerry Pettis, a return flight to Burbank and, early Friday morning, a flight back to New York.

What kind of man pushes himself this way? The same kind of introverted, self-contained, driven man who worked uncomplainingly one hot North Carolina summer for a law professor at Duke, handcranking an inky mimeograph machine eight hours a day in an airless cubicle, duplicating a manuscript the professor wanted to sell to his students. Nixon did the drudgery because it paid well and he needed the money to complete law school. Then and thereafter, the end justified the means.

For Richard Nixon, the end is power—specifically the incomparable power of the presidency. He moved toward it in a spectacular, meteoric career. Congressman at thirty-three, important Congressman at thirty-five, Senator at thirty-seven, Vice President at thirty-nine, only two-term Republican Vice President at forty-three, presidential nominee at forty-seven.

So often the prize seemed close. In 1955, the serious heart attack of President Eisenhower made Nixon, in effect, the acting President. A year later, Eisenhower contemplated retiring, a step that undoubtedly would have led to Nixon's nomination and very probably to his

"Gee Whiz, Pat . . . Some Men Go Bowling, Some Play Poker . . . I Just Happen to Like Running for President!"

Conrad, Los Angeles **Times,** Aug. 16, 1965. Reprinted by permission of The Register and Tribune Syndicate

election. Through other illnesses in Eisenhower's second term, Nixon was forced to prepare himself mentally for the task of national leadership that could at any moment have been thrust on him.

And then in 1960 came his chance, his shining chance. He campaigned flat-out for nine weeks, sparing himself nothing, trying to manage every detail of the race. He charged from Baltimore to Indianapolis to Dallas to San Francisco the first day, and rarely slackened the pace thereafter. He drove himself, his staff and his wife, who went every step of the way with him, to the edge of exhaustion, sustaining himself through the endless, weary days of parades and speeches and crowds in the only way a presidential candidate can survive the ordeal of the campaign—by knowing the value of the prize at the end of the road.

And then he lost. Lost by an eyelash—118,574 votes—less than one vote per precinct, two-tenths of one percent of a total vote of nearly 69 million.

He lost honorably. He debated his less-well-known opponent, although he knew it was not the politically expedient thing to do. He firmly dampened the religious issue among his own adherents, while Catholics were swinging over decisively to his opponent. He refused to challenge the results in Illinois and Texas, where there was substantial suspicion of vote fraud, and where a shift would have given him the election.

In almost two centuries of the American Republic, as Richard Nixon, amateur historian, knows, no man defeated for the presidency and denied renomination in the subsequent election has later been able to recover sufficient political strength to achieve either nomination or election. The man whose career most parallels Nixon's is the long-forgotten John C. Breckinridge of Kentucky. As presiding officers of the Senate, Vice Presidents Breckinridge and Nixon—exactly one hundred years apart—officially announced their own presidential defeats, the only two men to officiate at their own political wakes.

But unlike Breckinridge, who faded to obscurity after losing to Lincoln, Nixon may still prove to be a political Lazarus. Though Richard Rovere dismisses him as a "connoisseur of defeat," each time Dr. Gallup takes the pulse of the nation Nixon is right there on the "most admired" list. Gallup Polls between November, 1963, and July, 1967, showed that rank-and-file Republicans preferred Nixon as their party's standard-bearer sixteen out of twenty-two times. Polls of G.O.P. county chairmen and delegates to the 1964 convention also put him ahead. Above all else, Richard M. Nixon is durable.

The durability may, in a strange way, be related to the eternal puzzling over what makes Nixon tick. It is hard to think what else keeps Nixon on the top. Some politicians are pleasing of face: Nixon's looks have been likened to a Bob Hope carved out of walnut. Some politicians are entertaining: Nixon is basically a serious, even studious person, a grind. And everybody knows that nobody likes a grind. He has not won public office in his own right for seventeen years. He has not held public office for seven years. Since his move to New York, he has been as close to being a stateless person politically as there has ever been in this country.

And yet he persists. It is hard to avoid concluding that the "mystery of Nixon" has added years to his political life. Who, after all, still wonders about "the real Harold Stassen"? After dishonor, the worst thing a public figure can do is bore. And in a celebrity culture where the sway of an author is measured in weeks, of a pop singer in months, and of an athlete in years, Nixon's is measured in decades.

Meg Greenfield, Washington editor of *The Reporter* magazine, wrote in the spring of 1967 a savagely funny lament for herself and the 9,534,000 others who turned twenty-one in time to cast their first presidential vote in 1952—the members of what she called the Nixon Generation:

> At regular intervals now, ever since that first vote in 1952, my generation has either been supporting or opposing Richard Nixon. The psychological implications of this fact are staggering: half of us have lived our whole adult life as a series of dashed hopes and disappointments, while the other half have passed the same period in a condition of perpetual anxiety over the prospect that he would succeed. . . . What distinguishes us as a group from those who came before and those who have come after is that we are too young to remember a time when Richard Nixon was not on the political scene, and too old reasonably to expect that we shall live to see one.

The Washington *Star*'s astute Mary McGrory has said, "he has been around so long, he has almost ceased to be controversial." But she gave her opinion in a non-presidential year. Quadrennially, by the time the snow falls in New Hampshire, the 'name Nixon triggers the imagination of his friends and enemies, which means practically every American.

If Americans as a whole have long been almost equally divided between the fans and the critics of Richard Nixon, there is one subgroup in the society—the intellectuals—whose verdict has been a nearly unanimous vote of no confidence. As New York writer Victor S. Navasky said, "You can't have voted for Richard Nixon and be a member of the New York intellectual establishment."

Ironically, Nixon fancies himself as an intellectual. He told Jules Witcover of the Newhouse newspapers in a 1966 interview: "I wish I had more time to read and write. I'm known as an activist and an organizer, but some people have said I'm sort of an egghead in the Republican party. I don't write as well as [Adlai] Stevenson, but I work at it. If I had my druthers, I'd like to write two or three books a year, go to one of the fine schools—Oxford, for instance—just teach, read and write. I'd like to do that better than what I'm doing now." One of the few commentators who saw this side of Nixon was Stewart Alsop, who, in a 1960 book, noted that there was "an oddly academic flavor to much of Nixon's conversation" and credited him with having an "inquiring, absorptive mind" and being "a rather judicial-minded fellow, a bit academic in manner."*

Probably in the true sense, Nixon is an intellect but not an intellectual, at least if one accepts the distinction of R. H. S. Crossman, the Labourite Member of Parliament, that "what distinguishes the intellectual from other politicians is his application of theoretical arguments to the solution of practical problems."† For Nixon, like most politicians, has little interest in general and abstract theory. He probably would agree with novelist Saul Bellow, who told a startled group of Communist writers in Poland, "Ideology is a drag."

Yet Nixon is an intellectual to the extent that he thrives on the play of the mind. It is the part of politics that he enjoys most and at which he is best. Even in his agitated state during the so-called "last press conference," he reminded the reporters. "I have welcomed the opportunity to test wits with you."

He also has a claim to the respect of intellectuals on much of his record. If he has been consistently hard-line in his opposition to Communism, that attitude does not distinguish him from two men the intellectuals have admired, Nelson A. Rockefeller and Hubert H. Humphrey. His attitude has been firmly internationalist, including early and consistent advocacy of large-scale foreign aid, a position that was hardly designed to win him votes. On civil rights, Nixon had the solidest record of any man in the Eisenhower Administration

---

* Stewart Alsop, *Nixon and Rockfeller, A Double Portrait* (Garden City, N.Y.: Doubleday, 1960), pp. 46, 47, 50.

† See R. H. S. Crossman, "The Egghead as Leader," *New Statesman*, July 9, 1960, p. 60. Also of interest is Robert A. Nisbet, "What Is an Intellectual?" *Commentary*, December, 1965, pp. 93-101.

—and before that, a voting record in Congress that matched John F. Kennedy's and surpassed that of Lyndon B. Johnson. Moreover, he was one of the first Republicans in the country to take on the John Birch Society, again a stand that was hardly calculated to win him votes.

Nixon uses well the intellectual's own key tools—language and logic. His syntax is generally orderly, his arguments are systematically arranged, and he even has the ability to turn a phrase. The essay he submitted to meet the admission requirements for the New York bar was described as the finest of the thousands that have come in through the years.

Nixon rarely employs ghostwriters. Instead, on yellow, legal-size pads, he painstakingly outlines and re-outlines his speeches. Then, once the logic, the key phrases and transition points are firmly imbedded in his own mind, he normally throws away the notes and delivers extemporaneously.*

Why then the breach between Nixon and the intellectuals? The antagonism for many goes back to the Hiss case and the McCarthy era. Clearly no young politician could have more thoroughly damned himself from the start than the freshman congressman, lowliest member of the House Committee on Un-American Activities, when his persistence and constant probing led to the conviction of Alger Hiss.

---

* Flying across the continent to deliver a Lincoln Day speech in Seattle in 1966, the former Vice President spent five hours making notes that, in part, looked like this:

1. *Why are we there?*
   1. N.V. Nam tries to conquer by support of revolution.
   2. We are helping prevent.
2. *Why should we interest ourselves?* (The Stakes)
   1. S.V. Nam's freedom.
   2. Confidence of all free Asian countries.
   3. If aggression succeeds, it will be tried again.
3. *What is our goal?*
   1. Stop aggression.
   2. Independence for S.V. Nam.
      1. Not there for bases.
      2. Not there to interfere in Civil War.
      3. Not there to conquer N.V. Nam.
4. *Why not get out?*
   1. It will bring war.
   2. Our goal is to reduce danger of war.
5. *Will we succeed?* (cf. French)
   1. S.V. Namese on our side.
   2. China not powerful—

"My name, my career," Nixon was later to write, "were ever to be linked with the decisions I made and the actions I took in that case."

Urbane, conservatively dressed Alger Hiss, with impeccable educational and social credentials, had been a New Deal figure and was president of the prestigious Carnegie Endowment for International Peace. Whittaker Chambers, wrinkled and fat, was an admitted ex-Communist. The antagonists seemed created to be symbols. The accusation against Hiss was a challenge to all that liberalism had represented for over twenty years. Most intellectuals, feeling deeply threatened, reacted with the same hurt and righteous indignation Hiss himself expressed. Many whom the public would recognize as the "best people" rallied instinctively to his cause; the President of the United States called the investigation a red herring. But Nixon, the small-town lawyer, believed Chambers. When Hiss was finally convicted, some of the intellectuals saw in the conviction elaborate conspiracy theories—"forgery by typewriter," homosexuality, counterespionage. Wrote sociologist E. Digby Baltzell, "Many [intellectuals] refused to face the evidence, and most never forgave Richard Nixon for his part in the case."*

Nor did they forgive him for his equivocal relationship to the junior Senator from Wisconsin, Joseph R. McCarthy, and the style of politics that bore his name. Nixon, like most Republicans, found no reason to denounce McCarthy until McCarthy turned his guns on the Republican Administration of which Nixon was a part. Meantime, Nixon's own speeches from 1950 to 1954 frequently used the same techniques for which McCarthy was ultimately censured.

As Nixon biographer Earl Mazo wrote:

Politicians were not averse to hyperbole. But not many in modern times handled it so resourcefully. Take, for instance, his [Nixon's] much-debated manipulation of the word "traitor." In 1954 he charged that "real Democrats are outraged by the Truman-Acheson-Stevenson gang's defense of Communism in high places"; and Truman, Stevenson and Acheson were "traitors to the high principles in which many of the nation's Democrats believed." Was that nothing more than an appeal for the votes of "real Democrats," as the Republicans insist? Or was it

---

* See E. Digby Baltzell, *The Protestant Establishment* (New York: Random House, 1964), pp. 104-5. For an excellent summary of the Hiss case, see Eric F. Goldman, *The Crucial Decade—and After* (New York: Vintage, 1961), pp. 101-111.

slick juggling, meant to highlight "traitor" and "Communism in high places"?*

More recently, Nixon has been providing ammunition for his intellectual critics by his seeming insensitivity to First Amendment rights, particularly in cases involving academics. Campaigning for a lackluster Republican candidate for Governor of New Jersey in 1965, Nixon enthusiastically endorsed his demand that an obscure Rutgers University professor who had championed the cause of the Viet Cong be fired from the state-supported university. When challenged for his stand, Nixon contrived an elaborate argument about the limits of academic freedom, which succeeded only in convincing the critics that he was insensitive to their concerns.†

But the intellectuals' dislike of Nixon goes beyond these questions of substance. It involves something else on which they place great emphasis—style.

Nixon's public style is that of the college debater, small-town, rural and lower middle class—William Jennings Bryan, not Woodrow Wilson; Hubert Horatio Humphrey, not John Fitzgerald Kennedy. Nixon debates well, controlling his material and his environment as a good debater must. Like most good debaters, he learned the technique young, and its habits are almost impossible to shake. The debater strives for points, not images. Not surprisingly, Nixon's speeches are loaded with "my three-point program," "a seven-point plan." In an age of television, debater Nixon is geared to the big hall, not the living room.

The debater oversimplifies. Confined to a few minutes, his technique is to hit and run. It is quick and graphic to label Senator Fulbright and his supporters as the "appeasement wing" of the Democratic party. The equation appeasement-Munich-sellout may not be lost on the audience, although Nixon could claim that the dictionary definition is not pejorative. Over the years Nixon has made an art of the almost-innuendo, an art for which Democrats from Lyndon B. Johnson on down will not forgive him.

His choice of words is indeed strange for a man who has handled

---

* Earl Mazo, *Nixon: A Political and Personal Portrait* (New York: Harper, 1959), pp. 7-8.

† But sensitive, in turn, to their reaction, Nixon made a point in conversations in 1966 of noting that his first Supreme Court case put him on the side of individual freedom—specifically, the "right of privacy"—which his client maintained had been invaded by *Life* magazine. The case was still in the courts in early 1967.

delicate diplomacy well and who now is a successful international lawyer: Lodge is getting a *bum rap*. . . . Rockefeller is a *spoilsport*. . . . I'm not a *buddy-buddy* boy. . . .The United States should not be *mealy-mouthed*. . . . He uses slang for its ornamental quality, casually or deliberately employing street-corner expressions to startle his auditors, and to show that, at heart, he is really one of them.

Nixon's oratory depends heavily on the question mark and the interior monologue. A little old lady is forever coming up to him and asking a question, always preceding it with a respectful "Mr. Nixon . . ." (It used to be "Mr. Vice President . . .") In a major address before the American Society of Newspaper Editors in 1964 Nixon asked himself fourteen questions: "Now, what does this mean?" "Now, what should the policy of the United States be?" "How much are they willing to risk?" His writing style employs the same techniques. In a 1963 *Saturday Evening Post* article, for example, Nixon tells of a Budapest railroad worker who approaches him as his train is leaving for Vienna and says, "My brother left [Hungary] in 1956 and is now living in Columbus, Ohio. If you should see him, will you tell him he was right?" It is an obviously unverifiable encounter, as it is meant to be. "I ask questions to wake up the guy in the audience," Nixon says. "It's the Socratic approach. I didn't invent it. But it drives the intellectuals nuts." He is right.

What upsets the intellectuals even more is Nixon's tone, perhaps best recalled in the famous "Checkers speech" of 1952. After carefully outlining his "complete financial history" in response to a charge that he had accepted an $18,000 fund from a group of supporters, the then vice-presidential candidate concluded:

. . . Well, that's about it. That's what we have and that's what we owe. It isn't very much but Pat and I have the satisfaction that every dime that we've got is honestly ours. I should say this—that Pat doesn't have a mink coat. But she does have a respectable Republican cloth coat. And I always tell her that she'd look good in anything.

One other thing I probably should tell you, because if I don't they'll probably be saying this about me too, we did get something—a gift— after the election. A man down in Texas heard Pat on the radio mention the fact that our two youngsters would like to have a dog. And, believe it or not, the day before we left on this campaign trip we got a message from Union Station in Baltimore saying they had a package for us. We went down to get it. You know what it was?

It was a little cocker spaniel dog in a crate that he sent all the way from Texas. Black and white spotted. And our little girl—Tricia, the six-year-old—named it Checkers. And you know the kids love that dog and I just want to say this right now, that regardless of what they say about it, we're going to keep it. . . .

This sort of thing may be more than a bit unctuous and an easy mark for the satirist—Mort Sahl suggested a TV program where Nixon would read the Constitution to his two daughters while Pat sits knitting an American flag—but for Nixon, the Checkers speech undoubtedly saved his political career. What may disturb the Nixonophobes most is the belief that he is putting them on. They may shake their heads sadly at a "true believer" like Romney, but Nixon they quickly accuse of just saying the things that he thinks the electorate wants to hear. He is one of the few politicians—Lyndon B. Johnson is another—whose *motives* are always questioned.

Were the suspicions of Nixon limited to the eggheads, it would be a political handicap, but not an insuperable one. It is true that virtually the same characteristics that made Nixon a dirty word in the intellectual corridor from Cambridge to Washington have failed to offend millions of other Americans, especially in the Middle West, South and Rocky Mountain regions. But it is also true that the epithet "Tricky Dick" is instantaneously understood by Americans of all backgrounds and of all sections to refer to one man and one man only.

Those who have puzzled over the essential Nixon character have usually ended by writing about the changes in the man, not the constants. Nixon-watchers tend to see him always evolving from one stage to another. In the course of a long career, he has been called the New Nixon, the old Nixon and the New, New Nixon. A Baltimore *Sun* editorial, viewing Nixon as a 1968 presidential candidate, gave him yet another label: "The Renewed Nixon," suggesting "a certain renewal of spirit and confidence. . . ." Rather than any major substantive change, however, the renewed Nixon is a product of changed circumstances and refined techniques.

Only a hundred days after John F. Kennedy moved into the White House, the former Republican Vice President went on a national speaking tour and Arthur Edson of the Associated Press reported: "There's a new Richard M. Nixon politicking about the land. It's a Nixon most people never saw, a Nixon who is relaxed and quick with the wisecrack." Edson was the first to comment on a phenomenon that would be increasingly noted after 1962. But it is well to remember that Nixon's "newness" came *immediately* after he left office, deserted him during the California gubernatorial race, and returned when he moved to New York. The distinction, therefore, should not be between new and old Nixon, but between candidate Nixon and citizen Nixon. To date the relaxed Nixon has been evident only when the personal stakes were modest.

But in the techniques of political campaigning there has been a fine honing, which may give the impression of change. A Nixon tour, the context in which he is most often reported, is an operation of high standards. It bears little resemblance to Barry Goldwater's "puttering" around or the mass confusion that characterized the late Estes Kefauver's national efforts. Nixon advance men are experts at the details of politics: cars are at the ready when the plane lands; crowds "spontaneously" appear; room reservations have been made; excerpts of the night's speeches are available well in advance. And Nixon always is presented in the best possible light. A favorite "trick" of the Nixon advance men is to schedule their man into an auditorium that holds less than the expected audience so that it looks like his appearance has drawn an overflowing turnout.

The most notable "change" has been in Nixon's use of humor. Now his jokes are less forced, his delivery is better, and, most importantly, he has learned the value of poking fun at his own foibles. To some degree this development results from Nixon's friendship with Paul Keyes, who may wish as his epitaph, "I taught Richard Nixon to laugh." Keyes is one of the greatest gag writers in the world, but, because of a passion for anonymity, he is totally unknown outside of a select show-business circle. The former Vice President met Keyes in 1961 when he appeared on the Jack Paar show, where Keyes was a producer and writer. While Nixon is the essentially serious man in whose presence others have a tendency to be solemn, Paul Keyes, although always respectful, is constitutionally unable to suppress his often outrageous humor. Soon he had assumed the role of court jester, with its long tradition of saying wise things in the coating of nonsense. While Nixon might not have put up with a mere funny man, in Keyes he recognized finely-attuned political instincts, perhaps his birthright as an Irish Catholic from Boston. Nixon sees less of Keyes since the writer-producer moved to Hollywood to work for Dean Martin. But he left with the Republican leader a feeling for making a point with a laugh. This is not just a question of good material, for Nixon's reactions to the unexpected are what separate him from other

joke-telling politicians. While addressing an Atlanta dinner, the spotlight suddenly failed. Nixon jested, "You know, turning off the lights in
the White House is one thing, but that's going too far." In Kalamazoo,
while he was in mid-sentence, a balloon floated down from the ceiling
and bounced off Nixon's head. The crowd tittered. Nixon plucked the
balloon off his shoulder, examined it carefully, and remarked, "Why,
it says vote for Romney and Millikin—but I already mentioned them."
Two audiences at least believe there is a new Nixon.

If Nixon's humor on these occasions is spontaneous, there is little
else about him that is. Though he never has been described as "the
thinking man's candidate," he deserves the title, at least in the sense
that he rarely speaks or acts without premeditation. It is the calculating quality of Nixon's personality that affects everything from his
personal relationships to his public reputation.

Richard M. Nixon may well be the most ill-at-ease man to occupy
a public position of prominence since John Quincy Adams. Small
talk eludes him. An incident in the 1960 campaign, trivial in itself,
illustrates this vividly. Nixon, for some unexplained reason, had
decided to take a Sunday respite, in mid-campaign, in Billings, Montana, of all unlikely places. The manager of the hotel where the candidate stayed decided to throw a cocktail party on Sunday evening
for the reporters traveling with Nixon. As the party began, Herb
Klein, Nixon's able press secretary (and now editor of the San Diego
Union), passed the word that the candidate would like to come down
for a social visit—no interviews, nothing on-the-record, just a visit.
This was such a departure for Nixon, who had held himself aloof from
reporters throughout the campaign, that they were astonished; but
soon there was Nixon himself, drink in hand, at the center of a circle
of journalists. Shortly afterward, Art Buchwald, the humorous columnist, shouldered his way through the group, bringing with him two of
the pretty stewardesses from the chartered press plane. Buchwald introduced the girls to the Vice President and told him, "They're great
fans of yours [which was true] and they've never had a chance to meet
you before." Nixon looked at the girls, and said, "Oh, are you stewardesses? I thought you were B-girls." No one laughed, so he added
hastily, "I meant B-for-Billings girls."

To say that the conversation was awkward from that point on
would be an understatement. The stewardesses retreated in embar-

rassment, while Nixon and a knot of reporters lamely kept the talk going. Finally, providentially, someone asked Nixon about the difference between speaking at an indoor rally and at an outdoor stadium. It was as if a physical burden had been lifted from the candidate's shoulders. All business now, safely removed from the perils of social talk, he launched into a lengthy disquisition on the technical problems of outdoor amplifying systems, the placement of speakers to avoid echoes, and a number of other arcane matters on which he seemed expert. At the end of the dissertation, Nixon made his farewells and left; the party resumed—not without an almost-audible sigh of relief. (At a similar press party in 1962 Nixon gave an informal lecture on the proper method of ordering sliced tomatoes in a restaurant.)

Whether this fascination with technique is a source of strength or of weakness is debatable. An astute—and very conservative—Republican public-relations man considers it Nixon's fatal flaw. Using a baseball analogy, he says, "Nixon is like a baseball batter who is complimented on having a perfect swing. But he's not satisfied to accept the compliment. He's got to stop and show you exactly how he cocks the bat, how far forward he brings his hands before he snaps the wrists, how far he strides—and while he's doing that the pitcher is striking him out."

The publicist's theory is more than fanciful. The hardest thing for Nixon to achieve is the appearance of doing or saying something instinctively. In the 1960 campaign, and again in his 1962 California campaign, Nixon used a political technique called the telethon, which his advisers felt would best display his stamina and incredible ability to give lightning responses. The object of the TV exercise was to have viewers phone questions to the candidate for hour after hour. The programs were not entirely unrigged, for it was the duty of a backstage panel to take the essence of a listener's query and give it a sticking point. Since Nixon was never at a loss for words, it made for a better performance, the producers felt, if an effort was made to stump him. Nevertheless, his assistants soon were asking him not always to rattle off his reply but occasionally to grope for an answer. His mental reflexes were making the show looked fixed!

Nixon has other techniques that seem almost too perfect to be real. His mind appears to have some sort of stopwatch mechanism that enables him to give a scheduled speech of twenty-nine minutes and fifteen seconds without being cued. Television directors who work with him for the first time find it uncanny.*

But it is not just technicians who are simultaneously impressed and

WAITING ROOM

Scott Long, Minneapolis **Tribune**, Oct. 13, 1966

made wary by Nixon's mastery of technique. His reputation in his party and with the public also shows evidence that there are those who, in the old phrase, "think him too clever by half." In the summer of 1966, Nixon was sought out by a prominent Republican Senator

* Off camera, however, Nixon is little more successful than Lyndon Johnson or George Romney in braking his own rhetoric. His most effective length, he feels, is thirty-five minutes, but the more tired he is, the longer he is apt to go on, and he has been known to hold forth for more than an hour.

for an endorsement of Percy's plan for an All-Asian Peace Conference to seek an end to the Vietnam War. The Senator approached the task without optimism, for Nixon's public position up to that time was strongly contrary to the logic of such a conference; indeed, he had been warning that demands for negotiations in this country only encouraged the enemy to keep fighting and thus prolonged the war. But, the Senator said, "Nixon instantly grasped the importance of the proposal to Percy's campaign for the Senate. He left my office and walked into a press conference and, on the spot, constructed a better argument for the All-Asian Conference idea than I had ever heard before. The only thing that bothered me," the Senator added, "was that he probably didn't believe a word of it."

The Senator's reaction may be at the heart of the enigma of Richard M. Nixon: Strip away the technique and what is left? Where is the real man?

As we shall see, the same conundrum occurs in Nixon's relations with the press. No American politician understands better the techniques of using the press, yet few are more distrusted by the reporters. No man has studied and mastered the techniques of politics more fully than Nixon, yet few have made more serious and fundamental mistakes of political judgment than he did in losing the presidency in 1960 and in running for Governor of California in 1962. For all his shrewdness and calculation, it was not he, but John F. Kennedy, who made the instinctive decision to pick up the phone and call the wife of the Rev. Dr. Martin Luther King when the civil-rights leader was thrown in jail.*

* For this decision, as for others for which he was criticized in the 1960 campaign, Nixon has an explanation. He says that he had been erroneously told that Kennedy was going to telephone the judge in the case and, as an attorney, he considered this an improper gesture, but he would have called Mrs. King to express his sympathy if it had been suggested to him.

Nixon says that the decision to debate Kennedy was virtually made mandatory by a statement from Senator Thruston B. Morton, then the Republican national chairman, welcoming the debates. In 1966, new light was shed on a third controversial decision—to limit President Eisenhower's campaigning in the final week of the campaign. Nixon accepted criticism for the decision, saying the General "did everything we asked him to do." But in 1966 Eisenhower revealed in an interview for *The Saturday Review,* and Nixon then confirmed to the New York *Daily News* columnist Ted Lewis, that in late October, 1960, Eisenhower's physician, Major General Howard M. Snyder, told Nixon he and Mrs. Eisenhower were worried about the President's physical condition and feared he might take on "too heavy a load" in the final days of the campaign. Mrs. Eisenhower gave the same message to Pat Nixon. So at

Close as he was to the presidency for eight years, much as he had studied the office, when the crucial confrontation took place, it was Kennedy, not Nixon, who impressed the nation's voters as having the presence, the coolness, the courage—whatever the special quality is—that the office demands.

Richard M. Nixon is not, as his enemies suggest, a "hollow man" but his essential nature is equivocal and mysterious both to those who have observed him closely and to those millions more for whom he has become part of the political landscape. It is fifteen years now since Adlai Stevenson told a breakfast in Boston, "This is Sunday, and this is a day of rest for candidates. And, therefore, I am not even going to worry about Senator Nixon's conscience." But people continue to worry.

Conscience is a central concept of Quakerism, Richard Nixon's religion. The Society of Friends, popularly known as Quakers, is one of the smallest of the Protestant sects, hardly exceeding 200,000. Still it has produced an extraordinary collection of diverse public figures, including, in recent years, Herbert Hoover, Drew Pearson (Nixon's most personally bitter enemy among the syndicated columnists), Whittaker Chambers and Alger Hiss.

On January 9, 1913, Richard Milhous Nixon was born to the former Hannah Milhous, of an old Irish Quaker family, and Frank Nixon, a Methodist who converted to his wife's religion and subsequently became a Quaker Sunday-school teacher. Dick Nixon's cousin is Jessamyn West, author of the charming collection of Quaker stories, *The Friendly Persuasion,* which is about their common great-grandfather and his family. Young Nixon grew up in Whittier, California, a community founded by and for Quakers and named after the Quaker poet. His mother, when conversing with her sisters, used "thee" and "thou" and his grandmother only talked in "the plain language." As a child, Nixon went to church four times on Sundays and he graduated from Whittier, a Quaker college.

The two leading contenders for the 1968 Republican presidential

---

a White House meeting on October 31 Nixon insisted that Eisenhower do only three already-arranged speeches, in Cleveland and Pittsburgh and an election-eve broadcast from the White House, and not accept an invitation for a Chicago speech that was being pressed on him by party leaders and the White House staff. Eisenhower, who did not learn the real reason for Nixon's objections until much later, complied. Kennedy carried Illinois by 8,858 votes.

nomination, Nixon and Romney, have been strongly affected by their religious faiths, but in very different ways. Their churches, while both placing emphasis on individual responsibility, are in many respects at opposite poles among the Christian sects. While Romney can hardly deliver a speech without calling attention to his religion, Nixon never mentions his. Nor does Nixon often attend church services, called meetings, any more.* The two facts are not surprising. For, unlike the Church of the Latter-day Saints, the Society of Friends is not a missionary church. And the Quaker attitude toward the importance of churchgoing may be best explained by the story of the non-Quaker who wandered into a Quaker meetinghouse, found the congregants in absolute silence, and whispered to the man next to him, "When does the service begin?" To which the Quaker replied, "The service begins when the meeting ends."

While Mormonism makes every man a priest, Quakerism bestows priesthood on no man; Mormonism is founded on a detailed set of holy writings, Quakerism has never had a creed; the Mormons are famous for their Tabernacle Choir, the Quakers for silence.

The Quakers, with their unexciting view of Christian life, have tended to be stolid, solid, practical and plain. They have produced educators and scientists, but few novelists and musicians. Some of the best schools have been run by Quakers, and, unlike the fundamentalists, they have never seen a conflict between science and religion.

The Mormons and Quakers have a similar history as persecuted minorities. But, for some reason, this affected the two groups very differently. The Mormons emerged extroverted and energetic, the Quakers deeply serious and introverted. Until relatively recently, Quakers frowned on singing and dancing. Jess Birdwell, the redheaded Irish Quaker in *The Friendly Persuasion,* outraged his meeting by buying an organ for his home, while Dick Nixon as a student barely managed to negotiate off-campus dancing for the first time at Whittier College.

For those who know the work of the American Friends Service Committee for pacifist and humanitarian causes or the Friends Committee on National Legislation for liberal welfare measures, the applied Quakerism of Richard Nixon may appear to be the antithesis of

---

* Nixon has not joined a Friends congregation in New York, but his family occasionally attends the Marble Collegiate Church, whose pastor is Rev. Norman Vincent Peale.

all that these church organs represent. Nixon recognizes this irony. But he quietly states, "The three passions of Quakers are peace, civil rights, and tolerance. That's why, as a Quaker, I can't be an extremist, a racist, or an uncompromising hawk. While all this may seem to be the opposite of what I've stood for, I'm actually consistent."

An American President who was the product of Quaker forebears, Abraham Lincoln, wrote of the Quakers during the Civil War: ". . . opposed to both *war* and oppression, they can only practically oppose oppression by war. In this hard dilemma some have chosen one horn and some the other." Despite their belief in pacifism, during World War II a majority of draft-age Quakers, including Nixon, entered the armed forces. And, while Quakers have been in the forefront of the opposition to the Vietnam War, Nixon argues that their position in the long run would lead to greater war. That he has support within his church is evident from this view of the Quaker philosopher D. Elton Trueblood:

> Though a small minority of contemporary Quakers claim that they favor, for their own nation, unilateral disarmament *now,* they are by no means representative. Actually, most Quakers, including those who register as conscientious objectors and perform what is called "alternative" service, will say, if pressed, that they would not eliminate the armed forces of their nation, *at this moment,* even if they could. This is not because of any lack of devotion to peace. Indeed they can see, without much difficulty, that the immediate total elimination of our armed forces would, in all probability, *create* war, the very thing which they are seeking to avoid. It is obvious, for example, that the existence of the United States Fleet, in the Taiwan Straits, *prevents* an invasion of either the Communists or the Nationalists. It would be an extremely confused lover of peace who wished for the elimination of this means of prevention of something that would involve untold murder and violence.*

Nixon started life poor, yet the pursuit of riches has not been a major goal for him—any more than it has been for Romney, Percy or Ronald Reagan. Indeed, starting life rich was a more profound experience for Nelson Rockefeller than the reverse has been for the four prospective 1968 candidates. The reason may be that their poverty was not lower class; they were all, in fact, from the shabby *bourgeoisie*—Romney, the son of a general contractor; Reagan, the shoe-store manager's son; Percy, the son of a bank cashier; and Nixon,

* D. Elton Trueblood, *The People Called Quakers* (New York: Harper & Row, 1966), p. 202.

the grocer's boy. (When Nixon told Nikita Khrushchev that he had worked in his father's grocery, the Soviet leader replied, "All shop-keepers are thieves.") Nixon's younger brother Edward, when asked how impoverished his family had been, replied, "As children, we never had an ice cream cone, but we didn't feel poor." Money for Richard Nixon seems to make little difference. In his personal habits he is almost spartan. He is neither dandy nor gourmet, and until re-cently never even carried a wallet.

By almost any standard today Nixon would be considered a success-ful man. In 1963 he joined the New York law firm of Mudge, Stern, Baldwin & Todd. It soon became Nixon, Mudge, Rose, Guthrie, Alexander & Mitchell. Obviously the former presidential candidate's name on the door attracted clients. When Nixon arrived the firm had sixty lawyers; it now needs over one hundred and has moved into the nation's top ten firms in size. Its offices are spread over four floors of a Wall Street skyscraper. The clients include Pepsi-Cola, Warner-Lambert Pharmaceutical, General Precision Equipment, Gen-eral Cigar, Cargill (a firm that has sold large quantities of wheat to the Soviet Union, a transaction that Nixon is politically against), American Bulk Carriers (for whom the Nixon firm has registered in Washington as a paid lobbyist), Newfoundland Pulp and Chemical, and Mitsui, the Japanese trading combine. The partners who have given their names to the Nixon firm each earn a yearly income in the $150,000 to $250,000 range. The senior partner now pays an income tax that is twice what his salary was as Vice President of the United States.

Attorney Nixon sits on the boards of directors of important compa-nies, such as the Harsco Corporation; Mutual of New York, one of the largest in the life and health insurance field; and Minneapolis-based Investors Diversified Services, the giant mutual fund with net assets of over $5.3 billion. He belongs to impressive in-town clubs—the Metropolitan, the exclusive Links, Recess, a Wall Street luncheon club with a panoramic view of lower Manhattan; and fashionable country clubs—Blind Brook in Westchester, Baltusrol in New Jersey. When he traveled abroad the press reported that the Duke and Duch-ess of Windsor entertained in his honor and that his wife was seen at the showing of Pierre Cardin's latest collection. His daughters attend Eastern women's colleges and have had well-publicized debuts.

When he leaves his twenty-fourth-floor corner office, filled with

autographed pictures of heads of states, keys to cities, and other re-
membrances of its occupant's importance, his chauffeur drives him
home to a ten-room cooperative apartment on Fifth Avenue, where
the windows in the high-ceilinged living room face the park and the
fireplaces are wood-burning. The venerable building comes one apartment to the floor and the tenants include Nelson Rockefeller and
William Randolph Hearst, Jr. It costs Nixon about $100,000, plus
a yearly maintenance fee of $9,600 to live there.

It could be a nice life. Another small-town boy, Thomas E. Dewey,
made the transition from presidential politician to Wall Street lawyer
with ease and has aged elegantly. The little black mustache that
once made him look like the groom on a wedding cake now is a
distinguished, corporate gray.

Possibly at first there were signs that Nixon too would enjoy private life. When he left government at the age of forty-eight his net
worth was about $50,000, mostly in the equity of his Washington
home and his Federal employee's pension plan. He joined a big
Los Angeles law firm and signed a lucrative contract to write his
memoirs. An old Washington friend who dropped by his office that
first year found Nixon going over his income-tax returns. Looking up,
the former Vice President said, "Do you know how much I gave in
charity last year? $11,000!" He was not bragging; he was merely
delighted—and amazed—that a man who had never earned more
than $35,000 a year could suddenly give away nearly a third of that
amount. He took great pride in his new air-conditioned Oldsmobile
convertible and his new home in Trusdale Estates, a fancy Beverly
Hills subdivision. As he stood by his swimming pool, wrapped in
smog, he never tired of telling Eastern visitors, "On a clear day you
can see Catalina."

But he was never really tempted. After ten months Nixon had
made more money than his combined salary during fourteen years
in Washington. So he called a press conference to announce that he
was a candidate for Governor of California. His first reason for
running, he said, was a selfish one:

. . . I often hear it said that it is a sacrifice for men or women to serve
in public life. For me, I have found it to be the other way around. On
my return to private life, I found that, from a salary standpoint, the
income has been beyond anything I could ever have dreamed. And I
have found, of course, other things in private life that are very attractive.

But after 14 years as a Congressman, as a Senator, and as Vice President of the United States, I find that my heart is not there—it is in public service. I want to be in public service.

He was almost pleading with the people of his home state to relieve him of the monotony of riches. When they declined, he moved to New York and returned to the practice of law, not with exhilaration but with resignation.

Today, Richard Nixon, the immensely successful Wall Street lawyer, never goes to the stylish country clubs to which he pays dues, never takes in the theater or opera that New York offers, never even attends the sports event that he enjoys. For major chunks of each year he circles the globe, poking his head into trouble spots on personal fact-finding junkets, looking into situations that intrigue him, while restoring his credentials as a foreign-policy expert. For other parts of each year he circles the United States, ordering hamburgers alone in hotel rooms, talking in private to Republican functionaries and *en masse* to the party's rank-and-file, while restoring his credentials as a political leader. Perhaps this strange behavior is only because he is part of a unique breed, a race apart. As the great Kansas editor, William Allen White, said of President McKinley, "He had lived so long alone in politics that he sloughed off his attitudes as an individual and gradually became a public man." Or perhaps the puritanical Quaker Richard Nixon agrees with Calvinist James Reston of the New York *Times* that "Politics is like booze and women: dangerous but incomparably exciting."

Nixon ran for Governor of California in 1962 because he needed a hiding place. There were other reasons as well. His money men convinced him that they could raise funds to underwrite the considerable expense of his political staff only if he was a candidate for office. He was restless in private life. But basically he needed an excuse not to be the Republican presidential nominee in 1964.

Kennedy would be impossible to defeat, he believed. Nixon, who no longer held the exalted position of Vice President, certainly could not expect to do better in a rematch with an incumbent President. Yet he would surely be the candidate, if only because so many Republicans were anxious to make him the sacrificial lamb, unless he had a reason to decline the dubious honor. Moreover, it would have to be a pretty good one or else he would forfeit the right to be

taken seriously as a candidate for the nomination in 1968 when
Kennedy would be ineligible to run again.

So he ran for Governor of California. And he lost. He lost for a
lot of reasons: because his opponent was an honorable man, who
had avoided scandals, and at whom it was hard to get mad; because
nobody quite believed that the man who had lost the White House
by a fraction really wanted to be a state Governor (just as it is
dangerous for a politician to reach too high, so too is it to reach
too low); because, in a state that gains a person a minute, half the
electorate are new voters each decade, and the former Vice President
had been away a decade and a half; because the Cuban missile crisis
took the spotlight off the campaign and he needed the voters' undivided attention to make his case. He even lost because a home
team was in the World Series and it went seven games and Californians were thinking about baseball instead of politics well into the
middle of October.

But, reasonable as the defeat seemed in retrospect, the manner of
his losing was far more damaging to Nixon than his 1960 defeat.
Losing by an eyelash to a John Kennedy was one thing; losing to a
Pat Brown by 296,000 votes, when the polls showed Nixon well
ahead at the time he announced, was something else. The California defeat apparently still rankles with Nixon himself. At least he
goes out of his way to avoid referring to it either in public speeches
or in private conversation; by contrast, he now speaks easily and
without apparent pain of the 1960 presidential race.

More than anything else, California stamped Nixon with his
greatest political liability; the tag of being "a born loser." Moreover,
it showed in a particularly tawdry light some of the political devices
associated with his name. Nixon had been identified as a hard-line
anti-Communist ever since the Hiss case, and had made effective
use of the Communist issue in every one of his campaigns for Congress, the Senate, the vice presidency and the presidency. But, when
he came back to California and campaigned against a Communist
menace in the state that had escaped most of the residents' notice, he
was trying to sell a scarcely credible issue.*

* The lengths to which Nixon went to haul in the Communist issue are indicated by this exchange from his telethon in Oakland, California, in October,
1962. *Question:* "Do you think the 30,000 votes received by the Communist
Archie Brown for Supervisor will all go to Governor Brown or do you expect
to get any of them?" *Nixon:* "I should say Governor Brown should speak for

On election eve, facing defeat, Nixon staged a televised repeat of his famous "Checkers" broadcast, once again assembling his family on the set and claiming "in persecuted tones," as *Time* said, "that he had been the victim of the worst smear campaign in California history."

The morning after the election, the morning of November 6, 1962, came the famous "last press conference," unquestionably the low point of Nixon's public career. Nixon now dismisses the whole episode: "There had been some reporting errors, some deliberately prejudicial," he says. "I took a lot of it in fourteen years. I owed it to myself to say what I felt about it. Now I can take it another fourteen years." But he was anything but calm at the time. His staff had fought to keep him in his room, but Nixon strode onstage at the Beverly Hilton Hotel. "Now that all the members of the press are so delighted that I have lost," he began, "I'd like to make a statement of my own." The statement lasted seventeen minutes and in it Nixon managed to insult not only his audience of reporters but his victorious opponent and even his own volunteer campaign workers. "As I leave you," he said, "I want you to know—just think how much you're going to be missing. You won't have Nixon to kick around any more, because, gentlemen, this is my last press conference. . . ."*

After the California defeat, Nixon moved to New York, not to keep his presidential hopes alive, as one columnist mysteriously hinted in 1963, but because he had been totally demolished in politics. He was turning to a new career, corporate law, and in this field, said Nixon, who is partial to sports metaphors, New York "is the fastest track in the world."

On the morning of November 22, 1963, he flew out of Dallas, just hours before President Kennedy was to arrive on his political

---

himself. The coincidence in names is not his fault, let's make that very clear. Throughout my political life, I have never had the support—in fact, have always had the most violent opposition from the Communists and their functionaries. I'm proud to have had it; I've earned it."

* The problem was that only two papers in the entire state, the Los Angeles *Times* and the San Diego *Union,* had reporters assigned full time to Nixon and Brown during the campaign. The parochialism of California publishers in this regard is a continuing problem; in 1966, as in 1962, the candidates for Governor of California were normally accompanied by a much larger contingent of Washington reporters than reporters from their own state's newspapers.

fence-mending tour of Texas. Nixon learned that Kennedy had been shot when a passerby ran up to his cab while it was stopped at a traffic light in Queens, en route in from La Guardia Airport. The doorman of his apartment house told him when he arrived that the President was dead.

"I called J. Edgar Hoover," Nixon recalled in his interview with Jules Witcover, "and asked him, 'What happened? Was it one of the nuts?' Hoover said, 'No, it was a Communist.'

"I didn't think of it in personal terms," Nixon said, " 'there but for the grace of God go I'—I never thought that. It was mostly in terms of he was so young, so full of life. . . . We had been friends, as Senators are friends. I was as friendly with him as he was with any Senator on the Republican side. To some people he was President, to some a friend, to some a young man. To me he was all that, and on top of that, a man of history struck down in the tragic panorama of history."

Nixon has come to believe, and probably correctly, that his link with Kennedy from the 1960 campaign is an asset to him. In 1961, a Mrs. Gladys Steimat of Hingham, Massachusetts, wrote the *Christian Science Monitor* that during a televised presidential press conference her four-year-old daughter Ann asked, "Mommy, that's Kennedy, isn't it?" "President Kennedy, dear," the mother replied. "Where is his friend, Nixon?" asked the little girl.

Friend Nixon now believes his close race with Kennedy is no disgrace, particularly when set beside the pummeling that Barry Goldwater took four years later. "After the [1960] election," Nixon says, "somebody wrote to me that nobody had liked Jack Dempsey until he lost. It made quite an impression on me, even though losing isn't something I'd recommend." Furthermore, Nixon says of the 1960 contest, "That was the classic campaign of our era. It is part of everyone's life." He was delighted to find in 1966 that an audience of Seattle high school students would laugh at his standard joke about being a "dropout from the Electoral College because I flunked debating." "Those kids were only eleven or twelve at the time," he remarked while flying back to New York, "but they knew immediately what I was referring to."

Kennedy's death had another and more immediate effect than making the 1960 campaign a part of history. It also revived Nixon's interest in and prospects for the 1964 Republican presidential nomination. Like most other Republican professionals, Nixon's immediate conclusion was that the accession of the Southern-born Lyndon B. Johnson weakened Goldwater as a prospective Republican nominee and undercut the logic of Goldwater's "Southern strategy." His guess was confirmed by visits and conversations with other Republican pros. On December 5, 1963, less than two weeks after the assassination, the Washington *Star* reported "the first signs of an organized effort to gain the 1964 Republican presidential nomination" for Nixon. It quoted Leonard Hall as saying he had met during the previous week with both Nixon and former President Eisenhower "to discuss changes in the political situation." It said "persons who have talked to the former Vice President in the past 10 days say he has been receiving a stream of phone calls, letters and visitors urging him to enter the Republican race." The *Star* also quoted an unidentified "leading New England Republican" as saying that a slate of delegates favorable to Nixon would be entered in the March 10 New Hampshire primary.

What developed, in fact, in New Hampshire, was a write-in campaign, organized without Nixon's official approval by ex-Governor Wesley Powell. The results were a bit disappointing, Nixon finished fourth with 15,587 votes, trailing not only Goldwater and Rockefeller, who were on the ballot and campaigned, but Henry Cabot Lodge, far off in the Saigon embassy, who won with 33,007 write-in votes.

The Nebraska primary, on May 12, was considerably better for Nixon. Former Secretary of Interior Fred Seaton, a Nebraska newspaper publisher and long-time friend of Nixon's, arranged a last-minute write-in campaign which netted Nixon 42,811 votes compared to 67,369 for winner Goldwater, the only man on the ballot.

The final test came three days later, on May 15, in Oregon, where Nixon's name had been entered automatically, along with all other potential nominees, by the Secretary of State. Rockefeller was the only candidate to make a full-scale campaign, and he won with 93,032 votes. Nixon finished a disappointing fourth, with 47,721 votes, trailing Rockefeller, Lodge and Goldwater, just as he had in New Hampshire.

Throughout these maneuvers, Nixon was at pains to remain on good terms with Goldwater and the Goldwater backers, even though the Senator had picked up Nixon's trail early and publicly labeled him as "my last big hurdle before the nomination." His most open bid to the Goldwater forces came in a Lincoln Day speech in Cincinnati in which Nixon dropped his long-time advocacy of civil rights and assailed "the irresponsible tactics of some of the extreme civil rights leaders."

While calling the civil-rights bill, then moving slowly through Congress, potentially "a great step forward," he warned that "a law is only as good as the will of people to keep it. The hate engendered by demonstrations and boycotts . . . will make the new law a law in name only." Just in case any of Goldwater's Southern backers failed to get the message, Nixon spelled it out in plain terms:

> In this election year Republicans will be urged by some to outpromise the Johnson Administration on civil rights in the hope of political gain. I am completely opposed to this kind of political demagoguery. . . . We reject the idea that the way to reduce high Negro unemployment is to increase white unemployment. . . . We oppose segregation in our schools either by law or in fact. But this problem must be dealt with in an orderly transition. We believe it is detrimental to both Negro and white children to uproot them from their communities and to haul them from one school to another in order to force integration in an artificial and unworkable manner.

Nixon's courtship of Goldwater and the Goldwaterites was premised on the hope that Goldwater and Rockefeller would knock each other out in the primaries and that Goldwater's delegates—clearly destined to be the largest bloc in the convention—then could be wooed into Nixon's camp. For the strategy to work, Rockefeller would have to defeat Goldwater in the last big primary, California. The polls immediately after his Oregon victory showed Rockefeller ahead, so Nixon wired assurances to Goldwater that "I am not supporting or opposing either of the two candidates running the California primary," then phoned to repeat the same message.*

It did not, of course, work out as Nixon had planned. Goldwater won California by 50,000 votes out of more than 2 million—and suddenly was on the verge of a first-ballot victory.

Just as suddenly, Nixon switched sides and became the self-appointed leader of the stop-Goldwater forces. A week after California voted, on June 9, he flew into Cleveland for the National Governors' Conference, arriving to find the remnants of anti-Goldwater opposition in shambles after the fiasco of Governor William Scranton's in-and-out

---

* For a full account of Nixon's 1964 manuverings, see Rowland Evans and Robert Novak, "The Unmaking of a President," *Esquire,* November, 1964.

weekend dabbling with the possibility of entering the race. Nixon breakfasted with the sixteen Republican Governors and then astounded everyone by attacking Goldwater in a press conference. Citing the Senator's views on the United Nations and Soviet-American relations, his suggestion that social security be made voluntary, that the Tennessee Valley Authority be sold to private interests, that civil rights enforcement be left to the states and that a national right-to-work law be enacted, Nixon said, "It would be a tragedy for the Republican party in the event that Senator Goldwater's views, as previously stated, were not challenged and repudiated."

Nixon disclaimed any desire to run against Goldwater himself, but immediately plunged into a series of conferences designed to put pressure on Romney to undertake what was obviously a hopeless task. For a time that Monday he seemed to be making headway with the Governor, but late in the afternoon Romney's Michigan advisers reached the scene and hauled him back to his previous declaration that he would honor his pledge to the voters of Michigan to seek a second term.

Goldwater, observing the spectacle from Washington, was not amused. He told reporters that Nixon was "sounding more and more like Harold Stassen every day"—the worst epithet that can be hurled at a live Republican hopeful.

Nor did Nixon make any friends for himself among the anti-Goldwater Governors by his belated effort to identify himself with their cause. Scranton told reporters later that, in the course of urging Romney to run, Nixon even made the argument that "we owe it to the television audience to provide some kind of contest at the convention; otherwise, they'll be bored and turn it off." The Governor called it "the most cynical argument I've ever heard a serious political figure offer." Although Goldwater rather quickly forgave Nixon for his performance in Cleveland, most of the Republilcan Governors who saw him and heard him there have not yet changed their initial view that Nixon was simply trying to set up Romney as a stalking horse in a last, desperate effort to produce a convention deadlock from which he, Nixon, could emerge as the nominee. The Governors' antipathy to Nixon, as a group, is a major factor in his bid for the 1968 nomination.

Cleveland about finished Nixon's efforts to obtain the 1964 nomination for himself.

When Scranton finally and belatedly entered the race, Nixon took a position of studied neutrality. At a June 15 press conference, he praised the challenger for "making a fighting campaign," but consoled the almost-certain champion with the thought that "now, Goldwater will have a mandate, if he wins, and he will be the stronger man for it [than] if he won by default."

Privately, in the last two weeks of June, 1964, Nixon began to readjust his sights from the 1964 nomination to 1968. Meeting with two close associates at Montauk on the tip of Long Island, he set a strategy based on two interlocking (and valid) assumptions: Goldwater could not be denied the 1964 nomination nor could he be elected President. In those talks at Montauk, Nixon evolved a new role for himself: the apostle of party unity who would campaign doggedly for the ticket in 1964 and for all Republican candidates in 1966 as a way of rebuilding his political capital for 1968.

Three steps were taken immediately after the Montauk talks to put the plan into operation. First, Nixon, who had said flatly in March that he would accept the nomination for Vice President if it was offered, now declared in equally categorical terms that he would not under any circumstances run for his old job again. The disclaimer was not addressed merely to a theoretical possibility. When Scranton, who had been Goldwater's first choice as a running mate, became the anti-Goldwater candidate, Nixon was sounded out by a key Goldwater fund-raiser as to his availability for Vice President. With Goldwater doomed to defeat, in Nixon's opinion, it was essential from Nixon's own viewpoint that he not be brought under public pressure to join the losing ticket.

Second, Nixon issued instructions to his backers to discourage any delegates who might want to vote for him for the presidential nomination from doing so. Third, Nixon himself arranged to switch his convention speech from the time he had carefully procured on the night before the balloting, with the hopes of building a boom for himself, to the night after the balloting, just before the nominee made his acceptance address.

The speech Nixon made to the 1964 convention was one of the finest of his career, a masterful effort to blur the differences that divided the party, and to provide a bridge on which Goldwater and his critics could, at least temporarily, meet. "Before this convention," he said, "we were Goldwater Republicans, Rockefeller Republicans, Scranton Republicans, Lodge Republicans, but now that this convention has met and made its decision, we are Republicans, period,

working for Barry Goldwater for President of the United States."
Though Nixon's speech was adapted to the needs of the moment, it
was not inconsistent with his general approach to party affairs. Never
an ideologist, he is a firm believer in the "big-tent" theory of political
parties. He thinks a party is healthiest when it can attract a balance
of conservatives, moderates and liberals. Nixon has campaigned for
all three, so his chore at the 1964 convention was not foreign or distasteful to him.

That Goldwater declined to pick up Nixon's carefully orchestrated
cue is well known. Instead, the Senator invited his critics to stay out.
"Anyone who joins us in all sincerity we welcome," he said in his
acceptance speech. "Those who do not care for our cause we do not
expect to enter our ranks in any case."

But it would take more than a policy of intransigence on the part
of the nominee to turn Nixon from his new role as the Loyal Helper.
When Goldwater was criticized by General Eisenhower and a host
of others for his "extremism in defense of liberty" line, it was Nixon
who wrote him the necessary letter of inquiry which permitted Goldwater to explain, without embarrassment, what he had really meant
to convey by those fatal words. When the Goldwater managers finally
awoke in August to the need for some gesture of party unity, it was
Nixon again who was called on to give the summation at the Hershey,
Pennsylvania, "unity conference" of Republican leaders.

Most of all it was Nixon who took to the road campaigning for
Goldwater when many other Republican leaders were staying in their
home states, saying as little as possible about the national ticket. In
an almost perfect blending of self-sacrifice and self-interest, he plowed
through thirty-six states in six weeks, working harder for Goldwater—
because of his remarkable stamina—than Goldwater was able to do
for himself. At no time was Nixon under any illusions about the outcome, but he wanted the record to be clear on who helped and who
did not. Just in case the point had been missed, two days after the
election Nixon held a press conference in New York, looking, at
least to columnist Murray Kempton, "honestly ruddy with the satisfaction of having well and truly tried in a cause so conveniently lost that
there were very few other survivors." His purpose, as Kempton said,
was "to bind up the wounds of the Republican party with a tourniquet
around the neck of Nelson Rockefeller." Nixon called the Governor
a "party divider" and a "spoilsport," arguing that despite his pledge of

support to Goldwater "he proceeded to drag his feet [and] . . . contributed to the Republican defeat."*

In the same press conference, Nixon called for a moratorium on criticism of Goldwater and his chosen national chairman, Dean Burch. Throughout the next month, he cautioned and worked against the Republican Governors' efforts to dump Burch, until it became clear that the scales had tipped against the embattled party chairman. At that point, Nixon was instrumental in arranging the transfer of power from Burch to Ray Bliss on face-saving terms for Goldwater.†

Thus, when the Republican National Committee met in Chicago in January, 1965, it was Nixon, once again, who presided as master of ceremonies and apostle of party unity at the luncheon preceding the election of Bliss. The man he had called, six months earlier, another Harold Stassen was now saluted by Goldwater in ringing terms:

> I want to express my heartfelt thanks and gratitude to Dick Nixon [Goldwater said] who worked harder than any one person for the ticket this year. Dick, I will never forget it! I know that you did it in the interests of the Republican party and not for any selfish reasons. But if there ever comes a time I can turn those into selfish reasons, I am going to do all I can to see that it comes about.

In the 1966 campaign, following the policy established at the Montauk meeting, Nixon once again was the busiest of his party's national campaigners. During the Labor Day–Election Day period alone, he campaigned in thirty-five states for eighty-six Republican nominees for Governor, Senator and Representative. The work was congenial and the results even more rewarding than those in 1964.

In a sense, Nixon's adaptive skills and light burden of ideology are better suited to a variety of congressional campaigns, with their focus on local issues and local concerns, than to a presidential contest, where what is said in one state is amplified to all the others. At the Hershey conference in 1964, Nixon had said: "I want all Republicans to win; I am just as strong for a liberal Republican in New York as I am for a conservative Republican in Texas, and I can go and just

---

* Nixon, in the November 6, 1964, press conference made a point of exempting from criticism Republicans like Romney, Senator Kenneth B. Keating of New York and Representative John V. Lindsay of Manhattan, who also refused to endorse or campaign for the national ticket. "As candidates, they had the right and responsibility to run their own campaigns as they thought best," he said, implying that Rockefeller, who was not on the ballot himself in 1964, had a different duty to perform.

† For details of the Burch-Bliss struggle, see Chapter 2, pp. 39-42.

as enthusiastically campaign for both, because we need both liberals and conservatives to have a majority." Thus Nixon was able to face with equanimity and handle with style an assignment that might make other politicians boggle—such as campaigning within a three-hour period one day, with equal conviction, for staunch conservative congressional candidate (now Congressman) Donald E. Lukens in Ohio and liberal congressional candidate (now Congressman) Fred Schwengel in Iowa.

Though there were some Republican candidates on both edges of the ideological spectrum—conservative Ronald Reagan in California and liberal Edward Brooke in Massachusetts, for example—who sent polite but firm word to Nixon to stay out of their campaigns, most Republicans welcomed him with open arms. And no wonder.

First of all, he meant money to them. Since 1964, Nixon estimates, his name has been on programs that have attracted between $5 and $6 million to the G.O.P. Nixon as the featured speaker, thinks a Michigan congressional district chairman, means an extra sale of 150 to 200 tickets at his annual $100-a-plate dinner. Washington State Republicans chartered a jet airliner to take Nixon from Seattle to Spokane and enriched the party's war chest by selling passage on it to nearly 100 persons at $150 apiece. Five thousand people paid $10 each for the honor of having breakfast with the former Vice President at the Elks Country Club in Lake Manawa, Iowa.

Nixon also had a touch with the "fat cats." When congressional Republicans organized the Boosters Club to raise money in chunks of $1,000 or more for 1966 candidates, they automatically made Nixon its chairman—and he was helpful in bringing them an amazing $1.3 million. He even set up a little "Boosters Club" program of his own on the side, tapping Miss Helen Clay Frick, the elderly steel heiress from Pittsburgh, for some two dozen contributions of $1,000 each, which Nixon dispatched for her to worthy congressional candidates around the country.

His second contribution was publicity. "A candidate lives on publicity," says Nixon, "and a visit by a national figure gets him massive publicity." A 1966 Nixon stop in Casper, Wyoming, for example, generated eight stories in the local newspapers:

NIXON TO VISIT CASPER (September 14)
HUGE RALLY FOR NIXON PLANNED (September 16)
PLANS SETTLED FOR ARRIVAL OF NIXON (September 20)
PLANS READY FOR HUGE NIXON RALLY (September 21)

NIXON TO SPEAK IN CASPER TONIGHT (September 22)
NIXON GETS BIG RECEPTION (September 23)
NIXON SAYS LBJ "LOST CONFIDENCE" (September 23)
NIXON RAPS LBJ IN CASPER TALK (September 23)

Over a two-day period the *Times-Democrat* of Davenport-Bettendorf, Iowa, devoted 130 column inches and four photographs to Nixon's visit, while Nixon received over 101 column inches in Salt Lake City, pretty hefty coverage for a stop of three hours.

The third contribution was the intangible of enthusiasm for the candidate and his campaign organization. "Any national figure has a certain mystique," says Nixon. "He can stir up the enthusiasm of the workers, make them think that this particular election has a national importance beyond the local." Nixon does not flatter himself with the belief that he can actually elect local candidates. But, as Warren Weaver, Jr., noted in the New York *Times,* "hard statistics [for 1966] show that a G.O.P. House candidate for whom Nixon did not campaign stood only a 45 percent chance of winning, while a man he embraced stood a 67 percent chance. It is hard to knock a coach who raises the team average that much."

Not only did Nixon contribute handsomely to the Republican victory of 1966, he also called it with uncanny accuracy. Throughout the fall, he predicted Republicans would win a minimum of 40 seats in the House, 3 in the Senate, 6 governorships and 700 seats in state legislatures. What they won were 47 seats in the House, 3 in the Senate, 8 governorships and 540 seats in the legislatures.*

For a man who had not won even a piece of an election in his own right since 1956, these vicarious victories were glad tidings, indeed. A friend who spent the 1966 election night with Nixon reports that he was "like a kid who had won his first race for the state legislature."

With the successful conclusion of the 1966 campaign, Nixon was ready to put stage three of the Montauk plan into effect: gearing up his own campaign for the 1968 presidential nomination. Or was he?

---

* Nixon's overestimate of Republican gains in the legislatures is more apparent than real. The independent news-research organization *Congressional Quarterly* calculated that Republicans made a gross gain of 728 legislative seats in 1966, but lost 188 seats, chiefly through reapportionment, which reduced the size of several legislatures. The net Democratic loss of seats was 726, almost exactly matching Nixon's estimate.

Ever since his loss in California in 1962, there have been those who have argued that Nixon is a politically displaced person. "He is now a candidate without any base of his own," wrote columnist Joseph Alsop, "and it is very hard indeed to figure out how any man can win the presidential nomination with this handicap." Nixon himself commented with tongue in cheek: "Someone suggested that I get a house trailer and move around from state to state establishing residence. Then I could pick the best one as my base for 1968. Why not? I've tried everything else."

Nonetheless, there is something musty about this talk of political bases in an age of television networks and national magazines, where voters see the same programs, read the same articles, follow the same fads, and are influenced or revolted by the same so-called style setters. Barry Goldwater of Arizona (sixteen convention votes) easily defeated Nelson Rockefeller of New York (ninety-six convention votes). And even the Governor of Rhode Island has a right to dream big.

If Nixon's name calls forth little enthusiasm in his native state of California and virtually none in his adopted state of New York, he still has, through long and arduous wooing, many political allies across the country. A Gallup survey of Republican county chairmen in the spring of 1967 not only showed Nixon far ahead of Romney and all other rivals in their preference for the 1968 nomination, but showed him leading in every section of the country. "Any power base that I have politically," Nixon has said, "resides on a national basis." Columnist William S. White has even turned the "base" argument inside out, accusing Governor Romney, Nixon's likeliest rival, of having "no visible national constituency, a human commodity in which Nixon is, relatively, quite rich."

Within that national base of support, there are three elements of vital importance to Nixon's prospects: the support of Goldwater and the conservatives; the support of the South; and the support of Republican Congressmen for whom he has campaigned. Each is worth examining in some detail for its strength, its solidity and the conditions it sets on Nixon's candidacy.

The Conservatives' Candidate. There is about American presidential nominating politics a musical-chairs quality, with the chairs representing political postures. When the music stops each player jumps (or is shoved) into a chair. If the chair he wishes to sit in is occupied, he must find another in order to stay in the game. The rules require that each chair must be filled even if the fits are sometimes awkward. In the 1968 Republican contest, Richard Nixon holds the conservative chair.

That he holds it was ordained by the fact that Barry Goldwater himself, Mr. Conservative, early made it plain that Nixon was his favorite among the likely 1968 nominees. This was hardly an accident; in fact, as we have seen, it was an endorsement Nixon labored mightily to achieve. Still, his position as the candidate of the right is not without a certain irony. When the game was played in 1960, the New York *Times* noted that "the right-wing tags him as a liberal." In mid-1964, when Nixon was urging Romney to become a candidate, the conservative *National Review* said that Nixon "in full plumage," was "migrating with a flock of influential (and liberal) GOP birds." Even George Gilder and Bruce Chapman, themselves now on the Romney staff, decided in their review of the 1964 struggle that Nixon "must in the last analysis be counted with Rockefeller in the party's progressive and moderate camp."

The conservatives are for Nixon chiefly because he did not desert the campaign in 1964. Goldwater followed up his praise of Nixon at the January, 1965, Republican National Committee meeting with repeated statements of support. But frequently there was an oddly conditional quality to the endorsement. In a typical interview, this one with the *New York Times Magazine* in June, 1966, Goldwater said: "Nixon as of now would be the party choice. This could change. Come '68, there could be another logical choice. But Jim Farley told me once that a party owes nothing to a member who won't work for the party. And I agree with that. . . . That's why I have to say Nixon as of today seems to be the man. He is far ahead of some candidates who deserted the ticket in 1964."

Goldwater's modest enthusiasm applies generally to the conservatives' blessing of Nixon. There is a noticeable absence of the do-or-die spirit that usually characterizes a candidate's hard-core supporters. Goldwater, in the same interview, made the point that "the party is busting for a new face" and "if Reagan wins the governorship of California, [as he subsequently did] hell, that's a brand-new ball game." Nixon himself has been under no illusions about the solidity of his conservative backing. "They don't like me," he says, "but they tolerate me." And Nixon is also well aware that he will face a desperate fight even to hold a portion of his conservative base if Reagan becomes a serious contender for the 1968 nomination.

Clearly, Nixon would prefer not to have any opposition from the right flank, because he does not want to mortgage himself any more heavily to the conservatives than he already has. Even Goldwater's endorsement is a mixed blessing, one Nixon can accept in good spirit only because he has been careful to put considerable distance between himself and the more controversial of the attitudes associated with the 1964 nominee.

It took Goldwater until mid-1966 to discover that the John Birch Society had evil designs on the Republican party (and Reagan had not yet acknowledged that fact in 1967), but Nixon drew a firm line against the Birchers from the time they first started harassing him in his 1962 campaign for Governor. He refused then and has refused since to campaign for, appear with or accept the support of any known Bircher, a stand that unquestionably cost him right-wing votes in his 1962 race.*

Nixon has never come close to echoing the statements Goldwater made on social security, nuclear weapons, TVA and other matters that kept him in so much hot water in 1964. In part it is a matter of rhetoric. Where Goldwater is given to the declarative absolute, Nixon is a devotee of the "balanced sentence." President Johnson was right to use nonlethal gas in Vietnam, says Nixon, "on the other hand . . ." He would have voted for the 1964 Civil Rights Act, "however . . ." Students should be allowed to hear unpopular views, "but . . ."†

But there is more to this than just a rhetorical device. In the words

---

* In 1966, during a California visit, Nixon defended Reagan's policy of accepting and endorsing Republican Birchers because, he said, "Reagan has made it clear they are buying his philosophy, he is not buying theirs." Two days later, however, in Alaska, Nixon reaffirmed his own stand by refusing to endorse Lee McKinley, Republican candidate for the Senate and an acknowledged Bircher. McKinley stalked out of the banquet hall after Nixon snubbed him; in the election, McKinley lost, while two non-Birch Republican candidates for Governor and Congressman that Nixon endorsed won.

† The classic user of the balanced sentence was Theodore Roosevelt. During the Spanish-American War, the Rough Rider announced the death of a "singularly gallant young Harvard fellow," then instantly added, "An equally gallant young fellow from Yale was also mortally wounded." Washington observer Mark Sullivan wrote, "It became a little boring in time to hear him tell of appointing a Catholic to office, and add that he would have appointed a Protestant under similar circumstances."

of a member of his 1960 staff, "Nixon is Mr. In-Between," a true centrist by instinct and conviction.

From his days in the House of Representatives when as a member of the Herter Committee he helped write the voluminous report that paved the way for the Marshall Plan, Nixon has been an unhesitating internationalist. On domestic issues he has been mildly conservative. He can decry the dangers of "big government" as heartily as Reagan, but as one who made his career in government he does not have the same deep-bred and instinctive fear of bureaucracy that the actor-Governor displays. Like Romney, there is in Nixon a small-town or Western accent on "the American way" and "the things that made America great" that seems stodgy to some and pleasantly nostalgic to others. In fact, for all the ideological freight Romney carries into the race with him, it is difficult to find sharp differences between him and Nixon on major domestic issues. Or between Nixon and Percy. The three—Nixon, Romney and Percy—are probably more closely agreed with each other on domestic policy than any of them is with Reagan, who is far more of a true Goldwater conservative than Goldwater's choice, Nixon.

There are differences in emphasis among Nixon, Percy and Romney. Nixon is less exercised about Federal-state relations than Romney, less involved with urban problems than Percy. One senses that Nixon really does not have his heart in domestic questions. His most carefully considered speeches are on foreign policy. When he talks about Medicare or drug addiction it seems almost an afterthought—because he is expected to say something. It is hard to shake the impression that, operating within the Republican framework, Nixon somehow feels he can "buy" the right to be an internationalist by taking conservative positions on domestic issues, much as Lyndon Johnson, as a Texas Senator and Majority Leader, "bought" the right to be a liberal on some economic and international issues by taking very good care of his conservative constituents on matters like oil depletion, tidelands and natural-gas regulation. If this is so, Nixon would consider that he has made a good bargain.*

The Southerners' Candidate. This view of Nixon is contradicted, in the opinion of some observers, by the demonstrable fact that his

---

* While this is not provable, the same view is held by Professor Totton J. Anderson of the University of Southern California. See Frank H. Jonas, editor, *Western Politics* (Salt Lake City: University of Utah, 1961), p. 92.

second major source of support is the South. Joseph Alsop has written, for example, that

> Nixon is 'my man' to Barry Goldwater, beyond any doubt at all, because he has indicated to Goldwater that, if nominated, he will adopt the 'southern strategy' that Goldwater invented and still favors. . . . The

"I See It, But I Don't Believe It"

Haynie, Louisville **Courier-Journal**, Feb. 18, 1967, © 1967, The Los Angeles Times Syndicate

Nixon candidacy, perhaps characteristically, is by no means what it seems. It is not a compromise candidacy, calculated to unite two wings of the party. . . . Nowadays, the man who has the southerners in the bag is, almost by definition, the man the extreme right wing of the party is determined to nominate.

Alsop's implication that Nixon has won his Southern support by pandering to racial prejudice is not supported by the record of what Nixon has actually said and done on his frequent visits to Dixie. Early in 1964, in the Cincinnati speech, as already noted, Nixon certainly did make his bid for what later came to be called "the backlash vote," but even then did not deviate from his clear support of the pending civil-rights bill. In 1965 and 1966, as he systematically touched down in the eleven states of the Confederacy, he was at pains to make clear that he was not there to give comfort to the segregationists. In May, 1966, for example, he went to Jackson, Mississippi, to address a $100-a-plate Republican dinner, a visit condemned in advance by some liberal Republicans, because the Mississippi G.O.P. had in its platform a statement endorsing segregation as "absolutely essential to harmonious racial relations."

Nixon was, of course, asked about this matter at a press conference in Jackson. He said, "I will go to any state in the country to campaign for a strong two-party system, whether or not I agree with the local Republicans on every issue." He added: "I am opposed to any so-called segregationist plank in a Republican platform. I would fight it in the national Republican platform and speak against it in any state I appear in. I do not share the views of the Mississippi Republican party or elsewhere where it takes a segregationist stand." Nixon said that as far as he could see "there is very little to choose" between the Democrats and Republicans in Mississippi on that issue. Finally, he reiterated his support of the 1964 and 1965 civil rights laws.

At the banquet that night, for the first time in the memory of Jackson reporters, there was an integrated audience at a function sponsored by either the regular Democratic or Republican party organization— six Negroes and about a thousand whites.

The theme of Nixon's speech was spelled out in his syndicated newspaper column that week:

> The Republican opportunity in the South is a golden one; but Republicans must not go prospecting for the fool's gold of racist votes. Any Republican victory that would come of courting racism, black or white, would be a defeat for our future in the South. It would be a battle won in a lost cause. Southern Republicans must not climb aboard the sinking ship of racial injustice. They should let the Southern Democrats sink with it, as they have sailed with it.

The speech was applauded by the Mississippi Republicans, and an aide traveling with Nixon commented, "He's the only man in the party they would take that from." They take it from Nixon, and they give back not scorn but applause and support, not because they agree with him on the race issue—clearly they do not—but because they believe he has been their friend and earned his right to differ with them on this issue.

As one Southern G.O.P. chairman remarks, "It's not so much what Nixon says down here that counts; it's what he doesn't say and doesn't do up North." Unlike Rockefeller, Romney and Percy, he has never particularly sought, received or bragged about support from either prominent Negro leaders or large numbers of Negro voters. Unlike Rockefeller and Romney, he did not refuse to support the Republican nominee strongly backed by Southern Republicans, and unlike Percy he never condemned Goldwater for the quality of his Southern support. But, most important of all, Nixon has not, like the others, contented himself with lecturing the Southern Republicans from a distance; he has been down among them in good times and bad.*

That the cultivation of the South is a matter of calculation and expediency on Nixon's part goes without saying. But his close acquaintance with the region has taught Nixon something other Northern Republicans do not know: Southern Republicans come in all varieties, from racist to progressive and all shades in between, but, to a man, they crave the respectability of approval and acceptance by the national party and its leaders. They do not want to be pariahs or outcasts; where condemnation drives them further into their parochial prejudices, recognition coaxes them to come out and to conform.

Thus, what is vital to the Mississippi Republicans—and by extension to Republicans in other Southern states—is not what Nixon says at their dinners, but the fact that he comes at all; and Nixon has been coming steadily since 1952. In any given speech, Nixon will give them enough to agree with—his hard-line anti-Communist foreign policy, his generally conservative domestic views—so that they can forgive him his difference with them on civil rights, where it exists. In fact, there are wides ranges of opinion among Southern Republicans even on the race issue. And if the diehard Republican segregationists like Wirt Yerger, Jr., of Mississippi support Nixon as the "least bad" on civil rights, the progressive Southern Republicans who are trying to orient their parties to a genuinely biracial constituency,

* The contrast in attitudes is illustrated by the difference between Nixon's talk in Mississippi and one Percy made to a very different audience at the same time. See p. 221.

like Robert J. Corber of Virginia, regard Nixon as the national leader who best understands and will most consistently support what they are trying to do.

The South is immensely important to Nixon. Where Goldwater's influence and the weight of conservatives generally in the party remains to be proven in 1968, the power of the South can be stated precisely: the 11 Confederate states plus Kentucky and Oklahoma have 356 delegates in 1968—more than any other region and well over half the 667 needed for nomination. Some, and perhaps many, of those Nixon delegates would be siphoned off if Reagan becomes a serious candidate; he, after all, opposes the 1964 and 1965 civil-rights laws as fully as Nixon supports them; he is flatly on record against state or Federal open-occupancy laws, while Nixon's position in 1967 was still unclear. But if there is no Reagan raid Nixon can look to an almost Solid South to put him halfway to nomination.

The Congressmen's Candidate. His entree to the rest of the votes he needs he will have to find in his third element of strength—the Congressmen for whom he has campaigned. How useful they will be when the showdown comes may be questioned. Nixon's travels in every one of the last eight campaign years have been premised on the hope that he is acquiring political due bills, as well as applause, along the way; that he is doing good for himself while doing well for his party.

As he travels the fried-chicken-and-creamed-peas circuit he is nominated or elected by nearly every politician who introduces him:

—Athens, Ohio. Former Congressman Homer E. Abele, "Two years from now he will be the favorite son of the whole United States!"

—Seattle, Washington. Congressman Thomas Pelly, "I ordinarily wouldn't say this but I think Dick Nixon's greatest service to his country has yet to come!"

—Tulsa, Oklahoma. Republican County Chairman Bert McElroy, "Tulsa has been, is, and will be again a Nixon city!"

—Wilmington, Delaware. Republican National Committeeman Harry G. Haskell, Jr., presenting Nixon with a gift, "We hope that someday this pen set will grace the desk in the White House!"

—Columbia, South Carolina. Republican National Committeeman J. Drake Edens, Jr., "The one man around whom we can rally our party and the most qualified of the people I know now to be President of the United States, Richard M. Nixon!"

Whether gratitude in a "what-have-you-done-me-lately" profession will translate into convention delegates remains to be seen. During Romney's first 1967 political swing, he received near endorsements from the Governors of Alaska and New Mexico, two upset winners for whom Nixon (but not Romney) had campaigned. Winners, once in office, tend to think of their own new interests first—not of those who may have helped them up the first rung of the ladder. This is one reason why Nixon has said privately that "campaigning for a loser may gain you more points than campaigning for a winner. . . . This is something Democrats understand, but very few Republicans do." Certainly Nixon's own experience with Goldwater bears out the point. And certainly, in Nixon's case, he probably has his strongest support among those who are furthest from top power themselves—the freshman Republican Congressmen for whom he labored in 1966. They may or may not be delegates to the convention, but they almost certainly will not be the leaders of the delegations. Thus, Nixon's real return on his investment will probably depend, as so much else does, on how the party's power brokers—the senior Governors, Senators, Congressmen and party chairmen—assess his chances of winning the prize.

The Nixon balance sheet of assets and liabilities going into the 1968 race is very different from what it was in 1960. In 1960, he was the heir-apparent, the understudy to a popular incumbent President. When he ran for Governor in 1962, he hoped to enter the 1968 presidential contest as chief executive of the largest state, an enviable position in the old game of power politics. Instead, that post is held by a potential rival, Reagan, and Nixon must write a new scenario for the drama he hopes to unfold.

But, if there are disadvantages in his position, there are certain compensations, also. A sort of informal "statute of limitations" operates in national politics, set by the short memories of voters for even the more spectacular incidents in candidates' earlier careers. Thus a set of names once firmly and emotionally tied to Richard Nixon—like Jerry Voorhis, Helen Gahagan Douglas and Murray Chotiner, respectively his first two prominent opponents and his former campaign manager—now have little meaning for the average voter. The 1960 campaign with Kennedy, as already noted, is being skillfully turned into an asset by "Friend Nixon."

Even the disastrous "last press conference," tapes of which are

available to the Democratic National Committee, has been rational-
ized by some Nixon supporters into an asset—on the perhaps questionable theory that the outburst shows him to be "human," removing
that aura of cold impersonality that had plagued him and had earlier
been so harmful to Thomas E. Dewey's national ambitions.

As we have seen, Nixon has positioned himself well for the 1968
race. He has won the support of Goldwater and the conservatives,
without identifying himself with positions on emotional issues which
alarm the moderates and liberals. He has won the support of the
South without the stigma of being a racist. And he has gained, in his
dogged campaigning for congressional candidates, not only an army
of potential allies of indeterminate size, but an expertise on the nu-
ances of regional politics and a host of local associations that none of
his three potential rivals can begin to match. No one else but Richard
Nixon, it seems safe to say, has already campaigned four times in
Sioux City, Iowa.

Moreover, Nixon enters the 1968 contest singularly free of obligations that would hold him to a rigid position on any domestic issues
that may arise in the campaign. Unlike Percy, he has not had to cast
a record vote on any subject that has come up recently in Congress,
nor is it possible to fix him with direct responsibility for anything as
specific as Romney's tax policy in Michigan or Reagan's handling of
the California colleges. He has generally adopted for speaking purposes the "constructive alternatives" that House Republicans have
offered on tax sharing, the war on poverty and other domestic issues.
But he is not strongly identified even with these. As far as domestic
issues are concerned, he can move with the political currents, as
political prudence dictates.

Finally, his position as a party loyalist (one who has never defected
from the national ticket) is of far greater importance in his battle with
Romney than most laymen realize. The trend toward ticket-splitting
has become so pronounced in recent years that the average citizen is
inclined to think that "independence" is almost automatically a political virtue. "I vote the man, not the party label," is almost the first
principle of the typical middle-class suburban voter. But politicans are
old-fashioned and most people who are actively enough involved in
their party to want to become delegates to its national convention
have a fierce loyalty to the party. Like the Rockefeller divorce and
remarriage in the last campaign, Romney's 1964 apostasy puts a gulf

between him and the party regulars, a breach that Nixon can exploit even if he never mentions it.

Yet, much as the politicians value loyalty, they put an even higher premium on the capacity to win. And it is the loser's label that Nixon must shake if he is to emerge with the nomination. At the 1966 Gridiron Club dinner in Washington a character was dragged onto the stage who looked very much like the former Republican Vice President. Viewing this stage Nixon, another actor commented, "Every time he throws his hat in the ring, it turns out to be a towel." One conservative leader has characterized Nixon as "the Floyd Patterson of the G.O.P." To counter this image, it will be necessary for Nixon to establish "winner credentials" in the only elections open to him, the presidential primaries.

At least four states (New Hampshire, Wisconsin, Nebraska and Oregon) promise to be Nixon-Romney battlegrounds in 1968. Nixon carried all these states against Kennedy in 1960, ranging from a modest 51.8 percent in Wisconsin to Nebraska's 62.1 percent, his most impressive state victory. If he swept them again in 1968 against the challenge of Romney, Reagan and Percy, there would be little question that the nomination would be his.

In preparation for the test, Nixon in March, 1967, gave his tacit consent to the formation of a National Nixon for President Committee. Until then, his entire full-time staff consisted of his devoted personal secretary, red-haired Rose Mary Woods; a researcher, twenty-nine-year-old Patrick J. Buchanan, on leave from the editorial page of the St. Louis *Globe-Democrat;* and a receptionist. In March, 1967, Nixon added another writer, Raymond K. Price, thirty-six, former chief editorial writer of the New York *Herald Tribune.* He also has been aided by two of the younger members of his law firm, Thomas Evans and John Sears. And during peak periods, such as the months before the 1964 election, Pat Nixon comes into her husband's office every evening to answer the phone, type, bring sandwiches to the other volunteers, and wash the coffee cups. Callers who refused to give their messages to "Miss Ryan" (Mrs. Nixon's maiden name) because they wished to talk to "someone close to Mr. Nixon" might have been shocked to discover they had just brushed off an amused Mrs. Nixon.

The Nixon for President Committee was launched under the sponsorship of four old-time Nixon friends: Nebraskan Fred Seaton,

Eisenhower's Secretary of Interior; Robert C. Hill of New Hampshire, Eisenhower's Ambassador to Mexico; former Connecticut Governor John Davis Lodge, Eisenhower's Ambassador to Spain; and, probably the key figure, New York investment banker Maurice H. Stans, Eisenhower's Budget Bureau director and big-game hunter who has actually shot a bongo in the Congo.

In addition to Stans, who served as finance chairman of Nixon's 1962 campaign for Governor, the Nixon "fat cats" include: Peter Flanigan, a manor-born New York investment banker and head of the 1960 Volunteers for Nixon-Lodge; 82-year-old Elmer H. Bobst, the "Vitamin King," who rose from a $3-a-week drugstore job to a position as board chairman of Warner Lambert Pharmaceutical Company; Albert M. Cole and the DeWitt Wallaces of *Reader's Digest;* and Seattle mortgage banker Walter Williams, chairman of Citizens for Eisenhower-Nixon in 1952.

Names from the past cling to the Nixon campaign. Like the candidate himself, almost everybody around him is a former something-or-other. How effective they remain politically may be judged from an appraisal of Walter Williams by a man close to young Governor Daniel Evans: "Here in Washington State, we listen respectfully to Mr. Williams as a party elder statesman as long as he doesn't try to grab any real power."*

Aware of the dangers of senescence in his political organization, Nixon has entrusted the actual operation of his campaign to a group of younger and able operatives. As full-time chairman of the Nixon for President committee, his backers hired—with Nixon's approval—Dr. Gaylord Parkinson of San Diego, who wound up a spectacularly successful three-year term as California Republican chairman at the end of 1966. "Parky," an ebullient, extroverted forty-eight-year-old, who found politics far more fascinating than his practice of obstetrics, was "discovered" by Nixon when the former Vice President returned to California in 1961. First with Nixon's backing and then on his own, Parkinson put the moribund Republican State Committee back in busi-

* Two of the best-known old Nixon hands are beyond his reach for the 1968 campaign. Leonard W. Hall, one of the managers of his 1960 race, signed up early to work for rival George Romney. (See pp. 131-33.) The other 1960 manager, Robert Finch, was elected Lieutenant Governor of California in 1966 and was restricted by Ronald Reagan's favorite son candidacy from participating openly in the Nixon campaign, even if he were so minded. (See pp. 280-81.)

ness and began stamping out the fires of factionalism with both feet. He launched the "Cal Plan," a system of providing heavy financial support and organization help to a specially-selected, small number of legislative candidates each year, with the goal of overturning the Democratic majority in the legislature by the election of 1970. (After 1966, the Republicans were only two seats down in the state senate, four seats down in the assembly.) In 1964 and again in 1966, Parkinson, using the sanction of grass-roots organization support for his own views, successfully imposed his "Eleventh Commandment," otherwise referred to as "Parkinson's Law," on aspiring G.O.P. candidates and their principal backers: "Thou shalt not speak evil of another Republican." He did not end all factional feuding, of course, but the primaries for state office in both years were conducted in a way that produced exceptional unity behind the nominees. Parkinson is credited, and rightfully, with a major contribution to the election of George Murphy to the Senate in 1964 and of Reagan and a host of other candidates in 1966.

The good doctor's brand of non-ideological, commonsense politics fit perfectly with the approach Ray Bliss was trying to inculcate at the national level, so Parkinson was a natural choice to succeed Bliss in 1965 as head of the Republican State Chairmen's Association. In that role, he has come to know well the current group of party leaders in all fifty states, and he is liked and respected by them.

For his executive director, Parkinson turned to his old political partner, Robert C. Walker, a San Diego public relations man, who, like his boss, is a skillful and eminently up-to-date organization man.

A third leading figure in the group is A. Linwood Holton, Jr., forty-three, a personable Roanoke, Virginia, attorney for whom Nixon campaigned in his unsuccessful 1965 bid to be Governor of the Old Dominion. (Holton is another example of Nixon's theory that losers are more grateful for campaign help than winners.) Holton is as bright and articulate an exponent of modern, nonracist politics as the Southern Republican party affords, ideal from Nixon's viewpoint as a representative of the region that provides his political base.

The Midwesterner in the group is Robert F. Ellsworth of Kansas, a forty-one-year-old former member of the U.S. House of Representatives. Ellsworth lost a bid for a Senate nomination in 1966 and, in that same year, struck up a chance acquaintance on an airplane with Nixon, which left him deeply impressed by a man he had never previously known or particularly respected. Nixon, in turn, was much taken with Ellsworth and invited him to be his traveling companion on his European tour in the spring of 1967. Ellsworth, an expert on international monetary policy, was a bona-fide member of the liberal Wednesday Club group in the House (along with John Lindsay) and gives Nixon an entree to the Republican liberals that is a useful offset to his backing from Goldwater and the conservatives.

Joining Parkinson and Walker in the Nixon-for-President headquarters that opened in a converted savings-and-loan bank on Pennsylvania Avenue, just a block from the White House, in May, 1967, were another California political operative, Robert Clark; Nixon's twenty-six-year-old law firm associate, John Sears, and Drew Mason, a staff aide to former Governor Henry Bellmon of Oklahoma.

Ready to join the organization and capable of supplying it with a high degree of professional polish are the members of what has been called Nixon's Baker Street Irregulars. They serve the former Vice President in much the same manner as the runners whom Sherlock Holmes magically materialized when there were specialized chores to be done. Nixon's BSI are mainly in their late thirties and early forties. Some have been with him for many years, such as Charles McWhorter, a West Virginian and past national chairman of the Young Republicans, who now works for the American Telephone and Telegraph Company while taking an active role in the management of the Newport Jazz Festival, and Ned Sullivan, a Yonkers, New York, real-estate and insurance broker who is a cousin of Mrs. Nixon. But most of them first came in close contact with their candidate while serving as advance men during the 1960 campaign.

Typical of Nixon's cadre is John C. Whitaker, forty, an ex-Baltimorean with a doctorate in geology, who now represents a large aerial surveying company in Washington. He decided he would like to work for Nixon after reading Earl Mazo's 1959 biography. Whitaker volunteered his services, became infatuated with both Nixon and politics, and for the past seven years has given a portion of his time to the ultimate goal of making Nixon President. In 1966 Whitaker handled the complicated scheduling operation for Nixon's cross-country campaign swing. Others who will periodically leave homes and jobs to further the cause of Richard Nixon are stockbroker Nick Ruwe of Detroit, Seattle attorney John Ehrlichmann, New Yorker

John Nidecker of Cities Service, Roy Goodearle, a Houston oilman, and Sherman Unger, a partner in the large Cincinnati law firm of Frost & Jacobs.

The Nixon campaign, then, will not lack for talent. Two things, however, are in question. The key people in the organization—Parkinson, Walker, Ellsworth, Holton and the rest—are relatively inexperienced in presidential nominating politics. How quickly they will learn the ropes remains to be seen. The other question is how much latitude Nixon will give them even if they prove their competence. The trouble with past Nixon operations has been Nixon's desire to be candidate, manager and kibitzer all at once. In 1960 it might be said that he was his own Jack Kennedy, Bob Kennedy and Ted Sorensen. "He wanted to be the one to decide where he was going to speak and what he was going to talk about. It was a great mistake," said Nelson Rockefeller. "What you need is men you've got confidence in and a clear sense of common objectives." But Nixon is a loner, who finds it necessary to make all major decisions and a great many minor ones. This means, since his time is limited, that some decisions do not get made and others are made with insufficient deliberation. Since those around him lack real power, Nixon campaigns are notorious for internal palace politics—what one Nixon aide has called "cells and cells within cells."

Another question about his candidacy is whether Nixon can make an effective campaign against President Johnson on the issue some Republicans think may dominate the 1968 election—Vietnam.

The question is ironic, for if there is any asset Nixon has labored to keep intact, by incessant foreign travel and by repeated writing and speaking on the subject, it is his reputation as the Republican with greatest experience in the vital area of foreign affairs. In the winter and spring of 1967, Nixon journeyed through Eastern and Western Europe, Asia, Latin America and Africa, making little news but accumulating a new store of impressions and anecdotes that help him display his "One-Upmanship" on any Republican foolish enough to challenge him in this arena. That his rivals—Romney, Reagan and Percy—are all essentially Innocents Abroad should make his task easy, but Nixon leaves nothing to chance. Almost any speech will include a statement like: "I remember talking recently to an Asian Prime Minister about our problems at home and he said: 'Mr. Nixon, what does it mean when we read of protests against your government's policies in Vietnam?' And I said: 'Mr. Prime Minister . . .' "

The message he wants to hammer home is the one stated for him in a Cincinnati *Enquirer* editorial of December 5, 1966:

IT'S A BIRD! IT'S A PLANE! IT'S SUPERNIXON!

Miller, Des Moines **Register and Tribune**, Mar. 7, 1967

. . . Mr. Nixon deals with complex international questions with a facility that no other possible aspirant for the 1968 nomination can hope to possess. He has resisted temptations to make capital out of awkward international problems, but he has not shrunk from dealing intelligently and forcefully with the problems that beset us around the world.

Still, the extent to which foreign policy expertise will be an asset to Nixon could depend on something entirely beyond his control—what Lyndon Johnson is able to do in Vietnam between now and the time of the Republican convention. For the long Nixon record on foreign policy contains a lengthy set of statements on Vietnam that could, in some Republicans' views, come back to haunt him.

George Romney, for one, even in the midst of his own almost frantic efforts to define a Vietnam position in the winter and spring of 1967, kept insisting to his advisers that he wanted "to keep my options open, not get locked in like Nixon has." "Nixon," said Romney, "is a hawk and the Republican party may not want to be the hawk party of 1968." The Governor was not alone in thinking that the G.O.P. might well, as a matter of both national policy and selfish politics, want to fly with the doves in the 1968 campaign. Percy from the beginning of his 1966 Senate race in Illinois kept at least one foot firmly planted in the "peace camp," and sometimes seemed ready to hop in all the way. Nixon himself in an interview late in 1966 pointed out that if the war is still dragging on by the 1968 election Republicans would be under great temptation to campaign as the peace party.

If past statements mean anything at all, then Nixon, no less than President Johnson, is "locked in," as Romney would say, to the belief that America's vital interests require the war to continue until Communist aggression has been defeated in South Vietnam and an independent, popular government is securely in power. That has been Nixon's position at least since 1954, when he proposed an airdrop of American troops to relieve the embattled French garrison at Dienbienphu, a suggestion that was never acted on. But to gauge the likely political consequences of Nixon's Vietnam stand in 1968 it is necessary to define precisely what he has said and what he has not.

In respect to the "doves," Nixon has never opposed a negotiated settlement of the struggle; in fact, he has publicly endorsed all the Administration efforts in this regard as well as Percy's All-Asian Peace Conference idea. Privately he has been skeptical that the Communists would negotiate until faced with the imminence of defeat. Publicly he has opposed bombing pauses or any similar steps that use the search for a negotiated settlement as an alternative to continued military pressure. Most of all, he has warned against a settlement that would give the Communists a victory by diplomacy that they have not been able to win on the battlefield. He said, for example, that the offer

at the Manila Conference of November, 1966, to withdraw all outside troops from South Vietnam within six months of the time that
subversion subsides might result in handing over the country to the
Viet Cong.

In respect to the "hawks," Nixon has generally been a step ahead of
the Administration in urging successive steps to bring American air
power and sea power to bear on strategic targets and supply lines in
North Vietnam. He has argued consistently that there is minimal
danger that such steps will risk war with China or Russia, declaring
that Russia lacks the vital interest and China the capacity to go to war
with the United States over Vietnam. On the other hand, he has never
gone as far as Goldwater, Reagan or some of the retired military brass
in advocating attacks on Hanoi or other population centers in North
Vietnam, a declaration of war on that country, or the use or even
threatened use of nuclear weapons.

In respect to the Johnson Administration, while Nixon has endorsed
the American commitment in Vietnam and the President's statements of America's purpose there, he has been steadily critical of
the actual conduct of the war. He has opposed the basic strategy of
limiting air attacks on the North while increasing the scale of ground
fighting in the South, warning that this would increase American
casualties and, over the long run, destroy the South Vietnamese
society we are striving to save.

Thus, in political terms, Nixon actually has followed a policy of
minimal risk and maximum opportunity for himself. He is most
clearly susceptible to challenge from a Republican who would argue
that the United States should not have gone into Vietnam and should
get out as fast as possible. If that view should reflect the prevailing
Republican sentiment in the country, or even in one or more of
the presidential primary states, Nixon might well be defeated by an
all-out Republican "dove." But there is nothing in the 1967 opinion
polls to indicate that is the sentiment; on the contrary, most Americans
—and a very large majority of Republicans—agree with Nixon that
the war is necessary but should be ended by increased military pressure as quickly as possible.

In a presidential campaign against the incumbent, Nixon could not,
on his own record, blame the President for getting us into Vietnam.
But he has complete freedom to criticize Johnson's handling of the war
or the terms on which he might make peace. Nixon is free to argue

that he, who has had no direct responsibility for the situation since 1960, could have done or would do a better job of winding it up satisfactorily.

Campaign organization and Vietnam are two questions overhanging the Nixon candidacy. A third, and even more serious one in the view of some Republican leaders, is his relationship to the press. "We might forgive him for his past mistakes," one key Governor told a reporter early in 1967, "but you guys never would."

How grave a problem is press relations to Nixon? The question brings us right back to the central enigma of the man: Is he more than just a clever manipulator? The fact that Nixon, after so many years and setbacks, still is seriously considered for the presidency is to some degree the result of his talent for keeping his name in the news. Better than any other contemporary politician, Nixon understands the mechanics of newspapering and uses his knowledge to generate copy. He knows the elements that must be present to make a story; he knows about overnight leads and weekenders; about the problems of time zones for traveling reporters; about the unique needs of the wire services.

One of the keys to Nixon's extensive press coverage has been his foreign travel. A statement that might not be considered newsworthy if made in New York takes on new luster just because Nixon is in Kuala Lumpur. The unsurprising announcement, NIXON WILL DO AS PARTY BIDS, was a New York *Times* headline on April 1, 1964. The dateline was Bangkok.

But Nixon can manufacture news not only by juggling datelines and servicing reporters on the prowl for new leads by saying the same thing in a different or colorful way. He creates news by thinking like a newsman. For example, during a trip to Moscow in 1965 he got himself into a verbal tilt with some obscure university teacher. Wrote Baltimore *Sun* reporter Stephen E. Nordlinger on page one: "The argument recalled the former Vice President's celebrated 'kitchen debate' with former Premier Nikita Khrushchev six years ago. . . ." A good and legitimate story, even if Nixon had produced it by artificial insemination.

Yet, skillful as Nixon is in generating news, the Republicans are not foolish to be worried about his relationship with the press. In 1960, as Theodore H. White wrote, "the brotherhood of the press was considered by Mr. Nixon and his press staff, not as a brotherhood, but as a conspiracy, and a hostile consipracy at that." And whoever else may have forgotten the "last press conference" in 1962, the reporters who cover Nixon have not. In trying to overcome the reputation for hostility and aloofness that plagued him in the campaigns for President and Governor, Nixon has, in one sense, compounded his problem. In making himself more accessible to reporters, he has also made himself more visible, and what is perceived is Nixon the Manipulator, the man of technique, not of substance. It is Nixon's habit, for example, on his cross-country campaigns for congressional candidates, to brief the reporters aboard his plane about the political background, personalities, special issues and special problems of the district or state he is about to enter. The briefings are extremely useful to the press; were he not a politician, Nixon would make a superb political reporter, for his insights are shrewd, his information encyclopedic and his gift for summary and exposition exceptional.

But like the baseball batter in the story told earlier, Nixon is not content to be admired. Rather than let the reporters discover for themselves how he adapts his basic speech to the situation, he goes on to say, "Now, this is a pretty conservative district, so you'll notice I don't bear down as heavily on . . ." or, "The Democratic incumbent here has been a very good Congressman, so I'm going to have to stay away from personalities and concentrate more on . . ."

If there was ever any doubt in reporters' minds that there is always a covert motive for anything Nixon says or does, such conversations end it. And in their own minds the reporters can hear the same Nixon who explained to them why he has altered his speech for this district explaining to his political aides why he has altered his technique for handling the press. In some ways, to be sure, Nixon has improved his standing with the press. He *is* more accessible now—for interviews, conversations or visits. He has picked up the old Kennedy technique of complimenting reporters on stories he admires. He does not smother them with flattery, but neither does he let them think he thinks he can get along without them very well.

More than anything Nixon has done, however, the passage of time and the alteration of circumstances have worked to improve his standing with the press. Just as the "statute of limitations" operates on the public's memory, so does it on reporters'. The incidents of his early career and of the McCarthy era, which had soured so many of the Washington reporters who covered the 1960 campaign, are no longer vivid, burning issues. Many of those reporters themselves have moved off the political beat into executive jobs or retirement, and the younger reporters covering Nixon now have literally no association with those earlier battles.

Moreover, a candidate is always judged by comparison with his rivals, and Nixon is fortunate in this regard. Reporters may not like or approve all of what they hear from Nixon in a background interview, but at least they confirm that he is aware of motives and forces that operate beneath the surface of politics, and that he is a three-dimensional man, not a cardboard figure or tape recording of himself. By contrast, they learn that interviewing Romney or Reagan, in most cases, is absolutely no different from hearing them make a public speech. Of the four Republican contenders, only Percy now has better relations with the press than Nixon, and he is largely untested.

But most of all Nixon is helped, so far as the press is concerned, by the fact that his prospective Democratic opponent in 1968 is not John F. Kennedy but Lyndon B. Johnson, whose contempt for reporters and whose techniques for frustrating their pursuit of the news make the old war between Nixon and the press seem as naïve and innocent as a battle of slingshots in an age of nuclear weapons.

In 1964 one political leader called another political leader ". . . a master politician who works hard at it—that's the secret of his success. He has preempted the field when it comes to wheeling, dealing, fixing and picking the political situations that will satisfy everybody. . . . He's not only tricky but he's good at it."

Richard M. Nixon was speaking of Lyndon B. Johnson. But it might easily have been the other way around. Indeed, there are many parallels between the Democratic President and the Republican leader—small-town birth, impoverished childhood, high intelligence, suspicion of the press and the intellectuals, finely-attuned political antennas, heavy reliance on congressional allies. In a humorous speech before the Gridiron Club, Nixon suggested some others: "We both served in the House and Senate. We both served as Vice President. We both ran for President against John F. Kennedy—and we both lost."

A Johnson-Nixon contest would be a fascinating political exercise. The nation got a brief preview in November, 1966, when the President, at his last press conference before the midterm election, suddenly lashed out at Nixon's criticisms of the Manila Conference communiqué, calling him "a chronic campaigner," who "never did really recognize and realize what was going on when he had an official position in the Government," and even in private life "doesn't serve his country well." It was a peevish outburst, possibly aggravated by Johnson's

"It sure as hell looks like Nixon, but why would he be picketing the White House?"

Interlandi, Nov. 13, 1966, © 1966, The Los Angeles Times Syndicate

foreknowledge that the election returns would be gratifying to Nixon and painful for him.

Nixon, who had carefully refrained from criticizing Johnson while the President was overseas on his Asian trip, leaped at this opportunity. On national television time provided by the Republican party, Nixon looked deep into the camera and addressed himself directly to the

President: "I respect you for the great energies you devote to that office and my respect has not changed because of the personal attack you made on me. You see, I think I understand how a man can be very, very tired and how his temper can be very short. . . ." Warren Weaver, Jr., writing in the *New York Times Magazine,* called Nixon's speech "a masterful piece of genteel effrontery," in which Nixon "again [appeared] in the role of Injured Innocence. . . ."

Despite such comments, Nixon came away from his first encounter with LBJ clearly the winner. Columnists and editorial writers rushed to his defense and he even had kind words from some highly unusual liberal quarters. Wrote *The New Republic's* T.R.B., "We aren't accustomed to defending Dick Nixon, but we don't like any argument that impugns an opponent's patriotism."

Nixon would welcome a chance to test Johnson again in 1968. Unlike 1960, when circumstances dictated that he defend the Eisenhower Administration, Nixon the next time would have the debater's advantage of being on the attack. He might even, on the basis of the opportunity he gave Kennedy in 1960, be able to press Johnson to meet him in face-to-face debate.*

A Nixon-Johnson contest would operate on at least two levels. On the level of intellect and rhetoric, the contest of minds, the Republicans could hardly hope for a better champion than Nixon. No one in the party knows national issues better or can argue them more effectively. But on the level of personality—the contest of images—Nixon offers no such dramatic contrast to Johnson as the clean-cut

---

* There is some reason to think, conversely, that Johnson would welcome Nixon as his 1968 adversary. They have never been friendly. As Majority Leader, Johnson occasionally contrived tie votes in the Senate so that Vice President Nixon would have to vote on controversial issues. The President has often recalled that his mentor, the late Speaker Sam Rayburn, reversed his initial opposition to Johnson's going on the 1960 ticket because Rayburn despised Nixon and was determined he should not be President. In the 1960 campaign, Johnson took great pleasure in deriding Nixon, saying, "He couldn't even stand up to Nelson Rockefeller; how can he stand up to Khrushchev?" Johnson concluded one of the memorable whistle-stop speeches of his tour through Virginia by demanding, "What has Richard Nixon ever done for Culpeper?" A close friend of the President commented in 1967, "I think he'd like to campaign against Nixon in 1968, 'cause he knows how to; he doesn't know these others." But the suggestion advanced by some loyal White House aides that Johnson's 1966 press conference outburst against Nixon was "deliberately designed to set him up as the 1968 opponent" seems far-fetched. The President's anger was so genuine and his language so intemperate that even Mrs. Johnson, sitting nearby, was observed to be saying quietly, "Stop."

new faces like Romney, Percy and Reagan would afford.

At the Hershey conference in August, 1964, Nixon was advising his party on how to defeat Lyndon B. Johnson—"perhaps the most superb politician ever to occupy the presidency," he called him, "a man that is everything to everybody." Said Nixon, "The point we should make is this: Is that enough in this age, at this time? And, of course, the answer is, it isn't enough for America; it isn't enough for the world." What America wants, he said, "is a man of peace, a man of heart, but above all things . . . compared with the political man in the White House, a man of principle, a man of high courage, a man of idealism who will inspire America to lead the world." At the time, of course, Nixon was describing Barry Goldwater as he hoped the voters would see him. They did not see Goldwater that way. The description is still apt for the ideal anti-Johnson candidate, but the question is unanswered: Does Nixon fit the role?

When a reporter asked Jacob Javits, no friend of Nixon, about the former Vice President's chances of becoming the 1968 Republican presidential nominee, the New York Senator, using the parlance of the race track, replied, "Well, they don't run 'em till they're two years old, and they rarely run 'em after they're six or seven." Nixon sometimes seems to promote this image of himself as an over-aged politician, tottering on the brink of elder statesmanship. Looking out at the audience in Palo Alto on a fall day in 1966, he remarked that it was "nice to be back among old friends and also to meet the grandchildren of some of the people who were here when I started campaigning." Yet in 1968 Nixon will be only fifty-five, two years younger than boyish Ronald Reagan, six years younger than energetic George Romney, four years younger than the President of the United States. Despite the atmosphere of nostalgia that engulfs him, he barely will have reached the bloom of political middle age, a time of life when ambitious men are normally approaching the peak of their powers.

Perhaps he will never be President. If not, it probably will be because he suffers from an acute case of the Greeley Syndrome. (After Horace Greeley's defeat for the presidency in 1872, a careful observer noted, "He called out a larger proportion of those who intended to vote against him than any candidate had ever before succeeded in doing.") It is not easy to unify California Democrats, but Nixon showed in 1962 that he was capable of the feat. After he campaigned in Pennsylvania in 1966, the Democratic gubernatorial candidate commented, "This has helped me by 15,000 to 50,000 votes." And, in the same year, pollsters hired by the Democrats followed Nixon into New Jersey and Maine and discovered that while he produced a positive G.O.P. impact, his visits had strengthened the negative Democratic reaction to him. Most party-oriented of the G.O.P. hopefuls, Nixon has honestly inherited the late Senator Taft's proud title of "Mr. Republican." And it still is a Democratic country.

He may be destined to be one of those figures in American history like Clay or Blaine or Bryan or Stevenson who have an almost presidential impact on their times without ever reaching the White House. He may yet serve in other posts of influence, chairman of his party or Secretary of State. But he is one of those forces—whether major or minor—who will not allow themselves to be denied, and who, like the fabled Phoenix, are born to be consumed in fire, yet each time to rise again, young and vigorous, from their own ashes.

Sitting in a Los Angeles hotel room, sipping coffee with three reporters in 1966, Richard Nixon was asked, "What keeps you going?" He did not seem surprised at the question.

"Sometimes I wonder myself," he said. "I started in this thing when I was thirty-two. You know me, I'm not an extrovert type. I like people, but I am not one who lives on the adulation of the crowd. But I am one who believes that you pass this way only once, and when the great decisions are made, you want to be in on them. It's the Theodore Roosevelt thing—the man in the arena, facing the challenge."

Nixon then sketched without exaggeration the life he could lead as a successful Wall Street lawyer—high salary, privilege and position, long vacations at fashionable resorts.

"I'd be bored to death," he said. "I'd be dead mentally in two years and probably dead physically in four. No, that is not for me."

Haunted though he is by the dream of the Presidency, the answer to what makes Nixon tick may really be simpler than most observers suspect.

"The thing I enjoy is the battle itself."

7 CHARLES H. PERCY:

The Middle Man

IN SANTIAGO, capital of Chile, late in December of 1965, the American Ambassador arranged for a visiting industrialist from his country to speak to a group of leftist student leaders. While waiting for the well-heeled visitor to arrive, a U.S. embassy official decided to indulge himself in a little game. He would give the young Latinos some biographical data on the evening's speaker and then ask them to draw a picture of the man who fit the description.

Mr. X was Chairman of the Board of a manufacturing company that employed about 10,000 people and had yearly sales of nearly $175,000,-000.

He also was on the board of two major banks, two great universities, and the American Management Association.

The students worked with gusto for they knew the type well. Their composite showed a huge Goliath, old and fat; a cigar-smoking militarist and a tool of the C.I.A. In other words, exactly the caricature that Homer Davenport drew in a dollar-sign suit to represent "The Trusts" at the turn of the century.

When the door opened in strode a short, hard-muscled man with a square jaw, upturned at a jaunty angle; his hair, once pictured as green, for some unknown reason, on a *Time* cover, was dark blond and razor-cut. He was forty-six years old, looked a full decade younger, and, at a distance, might still have passed for a fraternity house president. "When I walked in," recalled Charles Harting Percy, "they were profoundly shocked."

Shock was not exactly the emotion that greeted Percy's victory a

year later, in November, 1966, over liberal Democrat Paul H. Douglas
of Illinois, a Senate fixture for eighteen years. For most of a decade,
Percy had been seeking a way into elective politics. After one setback,
he had gained the first rung on the ladder and now the question was,
where would he go—and how fast? On the day after his election, Percy
told a Chicago press conference that he saw "no circumstances what-

On Schedule

Moore, Waukegan **News-Sun**, Nov. 9, 1966

ever" that might point to his nomination for President in 1968. What
about a possible draft? No, he replied, drafts occur only when there is
a lack of good candidates, and the G.O.P.'s presidential cup was
presently running over. Would he consider 1972? Well, he answered,
he hoped to have done such a good job by then that the people of
Illinois would re-elect him to the Senate. "I have been without a steady
job for three years," wryly commented the millionaire Senator-elect,
"I'm going to stay right with that job." Clearly Chuck Percy had
already learned the becomingly modest answers that are expected of

a promising young politician about to enter his first elective office.

Yet, once in Washington, even before he had time to arrange the office furniture, hang pictures on the nails that protruded from the bare walls, or rent a house for his family, Senator Percy was holding a series of "get-acquainted" sessions with small groups of journalists. *U.S. News & World Report,* in an article entitled "A Dark Horse to Watch for the Presidency in '68," counted at least seven syndicated newspaper columns in the early weeks of the session that had kind words for him.

Almost before some of the other new legislators had boarded the Senate subway he had made a quick round trip to England.

Within a week, he began drumming up publicity and support for a clever proposal on housing written for his campaign use by a young intellectual named John McClaughry. Unveiled during the first week of the session, the National Home Ownership Foundation plan was peddled so successfully by Percy that when it was formally introduced in April, it enjoyed the patronage and co-sponsorship of every Republican Senator and 109 of the 187 House Republicans. What attracted this display of unprecedented political ecumenicism among Republicans was a plan for a private, nonprofit foundation whose (government-guaranteed) bonds would finance low-interest loans to enable slum families to purchase and rehabilitate their own homes or apartments. The means (private enterprise) appealed to the conservatives; the ends (improved living conditions for the poor) appealed to the liberals. The Democratic Secretary of Housing and Urban Development issued a special memorandum calling the plan impractical, but Percy enjoyed a publicity and political bonanza nonetheless. "Commendable . . . inventive . . . ingenious," wrote conservative William F. Buckley; "positive . . . a very fast start," wrote liberal Joseph Kraft. Moreover, in a country in which three out of four people live in cities and suburbs, as the Washington *Post* headline proclaimed: PERCY BUILDING AN URBAN AFFAIRS IMAGE.

By the time the cherry blossoms were in bloom, Percy had made speeches in Nebraska and New Hampshire, two states that hold key presidential primaries, as well as in Pennsylvania, Michigan, Florida, New York and Kentucky. Then, too, in private Percy was saying strange things about his fellow Republican moderates. He rarely missed an opportunity to needle George Romney, at the time desperately trying to find his sea legs in foreign policy, or to promote Nelson

Rockefeller. Since Romney and Percy represent the same region and the same political persuasion, one would have to fall if the other was to rise; while talk of the New York Governor as a potential presidential candidate, as he was the first to point out, only served to undermine front runner Romney.

It would appear that Charles H. Percy, who ranked ninety-ninth in Senate seniority, had his mind on opportunities other than the slow, steady rise to congressional leadership.

"His life sounds like a soap opera, doesn't it?" asks Percy's wife Loraine. Actually, it has more often been compared to a Horatio Alger novel, the rags-to-riches tale of a child of the depression working his way up to corporation president by the age of twenty-nine.

Born in Pensacola, Florida, September 27, 1919, Chuck Percy started running at age five when he began his business career as a magazine salesman in Chicago, where the family moved while he was an infant. He promptly proved that his abilities were exceptional, winning a plaque for selling "more copies of *Country Gentleman* to city people than any other urban salesman in the United States." Within a few years he had the largest schoolboy magazine route in the city. At the time Percy's father was doing nicely as the cashier of a small bank. It was not until the bank failed in 1931, when Percy was twelve, that the boy's drive was also motivated by necessity. Being poor did not make Percy run. It just made him run faster.

During his high school years he held as many as four jobs simultaneously. He stoked furnaces before school, worked in the registrar's office during school, delivered newspapers after school, and on nights and weekends ushered at a neighborhood movie theater. When the welfare truck brought the Percys a hundred-pound bag of sugar by mistake, his mother baked cookies and Chuck sold them door to door. But nothing stemmed the slide into poverty. The car was repossessed. The telephone was disconnected. Finally, Mrs. Percy sold her engagement ring.

Mrs. Percy told David Murray of the Chicago *Sun-Times* in 1966: "I don't believe we ever went to bed hungry. Oh, we didn't have as much to eat as we would have liked or often what we would have liked, and I did bake cookies for Chuck to sell. But we weren't any worse off than a lot of other poeple. We'd work and hope things would get better. We always felt there was a way out."

A surprised campaign aide found out about this period in the Percys' life when Percy was running for Governor in 1964. "Why didn't you *tell* me you had been on relief?" he asked. "You didn't ask me," the candidate answered. "You don't go around asking members of the Chicago Club if they've been on relief," his supporter replied. "After that," writer Hal Higdon pointed out, "Percy seldom failed to mention his former welfare status."

To one interviewer, William Trombley, Percy described the period when his father finally found a job as a night clerk at a rundown hotel on Chicago's Lawrence Avenue, where he made $35 for a seven-day, eighty-four-hour week. "To see him coming home then, he was so depressed . . . I'm sorry," Percy said, tears beginning to roll down his cheeks, "I didn't realize the memory of my father in those years could still arouse that much emotion."

"It was my mother's music and her religion that kept our spirits up," Percy now says. Mother's music was made on the violin. In fact, she had met her husband while on a concert tour of the South, he being from an old Southern family whose branches include a Governor of the Jamestown colony and a drummer boy at Robert E. Lee's headquarters. Mrs. Percy, now in her mid-seventies, still plays in the Evanston Symphony Orchestra and when her campaigning son toured the Illinois county fair circuit in the summer of 1963, she went along to entertain the crowds with her rendition of "Perpetual Motion."

Percy inherited only enough of his mother's musical ability to play the piano passably and to enjoy singing, but her religion, Christian Science, has been a major influence in his life. Mrs. Percy organized Sunday-evening prayer sessions, had readings from the Bible and Christian Science publications at breakfast, and said grace at all meals —customs that her son continues. Like the equally religious George Romney, whose Mormon faith is as patriarchical in its orientation as Christian Science is matriarchal, Percy does not smoke or drink or swear. He told writer William Barry Furlong that he could recall hearing his father (a convert to Christian Science) use an oath only once. It was at dinner during the 1930's; the family meal, for the sixth or seventh night in a row, was Spanish rice. As the elder Percy started to pick at his food, his wife said, "Edward, can't you wait a moment and express your gratitude to God for what He's given us?" "I'll be damned," he replied, "if I'm grateful for this."

Like Romney, too, Percy has a fetish about physical fitness, swimming daily if possible (he was a water-polo player in college), bounding up stairs two at a time, rather than taking an elevator. And like Romney he radiates an air of purposefulness and self-satisfaction that some find a bit too much to take. The Chicago *Tribune* once wrote that "Mr. Percy . . . affects an elaborate piety, like a figure in stained glass." But, however it strikes outsiders, Percy draws from his religious faith a confidence and sustaining power that are almost palpable. In both the tragedies of his life—the death of his first wife and the brutal murder of his daughter, Valerie—Percy has maintained a composure that has been remarked with awe by his associates.

Christian Science, like Mormonism, is a nineteenth-century American product, founded in 1879 by Mrs. Mary Baker Eddy at what is now known as the Mother Church, the First Church of Christ, Scientist, in Boston. Born on a farm in Bow, New Hampshire, in 1821, raised in the Congregational Church, the thrice-married Mrs. Eddy set forth the principles of her faith in *Science and Health with Key to the Scriptures,* published in 1875. The book was based on her study of the Bible and her own experience after a fall on the ice in Lynn, Massachusetts, in 1866, when she sustained what a doctor diagnosed as a brain concussion and spinal dislocation. Three days after the accident, still bedridden, she read the account in Matthew 9:2–8 of Christ's curing the paralytic, and, as she wrote, "The healing Truth dawned upon my sense; and the result was that I rose, dressed myself, and ever after was in better health than I had before enjoyed."

The church Mrs. Eddy founded has expanded now to embrace 3,300 branches in 48 countries, with a membership in the millions. (Church policy prohibits the publication of exact membership figures.) Like the Mormons, the Christian Scientists have no clergy; services are conducted by a First and Second Reader, elected by the membership for a fixed period of time. Unlike the Latter-day Saints, Christian Scientists do not conduct active proselytizing or missionary work, though their network of reading rooms around the world and their extensive publications program make Christian Science material widely available.

The distinctive feature of the religion—and the only one that could conceivably become a matter of public discussion if Percy ran for President—is its attitude toward medicine. Described in official publications as "Christianity in its most practical and scientific form," Percy's faith regards healing through prayer as central to its practice.

Testimony of healings, given weekly at Christian Science services, is the conspicuous proof to its adherents of the validity of their religion. A booklet *Facts about Christian Science,* distributed by the Christian Science Publishing Society, answers the question "Can Christian Science be combined with reliance on medical aid?" with a flat "No." "Experience has shown that the attempts to combine Christian Science treatment with medicine is fair to neither system and lessens the efficacy of both," it says.

But, as the same booklet goes on to say, Christian Scientists take medical examinations as required for insurance policies, for school admission or for the armed services. Doctors attend Christian Scientists in childbirth where specified by law. Christian Scientists obey regulations requiring reporting and isolating of contagious diseases. They sometimes use doctors to set bones, when no medication is involved.

Percy himself does not take drugs or place himself under doctors' care for routine ailments, but he and his family visit a dentist and use an eye doctor. When the present Mrs. Percy fractured her leg while skiing, a doctor set it, but she refused to let him insert pins to secure the bone. When Valerie Percy was found mortally wounded, her father telephoned both a neighboring physician and a Christian Science practitioner (a person specially trained in what is called "the healing ministry"). A physician was also summoned late in the terminal illness of Mrs. Percy's mother, who died in 1967.

Percy was asked how his religion might affect his public performance when he ran for Governor in 1964. He replied:

> It is a logical question: a Christian Scientist does not resort to medicine. Now, there's no law saying you can't. You don't withdraw from the church if you do. And, most important, you don't impose your beliefs on others. But your inclination is not to use medicine, and I never have. I personally believe in the power of prayer. But if someone does not believe in prayer for healing, doesn't choose to follow that route, then my position is he better follow *some* route, and if it is medical care it better be the best medical care. . . . There is nothing in my religious belief that would hinder me in my performance of the functions of Governor as they relate to the public health needs of all our people.

In an interview with the authors in 1967, Percy also noted that as a trustee of the University of Chicago he had voted for the expenditure of millions of dollars for medical research and as a candidate had advocated Federal and state programs for the improvement of health care for the needy and the elderly. He also said that during the Eisenhower Administration, Secretary of Health, Education and Welfare Oveta Culp Hobby and Under Secretary Nelson A. Rockefeller, urging him to become assistant secretary of the department (which he refused), had assured him there would be no criticism of his suitability because of his religious beliefs.

Actually, the religion-and-health issue has never received much notice in his campaigns, not even as much as the limited attention paid in Michigan to George Romney's Mormonism. In the 1966 senatorial campaign, according to his aide, Scott Cohen, the candidate received only five letters relating to his practice of Christian Science.

In the 1967 interview, when Percy was asked some "what-if-you-were-President" questions, he said that the public character of the office, his responsibility to others, would necessitate that he follow the custom of having a full-time White House physician. He also said that he could think of no case in the medical histories of the last three Chief Executives—Eisenhower, Kennedy and Johnson—in which he would have declined the medical attention they received.

"But I've been healthy," Percy remarked. "My family has been healthy; my parents have been long-lived." Then, discussing his religion, he made some remarks that offer an interesting insight into its place in his life and his own set of values.

"I find it a very satisfying thing," he said. "It depersonalizes what you are doing, makes it not just a matter of sheer will power, but makes you feel there is a source of guidance and strength you can draw on. There is a sense of optimism about it which appeals to me. Also it is a wonderfully organized church, and I admire organization. The publications come regularly and are of high quality. I love the *Christian Science Monitor*. It gives you a balanced viewpoint. I've never found them shading an article toward me. They've never endorsed me and they never would; but they are wonderfully balanced. ... An international business management firm once recommended to the Roman Catholic Church—*Time* wrote about it—that they look at the Christian Science Church as a well-organized, functional business, if you like. Ours is not a ritualistic church; I don't need ritualization of religion; Christian Science strips religion down to its fundamentals."

If Percy needed any additional reason to cherish his religion, he could find it in the coincidence that led to his big break in the business world. The rigid formula of the Horatio Alger story requires that the hero be, not only honest and hard-working, but also lucky. The man whose daughter he rescues must be a grateful capitalist; Alger's young worthies never save *poor* damsels in distress. For Charles Percy the lucky break came when he entered the Sunday-school class of Joseph McNabb, the president of a small camera company called Bell & Howell. (There is a persistent and totally erroneous story that Percy's first wife was the boss's daughter.) Percy asked his religious mentor if he would give his father a daytime job so that the family could have some time together. NcNabb, who liked the boy's pluck, complied. (The senior Percy retired from Bell & Howell as an office manager in 1957 and died two years later at the age of seventy-five.) McNabb also gave young Percy summer employment and during one such period Percy revolutionized the customer service department by designing sixty form letters that fit nearly every situation. ("I've just taken four rolls of film and they all came out blank." "Dear Madam: Please take off the lens cap.")

Percy attended the University of Chicago on a half-tuition scholarship and by his senior year in 1941, according to Chancellor Robert Hutchins, he was the "richest boy who ever worked his way through college." (Hutchins, who replaced football with Aristotle, also told Percy, "You're exactly the kind of student I'm trying to keep out of the university." A dozen years after graduation Percy was a U.C. trustee.) Besides the usual college odd jobs, waiting on tables and tending the library, Percy worked out two operations of considerable ingenuity and organizational skill. He took over a cooperative purchasing and servicing association for the fraternities. They had been paying local laundries 7.5 cents per pound but by hard bargaining and throwing all his business to one laundry, Percy was able to get the price down to 3.5 cents. He made similar savings on food and supplies by buying in large lots. After three years the business was grossing $150,000 a year and Percy's cut was $10,000. He also recruited potential students for small colleges that were particularly hard-pressed by the depression. "I got five cents for the name of every high school senior I obtained and ten dollars if he enrolled," Percy recalls. Later he hired others to do the legwork for him and paid them three cents a name and five dollars an enrollment. "That," said Percy, "was the value of being an entrepreneur."

Entrepreneur Percy went to work full time for Bell & Howell upon graduation and McNabb put him in charge of defense contracts, a relatively modest activity. Within six months, however, Pearl Harbor was attacked and Percy was soon supervising the bulk of his company's business. He was, on McNabb's recommendation, made a director before he was twenty-three, and before he left for the Navy.

In his three Navy years, Percy never got overseas, but suffered a permanent hearing impairment from his duties as a gunnery training officer. (He wears a hearing aid, either openly or concealed in the frames of his glasses, in places with bad acoustics, like the Senate chamber, and still suffers occasional embarrassment when he fails to hear a greeting or interrupts a conversation.)

During the war, Percy married Jeanne Dickerson, who bore him three children—twin girls, Valerie and Sharon, and a son, Roger. In 1947, Jeanne Percy, who was not a Christian Scientist, was operated on for ulcerative colitis. She was given penicillin, which caused a fatal reaction. She was twenty-three, her daughters were three, and her son was a year old the day she was buried.

Three years after his wife's death, Percy married a pretty twenty-one-year-old Californian (and fellow Christian Scientist), Loraine Guyer, whom he had met on the ski slopes of Sun Valley. They now have a son and a daughter.

Percy was informed by Joe McNabb, two years before his death in 1949, that he was leaving a sort of "corporate will" recommending that Percy, rather than his own son or any of the other executives, succeed him as president. Percy delights in telling the story of the tense days before the board of directors met to name McNabb's successor. "I tell you," he says, "it was *Executive Suite* all over again. I wasn't even a vice president then. McNabb's lawyer and I were the only ones who knew about the existence of the letter, and I wasn't sure whether it had been changed since Joe had told me of his plans." On the fateful day in 1949, the letter was opened and the board of directors— an august body of industrialists whose average age was in the sixties— then dutifully named McNabb's twenty-nine-year-old protégé as president of Bell & Howell at an annual salary of $40,000—plus appropriate stock options, which the young executive declined until he could prove himself. Percy led his company for fifteen years. During that period sales grew from less than $5 million a year to $160 million, company employment from less than one thousand to approximately ten thousand, salaries from an average of $2,000 per employee to more than $7,500. An employee profit-sharing plan was inaugurated and the company, which had been privately owned by three families, was listed on the New York Stock Exchange. Where Bell & Howell had been almost exclusively a quality camera maker, Percy diversified into business equipment, reproduction machines, automated-mailing systems, and instruments for the space and military programs. He pushed expansion into foreign markets. He also, in the manner of George Romney, went in for promotions with a flair. Living in the shadow of Eastman Kodak, just as Romney's company was dwarfed by the auto industry's Big Three—he tried harder.

To prove to his dealers that Bell & Howell was not stuffy, as had been reputed, Percy and three top executives went on a thirty-one-city tour during which they closed their "act" by donning skirts, wigs and padded bras while mouthing the words of a hit record by Bing Crosby and the Andrews Sisters. Percy made a point of shaking hands with every employee at Christmastime, a practice, he later said, that was an excellent preparation for politics. Realizing that Bell & Howell could not compete for sponsorship of expensive television entertainment, Percy's company pioneered as sponsor of controversial documentaries, such as programs on racial unrest and the population explosion, in prime evening time.

During the 1957–58 economic recession, when it was obvious that sales of a luxury item like a camera would be hard hit, Percy decided to "buck the trend." Instead of cutting back on development costs, he increased them in order to bring new products to the market ahead of schedule. Instead of reducing sales costs, he talked television stations and other media into giving him rate reductions if he would purchase larger dollar volumes. Orders to their own suppliers were increased in return for price reductions and the savings were passed on to the consumer so that the price of the least-expensive camera was cut from $50 to under $40. The result of Percy's gamble was that in 1958 his company increased sales by 15 percent, net earnings by 22 percent, and the price of the stock doubled.

Perhaps he had "conquered" the world of business and felt the need for new challenges. Perhaps his interests had grown. Perhaps he had been in one place too long. Perhaps it was that he now had all the money he and his family would ever need.* But by the mid 1950's

* During an interview in April, 1967, Percy estimated his personal fortune "conservatively" at $6 million. According to published reports, he sold 10,000

Charles H. Percy was becoming increasingly restless and anxious to find a new role, if not a new life, for himself. "I simply found I was reading the political columns in the paper ahead of the business page and I knew I was hooked," he says.

As if to prepare himself for this new life, Percy hired Robert A. Goldwin, a political science professor from the University of Chicago, to come to his North Shore estate every Saturday morning to give him a private course in political theory. Together they worked their way through the Federalist Papers, Locke and Mill.

He made extensive trips abroad, not for sport or casual sightseeing, but as part of his constant emphasis on self-improvement. Before he joined the Navy in World War II, Percy had never been further east than Grand Rapids or further west than Des Moines. As president of Bell & Howell he had traveled widely on business. Now his sole purpose was his own education. For a year before each trip he studied the chosen area, its government, agriculture, educational system, religion. In 1955, for example, he spent six weeks in India going from village to village, over six thousand miles by boat, train, plane and Jeep. As on his previous trips, Percy came back with a filmed record. It was no movie of snake charmers or moonlight on the Taj Mahal. Rather, it was the story, as narrator Percy saw it, of what the future of India could be. Back in Chicago he toured the civic and educational groups with his film.

It may not have escaped his notice that it was good advertising for a camera maker to show home movies. But what is wrong with doing well while doing good? And Chuck Percy was a do-gooder *and* a do-weller. Each day he began with a hymn—"We like to start the morning with a song." He was Poor Richard, the overachiever of the Protestant ethic, the American Dream. Going up a ski tow he read magazine articles. Sound body, sound mind. Time is money. Waste not, want not. When he was told that it was politically disadvantageous to be thought "too good to be true," he replied, "Well, that's my imperfection." He was every boy who had ever sent off for a course on "How to Succeed . . ." Only he had.

President Eisenhower, who was partial to the type, saw Percy as a

shares of Bell & Howell stock on May 18, 1966, for about $390,000, which left him with 82,017 shares, now worth nearly $5 million. When he entered the U.S. Senate in 1967 he turned over the management of his portfolio to Stein, Roe & Farnham with written instructions for them not to buy shares in any company that he might have an influence on as a legislator. The cost of his Kenilworth home has been estimated at $230,000.

comer. Right after New Year's, 1959, Percy, known to Ike as a major backer of his reciprocal trade program and as a top fund raiser for the Illinois Republican party, stopped by the White House. "The nation has moved into a new period of danger, threatened by the rulers of one third of mankind, for whom the state is everything and the individual significant only as he serves the state," the thirty-nine-year-old industrialist recalls that he announced to the sixty-eight-year-old President. "We need a new understanding of the problems, not only to meet a deadly menace and extend the area of freedom in the world, but also to preserve and enlarge our liberties." The President was excited; people did not usually burst into his office and deliver a Fourth of July speech. He called his speechwriters, then putting the finishing touches on the State of the Union Message. The speechwriters frantically sliced away at their lengthy draft to make room for Percy's ideas. And, standing before a joint session of Congress four days later, President Eisenhower—"permit me to digress long enough to express something that is much on my mind"—announced he would appoint a Presidential Commission on National Goals.

This "goals" business was heady stuff. Having set in motion the machinery that would at last give the United States a set of "national goals," Percy now turned his attention to "party goals." Shortly after the State of the Union Message, the President asked Percy to head a committee to provide the Republican party with a "concise, understandable statement of our party's long-range objectives in all areas of political responsibility."

The "concise, understandable statement" turned out to be a 190-page paperback, titled *Decisions for a Better America*. Its overall tone reflected the more liberal impulses left in the aging Eisenhower Administration, but, like any committee-produced manifesto, most of its assertions had all the cutting edge of a soft cliché. The Republican party, it courageously said at the outset, "must pursue definite goals, safeguard enduring values, yet be flexible and imaginative in welcoming change as the key to all progress." Later, it found that "if the working man and the employer are to enjoy fully the rich benefits of the American economic system, they must work as partners to produce more and better products with ever-increasing efficiency. Their interests are inseparable."

Still, the fact that it was written at all was something of an accomplishment. Percy, always fond of the academic style, almost scuttled the project at the start, by bringing two University of Chicago professors to the first session to lead a seminar-type discussion. Using the Socratic method, the professors tried to shock committee members into a sense of commitment to the job at hand. The committee's task is impossible, they argued. It is politically risky. Disband at once. But they were not in a classroom and their listeners were not college students, but old pros like Everett Dirksen and Charlie Halleck. "A lot of them," one participant recalls, "didn't know what the hell to think."

When the Percy Report was at length declared ready, Richard Nixon hailed it as "the most useful and constructive statement of goals and principles ever issued by a political party in the United States," and President Eisenhower said "every earnest Republican and every other dedicated citizen can benefit greatly by a reading of these papers."

It is a safe bet that very few of the earnest and the dedicated did so, but the report made Percy, in the eyes of Eisenhower and Nixon, the logical fellow to chair the 1960 Republican platform committee. It took some arranging. While Percy was valued for his fund raising (some $4 million) in Illinois, the state's conservative Republican leadership did not picture him as their logical representative on platform issues or anything else of consequence, for that matter. However, National Chairman Thruston Morton called the G.O.P. brass in Illinois to pass the word that both the White House and Nixon wanted Percy named the state's platform committee representative, and their request was honored.

The platform job proved easier to get than to perform. For, at the last minute, Nixon determined he should woo Rockefeller with a series of liberal platform amendments. Percy, like everyone else at the Chicago convention, was kept in the dark about the Rockefeller-Nixon meeting in Manhattan until it was over; then he was phoned and, as a platform committee aide recalls the scene, sat taking notes from the two men on a long yellow pad for more than an hour.

Percy now faced a full-scale revolt by the 104-member platform committee, which was more conservative than its leadership. Barry Goldwater, just emerging as the conservatives' spokesman, branded the Nixon-Rockefeller pact as "the Munich of the Republican party." Moreover, the committee's pride was affronted by what it took as a slight to its duly-constituted authority. In the crunch, Percy's political inexperience betrayed him. "He tried to do it all [get the Nixon-Rockefeller language adopted] with charm and personality," a conservative platform member recalls, "and this was a situation where you had to knock some heads. When you get right down to it, Chuck was naïve."

"Chuck's problem," said another, "was that in a controversial situation he had a tendency to agree with both sides. There was no room for a neutral there."

For a full day the revolt raged unchecked. Finally Nixon arrived on the scene, and the next morning Percy quietly handed over the gavel to the committee's vice chairman, Wisconsin's tough-as-nails Congressman Melvin Laird, who pounded the platform through, while Percy busied himself rehearsing the narration for the film that was to accompany its presentation to the convention.

As a man who disciplines himself to make use even of his painful experiences, Percy feels the lesson he learned from the platform committee was the need to do "total homework." "I knew the issues," he now says, "but I didn't understand how important tactics and maneuvers and parliamentary tricks can be. I learned a lot from that job, and the main thing I learned was that knowledge is power."

If that is the case, it was equally borne home to Percy that power itself is power—and the power that politicians respect is the power of public office. The talented amateur, the money raiser, the platform drafter got a polite brushoff in the 1960 election and he did not enjoy the experience.

Nixon, Percy says, asked him to head his national citizens organization (after hinting earlier, before the convention, that he might even be under consideration for Vice President), but Percy declined on the ground that an effort to lure independent and Democratic voters should be run by someone other than a prominent Republican. After that, he was asked to do very little. He was a member of Nixon's advisory board, but Nixon did not seem to require advice. He volunteered to make speeches in Illinois, but Republican Governor William G. Stratton, no friend of Percy's, kept him off the stump. On the weekend before election, he finally received a speaking assignment —in Colorado. Seeing Illinois go to Kennedy by 8,800 votes, Percy says he felt "a terrible sense of guilt. If I couldn't change that many votes in my own state . . ."

The way to have influence, he decided, was not to offer advice from the sidelines, but to get into the thick of the action by running for office.

But the next available office in Illinois was the Senate seat held by G.O.P. leader Everett Dirksen. Despite Dirksen's seeming invincibility, Percy set off on a tour of Illinois to explore the possibility of opposing his fellow Republican. "It was not an unthinkable thing for me to run against him in the primary," he says. "In the late 1950's the view was not nearly as unanimous as it is now that Everett Dirksen was invaluable. We had issues on which we disagreed and I believe no one has a license to hold political office for life." Whatever Percy thought, local politicos viewed the potential challenge as bordering on political suicide. But Percy says it was a conversation with New Jersey Senator Clifford Case, rather than the Illinois organization's indifference to him, that convinced him not to make the race. Percy had never met Case before, but he respected him and asked for a meeting. "I put the question to him: 'Do you think I would be performing a service if I ran against Dirksen?' He said it would be a disservice. . . ." So Percy waited a year and announced in 1963— seventeen months ahead of election—that he would run for Governor.

The odds against Percy's winning the gubernatorial nomination in 1964 were nearly as great, twenty to one, he later estimated. For the choice of those Republicans who had always done the hard work in Illinois politics was popular Charles F. Carpentier, Secretary of State for nearly a dozen years, whose well-known signature in Kelly green ink graced every driver's license, bookmobile and highway safety booth in the state. To counter this long lead, the always hard-working and confident Percy, better known in Eastern business circles than in Springfield political circles, began touring the state with his "Chuck Wagon" and his photogenic family a full nine months before the April primary. Then, as luck would have it, old Charlie Carpentier dropped dead. The conservatives put up a replacement, but now Percy was the favorite. Even a scurrilous broadside called "Mercy, Mr. Percy," whose center fold pictured Percy in amiable conversation with Soviet Premier Khrushchev, could not deny him the nomination, by a two-to-one margin.

The November election, however, was another story. Nineteen sixty-four, the year most Republicans would like to forget, proved especially distasteful for Charles Percy. Goldwater might claim he lost with honor and Romney that he won as best he could; but Percy, as he admits, lost with little honor. "The defeat for Governor," he now says, "was probably well deserved." There were three facets to Percy's campaign that caused distress to those who saw him as a bright hope of the party.

First, he ignored the highly structured Republican county organization, relying on his own volunteer committees, and generally convincing the regular party leaders that there was no particularly good reason for them to exert any extra effort on his behalf.

Second, Percy came across to the voters as stiff, cold and remote, rather, thought one reporter, "like the chairman of the board of a slightly dissident stockholders meeting." Recalling his 1964 performance, Percy says, "I was using statistics like an IBM machine." Percy is basically a very serious person—a former aide can recall only one joke he made in a year—but he is not dour. Yet in 1964 there was little of the amiable disposition he later proved capable of displaying.

Typical was the story of a businessman who talked with Percy on a private plane from St. Louis to Chicago only to have the Republican candidate walk by him without recognition several days later. (In 1966 Percy invented an almost fool-proof system for making sure that while on walking tours he did not shake hands twice with the same person —he pinned his campaign button on everyone he met and thus could easily spot whoever happened to pass his way again.)

Third, on substantive issues Percy managed to disturb those who had considered him a liberal without making a corresponding gain among the conservatives. He had been known as a progressive on civil rights. His record included nondiscriminatory hiring at Bell & Howell, strong backing for a state Fair Employment Practices Commission, and his name on a party platform with the most liberal civil-rights plank in recent G.O.P. history. Yet, while others—Rockefeller, Scranton, Romney, Scott—bled in the cause of civil rights at the San Francisco convention, Chuck Percy was strangely quiet. He was off the floor "in conference" when the civil rights amendments to the platform were offered. On the most important civil-rights issue of the year, he told an interviewer, "Right now we aren't ready to force people to accept those they don't want as neighbors. I was for FEPC because there was a consensus in the state for it. There is no such consensus in Illinois for open occupancy." So Percy came out against open-occupancy legislation, stating that, if elected, he would try to get compliance by voluntary means.

But what he calls "my biggest mistake" was his attitude toward Goldwater. So anxious was he to get the gubernatorial nomination that he abdicated his responsibility to try to get his party to choose an ideologically compatible presidential nominee, declaring repeatedly that he preferred "no other candidate before him [Goldwater]." He turned his back on Rockefeller when the New York Governor came to Illinois searching for delegates in late 1963, and he turned his back on Scranton when the Pennsylvania Governor's wife begged him for support at the convention. (No, he told the fiery Mary Scranton, it is not a moral issue. Didn't your husband tell the Illinois delegation he will support Goldwater if the Arizona Senator wins?) Percy pledged his neutrality. "I was having enough trouble getting the gubernatorial nomination," he now recalls. "It would have been presumptuous of me to try to make a President, too." Instead, he promised to support the majority decision of the Illinois delegation, an action that, in fact, committed him to Goldwater, a candidate with whom he had little in common and one who was to prove immensely unpopular with the electorate in whose hands he placed his own fate.

In the general election he stuck with Goldwater—sort of. Although he wore a Goldwater button in his lapel, it was an all-gold model on which the name "Goldwater" was visible at a distance of up to, but not more than, three inches. If he was not quite what "Czar" Reed once called "a straddle-bug," it was nonetheless true that his position was ambiguous enough for him to be caught in what has come to be known as a "sidelash." Badgered from both sides—by the moderates and the conservatives—Percy lost the election to Democratic Governor Otto Kerner by 179,299 votes, while President Johnson's winning margin over Goldwater was an extravagant 890,887. There was little doubt that had Percy—like Romney, Lindsay, Scott and others—forcefully disassociated himself from the national ticket, he would have been elected.

It did not dawn on Percy immediately that his loyalty to the national ticket might someday be of use to him, when he was contrasted with a bolter like Romney. Having lost *with* Goldwater, in defeat Percy turned *against* him and all that he represented. He jumped aboard the dump–Dean Burch bandwagon (after telling the embattled chairman to his face that he should resign) and generally heaped scorn on the Goldwater forces. By 1967, Percy realized that Goldwater's good will was something worth having, and he made a point of telling reporters that he had never blamed Goldwater for his own defeat in

Illinois. Earlier, however, when a too-inquisitive reporter asked whether he had voted for Goldwater, Percy snapped, "Not even my wife dares to ask me that question!"

While Percy in 1967 would insist that he never criticized Goldwater personally, the speech he prepared for the December, 1964, public-relations conference of the National Association of Manufacturers (but delivered, instead, to a press conference because the NAM objected to its partisan content) was as scathing an indictment of the Republican campaign of 1964 as any Romney or Lindsay ever delivered.

I want to make it plain [Percy said] that I am not criticizing the national ticket, but rather myself and others. Senator Goldwater had every right to present his viewpoint to the electorate and to pursue the nomination; he won it fairly, with hard work and adroit planning by his ardent supporters—and because moderates like myself made it easy for him. . . .

In retrospect, the Republican party made a critical error in 1964, not so much because we lost . . . but because we gave the leadership of our party to men who do not accurately reflect its attitude and aspirations, its tradition and philosophy. The philosophy of some of these men does not even reflect conservatism as it has been practiced in the GOP by such men as Senator Robert A. Taft, Senator Arthur Vandenberg, and President Herbert Hoover. . . .

An example of a new myth which should be nipped in the bud is the idea that 26 million Americans voted for the far-right brand of conservatism espoused by some of the more vocal supporters of our national ticket. . . . Nor let us deceive ourselves concerning our so-called breakthrough in the South. Face it: We won five States in the deep South on an implied, if not actually stated, rejection of the civil rights movement. . . . Let us not boast of these inroads, for they are nothing to be proud of.

One quality of Percy as a politician is that he is absolutely dauntless in the face of personal reversals. So, dusting himself off from the 1964 disaster, he looked around for the most productive way to employ his talents while waiting for the next electoral opportunity. He hit upon a novel plan: the New Illinois Committee. Why not try to do some of the projects, on a limited scale, of course, that he had proposed doing if elected? A sort of government-in-exile. A defeated candidate keeping campaign promises. The St. Louis *Globe-Democrat* called the idea "refreshingly new." With taxable funds contributed by Percy's friends, the former candidate began programs in literacy education, job-opportunity reporting, economic development, a family center in a Negro neighborhood. One program, "Call for Action," allowed slum dwellers to phone their complaints into a tape recorder from which volunteers took the information; they tried to get landlords to make the necessary corrections. When dialing 346-6667, the "Call for Action" number, a recorded voice answered: "This is Chuck Percy. . . ." The New Illinois Committee, "formed to pursue those goals and activate those programs outlined in 'the new Illinois' that Chuck Percy had envisioned," concentrated on the Negro ghettos, where Percy had run poorly in his bid for the governorship. It also undertook research reports on U.S. strategy in Vietnam and "a study of the 1954 Geneva accords on Indochina." Once again, Percy the do-gooder and Percy the well-doer were perfectly meshed.

In the late fall of 1965, Charles H. Percy sat on the dais of a Chicago Boys Club banquet. The featured speaker was Richard M. Nixon, national chairman of the Boys Clubs of America. The mimeographed text of the former Vice President's speech was on the table before Percy and he jotted some notes on the back of the Nixon handout. Chicago *Daily News* columnist Norman Ross, another guest at the dinner, discovered Percy was not reminding himself of points he would make in his own remarks. Rather, he was drawing up a list—really two lists. Percy, like Nixon, prefers things to be well-organized. Chaos disturbs him more than it does most men. Now he was listing all the reasons why he should run for Governor in 1968 and all the reasons he should run for Senator in 1966.

The reasons for running in 1968 for Governor probably boiled down to his often-stated position that he was more a man of executive ability and temperament, a former operating head of a corporation, who was better suited to be operating head of a state than a member of a large body of legislators.

His reasons for running in 1966 for the Senate were a little more complex, but they came down to the fact that 1966 was at hand and the Senate nomination was his for the asking, while 1968 was remote and promised another primary fight. The same conservative Republicans who tried to balk him in 1964 would oppose him again if he ran for Governor. Quite willing to see him run for the Senate— if he won he would be out of their hair and in Washington, if he lost he would be finished in politics—they were adamant in rejecting him

for the governorship, which would give him control of the party, its
policies, its patronage and its convention delegation. Percy had been
on the stump constantly since mid-1963, and his name was now
known to virtually every voter. In two years, with no real excuse to
remain in the news, he might be forgotten or simply old hat.

Charles H. Percy would run for the Senate.

But it was not a simple decision. In fact, like his decision to run
against Carpentier in 1963, it was an incredibly risky one. It was
the sort of choice that only foolhardy politicians or men of driving
ambition make, the same sort of decision that sent Kennedy into
West Virginia in 1960 and Nixon into California in 1962. What
made the move so fateful for Percy was that the race would pit
him against the greatest vote getter in modern Illinois politics—
Paul H. Douglas, a former University of Chicago professor whose
intellectuality and independence were of immense appeal to the
liberals, yet a man who had worked out an advantageous peace with
the Daley machine in Cook County, the only really powerful city organization left in the United States, and a man who, although a
Democrat, always ran amazingly well downstate.

When the old-guard Illinois Republican leaders instantly and joy-
ously united behind Percy, it was not hard to believe that they had discovered a painless way to be rid of this pushy newcomer. Even the
astute Evans and Novak team thought it "a fiendishly clever trap
prepared by his arch-enemies," and added, ". . . it will be a minor
miracle if he wins." A prominent Democrat, expressing the commonly
held estimation of Percy's situation, told Andrew Kopkind of *The
New Republic,* "Douglas is like Everest, you make the assault because he's there."

There was an added drama to the Percy-Douglas clash because
twenty-eight years before, Economics Professor Douglas had taught
a course in labor relations in which undergraduate Percy was enrolled.
At first they were both rather testy about the student-teacher relationship. When asked how Percy had done, Douglas said, "I had a large
class and I don't recall what his grades were." To the same question,
Percy replied, "All I know is I passed." (And the University of
Chicago administration was hardly about to refresh the memories of
Trustee Percy or ex-Professor Douglas.) However, as the campaign
warmed up, both candidates found some value in their past association.
Percy, in order to prove to a hostile union meeting that his interest
in their problems was not of recent vintage, cited as evidence that he

had once taken a course in labor relations—from Paul Douglas. While Douglas, somehow leaving the impression that the long-ago course had been something like Money Grubbing I, told delighted audiences, "I must have given him [Percy] a few hints, because he went out and made many millions and became rich beyond the dreams of avarice." Then he added: "I only wish I'd taught him political science and driven some of those Republican notions out of his head."

Now that he was a candidate again, Percy said, "Truthfully, I am much more qualified by inclination and past experience to be in Washington than in Springfield. I would make a better senator than governor." But his most interesting change of mind came on civil rights.

Only a month after the 1964 gubernatorial campaign, in which Percy was rewarded for his stand on open occupancy by losing 89 percent of the Negro vote, he told a meeting of Republican Governors that the G.O.P. would "never be known as the party of opportunity until we make it unmistakably clear where we stand as a party on civil rights." As a first step he proposed that the party "go on record to repudiate those who are not really Republicans, . . . who waved our party banner in 1964 only as a means to promote hate and bigotry, or only in the hope of discouraging the civil-rights movement." Later Percy delivered a similar message to the racially integrated Mississippi Council on Human Relations. After rejecting what he described as "heavy pressure" from some Southern Republicans to cancel the appearance, Percy was boycotted by Mississippi G.O.P. leaders. They missed hearing the Illinois industrialist tell more than five hundred persons in Jackson that "In 1964, the Republican party won five Southern states by setting foot upon what has been called 'The shifting racist sands,' and that was a triumph neither for Republicans nor conservatives. Such a victory will not serve the future success of our party, or of any party. For what we succeeded in doing in 1964 was to drive practically the entire Negro vote in the United States into the Democratic camp."

At the same time, Percy was speaking out with equal vigor in his own state. Appearing before the Illinois Press Association on May 14, 1965, he admitted that he had been wrong to believe the real-estate industry could be persuaded to adopt an effective fair-housing code and therefore he would now support state legislation "to eliminate the evil of discrimination in housing." Later, when it was also clear that the state would not act, Percy backed a Federal open-occupancy law, thus essentially taking the same position as Senator Douglas.

It was fair play in politics for Percy's opponents to chide him for switching positions. A University of Illinois coed picketed him with a sign reading, "Where will you stand tomorrow, Mr. Percy?" Paul Douglas felt that Percy was the first public figure "to raise vacillation to the level of moral principle." Those with less style, such as a Douglas hatchet man named Richard C. Wade, simply said that Percy "is a man of convenience whose views on important issues are governed by political calculation rather than by personal commitment." Percy was very sensitive to any charge that he was not completely sincere on civil rights. When a young man asked him about housing discrimination in the Kenilworth suburb where he lived, the Republican candidate responded in anger. "Are you suggesting I'm a bigot?" Percy asked. "If you find any family who wants to move to Kenilworth, see me. I'll take them around and see any real estate firm or any house they want. If you are saying I'm a bigot, have the guts to say it. You implied it." (Percy had told his Jackson, Mississippi, audience earlier that "I myself live in a village of three thousand persons where there is only one Negro family; this is not a sociological accident.")

The fact is that while Percy cannot be charged fairly with courting the "backlash" vote, he unquestionably benefited from the racial agitation in Chicago and Cook County engendered by the Rev. Dr. Martin Luther King's open-housing marches in the summer of 1966.

Thomas Houser, Percy's campaign manager, said in a postelection analysis written for the Senator, "It cannot be denied that the so-called backlash vote was a factor in some selected Cook County areas, but the case is rather clearly made that the backlash vote was not the major factor by any stretch of the imagination." More important, in Houser's view and that of many neutral observers, were such issues as inflation, Vietnam, the "credibility gap," imbalance of party strength in Washington and the difference in age between the two candidates. Percy's own pre-election surveys showed a sharp rise in public opposition to open-housing legislation after King's marches, but they also showed most voters discerned no difference between Percy's and Douglas' stand on that issue.

Indeed, Percy managed to make a larger percentage gain from 1964 to 1966 in Negro wards of Chicago than he did in the city as a whole. Citywide, his percentage increased only 5 percent, but in seven predominantly Negro wards it went up slightly over 6 percent. This was due only in part to his switch of position on open housing. Percy worked hard to woo Negro votes and improve Republican organization in Negro areas; he and his friends selected and financed a Negro opponent against veteran Negro Democratic Representative William L. Dawson in Chicago's South Side ghetto and gave him rent-free use of six joint store-front headquarters. To Percy's great advantage, the size of the vote in the Negro wards fell off more heavily than it did elsewhere in the city from 1964, in part because there was no emotional issue like Goldwater to bring out the Negroes and in part because civil-rights militants decided to take out their anger with Mayor Daley on Douglas, by organizing a boycott of the polls.

When all is said and done on "backlash," however, the principal fact remains that the vote shift from 1964 to 1966 was less marked in Chicago and Cook County than in downstate Illinois, where Percy discarded the personal campaign organization approach that had proved so abrasive and went out of his way to cultivate the regular Republican committees. He carried 93 counties in 1966, compared to 59 in 1964. Even Phyllis Schlafly, the ultraconservative G.O.P. women's leader from Alton, Illinois, worked for the whole state ticket.

While Douglas attacked him for being ambiguous and all things to all people—"like trying to locate a moving target covered in fog"— in fact, the Republican candidate developed some positions with considerable appeal, among them a plan for preschool education, the National Home Ownership Foundation plan, and a proposal for an All-Asian Peace Conference. Although Dirksen made a short speech on the Senate floor to remind his colleagues that the conference idea had already been proposed by a most anonymous Senator from Iowa, Jack Miller, the proposal was so firmly linked to Percy's name that a typical newspaper headline read: JOHNSON OKs PERCY's ALL-ASIAN PARLEY PLAN. When asked in March, 1966, by a St. Louis *Post-Dispatch* reporter where he stood on Vietnam, Percy replied, "In the controversy between hawks and doves, I would say that I am an American eagle—somewhere in between." But there was no doubt where ex-Marine Paul Douglas stood and his stringent hawkishness was increasingly out of line with the views of his liberal following. Percy's peace-conference position served to underscore the widening gulf between Douglas and his natural allies.

There was another issue that Douglas could do little about—his age. He was seventy-four and Percy was forty-seven. Percy's slogan

("A Strong New Voice for Illinois") was a play on this difference, while all of Percy's advertisements and campaign literature featured a photograph of him, shirt open at the collar, looking rugged and youthful. "It seemed to have just the right combination of firmness, dynamism, and intensity," commented the advertising executive who handled the Percy account.

But the main difference between the 1964 and 1966 campaigns was Percy himself. As Howard James, the able Midwest bureau chief for the *Christian Science Monitor* wrote somewhat effusively on election night, "There is little question that Mr. Percy is a far different man from the business executive who tried and lost in 1964. Warmer, more knowledgeable, with greater feeling for the problems of the people of Illinois, white and Negro, he won because he had the people on his side. . . ." Newspaper photographs showed Percy Indian-wrestling in Franklin Park, Percy in the middle of twelve hundred costumed Lithuanians at a folk song festival, Percy joining an Assyrian chain dance. Arthur Schlesinger, Jr., bitterly commented when he flew to Chicago to try to hold the eggheads for Douglas, "He is a product of the black art of public relations." And perhaps Percy the back-slapper, Percy the handshaker, Percy the seeker of advice from county chairmen was a "synthetic character," as the historian and former Kennedy aide called him. But on the morning of September 18 there was no room for doubt that Charles Percy was anything other than a dreadfully troubled, grief-stricken father. Sometime about 5 A.M.— five hours after Percy himself had returned to his lakefront home— someone cut through a screen, slipped into the house, up the stairs past the bedroom where twin sister Sharon was sleeping, and assaulted twenty-one-year-old, honey-blonde Valerie Jeanne Percy, fractured her skull with two blows from a blunt instrument and stabbed her more than ten times. Valerie resisted and her cries and moans woke her stepmother, sleeping in the master bedroom thirty-five feet down the corridor. Loraine Percy padded down the hall to investigate and confronted the murderer, standing over Valerie's body; he blinded her with the beam of a flashlight, and escaped while Mrs. Percy ran back to the bedroom to awaken her husband and sound the burglar alarm. Sensitive, lovely Valerie Percy was dead.

The funeral was private, but the glimpses the public had of Percy through news cameras showed a man of stoic strength, his grief mingled with resignation. The campaign halted for seventeen days; Douglas had immediately wired Percy his sympathy and his pledge that he would not resume campaigning until Percy did. And in those seventeen days, while the unsolved murder dominated the headlines, Illinois voters had time and reason to think again about the two men, Douglas and Percy, whom fate had cast in this strange contest. Earlier in 1966, John Dreiske, political editor of the Chicago *Sun-Times,* had described Percy as he was seen by Republicans across the state. "When you see him standing there," wrote the veteran newsman, "he seems so self-sufficient it is quite obvious he doesn't need you."

That picture disappeared with Valerie's murder. There is no such thing as a self-sufficient father looking down at the battered body of his first-born. Poll takers in Illinois found little evidence of a sympathy vote. But one had to be less than human not to feel a cold shiver and the start of tears when Percy, resuming the campaign with a bodyguard at his side, introduced his family from the back platform of a train, at his first whistle stop, Joliet, and said, "I want you to meet my wife, Loraine, my daughters Sharon and Val . . ."

He won by 422,302 votes—55 percent. It was an important victory because the candidate was already a national figure, because he had beaten a powerful and widely-admired incumbent, because he would represent a major industrial state, because he had that elusive quality that makes reporters add the supportive clause to his name—Charles H. Percy, "a potential presidential candidate."

On election day, 1966, while waiting for the returns to come in, a Percy aide began to think ahead. In a memo to his boss—"Subject: Senate Committee Assignment"—he told the soon-to-be-elected candidate:

> As a Senator-elect, there is one quality you *must* refine to perfection: HUMILITY. No matter what you were or may be, as a newly elected Senator you are a wretched worm. The Senate absolutely delights in destroying big-shot, small state governors and red-hot businessmen-politicians. The rules for success are these:
> 1. HUMILITY
> 2. DO YOUR HOMEWORK IN COMMITTEE
> 3. LISTEN, DON'T TALK
> 4. SHOW GREAT DEFERENCE TO YOUR INCUMBENT COLLEAGUES
> 5. DISCLAIM ALL EXPERTISE
> 6. HUMILITY

It was sound advice—if one's ambition was a long career of Senate preferment. But on November 22 Percy flew to Washington for his

first meeting with the capital's press corps, and the next day's headlines around the country proclaimed: A PRESIDENTIAL DARK HORSE
TALKS (Baltimore *Sun*), PERCY DISAVOWS PRESIDENTIAL AMBITION,
BUT—(New York *Times*). It was not really what the newcomer
said; rather it was the mood, the feel, that the reporters brought away
from the session.

Over the next months Percy complained that the newsmen had
him all wrong; he was "just a fellow trying to be a good Senator." Yet
he lengthened his national speaking schedule, and of his first nineteen
speeches away from the capital only eight were in his home state.
When a junior Senator from Massachusetts, John F. Kennedy, started
to appear with some frequency around the country in 1957, another
Senator remarked, "When you see a Senator doing much speaking
outside his own state, it means one of two things. He needs the money
or he's got his eye on higher office. And Jack doesn't need the money."
The same could be said of Percy.

Before the Women's National Press Club annual dinner on January
12, 1967, Percy told his standard joke about the time his campaign
manager in 1964 went on TV to counter the charge that the Republican candidate only wished to use the Governor's Mansion as
a stepping-stone to the White House. "I've known Chuck Percy all
his political life," said attorney Tom Houser, "and I can tell you that
the only job he wants is to be Governor of the United States." It was
a good story because it was so plausible. But some found the sweet
smell of ambition a bit overpowering, as Boston *Globe* reporters
Martin Nolan and James Doyle indicated when, after reviewing
Percy's first days in office, they wrote that his "candid display of self-
promotion was remarkable." And Charles Nicodemus of the Chicago
Daily News's Washington bureau interviewed one Senator (not named,
but described as "a veteran, widely respected political craftsman"),
who was "irritated in the extreme by what he considered to be Percy's
proclivity for showboating."

If Percy did not listen very carefully to his aide's election day advice
on how to get along as a Senator, there was another bit of information
in the same memo that he took very much to heart. Wrote the assistant, who knew his way around Capitol Hill: "Obtaining choice
[Senate committee] assignments is not a matter of chance. You will
have to lobby aggressively with Republican Senate leaders to get the
seat you want. If you do not, you will find yourself on District of

Columbia, Aeronautical and Space Sciences, and maybe the Joint Committee on the Navajo-Hopi Indian Administration. Your first resource is, of course, Senator Dirksen. . . ."

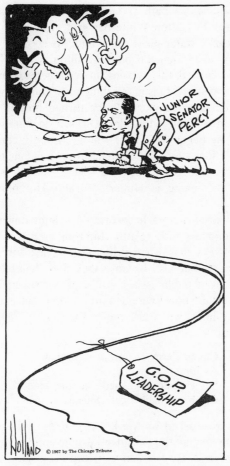

Holland, Chicago **Tribune,** Feb. 5,
1967, © 1967, The Chicago **Tribune**

Dirksen did help Percy get the assignment he wanted, on the Banking and Currency Committee, which has jurisdiction over his pet project, the Home Ownership Foundation. (He also got, as his assistant had warned, Aeronautical and Space Sciences.) But the care and cultivation of Everett McKinley Dirksen goes well beyond the question of choice committee posts. As the senior Senator from Illinois, as well as the Senate G.O.P. leader, Dirksen is in a strategic position not only to smooth the way for his junior colleague, but, perhaps more important, to block his path should he feel the whim. As veteran political manager F. Clifton White has said, "If I were Chuck Percy, I'd watch Dirksen's water glass every day. As soon as the level went down a quarter of an inch, I'd be there filling it up." In at least one case Percy has carried this wooing to a rather extravagant length. Speaking to 2,200 sports fans at Washington's Touchdown Club, when Dirksen was the honored guest, Percy turned himself into a cheerleader doing an Everett McKinley Dirksen locomotive. "E is for Effectiveness," he began. "V is for Valor." Twenty cards later, when he reached the final "N," the audience was howling to get on with the game. (Percy was followed by the Vice President, who announced with a grin, "My name is Hubert Horatio Humphrey—H is for HELP!")

The two Illinois Senators have opened a joint downstate office in Centralia. Nonetheless, their relationship is inherently sticky—not only because it is always thus when prima donnas are forced to perform in close proximity, but also because they find themselves frequently on opposing sides of public issues. An actor portraying Dirksen at the 1967 Gridiron Club show expressed an opinion that many believe the Senator secretly holds when he sang to the tune of "My Bonnie Lies Over the Ocean":

> Chuck Percy is only a freshman,
> As junior as junior can be.
> So why does he act like the leader?
> Oh, bring back Paul Douglas to me.

When Percy was asked in April, 1967, if he had any plans to be Illinois' favorite son at the presidential convention, he replied, "As far as I'm concerned, Ev Dirksen is favorite son. He's up for re-election [in 1968] and if this will help him I'm all for it." This was a gallant gesture, but it is far from certain how much, other than his own vote, Percy will control in the Illinois delegation. All but ten of the fifty-eight delegates are chosen in their congressional districts; contests are possible in the June 11 primary, but normally the selection of district delegates is arranged by the local Republican powers. The ten at-large delegate places are reserved for prominent officeholders and state party officials, including Dirksen and Percy, but the dominant influence on the delegation is usually the Governor or candidate for Governor.

In 1967, four men were under discussion as Republican candidates for Governor. The first name on almost every list was John Henry Altorfer, a wealthy Peoria businessman who was Percy's running mate for lieutenant governor in 1964. Altorfer is more conservative than Percy but the two men have no insuperable differences. A second man regarded as an almost-certain contender is Richard B. Ogilvie, former sheriff and now president of the patronage-rich Cook County Board of Commissioners. Ogilvie, too, has had his differences with Percy, but most were patched up before 1966. The two other possibilities—Illinois House Speaker Ralph Smith of Alton and state Senate President Pro Tempore W. Russell Arrington—are not regarded as Percy partisans.

In 1967, most observers assumed that Nixon would have the bulk of the Illinois delegation unless Dirksen and the gubernatorial nominee decided jointly it was in their interest to line up the delegation behind Percy. Thus the progressives' backup candidate for President, unlike Ronald Reagan, his right-wing counterpart, cannot automatically assume he will go into the 1968 convention in control of a sizable bloc of votes from his own state.

Nor, however, can those who are watching his moves with interest and some apprehension—like George Romney—assume that he will not. Percy has built up a considerable organization in the state, and Dirksen, facing a re-election campaign in 1968 against the possible opposition of a "name" Democrat like state Treasurer Adlai Stevenson III or poverty director Sargent Shriver, might decide it would be helpful to have Percy on top of the ticket for President or Vice President. Indeed, if Percy can light enough fires elsewhere, he can almost compel his own state G.O.P. to support him, just as his alliances in Washington compelled Illinois Republicans in 1960 to name him their representative on the platform committee.

While it is conceivable for a freshman Senator to seek the presidential nomination actively—Robert Taft did it in 1940—the odds against it are very long. Any calculus of the odds against Percy would have to take into account at least some of these assets:

Glamour and Youth. At forty-eight, Percy is the youngest of the four Republican presidential prospects—and looks even younger than he is. He has a pretty wife, whose breathless voice and wide-eyed wonderment at the strange ways of politics are not unlike those of Jackie Kennedy. Percy also has the Kennedy flair for providing the sort of *happening* that mass-circulation magazines dote on. When Sharon Percy, Valerie's twin, picked a husband, he turned out to be handsome John D. Rockefeller IV, who went from the Peace Corps to a poverty program job in West Virginia (the perfect career line for a "tuned-in" younger-generation doer), and then got himself elected to the West Virginia legislature as a Democrat. When Sharon and Jay were married in Rockefeller Chapel on the University of Chicago campus in the spring of 1967, the guest list was a who's who of American politics and society—and the whole event was recorded in living color on page after page of *Life*.

Percy plays the Kennedy-generation identification quite consciously, by way of unspoken contrast to his older Republican rivals and President Johnson. His speech to the City Club of Chicago in October, 1966, bore a startling resemblance in rhythm, in rhetoric, and even in phraseology to John Kennedy's speech in Granite City, Illinois, in the 1960 campaign.

Said Kennedy (1960):

I run for the office of the Presidency with full recognition of the tremendous responsibilities which the U.S. Constitution and events gives the President of the United States. . . . I think one of the chief tasks of the next President of the United States is to set before the American people the things we must do in order to protect ourselves, in order to maintain our freedom, and in order to meet our commitments to freedom around the world. I am not satisfied as an American to be second in space. . . . I am not satisfied with the drift of events today. I am not satisfied to be reading every day that Khrushchev and Castro and the Chinese are on the upward march. I want to read that the United States is once again asserting its leadership as a great and free country, which offers a ray of hope to all those who wish to follow the example.

Said Percy (1966):

I run for the Senate because I believe fresh voices are needed in Washington. I run because I believe the next decade will require vigorous and effective leadership in Congress. And I run because I am not satisfied with things as they are. I am not satisfied when little children are bitten by rats in the slums of Chicago and East St. Louis. I am not satisfied when the war in Vietnam drags on without discernible progress. I am not satisfied when our children's schools are overcrowded and understaffed. I am not satisfied when the dream of equal opportunity for all Americans is yet unfulfilled. . . .

Said Kennedy (1960):

I can assure you that if I am successful in this campaign, I do not run saying life will be easy, because I think the difficulties of the sixties will press upon us. . . .

Said Percy (1966):

My friends, the next decade will not always be easy. There will be tough trying questions to be answered by this nation. . . .

Said Kennedy (1960):

We can take action to provide aid to education. We can take action to provide medical care for our older citizens. We can take action to try to stimulate the American economy. . . .

Said Percy (1966):

I stand for the establishment of universal preschool education for all children beginning at age four. . . . I stand for broad improvement of elementary and secondary education. . . . We can extend the nuclear test ban treaty. . . . We can cooperate more fully with the United Nations. . . .

After his election in 1966, Percy borrowed—again without acknowledgment—from Robert Kennedy. In early 1967, he delivered a stream of very funny anti-Bobby jokes to a Republican audience in Hastings, Nebraska. What Percy failed to tell the Cornhuskers was that they were the jokes he had heard Kennedy tell on himself at the Gridiron Dinner in Washington the week before.

Republicans might overlook such imitation by noting that since Robert Kennedy himself had ruled out running against Lyndon Johnson in 1968, a whole anti-Johnson generation might be lured to vote for a crypto-Kennedy Republican named Percy. In May, 1967, Percy visited the Berkeley campus of the University of California and told the students at that symbol of youthful dissent: "Some of us hear you, and we do not dismiss the questions you raise. In the midst of war and injustice and poverty, our consciences do not sleep."

Brains, Ability and Salesmanship. The one charge that has never been made against Percy is stupidity. Nobody cracks about him, as they do about Romney, that "Down deep, he's shallow," or, as they do about Reagan, that "behind that glittering façade there is—a glittering façade." His mind may be almost as facile as Nixon's, and, like Nixon, Percy does his homework. He scurries after new ideas with the persistence of a squirrel. Between his campaigns for Governor and Senator, he resumed his private political-science seminars—this time inviting mixed groups of two dozen academics, journalists and politicians to meet with him for two and a half days of intensive discussion of liberalism, conservatism, urban problems, reapportionment, civil rights and other weighty topics, in a windowless conference room at the University of Chicago's Center for Continuing Education.

But his skill goes beyond just research in the realm of ideas. As a former manufacturer of consumer goods, Percy brings to politics a healthy respect for "product development." One man who has worked closely with him for the past few years says, "Basically, he is a merchandising man. He thinks in terms of a mix of activities—research, engineering, advertising, promotion and sales." And when Percy latches onto an idea—like the All-Asian Peace Conference or the Home Ownership Foundation—he does not rest until it has been sold to the widest possible audience, and always with the Percy label plainly in view.

Television Presence. Percy, like Reagan, appears to be a man born for the television era. No ugly beard shadows, no squinty, close-together eyes. No endless sentences, either, but crisp, almost always grammatical phrases, not flashy but clear; and always delivered with a look of total sincerity. The voice is almost too professional, deep, devoid of regional accent, with a way of talking without seeming to need to breathe. (Percy was a public-speaking champion in high school; not a debater like Nixon or a missionary like Romney.) The small stature that surprises and disconcerts some people on first meeting—Percy is five feet, eight inches tall, the shortest of the four presidential prospects—is not apparent on television. There Percy looks cool, muscular and virile.

Staff and Mentors. Though untested in national politics, the Percy staff is young and capable—bigger than most and better paid because Percy puts his entire government salary into supplemental staff payrolls. Thomas Houser, thirty-eight-year-old former counsel for the Burlington Railroad and personal campaign manager in both

1964 and 1966, is running Percy's Chicago office and quarterbacking his early political excursions into other states. Houser's main responsibility in 1967 was to secure Percy's home base for any national plans that might develop. Allen J. Marrinson, thirty-six, like Houser a Northwestern University law graduate, former Assistant District Attorney in Cook County, later vice president of the American National Bank and Trust Company of Chicago, came to Washington with Percy as administrative assistant and office manager. Top man on the foreign-policy side in the Washington office is dapper forty-two-year-old Scott Cohen, former newspaperman and fourteen-year veteran of the Central Intelligence Agency, who has been with Percy since 1964, dividing his time between research and press relations. Martin R. Hoffman, formerly Republican counsel to the House Judiciary Committee, was hired by Percy as his legal counsel and domestic legislation specialist after the election. Mrs. Carol M. Khosrovi, a veteran of several congressional offices, including that of Representative Robert Taft, Jr., is his legislative assistant. Lanky, well-connected Calvin Fentress, III, a *Newsweek* alumnus in his late twenties, is speechwriter and part-time press aide.

A man with great influence on Percy is Robert A. Goldwin, the research director of his first campaign. Goldwin spent the past year in England doing research on John Locke and was scheduled to resume teaching in the autumn of 1967 as associate professor of political science at Kenyon College.

From the days of the 1959 Percy committee report, the young Senator has had a close relationship with Senator Thruston B. Morton of Kentucky, as wise in the ways of the Senate and of the Republican party as anyone alive. Morton has taken such a special interest in Percy's Senate career that there has been steady speculation that he sees him as his favorite for the 1968 nomination. A member of Morton's staff, Duff Reed, a veteran Washington publicist, has worked almost full time ballyhooing Percy's legislative projects and political prospects from the day he entered the Senate.

In the House of Representatives, one of Percy's closest allies is Robert Taft, Jr., of Ohio, who shares with him the experience of a costly defeat in 1964 and a political comeback in 1966. Percy's best friend in the House is probably his home-district Congressman from Illinois, Representative Donald Rumsfeld, a crew-cut thirty-five-year-old, who came out of Princeton and the Navy air arm to work as a staff member for two young Congressmen, one of them Representative (now Senator) Robert P. Griffin of Michigan. In 1962, Rumsfeld beat the Republican organization choice for a vacant House seat. In less than three terms, he has made a reputation as a party spokesman on space matters and as a chief sponsor of the freedom of information bill. Another Illinois Congressman, forty-six-year-old downstate publisher Paul Findley, is also an eager promoter of Percy's ambitions. Findley, a House member since 1961, is a classic Illinois conservative on domestic issues, with a 90 percent ACA rating. But his views on foreign policy would make the old Chicago *Tribune* wince. Besides displaying considerable independence in the area of U.S.-European relations, he also has advocated immediate diplomatic relations with Communist China. Findley would like very much to move up to the Senate—a goal that is blocked as long as Dirksen and Percy occupy Illinois' seats.

Percy's 1966 finance chairman was A. C. Nielsen, Jr., son of the founder and president of the giant market research corporation that provides television's life-and-death ratings. Finance chairman in 1964 and a vice chairman in 1966 was Robert Galvin, head of Motorola, a conservative Republican and board member of Barry Goldwater's Free Society Association.*

Issues. Percy, like Nixon, is inherently a centrist; his tendency is to shun the extreme. But the homing instinct competes in him with a flair for dramatic improvisation that is also part of Percy's concept of "dynamic" leadership. In juxtaposition, the two tendencies give Percy a unique and probably advantageous identification in the field of 1968 presidential prospects. His eagerness for innovation in dealing with specific problems pleases progressive Republicans; his instinct for the middle of the road reassures conservatives.

The same talents, however, leave Percy open to charges of "showboating" some of his stands and, conversely, of "trimming" others. Both accusations followed him from the business world into the Senate.

---

* The Percy-Galvin friendship survived intact a bitter controversy between Galvin's company and the Illinois FEPC, which Percy helped lobby through the legislature and whose first head, Charles Gray, had been a Bell & Howell executive. The FEPC accused Motorola of administering examinations to prospective employees in a discriminatory manner, a charge which the company hotly denied. Percy backed Gray, but the dispute did not appear to damage his long friendship with Galvin.

As president of a camera company that faced serious competition from German and Japanese imports, Percy nonetheless took a strong stand for a freer U.S. trade policy. The plaudits this position won for him from government officials were marred by the complaint from some quarters that Percy was everlastingly pointing out what a noble stance he was taking.

Something similar happened during the Senate debate in 1967 on the consular treaty with Russia. When Morton took the lead in challenging Dirksen's initial opposition to the treaty, Percy promptly supported the Kentuckian, and made several effective speeches urging ratification. But while sixty-six Senators (including Dirksen) ultimately voted for the treaty, only Percy found it necessary to tell television viewers, "I've had 7,400 letters against the consular treaty ratification and forty-six in favor of it, and yet I'm going to vote in favor of it because it is in the best interest of the United States of America. . . ." (A member of Percy's staff estimated that 70 to 80 percent of the opposition mail was mimeographed form letters from a few sources, the largest being the toothless Liberty Lobby, an ultra-rightist group.)

While Percy was accused of "grandstanding" on the consular treaty vote, others criticized him for failing to come down hard on other issues. On the question of cloture in the Senate, Percy voted twice with the conservatives (and Dirksen) to block a liberal-backed move for a direct vote on a change in Senate rules to make it easier to cut off a filibuster, then turned around and voted with the liberals (and against Dirksen) on a later, but also unsuccessful, effort to bring the question to a test.

One former Percy staff member, who is not completely enamored of him, thinks the Senator gives a "wishy-washy impression" on some questions because of his "utter reasonableness. . . . He is unable to take a firm, unequivocal stand, because he sees all sides."

How much calculation entered into such compromises is impossible to say, but Percy made an interesting comment to United Press International in March, 1967. Discussing anyone's problems in winning the 1968 presidential nomination, he said that "if you isolate or polarize yourself too much with a particularly ideological point of view, I think it will be more difficult to break through."

In view of his position as a lively dark-horse possibility for that nomination, fellow Republicans watched with fascination as Percy developed his position on the key issue of Vietnam.

When the five freshman Republican Senators appeared together on *Meet the Press* in January, 1967, each was asked whether he favored cessation or continuation of the U.S. bombing of North Vietnam. Mark Hatfield and Edward Brooke favored cessation.* Howard Baker and Clifford Hansen favored continuation. Percy said, "I would like to see it stopped if we get something back for it . . . ," which provoked an observer to comment, "That makes the score 2½ to 2½."

As 1967 wore on, Percy flirted more and more openly with the "dove-ish" minority of his party, represented by Hatfield, Senator George Aiken of Vermont and Senator John Sherman Cooper of Kentucky. With Nixon and Reagan firmly identified as "hawks," Percy waited until Romney gave general support to the Johnson Administration's conduct of the war, then moved to occupy the largely vacant ground of restrained "dove-ish" dissent. The same April night that Romney told a Hartford audience that American withdrawal from Vietnam would be "unthinkable," Percy told a Concord, New Hampshire, press conference, "anything is thinkable," but added that a unilateral, precipitate American pullout would be "incomprehensible."

Later in April he called for a limitation in American bombing of North Vietnam, declaring that "escalation has hardened the determination of the enemy to resist . . . and alienated world opinion" without achieving the promised military results. In a joint statement with Senator Jacob K. Javits of New York and Senator Hugh Scott of Pennsylvania, he called for "more vigorous" efforts to achieve a negotiated settlement and warned against military actions that risked bringing Communist China into the conflict. On his own, he proposed as part of the "peace offensive," that "the Viet Cong be assured of participation in South Vietnamese political life as a legal political party competing peacefully at the polls and shunning violence."

Percy's position in the spring of 1967 was not in the middle of the Republican road; the majority view was unquestionably that of Dirksen and Ford, who kept reiterating their "four-square and wholehearted" support of the Commander in Chief, the generals and the troops in Vietnam. His "dove-ish" statements drew an open rebuke from Barry Goldwater, previously a Percy booster. But there were many Republicans who believed that as election day drew closer the party would be driven by the force of public opinion to present itself and its policy as an alternative to, not an echo of, Johnson's conduct

* Brooke later changed his position after a trip to Vietnam. See p. 305

of the war. In that case, Percy may well have staked out ground for as broad-based a Republican position on Vietnam for 1968 as his All-Asian Peace Conference proposal proved to be for 1966. That plan, calling for a convocation of Communist and non-Communist Asian nations to work out a Vietnam settlement, appealed to Republican "doves" because it aimed at peace and reflected their view that the Vietnam war had been over-Americanized. It also appealed to Republican "hawks" because it gave them a way of being for "peace," through a rather remote device, without requiring them to stop urging an intensification of the war. Like his Home Ownership Foundation bill, it became something on which every Republican could hang his hat.

One problem with such successes is that they strike some people as being just a little too clever. "Chuck's problem," one friend says, "is that he wants to be liked by everybody." Another strong Percy booster says that "in the business world Percy came from, a perfect product is what you aimed for; in politics, perfection is not the ideal, and Chuck hasn't learned to settle for being something less than perfect." A side effect of the constant polishing and shaping of Percy's positions is the charge that he is shifting his stand. For one who does not welcome the suggestion that he is a smooth-shaved version of Nixon, the number of stories already written about "the *new* Chuck Percy" is an ominous warning.

Taken together, the penchant for pleasing all factions and the talent for self-promotion—which are two of Percy's major political assets—add up in the eyes of his critics to the rather unpleasant word that George Romney applied to him: "opportunist." The specifics of Romney's charge—that Percy failed to support him in his fight for platform changes at the 1964 convention—were in part inaccurate and in part unjust. But the general description was not so far off target that Percy could afford to ignore it. "Shocked" and "hurt" though he said he was by the incident, the more lasting damage from Percy's point of view would come if the label stuck.*

Another and more pressing problem for Percy in 1967 was the choice of political strategy for the 1968 nomination contest. As 1967 began, Romney was the front runner in the polls, committed by his position to a flat-out, headlong assault on the nomination, taking the

---

* For a discussion of the "opportunist" incident's effect on Romney, see pp. 101-02.

presidential primary route. Nixon was lagging slightly in the polls, but was ahead in the preference of organization men; his position dictated concentrating on the delegate roundup and, hopefully, tripping up Romney in one or more primaries. Reagan was the dark horse, an untested quality, who might, as Barry Goldwater said, be nominated "if after five or six ballots, he seemed to be the only one left."

But Percy had some options, and, as the calendar drew toward the inevitable day of reckoning, he faced three alternative courses. He could be:

1. The Fall-back Candidate of the Liberal Republicans. As Cook County Republican chairman Timothy Sheehan put it, "We all know that the East Coast Establishment is bankrupt for a presidential candidate. They have hooked their star [*sic*] to Romney of Michigan, who may rise or fall in time. In Chuck Percy we have a man who would make an excellent candidate for President, if the convention becomes deadlocked or if the party leaders agree on him. He is acceptable to the people and even to the Eastern Establishment."

Actually, the so-called Eastern Establishment made Romney its candidate with a minimum of enthusiasm. As one prominent financier told a Wall Street luncheon meeting in December, 1966, "The difference between George Romney and us is that he prays before he makes a decision; we pray after." Percy's ties with the Establishment are older and more intimate than Romney's. Even before he became an in-law of the Rockefellers, he was a member of the board of David Rockefeller's Chase Manhattan Bank and a member of the 1956 Rockefeller Brothers public policy panel. He "belonged" to the traditional base of liberal Republicanism in a sense that Romney never would.

The problem with the fall-back-candidate strategy was that Romney was already occupying the ground Percy would have to seize, and showing no sign of relinquishing it. Romney might stumble, but even if he did there was no certainty that he would remove himself from the race and help Percy. Meantime, those, like Nelson Rockefeller and William Scranton, who could have triggered a massive shift of liberal support from Romney to Percy, were conspicuously refusing to do so. In the spring of 1967, their constant refrain to other liberals was: unite behind Romney or you will lose control of the nomination. In a switch from Romney to Percy, they said, enough time, votes and momentum would be lost to allow Nixon to seize the prize.

Personally, Percy made it plain he would have no reluctance to battle Romney for leadership of the liberal Republican cause. Even before the "opportunist" incident gave him all the excuse he would ever need for disliking the Michigan Governor, Percy was visibly

'-AND NOW I'D LIKE TO INTRODUCE MY GOOD FRIEND, THE WELL-KNOWN OPPORTUNIST, CHARLES PERCY!'

Crockett, Washington *Star*, March 2, 1967

needling Romney. Before Romney left on his Western tour in February, 1967, Percy publicly second-guessed him, telling a group of reporters, "I frankly thought that this Western trip was scheduled too early. Now he has got to come back with a success."

The next month, in a television interview, Percy adroitly fielded several foreign-policy questions and then was asked if he thought Romney should be more specific about Vietnam. Instead of saying, as would most politicians, that it was not his function to offer advice to others, Percy replied: "Well, I think that Governor Romney should not speak out on Vietnam until he has all the facts, and it would be irresponsible for him to take a position until he has those facts." As Thomas J. Foley of the Los Angeles *Times* noted, "The inference that any but the casual listener could draw was clear: Percy has the facts and Romney doesn't."

But the problem for Percy was that as long as Rockefeller, Scranton and other leaders of the liberal wing stuck with Romney, his tactics left him open to the charge that he was a "spoiler." The fall-back-candidate strategy, in short, while possibly a workable one in the end, ran serious risks of antagonizing those in the party who were his natural allies.

2. The Compromise Candidate. A second possibility was to be, not second choice for one wing of the party, but final choice for both wings. In the spring of 1967, a coincidence of two events made this strategy look very appealing.

On March 22, Governor Tom McCall of Oregon, a newcomer to the liberal ranks, wrote a round-robin letter to his fellow Republican Governors urging them to withhold endorsement of any presidential possibility until they could act in concert. For himself, McCall said, "as of today," he would be inclined to favor Percy over Romney, whose Vietnam position he described as "vague."

The same day McCall made public his letter, the *Saturday Evening Post* published an interview with Barry Goldwater, in which the 1964 nominee—nominally committed to Nixon for 1968—said some rather remarkable things. Nixon, his supposed favorite, "will have the most delegates, but probably not enough for a majority. . . . The trouble is everybody says Nixon is the best trained man for President, and then everybody turns right around and says he can't be elected. I don't believe that's true, but I don't see how to tear that image down." As for Percy, Goldwater said, "He's one of the smartest men who ever came to the Senate . . . and he's a fine, decent, attractive guy, too. He might be the most dangerous against Johnson, provided he could show he was really knowledgeable about foreign policy. Maybe more dangerous than a guy who had been around the woodpile too long."

Simultaneous testimonials from the conservative 1964 nominee and a liberal Governor who refused to support the national ticket in 1964 were enough to set anyone thinking. Conceivably, a moderate who went down with the G.O.P. ship in 1964 rather than jump overboard for safety might yet reap a reward for his action.

The problem with the compromise-candidate strategy was that some conventions—as Stuart Symington learned in 1960 and Richard Nixon in 1964—never get beyond the first ballot. For Percy to do all in his power to promote a deadlock and wait for Nixon and Romney to kill each other off was tempting, but it was no guarantee of success.

3. The Man of Tomorrow. The third possibility was to skip 1968 and adopt a strategy most likely to succeed in 1972 and 1976. At forty-eight, nearly six years younger than Nixon, eight years younger than Reagan and twelve years younger than Romney, Percy could well afford to decide that 1968 was not his year. Or he could position himself to be the vice-presidential nominee, as Kennedy tried to do in 1956, knowing that if the ticket lost he would be the logical contender for the top job in 1972, and that if the ticket won he would still be young enough to run for President even after eight years in the number-two job.

As a vice-presidential prospect, Percy has obvious appeal to both Nixon and Reagan. One top Nixon strategist said in the spring of 1967, "If Dick wins, I think he's *got* to have Percy with him." Conversely, Percy himself suggested to a group of Washington reporters early in 1967 that Nixon would be a good *vice-presidential* nominee to lend weight to a ticket with a more glamorous top man; moreover, Percy told them, he was sure Nixon would run again for his old job. The Nixon-Percy relationship is an amicable one, considering that neither man particularly seeks intimacy with fellow politicians. Percy considers Nixon "a tremendous party worker" who might have "an easier time" than Romney getting nominated, but who does not have Romney's appeal to Democrats because "Nixon has been on the firing line and has made enemies."

A combination of Romney and Percy is less logical in terms of geography and ideology, but not impossible, if Percy should turn out to be the man who controls the votes that could make Romney the nominee.

Characteristically, Percy's solution to the problem of choosing a strategy for 1968 was to follow all three paths at once. He solidified his position as the fall-back candidate of the liberal wing by championing the cause of expanded East-West trade, by advocating a variety of approaches to a peace settlement in Vietnam, and by attempting to identify himself as the party's urban expert in the Senate.

At the same time, he heightened his hopes for being the compromise choice by careful courtship of conservatives—raising money for New Hampshire Senator Norris Cotton's re-election campaign, for example, or telling a Nebraska Republican audience that "I haven't always voted with Carl Curtis and Roman Hruska [the state's conservative Republican Senators] but I've always marveled at how well they do their homework and research, and I've learned a lot by listening to them."

Percy made no overt move to launch a candidacy for 1968, and, indeed, denied whenever asked that he had any intention of doing anything but being "the very best Senator I can be." But he also kept the door wide open for a last-minute dash into the race.

Visiting New Hampshire eleven months ahead of its first-in-the-nation presidential primary, Percy was asked what he would do if his backers entered his name there. "If it were next week," he said, "I would withdraw. But since it is a year off, I see no reason to commit myself. I don't want to remove any options now when I don't have to."

In 1962, Percy met with a presidential assistant at the White House in connection with his support of the reciprocal trade bill. When President Kennedy heard that the Chicago industrialist was in the building he asked him to drop by his office. It was lunchtime and as Percy arrived outside the presidential office the Joint Chiefs of Staff were just leaving. He expected to engage in two or three minutes of pleasantries, but instead found himself answering a barrage of presidential questions about the future of technology, the development of the electronic industry, automation and its effect on manpower and job skills. After forty minutes, Percy rose to leave for the third time, saying that he felt he had taken too much of the President's time. Kennedy walked his visitor to the door, put his hand on Percy's shoulder, and said, "One last question. What are your political intentions?" Percy replied that he did not know. "One of the exciting things about the future, Mr. President, is that none of us can really prescribe what will happen to our lives." Percy said he had a deep interest in politics and in public life, but he was not sure he would follow the elective route.

John F. Kennedy must not have been satisfied with the answer to his final question. For sometime later, as he and Senator Dirksen strolled in the White House Rose Garden, Kennedy suddenly asked, "What's Chuck Percy up to?"

The usually loquacious Republican leader, by way of reply, simply pointed a finger at the open French doors that led into the oval office of the President of the United States.

8 RONALD REAGAN:

The Man of Parts

THE National Press Club in Washington prides itself on being one of the toughest audiences in the country. Though the membership includes probably two or three lawyers, lobbyists and public-relations men for every working reporter, the denizens of the thirteenth-floor redoubt atop the capital's tallest office building flatter themselves with the belief that nobody can fool them. Through the years, the great names of the world—Presidents and princes, financiers and frauds—have come when bid to its rostrum, and each in turn has been carefully measured and scored a success or failure.

On June 16, 1966, the club's ballroom was packed to its white walls, the tiny balcony bulging with overflow spectators, for the first Press Club appearance of Ronald Reagan. A week earlier, Reagan had won a surprisingly easy primary election victory to become the Republican candidate for Governor of California. But the aging ex-film actor and host of television's *Death Valley Days* had never held public office. The notion of him as chief executive of the nation's most populous state was risible. When Jack Warner was asked his opinion, he supposedly said, "No, Jimmy Stewart for Governor—Ronnie for Best Friend." And the six hundred Press Club members were as skeptical as Warner about this latest product of California's Pop Culture.

Standing tall and relaxed just two blocks from the White House, Reagan set forth the blueprint of a "Creative Society" that he described unblushingly as a "constructive alternative" to President Johnson's Great Society. The Great Society costs Americans "an ounce of personal freedom for every ounce of Federal help we get," Reagan said. The Creative Society he has envisaged for California would "discover, enlist and mobilize the incredibly rich human resources of . . . the best [men and women] in every field . . . coordinating the creative energies of the people for the good of the whole." The concept may have been murky but the rhetoric rang, and the hard-boiled Press Clubbers found themselves applauding like schoolboys. By the time the question period was reached, it seemed entirely natural for Reagan to be asked if he was "interested in taking on LBJ in '68." Flashing his boyish grin, he replied: "Gosh, it's taken me all my life to get up the nerve to do what I'm doing. . . . That's as far as my dreams go." Leaving the luncheon, the reporter who had asked the question turned to a companion and inquired, "What do you think?" His friend said: "I think the answer is yes."

Fifty-three weeks later, on June 23, 1967, that tentative yes had become far more affirmative. Ronald Reagan, six months in office as Governor of the nation's largest state and daily applying his Creative Society precepts to the management of its affairs, came to Nebraska for a two-day tour of that vital presidential primary battleground. His first stop was the closing banquet of the biennial convention of the national Young Republican convention—the same forum where Barry Goldwater really launched his campaign for the 1964 presidential nomination in the summer of 1963. For three days before his arrival, youthful Reagan partisans—their activities supervised by an aide to Thomas Reed, Reagan's unofficial "liaison man" with national politics—had been plastering hotel lobbies and auditorium walls with "Reagan in '68" banners. And that Friday night, when Reagan finally arrived, the 1,500 delegates and guests shouted themselves hoarse: "We want Reagan! We want Reagan!"

"I am," said the Governor, surveying the enthusiastic delegates, "deeply honored and flattered. . . ." No longer nervous and no longer limiting his dreams to the borders of California, Ronald Reagan said, "It is our destiny—the destiny of our party—to offer a banner for the people of all parties to follow."

Americans have always had a sneaking weakness for electing celebrities to public office. They sent to Congress John Morrissey, heavyweight boxing champion of the world, and Daniel E. Sickles, who murdered his wife's lover. The composer of "You Are My Sunshine" was made Governor of Louisiana and the composer of "Mexicali Rose" went to the California state Senate. The skipper of the first atomic submarine sits in the U.S. House of Representatives and astronaut John Glenn, had he not withdrawn from the race because of poor health, probably now would be in the U.S. Senate.

Ten generals have been Presidents. Other public officials have been hereditary celebrities, heirs to great political or financial estates. Three of the last four elected Governors of New York counted their inheritance in millions; at least two members of the present United States Senate owe their initial election to distinguished relations.

Yet thespians, professionals who have more in common with elected officials than have boxers, composers, astronauts, war heroes, heirs or murderers, have been singularly missing from the list of celebrity-politicians until recently. This may be because the acting profession was once considered socially *déclassé*. First Families of Virginia were shocked when George Washington's stepson wrote for the theatre. Early Greeks and Elizabethans, rather than expose their women to life on the wicked stage, had boys play the female roles. And then too, actors—from Nell Gwyn to Fatty Arbuckle—have been so disreputable!

In 1944 an actress–opera singer was elected to the U.S. House of Representatives. Twenty years later a "song-and-dance man" was elected to the U.S. Senate. But Helen Gahagan Douglas and George Murphy were long-time political activists: she had served on the Democratic National Committee; he had been Republican state chairman. Both represented California, center of the motion picture industry, and a state in which the high mobility rate leaves many voters feeling that they know the movie stars better than their neighbors. Moreover, Murphy was a very distant star who was running against a man more celebrated at that moment. For his opponent, ex-White House press secretary Pierre Salinger, belonged to a new category of the famous, the Kennedy Celebrity.

Part of the film actor's previous isolation from politics was employer-imposed. The moguls at Metro-Goldwyn-Mayer, 20th Century–Fox, and Warner Brothers believed that a star's political activities might offend potential moviegoers. So it was not until the post–World War II breakup of the rigid studio system that actors plunged into politics. In an industry noted for its fads, it soon became as fashionable to have a political party affiliation as a favorite charity.

Once in politics, the overwhelming majority proved to be liberal Democrats. The high priestess of the Democratic party in Hollywood became Mrs. Milton Berle, and among her more active campaigners were Eddie Fisher, Steve Allen, Danny Kaye, Sammy Davis, Jr., Frank Sinatra, Jimmy Durante, Anthony Franciosa and Gene Kelly. But there were also Republican stalwarts, including Irene Dunne, John Wayne, Jimmy Stewart, James Cagney, Walter Pidgeon, Mary Pickford, Lloyd Nolan, Robert Taylor and Eddie "Rochester" Anderson.

As actors became more political, politicians were becoming increasingly aware of the beauty of celebrities as candidates. Campaign costs were skyrocketing. Television, although hardly the only culprit, could devour money at the rate of $2,900 a minute in prime evening time on one New York station (exclusive of production costs). Clearly, if a candidate were "pre-packaged," a celebrity, costs might be kept down. And since TV primarily was an entertainment medium, what better celebrity than an actor? "A natural candidate," thought the liberal Catholic magazine *Commonweal,* was someone whose "old movies were still running on the late show."*

Yet many viewed such candidates as jokes. Bob Hope quipped, "With George Murphy in the Senate, if Ronald Reagan becomes governor, California will have to join Equity." College students picketed with placards reading, "Elizabeth Taylor for Superintendent of Public Instruction." The political director of the International Ladies Garment Workers Union proposed that Congress might pass an APEX, an Act for the Political Education of Actors. "X stands for those actors who sign their name with an X." Even *The Christian Century,* which bills itself an "An Ecumenical Weekly," could not resist calling Reagan "The Borax boy." Emmet John Hughes told his *Newsweek* readers, "The idea of an actor named Ronald Reagan becoming the

---

* Commenting on the assets of Murphy and Reagan as political candidates, Jessica Mitford wrote in *Ramparts,* "Above all, both are seen *night after night,* albeit twenty or thirty years younger, in revivals of their old movies on the late-late show, invariably cast in good-guy roles—*a television saturation that would cost astronomical sums were it paid for at political time rates.*" (Italics added.) Since this often-heard opinion goes unquestioned, we checked the schedules of all movies shown on television in Los Angeles, San Diego and Santa Barbara from January through July, 1965. *Murphy's films were shown only seven times; Reagan's, seventeen.* In other words, Murphy could be seen once a month and Reagan about two and a half times a month in the major Southern California market. Perhaps not insignificant exposure, but hardly "saturation."

next governor of America's largest state evokes a political vision approximately as radiant as a nomination of Rock Hudson to be the next Secretary of State."

Yet on November 8, 1966, the people of California elected Ronald Reagan, an actor, as their governor by a plurality of nearly one million votes. And as the chief executive of the nation's most populous state he became automatically a potential candidate for the office of President of the United States.

He calls it *Where's The Rest of Me?*—the question being a line from his starring role in *King's Row*—and for the first 138 pages there is no reason to suspect that it is not just another actor's (as told to . . .) autobiography. "The story begins with the closeup of a bottom. . . ." (Those really are the book's first nine words!) So now the reader should be emotionally prepared for an evening of fun at least as vulgar as *My Life with Chaplin* or *The Big Love* (Mrs. Aadland's account of her daughter Beverly's affair with Errol Flynn).

Here is all you've been waiting for. What it really feels like to kiss a silver screen siren when the director calls, "Action!" (Answer: Not much. If you do anything more than brush lips "it shoves her face out of shape.") And then I did *Juke Girl* ("a serious story about the migrant crop-pickers in Florida"). And then I did *This Is the Army* ("George Murphy played my father").

But in chapter nine something very strange happens to "The Ronald Reagan Story" (the book's subtitle), and it turns into the most schizophrenic scenario since Joanne Woodward played *The Three Faces of Eve*. Suddenly the prose changes from *Photoplay* to Ph.D. Names of stars are replaced by an array of initials that would be the envy of a Washington interoffice memo writer—IATSE, AFL, SAG, IBEW, FMPC. Actor Reagan becomes unionist Reagan, six-term president of the Screen Actors Guild (SAG). The Glamour Boy in gold-buttoned blazer emerges in a gray flannel suit as Political Man. The public mind often has been unable to fuse these coexisting Reagans; it sees Glamour Boy when the script calls for Political Man, thus causing Reagan to be both attacked and supported for the wrong reasons.

1. Glamour Boy. "Don't forget his background," reminds one of his closest friends. "He was playing the role of All-American boy long before he got to Hollywood."

Ronald Wilson Reagan was born February 6, 1911, in Tampico, Illinois, a town so small that the city hall is open only sporadically, to an Irish Catholic father of alcoholic proclivities and a Protestant mother of English-Scottish ancestry. (Reagan, like Lyndon Johnson, now belongs to the Christian Church.) Despite his family's humble income—his father was a quasi-itinerant shoe salesman—young "Dutch" (Ronald's nickname) became a Big Man on Campus, earning high school letters in football, basketball and track, while being elected president of the student body.

Lots of hard work (waiting on fraternity house tables in winter, lifeguarding in summer, where he rescued a future California Republican Congressman!), plus an athletic scholarship, got Reagan through tiny Eureka College, twenty miles from Peoria. He was a middling-to-good student (majors in economics and sociology), and again was elected president of the student body. After graduation in 1932, he became a sports announcer, first in Davenport, Iowa, then in Des Moines, where he was known as "the voice of the Chicago Cubs." On a 1937 trip to California, to watch the Cubs' spring training, Reagan was given a screen test by Warner Brothers and signed to a $200-a-week contract.

His film career really wasn't much; some twenty B pictures ("The studio didn't want them good, it wanted them Thursday," is the way he now says they were made) before he moved to modest stardom as the Gipper in *Knute Rockne—All American* (1940). Then another thirty pictures, mostly in parts that were soon forgotten. After seeing Reagan in *The Girl from Jones Beach,* the New York *Times*'s Bosley Crowther wrote that "he is a fellow who has a cheerful way of looking at dames." But that is about as close as he came to critical acclaim.

There are old friends of Reagan's in the motion-picture business who think the failure to win full stardom is what spurred his ambition for a second career in public life; but if Reagan harbored a sense of disappointment, he kept it to himself. A publicist who worked with him says, "Ronnie believes in fairy tales. And why shouldn't he?" He showed up in Hollywood at a time when moviegoers demanded little more from an actor than broad shoulders, wavy brown hair, blue eyes and white teeth. It was a time, also, when even mediocrity commanded phenomenal incomes.

During World War II, when poor eyesight (corrected now by use of contact lenses) kept Reagan from combat, he served as an Army

Air Corps captain working at the Hal Roach studio as an administrator and narrator of training films. After the war, he made an agile leap from his waning film career to the new medium of television, performing as host and occasional star of *The General Electric Theater* and then in *Death Valley Days*. His income was in the $150,000-a-year range, much of which he wisely invested in real estate.* He married beautiful women: first, actress Jane Wyman (1940-48; two children); second, actress Nancy Davis (1952-present, two children). And he lived in a sumptuous home on the Pacific Palisades, the very embodiment of a mid-twentieth-century success story, with a Southern California twist.

And no one could think of a valid reason to elect him to anything until he turned into. . . .

2. Political Man. The headline in the Los Angeles *Times* of June 29, 1948, read: "Jane Wyman Divorced; Blames Rift on Politics." Beneath it was a story of how Miss Wyman was leaving her husband, Ronald Reagan. (She was more famous and hence got top billing.) As she told the court, they were continually arguing about politics and she simply could not match his enthusiasm. Yet, despite her disinterest in his political activities, which centered around the Screen Actors Guild, Reagan insisted that she attend meetings with him and be present during discussions among his friends. "Finally there was nothing in common between us."†

Other actors gave Hedda Hopper items about parts and parties. Reagan gave her a long treatise on "the cultivation of freedom of the individual." On May 18, 1947, the gossip columnist reported him as saying:

Our highest aim should be the cultivation of freedom of the individual, for therein lies the highest dignity of man. Tyranny is tyranny and

---

* After his election as Governor he sold 250 acres of his 305-acre Malibu ranch, "Yearling Row," to 20th Century–Fox studios for about $2 million, with the purchaser also taking options on fifty more acres at $8,000 an acre.

† In his autobiography, Reagan gives Miss Wyman less than a page. Their divorce gets a paragraph: "I arrived home from the Washington hearing [of the House Un-American Activities Committee, where he had testified] to be told I was leaving. I suppose there had been warning signs, if only I hadn't been so busy, but small-town boys grow up thinking only other people get divorced. The plain truth is that such a thing was so far from even being imagined by me that I had no resources to call upon. . . . I have never discussed what happened, and I have no intention of doing so now."

whether it comes from Right, Left or Center, it's evil. I suspect the extreme Right and the extreme Left in political ideologies, though seeming to branch off in opposite directions, curve to a common meeting point.

I believe the only logical way to save our country from both extremists is to remove conditions that supply fuel for the totalitarian fire.

Right now the liberal movement in this country is taking the brunt of the Communist attack. The Reds know that if we can make America a decent living place for all of our people their cause is lost here. So they seek to infiltrate liberal organizations just to smear and discredit them.

I've already pulled out of one organization that I joined in completely good faith. One day I woke up, looked about and found it was Commie-dominated.

You can't blame a man for aligning himself with an institution he thinks is humanitarian, but you can blame him if he deliberately remains with it after he knows it's fallen into the hands of the Reds.

There were some who thought Reagan foursquare; most in the Hollywood set just thought him square. "Always a Boy Scout," privately said an intimate friend.

To understand Reagan as Political Man, it is necessary to keep in mind his small-town roots, which are deep. "In a small town," he says, "you can't stand on the sidelines and let somebody else do what needs doing; you can't coast along on someone else's opinions. That, really, is how I became an activist." As a college freshman in 1928 he led a successful strike of the students against the school's president; in 1959, as a union leader, he led a successful strike of the actors against the film studios.

Nor was Reagan a mere figurehead during his twenty-two years on the board of the Screen Actors Guild, six years as its president. For the Guild is a working union with fifteen thousand members, whose gross earnings are around $60 million a year; a Los Angeles office with an annual budget of over $250,000; and other offices in New York, New Orleans and San Francisco. Moreover, he was SAG president during the most troubled time in Hollywood's history, when the question of Communist party membership triggered congressional investigations, blacklists, and jail sentences for ten members of the industry. Under his leadership SAG officially condemned all members "who have been named as past or present Communist party members and in appearing before the House Committee on Un-American Activities refused to state whether they are or ever have been members of the party." The Guild also declared that applicants for membership must attest that they are not members of the Communist party "or of any other organization that seeks to overthrow the government of the United States by force and violence."

When Reagan was asked directly if the Guild had a blacklist, he indirectly replied, "The fact is the Guild protected its members from unfair accusations. The public had lists, many of them wrong. We in the industry worked hard to oppose *unofficial* lists." Apparently under Reagan's presidency, the union's policy was to protect the innocent and offer redemption to the guilty if they cooperated with the F.B.I.

Mervyn Le Roy, the director, wanted Reagan to straighten out a situation in which a young actress under contract to MGM was afraid of being blacklisted because her name appeared on the roster of Communist-front organizations. The SAG president cleared Nancy Davis of any leftist taint and also married her.

Until 1952, however, Reagan officially was a left-leaning Democrat. It has been said that Helen Gahagan Douglas, in her 1950 Senate race against Nixon, kept Reagan's name off her letterhead because of his radical connections. He called George Murphy an "archreactionary." Looking back on this period, Reagan now says, "I was a near-hopeless hemophilic liberal. I bled for 'causes.' " But in 1952 he voted for the Eisenhower-Nixon ticket and by 1964 he was co-chairman of the Goldwater campaign in California. At least three causes contributing to Reagan's left-right shift are identifiable:

—Some note the metamorphosis coincided with his marriage in 1952 to Miss Davis, a petite, wide-eyed, Smith College graduate, whose father, a world-renowned neurosurgeon, holds political views to the right of Herbert Hoover and whose own opinions, according to intimates, are both conservative and emphatic.

—Reagan, himself, credits his new conservatism to his bouts with the Communists and Communist-front organizations that were blossoming in the motion-picture industry during the late 1940's. "Light was dawning in some obscure region in my head," he wrote. "I was beginning to see the seamy side of liberalism." Reagan the anti-Communist crusader was threatened by acid throwers and, for self-defense, Warner Brothers made him wear a shoulder holster with a loaded .32 Smith & Wesson. Later, when a congressional committee asked actor Sterling Hayden what tripped up Communist maneuvers in Hollywood, he replied, "We ran into a one-man battalion named Ronnie Reagan."

—There were also his speaking tours for General Electric. When asked whether "this contributed to your conversion," Reagan answered, "No question about it. I came home one time and told Nancy: 'You know, I go out there and make speeches and I'm coming to the realization that I turn right around and vote for the people who are responsible for the things I'm criticizing.' " Then he added: "I also think that a large part of my conversion came through my own research for my speeches." But some others, such as San Francisco professor Leo E. Litwak, credit Reagan's shift to the right more to his ability as an actor than as an empiricist. "Perhaps you can become a George Gipp by pretending to be him," mused the professor. "Or you may become a rancher by being cast as one. . . . A good actor is told to be a garrulous newspaperman and, if he is like Reagan, he *is* a garrulous newspaperman." Be a spokesman for free enterprise. . . .

While humorist Art Hoppe has called him "a former left-wing right-winger," Reagan contends that his political shifts have been of fewer degrees than many people realize; that he was neither as far left nor as far right as pictured. There are old friends who will agree, saying that even during his most "liberal" days he held some remarkably conservative notions, notably his opposition to the income tax.

When Reagan signed on as "host" of the *The General Electric Theater* in 1954 it was understood that he also would take to the road for about twelve weeks each year as a "goodwill ambassador," visiting the company's plants and talking to its employees. Though some remember it differently now, at the time the agreement was nothing more than the standard use of a "celebrity" to jolly the workers. The company expected its star to tell mildly "inside" stories about life in Hollywood. GE management was as surprised as GE labor when instead Reagan's set speech was about the "dangers of Big Government." Big Government, in fact, was a major GE client.

For eight years Reagan made the company circuit, talking to all 250,000 GE employees in thirty-eight states, often giving as many as fourteen brief speeches a day. Logistically, it was a presidential campaign in miniature.

It was the basic GE-tour speech, now titled "A Time for Choosing," that Reagan delivered on nationwide television during the 1964 presidential campaign. Ironically, according to Stephen Shadegg, Goldwater's chief advisers, campaign director Denison Kitchel and adviser William Baroody, Sr., tried to have the filmed talk can-

celed "primarily because it discussed the inadequacies of the present Social Security program. . . ." Estimates of the contributions that
flooded Republican headquarters in the wake of Reagan's appeal range

"Take up Our Quarrel With the Foe! To You
From Flaming Hands We Throw . . ."

Haynie, Louisville **Courier-Journal,** June 10, 1966, © 1966,
The Los Angeles Times Syndicate

from a quarter of a million dollars to two million. A probable figure
is $600,000. It was the most successful national political debut since
William Jennings Bryan electrified the 1896 Democratic convention
with his "Cross of Gold" speech (which also had been carefully

pretested on the lecture circuit) and it made Reagan a political star overnight.

The day after Barry Goldwater's sun sank slowly in the West— November 4, 1964—a group of conservatives formed "Republicans for Ronald Reagan" in Owosso, Michigan (birthplace of Thomas E. Dewey). It was the first step, they said, in a campaign to make him President.

In Southern California, a group called "Friends of Ronald Reagan," was organized in June, 1965, with the more limited goal of making him Governor. Their plan was to raise the funds necessary—nearly $140,000—to allow Reagan to send up a six-month trial balloon. If it was still aloft by January, 1966, Reagan would formally become a candidate.

Looking back on his lifetime of political interest and his activities as a union president, in the fall of 1965 Reagan told an interviewer: "I think I've had a reasonable amount of experience, more than perhaps a great many businessmen, certainly more than the average lawyer who is considered the logical choice for a political job."

On January 4, 1966, he was a month shy of fifty-five years old, still looking ruddy and at home in the outdoors, his more than six feet still slim and erect, his face still incredibly boyish, although at very close hand the neck was corded and the corners of his eyes sent out a stream of thinly-etched lines. Alone on the set that looked like a family den, he spoke quietly, earnestly into the camera. Fifteen television stations, from Redding in the north to San Diego in the south, carried forth the message to the people of California: Ronald Reagan, describing himself as a "citizen-politician," was officially a candidate for the Republican nomination for governor.

About the state that Ronald Reagan wished to govern Lord Bryce had once said, "California, more than any other part of the Union, is a country by itself." Its hundred million acres are compressed within natural boundaries—forests on the north, desert on the south, water on the west, mountains on the east. Its land mass would stretch from Boston to Charleston, South Carolina, or from Amsterdam to Rome. In gross national product it is exceeded by only eight nations in the world.

Every minute California adds one new resident; 1,460 new Californians a day; enough new citizens each year to fill a city the size of Oakland or San Diego. There are over 19 million people now; the population tomorrow, says the state's Department of Health, will be 25 million in 1980, 50 million by the end of the century. Never in history has population multiplied at such a rapid rate for so long. "Over 1.5 billion people would be living in California within 100 years if the state's population continues to grow at the rate of the last ten years," concludes the Population Reference Bureau. "This would be nearly half of the population of the planet today."*

If California could have been one nation, it also could have been two states, divided east to west, at the Tehachapis. The state always has been a study in contrasts. Geographically, it contains both highest and lowest points in the continental United States. It has some of the flavor of Western rugged individualism while accepting twenty cents of every Federal dollar spent on defense contracts. It has burgeoning cities and lonely ghost towns, such as Bodie, which once maintained two burying grounds, one for "decent folk," the other, much larger, for the rest.

Southern California has the majority of the people; the population of Los Angeles County alone is greater than that of forty-two of the fifty states. Here the people register Democratic and vote Republican, partly because the Southern immigrant brought along his party label and his conservative orientation. Southern California is Republican and Northern California is Democratic, but this is just today's rule of thumb: the hallmark of a California voter is fickleness.

Governing such a state under any circumstances would be a challenge. What makes the job for the mid-twentieth-century leaders of California, in both parties, infinitely more painful are the "reforms" they inherited from Hiram Johnson, who, in typical California fashion, took the concepts of the Progressive movement and pushed them to a point of exaggeration from which the state has not yet recovered.†

At the turn of the century, San Francisco was run by one Abe Ruef,

* See Robert C. Cook, "California: After 19 Million, What?" *Population Bulletin* XXII, No. 2, June, 1966; also Kimmis Hendrick, "California: Big, Bigger . . ." *Christian Science Monitor*. March 24, 1962.

† Among the books helpful to an understanding of California politics in this century are Bernard L. Hyink, Seyom Brown, and Ernest W. Thacker, *Politics and Government in California* (New York: T. Y. Crowell, 1965); George E. Mowry, *The California Progressives* (Berkeley: University of California, 1951); James Reichley, *States in Crisis* (Chapel Hill: University of North Carolina, 1964); Frank H. Jonas, editor, *Western Politics* (Salt Lake City: University of Utah, 1961); and John Gunther, *Inside U.S.A.* (New York: Harper, 1947).

a debonair little crook, who, with the aid of his puppet Mayor, a professional violinist by the name of "Handsome Gene" Schmitz, extracted payoffs from prize-fight promoters, bordello operators, saloon keepers, and less colorful businessmen. One member of the Ruef machine was Grove L. Johnson. He had migrated to California from Syracuse, New York, during the Civil War, served a term each in the penitentiary and the United States House of Representatives, and then became the Southern Pacific Railroad's chief lobbyist in Sacramento.

In a classic case of family rebellion, Grove Johnson's son Hiram, fresh out of the University of California, became a leader of the "reform" elements in Sacramento and, later, the special prosecutor who put Ruef and Schmitz behind bars. Identifying himself with the "progressive Republicans" of Teddy Roosevelt, he was elected Governor in 1908 over the bitter opposition of the Southern Pacific, which had run the state government for years.

In Hiram Johnson's view, the partisan politics his father had manipulated so skillfully was evil. He devoted his two terms as Governor to scrambling party lines and instituting a series of structural changes designed to insure that future Californians would be uncorrupted by meaningful political parties. He was a man of strength and guts and he did his job well. The Johnson program included: the direct primary, with a prohibition of pre-primary endorsements by political parties; the referendum, initiative and recall; nonpartisan local elections; and the almost complete elimination of patronage.* It also included cross-filing, a unique system which permitted a candidate to enter the primaries of *both* parties and, if successful, to spare himself and the voters the embarrassment of a partisan contest in the general election. During one period, from 1940 through 1952, 84 percent of the state Senate races and 72 percent of those for the Assembly were decided in the primaries. It was a particularly useful system for incumbents, since they were better known, and during the first half of the century incumbents in California were usually Republicans. In the 1922 election, for example, Democrats won only three out of seventy-seven seats in the state Assembly. When they finally came to power in 1958, the Democrats' first step, understandably, was to abolish cross-filing.

The rest of the Johnsonian anti-party system remains intact, how-

---

* Out of 160,000 state employees, the bulk of the Governor's patronage consists of 31 department directorships and an equal number of deputies.

ever, and its consequences shape the pattern of California politics—the pattern that produced, in 1966, the Governor named Reagan. The genius of the American two-party system is that it provides a delicate but effective set of interlocking power relationships that bridge the constitutional gaps between local, state and national governments, between legislative and executive branches, between the voter in his precinct and the official in his public post. The key to the party system is the nomination and election of officers at all levels on a common ticket. Johnson broke that system into bits. By ordaining that local offices be nonpartisan and by encouraging cross-filing for partisan posts, he weakened the office holders' and voters' loyalty to the ticket. By denying parties the right to make their own endorsements of candidates, he destroyed their capacity to defend their own institutional integrity. By stripping the Governor of virtually all patronage, he guaranteed that his power would be inadequate for his responsibility in party leadership. And, by hedging the official party organizations with minute restrictions, he guaranteed they would lack the tensile strength to resist the centrifugal forces of the conflicting economic, ideological and local interests of the burgeoning society that is the California of today.

What Johnson and the Progressive reformers forgot is that politics—like nature—abhors a vacuum. The power they denied to political parties did not disappear; it was simply seized by others. Four vital functions normally fulfilled by the parties went elsewhere:

Finance. Since the party treasuries were meager, every candidate or prospective candidate had to find his own "angels." Lobbyists, the original target of Johnson's reforms, provided the financing for most legislative candidates; "money men" of varying ideologies and intents moved in to exert their influence through the selection and financing of statewide candidates.

Publicity. Since voting the party ticket was almost impossible, every candidate depended on his personal name appeal. Incumbents, of course, had the great advantage; those challengers who were favored by the newspaper publishers and, later, those most adept at the new medium of television also had a head start on their competitors.

Endorsement. Since the party officially could not indicate its choice of those seeking office under its label, a variety of "volunteer" groups

were formed whose endorsing process gave them a power dis-
proportionate to their numbers.

Management. Since the party was too weak and impecunious to provide campaign direction for its nominees, private firms of professional
campaign managers developed in California earlier than they were
known in any other state.*

The characteristic quality of the system that Johnson's "reforms"
produced was the disparity between responsibility and power. Those
who had the most responsibility—chairmen of the formal political
parties, Governors, Mayors, leading legislators—normally had little power to command or even influence their nominal subordinates.
Those who had power, through the happenstance of money, or access
to publicity, or activity in the "volunteer" endorsing groups, or
possession of management skills, were characteristically responsible
to nothing but their own whims. Incumbents were subject to a certain
self-restraint because of their day-to-day governmental responsibilities,
but the system was made to order for the activists of all political extremes.

The Democrats—the "out" party in the thirties and forties—were
buffeted by recurrent internal battles between their conservative
money men and their radical political activists. More often than not,
the radicals won the nomination fights and the conservative and
middle-road Democrats would thereupon vote Republican. So fixed
did this pattern become in this era that Republican incumbents, en-
joying the privilege of cross-filing, became not just "moderates" in
terms of a normal Republican lexicon, but "neuters," nonparty personalities.

One such figure was Earl Warren, who became Governor in 1942,
won both party nominations for re-election in 1946, and in 1950 became the only three-term Governor in California history. Warren,
unlike Hiram Johnson, was neither flashy, dashing nor mean. He was
a big fellow of Scandinavian stock (the family name originally was
Varran), likable and friendly. Californians could feel comfortable
having him in Sacramento, and from his genial image was cast the
pattern of the successful candidate for state office.

* See page 62 for a discussion of how the California-style professional
political management firms have set the pattern for similar developments in
other states.

In the year 1950, when Warren won his third term with 65 percent of the votes, California Republicans might have been excused for believing that they were nearing the millennium. Goodwin J. Knight, once a hard-rock miner, was re-elected Lieutenant Governor after abandoning plans to oppose Warren, whom he considered too liberal; a young Los Angeles county Congressman, Richard M. Nixon, was elected to a U.S. Senate seat formerly held by a Democrat. He joined William F. Knowland of the conservative Oakland *Tribune* family, who had been appointed to the Senate in 1945 by Warren. The only Democrat in the whole state to hold major office was Attorney General Edmund G. Brown.

Nineteen fifty-two saw Nixon elected Vice President; his Senate seat was filled by State Controller Thomas H. Kuchel, a Warren protégé; and, when Warren was made Chief Justice of the United States in 1953, Goodie Knight was elevated to the governorship, proving, once in power, to be even more liberal than his predecessor. Knowland, Knight, Nixon and Kuchel were all re-elected between 1952 and 1956. The party was in the presumably happy position of an impresario with too many stars.

But when Big Bill Knowland came charging home from Washington in 1958, intent on wresting the governorship from Knight as a launching pad for his presidential ambitions, he triggered a chain reaction of seriocomic catastrophes: Knowland bumped Knight into the Senate primary, where Knight bumped San Francisco Mayor George Christopher. Both Knowland and Knight then were mauled in the general election, and Pat Brown, the inoffensive son of a poker-parlor operator, became Governor by a million votes. The Democrats gained control of the legislature for the first time since 1888 and their popular vote margin was the largest won by either party since 1883. When Nixon returned to California after losing the presidency—although he carried his home state by a whisker of absentee ballots—and promptly was defeated for Governor, carrying running mate George Christopher down with him, the shattering of Republican fortunes was virtually complete. Like a Greek tragedy, it was particularly poignant because of the great heights from which the mighty had fallen. Only Tom Kuchel, by following the nonpartisan lesson he had learned at Warren's knee, retained office.

Defeat also opened the ideological floodgates. So long as they were the party of government, the Republicans had remained in touch with reality; but when the catastrophe in 1958 was followed by Nixon's loss in 1960 the restraints of responsibility were cast off, and the G.O.P. entered a whirlpool of extremism. Southern California had always been susceptible to "true believers" of every shade. In 1962 the radical-right extremists there provided opposition in the primary to both Kuchel and Nixon. Reagan was active in behalf of the anti-Kuchel candidate, whose challenge the Senator tossed back with ease. Nixon was less fortunate; his opponent, Assemblyman (and oil millionaire) Joseph Shell, received one-third of the votes. And, when Nixon attacked the John Birch Society, many of the Shell supporters decided to sit on their hands in the general election. They were delighted when he lost, and even more delighted when their new hero, Barry Goldwater—the candidate of Knowland, Reagan and Shell—cinched the 1964 Republican presidential nomination by defeating Nelson Rockefeller in the California primary.

In six years, the party of Warren, Kuchel, Nixon and Knight had been taken over by the militant right. The right wingers also captured the volunteer organizations that provide much of the manpower for the nonparty politics of California. The largest and most influential of these was the California Republican Assembly (CRA), founded in 1934 and long the pride of Earl Warren. Its 1965 "scorecard" awarded the top grade (97 percent) to Senator John Schmitz, the only member of the John Birch Society in the legislature, while the Republican Senate leader, a moderate, earned a failing 29 percent. By 1966, five of the organization's sixteen key leaders were Birchers, and the Los Angeles *Times* concluded CRA "apparently has relinquished its final clutch on political reality."

The United Republicans of California (UROC) was formed in 1963 by conservatives who felt the CRA was not far right enough. However, by 1966 debating which was the farthest out, CRA or UROC, was like the medieval conundrum about how many angels can dance on the head of a pin. UROC's 1966 president was not a Birch member, but his wife was, as were the group's Southern California vice chairman and sergeant-at-arms. Executive Director Rus Walton, who had been responsible for the banned Goldwater film, *Choice,* resigned from UROC because its policy positions, he said, represented a triumph for "rigid militants over those who learned our lesson in 1964."

The California Young Republicans (CYR) in 1966 were headed

by Mike Djordjevich, a twenty-nine-year-old Yugoslav refugee, who favored U.S. withdrawal from the UN and the abolition of the Federal income tax. The CYR executive vice president, national committee-man, and treasurer were Birch members. Their election was viewed by the Republican state chairman as "the first concrete evidence that there may be conspiratorial activity by the John Birch Society to take over a segment of the Republican party." But they remained in office. However, when the Long Beach chapter elected as its president a man who had been arrested by the FBI for attempting to sell a 9-millimeter British Sten gun and a 50-caliber machine gun to Treasury agents posing as members of a secret private army, the parent organization felt this had gone too far. The young arsenalist was quietly deposed.

The moderates who were ousted from control of the CRA and the CYR formed their own volunteer group in 1965, the California Republican League, which excluded Birchers from its ranks. But the new organization achieved only a modest membership and its founder was taken out of politics when President Johnson appointed him in 1966 to the Federal bench.

While the ideologues were having a field day in the volunteer organizations and making mischief in Republican primaries, a counter-vailing trend was taking place. A small group was trying to return the G.O.P. to old-fashioned political pragmatism. The key movers were two Nixon protégés, Dr. Gaylord Parkinson and Robert Finch, left behind to salvage the ruins after Nixon fled to New York. Finch, a ruggedly handsome Los Angeles lawyer, who was only thirty-four years old when appointed campaign director of Nixon's 1960 presidential bid, became the manager of George Murphy's 1964 Senate race. A centrist by instinct, Finch easily steered the old musical-comedy star through a blessedly non-acrimonious primary with Leland Kaiser, a wealthy, conservative but non-strident businessman. Throughout the fall, he kept Murphy smilingly detached from the perils of the Gold-water campaign—never repudiating the head of the ticket, but never getting caught too close to him either. Parkinson, the obstetrician-turned-politician, did his part as state chairman to spare Murphy the cross fire of pro- and anti-Goldwater Republicans, while scores of party workers, appalled by the amateurism and ideological excesses of the Goldwater campaign, pitched in to help the strictly non-ideological senatorial candidate, who soft-shoed his way through the issues,

serenely confident that "everybody likes George Murphy." As Finch
was later to remark, in a year when Republicans were assailing each
other, and being assailed by the Democrats, with every kind of ammunition, "the Murphy campaign was the best political bomb shelter
there was." Under the skillful tutelage of Finch and Parkinson,
Murphy defeated appointed Senator Pierre Salinger by 216, 643 votes,
while Barry Goldwater, despite the speeches of Ronald Reagan, was
losing California by 1,292,769 votes.

In the winter of 1965, the ideological and the pragmatic streams of
California Republicanism met, intermingled and produced an organization called "The Friends of Ronald Reagan." Its target was the
governorship; its tactic was to unite behind a man whose ideology was
satisfactory to the radical right and whose personality and political style
had the soft-sell ingenuousness of the successful George Murphy.
Ronald Reagan was the man and the four elements of political power
that Hiram Johnson had sought to disperse soon coalesced on his
behalf:

Finance. Besides such Reagan show-biz buddies as Walt Disney, James
Cagney, Randolph Scott and Robert Taylor, there were a number of
ultra-conservative businessmen, the most conspicuous being Henry
Salvatori, designer and developer of oil exploration and drilling equipment, previously a backer of Nixon, Goldwater and the Anti-Communist Voters League; the late A. C. (Cy) Rubel, a retired oil-
company executive, Goldwater delegate and finance chairman for
Joe Shell's campaign against Nixon in 1962; Holmes Tuttle, Los
Angeles auto dealer and Goldwater delegate; and Walter Knott, developer of Knott's Berry Farm, and fund raiser for conservative causes
from the "Christian Crusade" to the Liberty Amendment Committee.

Management. For a fee reported to be $150,000, Salvatori & Company
retained the top-rated political public-relations firm of Spencer,
Roberts and Associates. Stu Spencer, thirty-eight, bouncy, with close-
cropped brown hair, a heavily lined face, and Bill Roberts, forty,
balding, fat, in a perennially rumpled suit, had been paid organizers
for the Los Angeles County Republican Central Committee until they
formed a partnership in 1960. In the next five years they handled
forty campaigns, winning thirty-four. They helped elect John Rousselot
to the U.S. House of Representatives in 1960 (but dropped him
after he revealed he was a member of the Birch Society and before

he was defeated in 1962), handled the Southern California campaign for Kuchel in 1962, and in 1964 ran Rockefeller's unsuccessful California primary race. (Goldwater also bid for their services, but got there too late.)

Endorsement. Reagan was the featured speaker in 1965 at conventions of the California Republican Assembly, the United Republicans of California and the California Young Republicans. Leaders of all three groups made it plain he was their choice for Governor. The Friends of Ronald Reagan committee included the most recent past president of CRA, the founder of UROC and a former president of the Los Angeles County Young Republicans.

Publicity. Like Murphy, Reagan was an established celebrity. He kept his own weekly television show, while winning reams of newspaper publicity as he toured the state "to determine if I have broad-based support for the nomination." As the Los Angeles *Times* headlined this phase: "Reagan Gets Star Role in 'Will He Run?' Saga."

It was during the buildup year of 1965 that Reagan, counseled by Bill Roberts and guided by his own strongly conservative instincts, shaped the basic approach that was to characterize his brilliantly successful campaign. They recognized from the start that Reagan's greatest problem would be to counter the argument that, as an actor who had never held public office, he had no visible qualifications to administer the affairs of the nation's largest state. Their answer was to convert this liability into Reagan's greatest asset by making him the spokesman and the symbol for the millions of others who were convinced that somehow, somewhere, something had gone basically wrong in government.

"I am not a politician," Reagan said in an early speech that he was to repeat with minor variations throughout the campaign. "I am an ordinary citizen with a deep-seated belief that much of what troubles us has been brought about by politicians; and it's high time that more ordinary citizens brought the fresh air of common-sense thinking to bear on these problems."

The attack on big government was central to his campaign. In Pat Brown's two terms, as in Warren's and Knight's earlier administrations, California had won the reputation of being in the forefront of state programs in every vital area. In the field of resource development, it undertook the largest state-financed public-works program in history, damming rivers and building a vast aqueduct system to carry the surplus water from the north to the booming but arid south. In the area of transportation, it built the greatest system of freeways and highways in the world. In the field of education, it became the first state to undertake to provide a tuition-free college education for the top 25 percent of its high school graduates, a program that involved the biggest college construction program in history. (Nor was quality sacrificed to size in California's education experiment; the state-supported University of California was rated best in the nation, the public elementary and high schools paid teachers the highest salaries in the county.) In the fields of welfare, recreation, rehabilitation and race relations, too, California moved ahead of the rest of the country. While other state governments declined, California's—like New York's—was the exception that disproved the rule of invariable failure.

But even success breeds discontent, particularly in a state where mushrooming population allows no respite from the demands on the government. The efforts California was making to keep apace of its growth—and to improve the quality of governmental services—were expensive. Taxes went up, particularly local property taxes to finance schools. In a mobile society, crime and welfare costs also skyrocketed, despite the fact that California was investing more to prevent crime and rehabilitate the needy than any other state. State pride in the University of California was rocked when "free speech" and "filthy speech" demonstrators disrupted classes at the Berkeley campus. Race relations were badly damaged by the 1965 riots in the Watts section of Los Angeles, and by later eruptions in Bakersfield, Oakland and San Francisco.

Strong racial and class lines emerged in the politics of the Golden State. The California middle class, the youngish World War II veterans and their families who filled the developments in Orange, San Diego and Los Angeles counties and around Fresno, Sacramento and the cities of the Bay Area, came to conclude that government was costing them more than it was worth. Now in their forties, with two cars in the garage, many of them forgot that they once had been beneficiaries of welfare programs—the GI Bill that paid for their educations, the Cal-Vet loans that enabled them to make the down payments on their first houses. Twenty years of progressive government had produced a conservative counterrevolution in the white suburbs. Riding this revolution, speaking for it, was citizen-candidate Ronald Reagan.

"No small part of the heavy tax load that is borne by the working men and women of our state is a welfare load which doubled in the last five years and is increasing faster than our spending on education," he said. "Those who administer welfare at the county and local levels have their hands tied by excessive regulations and red tape imposed by both Washington and Sacramento."

In California—that most American of all the states—"the alienated voters," those who wanted nothing from government but to be let alone, found their voice in Ronald Reagan.

"Cheating and stealing isn't cheating and stealing if it takes place in the halls of government," he said. "Then, it's just politics. . . . Well, we've had enough of the wheeling and dealing and enough of schemers and schemes. I think it's time now . . . to re-implement the original idea that you and I have the capacity for self-government, the dignity and the ability and the God-given freedom to make our own decisions, to plan our own lives and to control our own destiny."

This antigovernment theme runs through everything that Reagan said in the campaign and says still. In his inaugural address:

> We have come to a crossroad—a time of decision—and the path we follow turns away from any idea that government and those who serve it are omnipotent. . . . For many years now, you and I have been shushed like children and told there are no simple answers to the complex problems which are beyond our comprehension. Well, the truth is there are simple answers—there just are not easy ones. The time has come for us to decide whether collectively we can afford everything and anything we think of simply because we think of it. The time has come to run a check to see if all the services government provides were in answer to demands or were just goodies dreamed up for our supposed betterment. . . . The cost of California's government is too high.

Once the main theme of the campaign had been defined, there remained the question of how to handle the inevitable effort to link Reagan to the extremists of the radical right. The obvious answer was for Reagan, like Nixon and Kuchel before him, to reject the support of any Bircher and to refuse to campaign with any Bircher on the G.O.P. ticket. Such a course was urged on him, but Reagan simply refused to follow the advice. "I refuse to accept," he said, "that the Birch Society is a Republican problem. . . . I see no reason to blanket indict or repudiate an organization of which I am not a member and have no intention of joining. . . . I am going out to solicit the support of individuals and I assume that if they vote for me, they are buying my philosophy, I am not buying theirs."

Whether Reagan took this position simply as a matter of philosophy or—as the Democrats were quick to suggest—because his conservative financial backers would permit him no other is not certain. But even the political advisers who first argued against it came to accept the decision, because every survey showed that the "extremism" issue had far less impact on California voters than two others which Reagan had going for him.

One was Berkeley, where University of California students, Reagan assured enthralled audiences, conduct "sexual orgies so vile I cannot describe them to you," though the demonstrations that took place on the campus were, Reagan conceded, the work of "a small radical minority." Governor Brown's direct authority over the university, administered by a board of regents of which he was one member, was almost nil. Yet Reagan, attacking conditions at the university in every speech, insisted that "this is no false issue concocted by the candidates for political advantage." He accused Brown of ordering "appeasement of campus malcontents and filthy-speech advocates under the pretense of preserving academic freedom" as part of a "policy of appeasement . . . dictated by political expediency." Where Brown opposed any outside investigation of the university as likely to endanger academic freedom and increase the threat of political interference, Reagan advocated, first, a legislative investigation and, later, an investigation by a citizens commission to be headed by John McCone, the former director of the Central Intelligence Agency. (After the election and the ouster of Clark Kerr as president of the university, Governor Reagan decided the situation did not require a special investigation.)

The other issue was even more emotional—open housing. In 1963 the legislature had passed a state fair-housing law, forbidding discrimination in new apartment units. Brought to referendum in 1964 by real-estate groups strongly opposed to its provisions, the law was repealed by an overwhelming two-to-one majority. Salinger campaigned in support of open housing and felt the issue played a major part in his defeat by Murphy, who steadfastly refused to take a stand. The issue was revived for the 1966 campaign by a California Supreme

Court decision invalidating the referendum.* Brown, who supported the open-housing law in the 1964 referendum, came out flatly against its repeal, though expressing willingness for a blue-ribbon commission to study possible modifications in its provisions.

Reagan had previously stated his opposition to the Federal Civil Rights Acts of 1964 and 1965 on constitutional grounds. He now opposed state legislation against housing discrimination and favored the repeal of the Rumford fair-housing law. On *Meet the Press,* he explained why:

Well, I agree with you he [a Negro] has a right to live where he wants to live. The unfortunate thing in my mind with regard to those people who are entrenched with the sickness of prejudice and discrimination is that they have certain consititutional rights that even though we disagree with them and even though we disapprove of their use of discrimination and bigotry, I believe the great danger in violating any individual's constitutional right is the precedent it establishes.

Now, while I say I am opposed to those provisions of the Rumford Act which invade the individual's right to the disposition of his property I have also been on record throughout my life as opposing restrictive covenants. I oppose restrictive covenants morally because I don't believe in prejudice and discrimination but I oppose them legislatively because I think there are certain rights you and I are endowed with from birth that we cannot submit to a majority rule and therefore when in a neighborhood a group of people get together and pass a ban by majority rule and say, "Well, no one in this neighborhood can sell their property to this group or that group," they have invaded the individual's right to the disposition of his property. So I always opposed restrictive covenants. I don't believe that even for the noble motive of the Rumford Act that you can turn around and make it any more right to violate that individual right in this kind of legislation. I would use the prestige and the power of the Governor's office to do everything I could do to convince everyone that needs convincing how evil this is, but I do not believe that we can without seriously endangering our basic freedoms, violate this constitutional right of the individual. But I myself, I will tell you now, do not subscribe to it. I am willing to sell my house . . .

When all the constitutional explanations were over, the political results were plain. Reagan ran about as poorly in Negro precincts as Barry Goldwater had. But in the white neighborhoods, particularly those near Negro ghettos, Pat Brown's margins were down sharply

* The decision was affirmed in 1967 by a 5-4 vote of the Supreme Court of the United States.

from 1962. Early in the spring of 1966, a top Reagan staff man had said, half whimsically, "We'll settle for the white vote." That is what he got.

If Reagan himself had written the script for the primary and general-election campaigns, it could not have been more to his liking. Hired early, Spencer and Roberts had plenty of time to do what they are best at—recruiting a political work force in a state where the parties themselves have none. As John Rousselot has said of the team, "They know practically every Republican worker in the state and they know who can produce and who cannot." Besides a precinct organization, under S-R's charmed touch a host of specialized committees sprang to life: Lawyers for Reagan, Athletes for Reagan (headed by former professional football star Jon Arnett), Young Businessmen for Reagan, Californians (i.e., Democrats) for Reagan, Insurance Agents for Reagan, Senior Citizens for Reagan (with Mrs. Francis X. Bushman as chairman), Sportsmen for Reagan (press release: "With a blast that nearly equalled a shot from their own guns, the California Sportsmen's Fish and Game Committee made it loud and clear that it is backing Ronald Reagan for Governor").

Birchers were carefully screened out of the campaign organization and, as a rule of thumb, at least one-fourth of the members of all committees were to be former Rockefeller or Kuchel supporters. For Spencer-Roberts well knew that in order to win the general election all of the primary election's wounds had to be self-sealing. Historically, votes lost by a candidate in a California primary tend to stay lost in November. And a Republican to win must have 90 percent of his own party's support and an additional 20 percent of the Democratic vote.

Reagan got a major break when, after months of wavering, Senator Kuchel, the strongest figure in the moderate Republican wing and practically the sole survivor of the Warren era, decided in the fall of 1965 not to run for Governor. That left the task of opposition to millionaire dairy operator George Christopher, a loser in his two previous statewide races, who looked and sounded like a tired TV wrestler. Pressed repeatedly by State Chairman Parkinson to honor "Parkinson's Law" (not to criticize a fellow Republican), Christopher stayed meek as a kitten. Except for some hardly embarrassing questions—"Did Mr. Reagan ever belong to Americans for Democratic Action, and when? Did he ever belong to the United World Federalists, and when?"—to which everyone knew the answers, Christopher had not a single harsh thing to say about his rival. This was a basic mistake, thought Reagan's managers. "We started in front," they explained. "We had the advantage in organization and money. He [Christopher] certainly couldn't hope to beat Reagan in a personality contest. The only way he could catch up was to chop Reagan down, and he didn't do that."

Instead, the hapless Christopher found himself in the closing weeks of the primary defending himself against a smear attack from columnist Drew Pearson, who had been fed legal records on a twenty-year-old law case involving Christopher's dairy by some overeager Brown campaign aides. The Brown operatives figured moderate Christopher as a tougher general-election opponent than conservative Reagan— a measure of the degree of wisdom that they displayed throughout the year. All they succeeded in doing was destroying Christopher and giving Reagan an opportunity to show his high-minded disapproval of the Democrats' underhanded tactics.

So when Reagan won the June primary by an amazing two-to-one majority, the party was more united than it had been in a decade. The very decisiveness of the victory was in reality a healing factor. As a prominent liberal Republican told columnists Evans and Novak, "If Reagan had won by 50,000 or 60,000 votes [instead of his 600,000 margin], we'd be scratching each other's eyes out. But with the size of his win, we have no choice but to accept him." Moreover, most Republican politicians were emotionally ready for a popular front: bone-tired of bitterness, they were happy, at least for the moment, to cast off the heavy mantle of contention. Then, too, here was Reagan playing the good winner, jumping over the net to embrace his opponent's supporters. Letters to Christopher leaders were in the mail before the last ballot was counted. Where Goldwater in victory had moved closer to his friends, Reagan was reaching out for the Christopher supporters, who blamed Brown most for his defeat. In a state that has always preferred genial candidates, it was a downright irresistible gesture.

The Democratic primary results, on the other hand, showed Governor Brown to be in deep trouble. He defeated Samuel W. Yorty, maverick Mayor of Los Angeles, by the shaky margin of four to three, actually receiving fewer votes in his primary than Reagan did in his.

The almost-million votes that went to Yorty, a nominal Democrat who had supported Nixon for President in 1960 and echoed Reagan's stand on the race issue, were an ominous portent for Pat Brown.

There were others. After eight years in office, Brown was tired and

A STAR IS BORN

RONALD REAGAN

SCRIPT FOR "NOVEMBER VICTORY"

Miller, Des Moines **Register and Tribune**, June 9, 1966

so was his administration. He had been a good Governor, but his was not the personality to rally the troops for one last charge over the ramparts. A product of the bland-personality politics of the Warren era, Brown had never established effective command of the Democratic party. Yorty was not the only Democratic leader who would just as soon have seen Sacramento without Brown. There was Assembly Speaker Jesse M. Unruh, the one-time "Big Daddy," now minus his excess poundage and wearing a lean and hungry look. The sharecropper's son, who commuted to seminars at the Eagleton Institute of Rutgers University, was one of a rare breed—the erudite boss. The political arena had not seen the likes of him since Willie Curran of Baltimore chose Latin as the language in which to decline a governorship: *Res ipsa loquitur.*

Brown seriously considered retiring at the end of his term, and probably would have, had Kuchel sought the Republican nomination for Governor. But, as he surveyed the scene, it became clear that the Democratic pary had reached a state of dissension where no one other than Brown had even a hope of pulling it together. The volunteer California Democratic Council, which in the 1950's had used its endorsing power to bring a modicum of discipline to the feuding Democrats, had itself fallen victim to the same sort of extremism that plagued its Republican counterparts. CDC conventions increasingly became debating forums for various factions of the New Left, while its membership dwindled steadily.

Meantime, on the other flank, many of the party's financial supporters were developing their own feuds with the Governor. Harvey Aluminum heiress Carmen Warschaw, known as "The Dragon Lady" for her pulchritude and viper tongue, broke with the Governor completely after blaming his henchmen for blocking her bid for the state chairmanship in 1966. In the final weeks of the election campaign, Mrs. Warschaw was socializing with Reagan, Mayor Yorty was in Mexico, Speaker Unruh was in South America, and many CDC members were too busy demonstrating against the Vietnam War to help their embattled Governor.

"Somehow in Pat Brown's campaigns," commented *Newsweek,* "the issue always becomes the other guy." Twice he had been elected Governor by turning his opponents into the villains. This time, his strategists figured, he would pull the hat trick by painting Reagan as "Pure Goldwater." As the Reagan managers had anticipated, Brown labeled his rival "the crown prince of the extreme right" and reminded elderly voters that Reagan "got his start in ultra-conservative politics fighting the aged of this country." The Democratic State Central Committee put out a pamphlet, made to look like *Time* magazine, entitled "Ronald Reagan, Extremist Collaborator, An Exposé" —a thirteen-page collection of guilt-by-association. If Mrs. McClarty

Harbison, identified as "Sponsor, John Birch Society's front, 'Truth About Civil Turmoil,' " contributed to Ronald Reagan's campaign, *ergo* . . .

But trying to make Reagan into a Birch sympathizer was a task beyond the capacity of genial Pat Brown. Extremism is a matter of both content and manner. Not only was Reagan now telling audiences that he was for expanded social security benefits and against right-to-work laws and the Liberty Amendment, but the star of so many "All-American boy" movies just did not look right for the part of kook. Rather, what the heavy-handed Govenor did was to turn himself into the villain. And in so doing he lost his slim chance of being re-elected.

Brown's other key point, his opponent's inexperience, might have been more effective if the Governor had not managed to mangle it into an anti-actor issue. He began promisingly enough with a take-off on Reagan's "citizen-politician" concept in a speech before the Associated Press, in which he compared his opponent to a pilot telling his passengers that this was his first flight, "but don't worry—I've always had an active interest in aviation." Later on, however, Brown settled into a routine of continuous cracks about Reagan films. "And what have my opponent's contributions been to this growing, thriving state of ours?" Brown's answer: "Starring in such unforgettable screen epics as *Bedtime for Bonzo.*" His TV spots were of the same genre. A typical one had Dan Blocker, *Bonanza's* Hoss, saying, "I earn my living in front of a camera—pretending to be somebody I'm not. But one of my colleagues is having trouble separating fantasy from reality. . . ." Finally after a Brown film reminded voters that "it was an actor who shot Lincoln," Jack Palance, a strong Brown supporter, announced that he was "disgusted" with his candidate. "Attack him [Reagan] if you wish for his lack of experience," said Palance, "but don't go after him just because he's an actor."

As a last resort, Brown attacked his opponent's managers. "I'm not running against Reagan, I'm running against Spencer-Roberts," said the Governor, part of whose campaign was being run by Baus and Ross, the firm that represented Goldwater in the 1964 California primary. And, for good measure, Brown dusted off the issue that had worked so well against Knowland and Nixon—accusing his opponent of using the governorship as a stepping-stone to the White House. But Reagan, when asked if he would complete a four-year term, answered, "Let's not tempt fate. [He looked heavenward.] The Lord willing, I'll complete my term." And everyone believed him.

As a campaigner, Ronald Reagan proved to be no crowd-plunging handshaker, à la Nelson Rockefeller and George Romney. Unlike his opponent, he was no baby kisser. (He is known to have kissed only one toddler, three-year-old Rose Marie Orlando, who, while Reagan was speaking at the Santa Cruz Municipal Auditorium, mounted the platform and took up position alongside the candidate.) He seemed shy and diffident when meeting voters on street corners or outside factory gates. He was almost incapable of making small talk with strangers.

But when Reagan mounted the rostrum he was a different person. He was forceful, yet relaxed; serious, yet witty. His jokes, according to one reporter's stopwatch, came at a rate of one every seven minutes, and, except for a penchant for anal humor ("The government is like a baby's alimentary canal, with a healthy appetite at one end and no sense of responsibility at the other"), they were of a fairly high level for the *genus* political. Herewith a modest chrestomathy of Reagan campaign humor:

—Watching myself on the late, late show is like looking at a son you never knew you had.

—We are told God is dead. Well, He isn't. We just can't talk to Him in the classroom any more.

—Our Governor has a native capacity for using the microphone as a shoe horn to get his foot in his mouth.

—There's nothing closer to eternal life than a government agency.

—He [Brown] recognizes that there are two sides to every question and if you give him time he'll take both.

—The Governor talks about *his* dams and *his* lakes and *his* reservoirs; you have the feeling that when he leaves office he'll take them with him.

—Sure it [my chance of winnning] looks good, but President Dewey told me not to be too confident.

As a speaker who was a professional actor, he appeared to play counter-image, using few gestures—except an occasional John F. Kennedy jabbing right forefinger—and few rhetorical gimmicks, his best being a devastating imitation of his opponent. His platform voice was somewhat higher than his conversational voice, and lacked the tonal richness of Charles Percy or even Richard Nixon.

In other subtle ways Reagan's appearances dispelled the "he's merely-an-actor" issue. He always spoke from notes, written on three-by-five index cards, which he rarely glanced it, while chiding Brown for using ghostwriters. (His TV spots were film clips taken from rallies, thus underscoring that they were not studio staged.) He quoted extensively from the greats and near greats, La Rochefoucauld to Hilaire Belloc—a sort of wisdom-by-association technique also used by President Kennedy—and he reeled off statistics like a train con-

'I'll Never Smile Again'
Green, Providence Sunday Journal, Oct. 30, 1966

ductor calling out stations on the Berlin-to-Baghdad Express, often rounding off at the tenth of a hundredth ("narcotics arrests of juveniles up 39.9 percent").

His main thrust, as the "out" candidate, was *Ya, basta!*—a slogan coined by Dr. Francisco Bravo, an ex-Brown supporter, who headed Reagan's highly successful Mexican-American drive. It meant, literally, "enough already." Running under the banner of this ethnic "Time for a Change," the Republican candidate won by 993,739 votes.

In the course of a seventeen-month campaign, Ronald Reagan displayed an almost flawless political instinct. He made no more serious error than to misplace a California river. ("This is a man running for Governor," Governor Brown, chuckling, told his audiences, "who doesn't even know where the Eel is." But, since few other Californians probably knew either, he did not score many points.) Reagan had successfully leaped the "credibility gap," picturing himself as something more than just an actor. He had successfully dodged the extremist label. He had successfully patched a party torn by ideological bickering. He had beaten the man who had beaten William Knowland and Richard Nixon.

On election night in Los Angeles Pat Brown thanked his loyal supporters, while, two miles away in the ornate ballroom of another hotel, fifteen hundred uproarious Republican workers cheered as a five-piece band struck up a jazz version of "California, Here I Come." And at 10:47, when the Governor-elect and his wife made their appearance, the first hand-painted "Reagan for President" banner was unfurled.

Thoughts of a presidential campaign were anything but alien to Reagan. A savvy California Republican, later to become heavily involved in the Reagan-for-Governor drive, remarked after his first meeting with the actor in early 1965 that "Ron's problem is that he doesn't know whether to bother with running for Governor or just to start with the presidency." The remark was not as foolish as it sounds. Reagan had been publicly talking national issues for ten years, and his political reputation rested far more on the nationwide speech he had made for Goldwater in 1964 than on anything he had ever done in California politics. As a matter of fact, he found it difficult at first to de-escalate his rhetoric from the national to the state level. The "Creative Society" theme he finally chose for his gubernatorial campaign was deliberately double-edged; it could serve, without change, as a counter-slogan to President Johnson's Great Society.

Nor was it Reagan alone who saw his candidacy in these terms. After his primary victory, he paid the customary courtesy call on General Eisenhower in Gettysburg. Reagan smiled shyly when a reporter asked the former President if he thought Reagan a presidential possibility.

"Any Republican," said Ike, "that wins a governorship and conducts it efficiently and on the basis of the welfare of all the people—you bet he's a possibility."*

* In March, 1967, General Eisenhower met again with Reagan and once again said some flattering things. While "there are a number of men who would make fine Presidents in our party," Ike remarked, "Governor Reagan is one of the men I admire most in this world."

The first faint rumblings of a Reagan presidential boom came from the same youthful quarters that saw in Barry Goldwater a candidate of shining valor and unblemished high principle. Lee Edwards, a bright, thirty-three-year-old publicist for right-wing causes, wrote in

"... Perfect, Ronald ... enter stage right ...
you're doing fine ..."

Conrad, Los Angeles **Times**, Jan. 6, 1966. Reprinted
by permission of The Register and Tribune Syndicate

Human Events of February 19, 1966: "If Ronald Reagan wins [the governorship] . . . he will be an obvious candidate for the Republican nomination for President—if not in 1968, then certainly in 1972. . . ." The same author, the same month, wrote in *The New Guard,* house organ of the Young Americans for Freedom: "I suggest there is one Republican, overlooked until now, who possesses an image more reminiscent of John F. Kennedy than any other. His name: Ronald Reagan." The message got through: 53 percent of the YAFers at a 1966 summer school made Reagan their first choice for President, with Goldwater second and Nixon a distant third. Reagan's national debut following his election was dramatic. He and his wife flew to the Colorado Springs G.O.P. Governors' meeting in chartered "his" and "hers" jets. But, as Paul Hope of the Washington *Evening Star* noted as their planes touched down, there was "surprisingly little talk about the possibility of Reagan becoming a presidential contender."

The eyes of the press and the other Governors were focused on George Romney. However, Romney managed to say only that he was not looking for support and that he planned to explore the Vietnam issue "in depth" before saying any more about it. Reagan, on the other hand, had no reluctance to give his views on Vietnam or any other subject. "I just don't recognize that a nation of our size can choose to be in a little war or a big war. When you consider the size of our country and of Vietnam, how can we talk with a straight face about spending ten years on this war? I think we should go in and get it over with." In a lengthy press conference, Reagan also recommended that the national Republican party adopt California's "Eleventh Commandment," and proceeded to put it into practice by ending his own feud with Romney. In the first flash of bitterness after Goldwater's 1964 defeat, Reagan practically had read Romney out of the party, telling readers of the *National Review*: "I don't think we should turn the high command over to leaders who were traitors during the battle just ended." Later, he hinted that a "repentant" Romney might be acceptable to him. And at Colorado Springs, he said magnanimously that he would not "disqualify" the Michigan Governor from anything. "I think all Republicans should repent for anything done in the past that did not help the party," Reagan said, "but I don't know of any Republican that isn't acceptable to me as the 1968 nominee."

There was more than sweet charity behind Reagan's new attitude of forgiveness. He had been visited already by two other potential 1968 favorite sons, Texas Senator John Tower and Ohio Governor James Rhodes, and absorbed from them the wisdom of staking out a bargaining position well in advance of the 1968 convention. Tower and Rhodes, like Reagan, were much closer philosophically and much more comfortable personally with Nixon than with Romney. But, above all, as practical politicians they could see the potential advantage of arriving at the convention uncommitted, with a sizable hunk of votes available for trading.

Reagan's bloc of eighty-six California delegates was second only to New York's ninety-two, but to control them he had first to make sure that he would have no competition in his state's binding presidential primary. By February, 1967, he had made it clear that he intended to be the favorite-son candidate in the primary and wanted no outsider—whether Nixon or Romney—contesting with him for control of the delegation. His stated reason for this tactic was to guarantee "California the voice it is entitled to in determining the party policy." But in short order this decision was cited as the grounds for refusing to remove his name from other presidential primaries where it might be entered. Vowing not to "lift a finger" to have his name entered anywhere or to campaign actively for votes outside California, Reagan nevertheless said it would be "arrogant" and inconsistent for him to be a favorite son in California and to reject any votes or delegates that were voluntarily offered elsewhere. Thus by March of 1967, barely two months in office, he had virtually assured that he would be on the ballot in at least four important primary states—California, Wisconsin, Oregon and Nebraska—and perhaps a good many more.

On March 1, he flew across the continent for a five-minute speech to the Republican Victory Gala in Washington, where he was escorted to the television cameras by the supposed Nixon stalwart Barry Goldwater. Reagan's speech and quips completely captured the audience from Romney, who made the mistake of competing with him as a funny man, and from Nixon, who prudently chose to take his bow and remain silent.

Reagan aides were busy assuring visitors to Sacramento that the Governor could repeat his platform triumph over Romney and Nixon any day of the week, in any state, and leading Republicans in the legislature and even in his own administration confided their belief that Reagan was more interested in adulation from the country than in the day-to-day details of running California. "He's acting the part of the Governor," one Republican remarked, "but really he's still campaigning—this time for President."

Reagan again flew cross-country in late March, this time for the star spot in a forum any presidential prospect covets, as spokesman for his party at the annual Washington Gridiron Dinner. The Governor was matched against Senator Robert F. Kennedy and, before an audience that included almost every major politician and influential member of the press, he had one of his rare flops. A guest, encountering Reagan afterward, sought to congratulate him on his speech, but was cut short by the Governor's remark: "I blew it." Kennedy and his New York gag writers simply outshone Reagan and his homespun West Coast humor. Typically, Reagan did not take the defeat lying down. The next time he and Kennedy were booked for the same show—a satellite television interview in May, where they answered questions from an audience of European students—Reagan did his homework on Vietnam policy far more thoroughly than Kennedy and easily dominated the program with his firm and well-documented defense of the American military involvement in Vietnam.

Indeed, as Sacramento reporters came to know, Reagan frequently seemed far more certain about what was going on in Vietnam than in his own capital.

On May 2, for example, Reagan was asked at his press conference about his administration's position on repeal of the Rumford open-housing law. The transcript reads:

REAGAN: No, I'm waiting to see what—what comes down to the desk. I know that the—there have been some amendments proposed. Now, whether they have been taken up yet or not, I'm familiar with certain amendments or have been told to, certain amendments that they are looking to the Burns Bill to add to this bill. And I'm watching this. I want to see what—what happens with it, and—and this would repeal the features that I think the people voted against in the state. But they are—it would also add other amendments to the bill, and I would—I'm waiting for that one. I'd rather not get in now with specifics until I see what's going to come downstairs.

QUESTION: Are you saying some of Bagley's amendments may be worked into the Burns Bill? Single-family dwellings and single-family—

REAGAN: I can't—I can't—as I try to recall, now, the one meeting we had on this, I can't recall whether—I think some of the amendments would be similar to some of the provisions of his bill.

Three questions later, Reagan was asked about the Vietnam war as a 1968 issue and there was no stumbling in the answer:

I have insisted for a long time that our goal should be to win and I think you win as swiftly as possible, that attrition over the long period of time will cost us more in lives than a sudden strike for victory.

Still fifteen months before the presidential convention, the rival ideological groups, the American Conservative Union and the Ripon Society, led off their March newsletters by noting what both called "The Reagan Phenomenon." The ACU *Battle Line,* enthusiastic over the way "Reagan wowed the party faithful" at the Gala, said that "if that was a Goldwater-Reagan crowd . . . then so is the Republican party." And the *Ripon Forum,* agonizing over the same event, said, "Ronald Reagan's presidential ambitions must be taken seriously, not because they are justified by the candidate's own experience or by his vision for America, but because he threatens, by the same combination of organizational maneuvering and narrowly based programs, to make 1968 another year of disaster and disunity for the Republican party."

A point that both the agonizers and the ecstasizers missed was that Reagan's real weight at the 1968 Republican convention would depend, not on how much he dazzled the diners in Washington, but on how well he fared as Governor in California. And there the first returns were decidedly mixed. If John Lindsay, confronted with a subway strike on the day he took office as Mayor of New York, was denied any political honeymoon at all, Reagan's honeymoon can be calculated at one week. Sworn into office in a midnight ceremony on Monday, January 2, 1967, on the following Monday he was hanged in effigy by students at Fresno State College.

Part of the problem that plagued him was the inexperience natural for any new administration, but naïveté was compounded by the anti-politician, anti-bureaucracy biases which Reagan brought with him to office. Two very experienced politicians were elected on the ticket with him, but he made little use of their talents. One of them was Nixon's and Murphy's manager, Robert Finch, now Reagan's Lieutenant Governor. Finch worked quietly behind the scenes for Christopher in the primary, but so skillfully that he attracted little antagonism from the Reagan forces. In the general election, he campaigned as hard for Reagan as for himself, but differed with the gubernatorial candidate on two key issues. Finch rejected Birch Society support and opposed, as unconstitutional, an anti-pornography amendment which Reagan backed and the voters turned down. Finch lagged far behind Reagan in the public-opinion polls until the end of the campaign, when the Reagan backers finally heeded his pleas for some financial support. On election day, to everyone's surprise, he led the ticket, running 230,000 votes ahead of Reagan.

California gives its Lieutenant Governor wider statutory authority than most states; he sits on thirteen boards and commissions and presides over the Senate. In addition, Reagan gave Finch special duties in overhauling welfare and urban programs. But, despite the pledges of unprecedented teamwork, the usual barriers appeared between the Governor's staff and the No. 2 man. "The one problem I never anticipated," Finch ruefully confessed, "was what might happen if I ran better than Reagan."

If Finch was somewhat suspect in the eyes of the Reagan men, that was nothing compared to the coolness between the Governor and the third member of his winning slate, thirty-six-year-old State Controller Houston (Hugh) Fluornoy, who scored the most implausible victory of the whole Republican sweep. Early in 1966 Fluornoy announced that he was quitting the Assembly after three terms to return full time to his academic career as associate professor of government at Pomona College. At the last moment, some of his Assembly friends backing Christopher against Reagan prevailed on Fluornoy to permit them to file his name as candidate for Controller in hopes it would help Christopher in Fluornoy's part of Southern California. No one wanted the nomination for Controller because the Democratic incumbent, Alan Cranston, was regarded as unbeatable. Without bothering to campaign, Fluornoy became the Republican nominee. He made a bit more effort in the general election, but kept his distance from Reagan, and eked out a narrow victory. Fluornoy's office in the capitol is right across the corridor from Reagan's, but there is virtually no communication between the liberal, intellectual Controller and the conservative movie-star Governor.

To some extent, the same gulf exists between Reagan and the Republican leaders in the legislature, Assemblyman Robert Monagan and state Senator Jack McCarthy. Both Monagan and McCarthy are moderates; both preferred Rockefeller to Goldwater in 1964 and Christopher to Reagan in 1966.

Instead of looking to Finch, Fluornoy, Monagan and McCarthy, Reagan seeks his advice and counsel from men who were part of his own campaign staff. Chief among them is balding, freckled, thirty-two-year-old attorney Philip M. Battaglia. Battaglia, smart enough to win admission to the University of Southern California Law School after only two years of undergraduate work, energetic enough to be successively student body president, law-school alumni director and president of the Los Angeles Jaycees, is the strong man of the Inner Circle. Blooded in the Kuchel-for-Senate campaign of 1962, Battaglia was picked by Spencer and Roberts as Southern California manager of Reagan's primary campaign, moved up to be statewide chairman during the general election and was named as executive secretary of the new administration the day after Reagan's election.

Second in importance is Franklyn C. (Lyn) Nofziger, a forty-two-year-old newspaperman of generous proportions, whose trademark is a steady stream of outrageously bad puns and good humor. Nofziger took a leave of absence from his job as chief Washington political correspondent for the Copley Newspapers (San Diego *Union,* Sacramento *Union, et al.*) to become Reagan's campaign press secretary in early 1966. Conservative in his own political leanings, Nofziger quickly established close personal rapport with his candidate and stayed on as "director of communications" for the Reagan Administration—a title that understates his real influence. He sits in on almost every meeting of Reagan's where Battaglia is not present, travels with the Governor and contributes heavily to almost every major Reagan speech.

Major appointments of the Reagan Administration were of generally high quality, though a few of them looked suspiciously ideological: Rus Walton, former head of the conservative United Republicans of California and producer of the banned Goldwater campaign film, *Choice,* was given a patronage job as deputy director of motor vehicles; a bakery company executive was named as state labor commissioner, the first time in modern history that the post was given to a man from management rather than labor; the head of the California Real Estate Association, an opponent of open-housing legislation, was named real-estate commissioner. The first two appointments on the state Board of Education went to conservative physicians, but Reagan had to withdraw one of them, an outspoken advocate of the teacher-led prayers in schools, when the liberal Republican state Senator from his home county threatened to fight his confirmation.

For the key fiscal post of director of finance, Reagan chose a nonpolitical figure, Gordon Paul Smith, vice president in charge of the Los Angeles office of Booz, Allen & Hamilton, the national management-consultant firm. Smith showed his political naïveté in several of the early budget-cutting crises, but impressed even his critics as being competent with the balance sheets.

Spencer Williams, defeated Republican candidate for Attorney General, was named administrator of Health and Welfare; Gordon Luce, a San Diego savings and loan executive, was put in charge of transportation and regulatory agencies; Norman B. Livermore, Jr., a San Francisco lumber executive with a reputation as a conservationist, was named administrator of the State Resources Agency. The most-applauded appointment was that of William R. Gianelli, a respected and experienced Democrat, to head the Department of Water Resources.

Given time to settle into their new jobs, the Reagan team probably would have managed a smooth transition. But neither circumstances nor Reagan's interpretation of his own mandate allowed them that luxury. Committed by the campaign to the view that California's government was swollen and its tax burden too high, Reagan had only thirty days, under law, to submit his first round of budget proposals. Obviously that was inadequate time to cope with a fiscal crisis which Reagan pronounced "far worse than anything we ever imagined we would find." Carryover commitments from the Brown Administration, he said, were costing the state $1 million a day more than it was receiving in taxes. Though Democrats claimed he was exaggerating the situation, Reagan and Finance Director Smith ordered a 10 percent slash in projected state spending.

The outcry was sharpest from the educators, already on edge because of Reagan's campaign attacks on conditions at the University of California. The university system had asked $278 million from the state for fiscal 1968; the separate state college system, $213 million. Instead, Reagan offered $196 million for the university and $154 million for the colleges, proposing that the shortage of $141 million in their combined budget of $491 million be made up in part by economies and in part by imposing tuition—$280 per student in the colleges and $400 in the universities. It was the tuition proposal, unintentionally leaked by Finance Director Smith to a meeting of educators, that led to Reagan's being hanged in effigy his first week in office.

Clark Kerr, the president of the nine-campus university, and Glenn S. Dumke, chancellor of the eighteen state colleges, warned that Reagan's economies would force either a reduction in quality of education or abandonment of the unique California guarantee of tuition-free higher education for every qualified high-school graduate in the state. Both men ordered new enrollments suspended until the finance situation was clarified. On January 20, three weeks after his inaugura-- tion, Reagan attended his first meeting of the university board of regents. Before the meeting, Kerr, who had tried with little success to defend the university's reputation during the campaign, sought out Theodore R. Meyer, chairman of the regents, and Mrs. Dorothy Chandler, a member of the board and wife of the publisher of the powerful Los Angeles *Times*. Kerr told them that since it was clear the university was in for a hard fight, the regents should determine *now* whether they thought he was the man to defend it. As Reagan later commented, "It was Kerr himself who made the proposition that he wanted it settled one way or the other." Once Meyer and Mrs. Chandler put the question to the full board, the result was probably inevitable. The vote to dismiss Kerr was fourteen to eight, with Reagan, Finch and the Reagan-appointed president of the state Board of Agriculture, Allan Grant, all among the anti-Kerr majority. The ousted president later said, "I became to many people a symbol of tolerance of expression of opinions that they didn't like." The state's top Democrat, Assembly Speaker and university regent Jesse M. Unruh, who voted against Kerr's dismissal, said, "It is bad precedent to fire a university president concomitant with a change of political party in the state administration. It will be interpreted as a political move."

The prediction was quickly verified as anti-Reagan rallies spread from campus to campus and large groups of students and teachers protested on the lawn of the capitol. Educators across the country took up the criticism. The American Association of University Professors dispatched two men to California, who interviewed Reagan and reported: "An anti-intellectual political reactionary now governs California and is determined to bring higher educational growth to a grinding halt." Though the Los Angeles *Times* had backed Reagan for Governor and Mrs. Chandler had voted with him to dismiss Kerr, by March the paper was in outright disagreement with his education policies. In an editorial, "The Education of Ronald Reagan," it said:

. . . Reagan has shown an apparent disdain for values far more important than temporary economic gain. He has demonstrated that he does not believe it is vital for society to enable each citizen to achieve the best in knowledge and skill and understanding of which he is capable. . . . In what other spirit could a public official scorn the universities for "subsidizing intellectual curiosity" as Reagan did at his last press conference? If a university is not a place where intellectual curiosity is to be encouraged, and subsidized, then it is nothing. . . . Informed people across the country believe that Gov. Reagan's budget cuts, following in the wake of his campaign attacks on UC and the subsequent firing of Clark Kerr, have started the university and the colleges on a downward plunge that will be difficult to reverse. If the governor is seeking to transform the University of California overnight into an institution of the second rank, and if he desires to hold back the development of a strong state college system, he has chosen the right path to reach those goals.

If Reagan was daunted by the turmoil and the criticism, he did not show it. Even Democrats who disagreed with him conceded that "he took the heat better" than they thought he would. In a televised February "report to the people," he said:

Education through high school is compulsory and therefore properly paid for by all of us. But the college and university levels present a different picture. There, traditionally, we have also offered a free education. But remember, on that level education is not compulsory. It is a gift to a limited number of our young people, paid for by all of us. It is a worthy and unique gift, to be sure, and we did not object to giving it in the past. And while some of us may think philosophically tuition is a good thing, I'm sure we would not object to free higher education now, if we could afford it. But we cannot.

Nor was it just talk. Each month, Reagan confronted the university regents at their meetings, fiddling with a rubber band on his fingers, while they debated hour after hour on how to trim their programs to meet his demands. The old union president proved an adept bargainer; in February, when the regents agreed to take $20 million of outside income from special projects and apply it to the general costs of the university, he agreed to provide $20 million more from state funds in lieu of the tuition payments which it was manifestly impossible to extract for the coming school year. But at the same time he warned the regents that if they balked indefinitely at imposing tuition for later years "we're going to have to review our entire approach to the financing of the university. . . ."

That was the first fight of his first legislative session, but it was not the only one by a long shot. Early on, Reagan dreamed up the idea of dramatizing the fiscal squeeze by "inviting" state employees to donate two days' work on the normal Lincoln's and Washington's birthday holidays. A bare handful of employees came to their offices, but dozens showed up outside the state office buildings in Sacramento, San Francisco and Los Angeles to picket in protest against Reagan's stunt. Two months later, the "stunt" seemed less phony when Reagan announced a cutback of almost eight thousand "surplus" state jobs, many of them in mental hospitals, to save $50 million in salaries. Both the "working holidays" plan and the reduction in state job rolls were announced by Reagan without prior consultation with his own Republican legislative leaders—and both produced emergency caucuses in the legislature and protests to the Governor's office. There were other "misunderstandings" with the Republican legislators in the early months over budget, patronage and revenue matters. The Democrats under Unruh were predictably critical, particularly when Reagan said that the Brown Administration had "looted" the state treasury, a word that he later apologized for using. At the end of his first three months in office, the Los Angeles *Times* said editorially, "The legislature is in a bind. Responsibility for the bind . . . rests squarely upon the administration. If the governor and his advisors hope to see any substantial part of their program get through, they must get the glue out of the works and move promptly to establish now virtually non-existent liaison with the Legislature."

The *Times* editorial reflected the judgment of most Sacramento observers. A veteran Republican official said that "Reagan's problem is that he doesn't realize his constituency has shrunk from 20 million [Californians] to 120 [the number of Assemblymen and Senators]." If that was true, it was also true that Reagan was playing brilliantly and successfully to the larger audience. The very Republican legislators who criticized his methods of operation conceded that their own mail was heavier than ever, and strongly weighted with admonitions to "help the Governor."

Reagan's office was so inundated with letters—sixty thousand in his first month—that volunteers had to be recruited to help the secretaries acknowledge them. "Overwhelmingly," Reagan said, "they support what we are trying to do." Public-opinion polls told the same story, recording majority support for his economy efforts, for his call for tuition payments, and for the ouster of Kerr. In March, 1967, Reagan did the hardest thing a new Governor can do. When all the economies he could find had been exhausted, he still had to ask for a record-breaking $946-million tax increase to finance a record-breaking $5-billion budget and to permit a modest $120-million start on the property tax relief he had promised in his campaign. By June, Reagan was forced to raise the ante again, seeking $1.07 billion in new taxes to finance a $5.15 billion budget. He handled the politics of the situation skillfully, blaming the stiff tax hike on the "spendthrift policies" of his Democratic predecessor, while milking every bit of publicity from the small, visible economies he was able to make. He sold the state airplane (and traveled on commercial or chartered jets), even ordered a halt to the printing of state road maps to save $192,000. The technique worked. The State Poll reported that after seven months, a record 74 percent approved of Reagan's performance in office.

Moreover, the controversy of his first months in office made Reagan even more a national figure than he was when elected. (A Gallup Poll in November, 1966, found that 75 percent of Americans could identify Reagan, compared to 57 percent who had known Romney in a similar quiz a few months earlier.)

Outside reporters came, and saw, and were impressed. Said columnist Roscoe Drummond: "He has shown that he is not afraid to tread on some toes, that he can make decisions and stand behind them, that he intends to redeem his campaign promises. He is proving in practice that the idea he is an empty-headed actor reading somebody else's script is bunk." *Newsweek,* in a cover story on the "rising star in the West," conceded "Reagan is no intellectual" and noted that his Cabinet secretaries were under orders to reduce all problems to single-page, four-paragraph memos, but nonetheless concluded that "he is playing his new role with more conviction and better results than he ever achieved as an actor." The *Wall Street Journal* said Reagan "is demonstrating a flexibility toward the state's problems that bodes well for his future." And the Washington *Star*'s Mary McGrory, an old hand at cutting up conservatives, was so charmed by Reagan that she wrote that "the crown prince of Goldwaterism" was being transformed by responsibility "into a moderate Republican," a change she called "one of the most interesting phenomena in American politics today." If reporters were intrigued by Reagan, it was nothing compared to the fascination he held for the television cameras. In one period in mid-February, Reagan's special staff assistant for television, pretty Nancy Clark Reynolds, reported the new Governor was on network news shows eight consecutive nights, facing down angry student pickets, coolly answering questions from hostile reporters.

"What Reagan is doing, pretty obviously," said Assemblyman Charles Warren, the state Democratic chairman, "is using his job to develop a national forum for himself. I used to think he was proceeding from ignorance, but it's perfectly clear now he wants to use the same things in a national campaign in 1968 he used to win California in 1966."

The original Reagan backers—Salvatori, Tuttle, *et al.*—were frequent visitors to Sacramento, and they did nothing to discourage Reagan's faith that a conservative counterrevolution was possible in America. Neither did his principal staff men, Nofziger and Battaglia. Reagan himself, in this period, concluded almost every speech with this thought:

> As a result of our victory, we started something in this state. We are being watched, watched by those all across this land who once again dare to believe that our concept of responsible, people-oriented government can work as the Founding Fathers meant it to work. If we can prove that here, we can start a prairie fire that can sweep across this country.

The flavor of Reagan's noble enterprise was brilliantly parodied by San Francisco *Chronicle* columnist Art Hoppe. He recounted the adventures of "Sir Ronald of HollyRood," who, in quick succession, "vanquished the evil Governor; freed the Golden State; banished Kerr, the Wicked Wizard from the Castle of Cal; awoke the sleeping Civil Service and marched boldly into the Thorny Thicket of the Legislature, in whose tangled depths dwelled The Unruh, feared by one and All."

It is while "cutting a brave swath through the Bureaucratic Brambles," Hoppe recounts, that Sir Ronald first espies "far off to the east . . . a big White House that somehow shimmers and glitters, advances and recedes, looms large and fades. A mirage if I be not mistaken."

"Oh, no, Sire," cries his faithful servant, Sancho Nofziger. "It is the Tantalizing Treasure. . . . Quick, to horse! We must pursue it lest some other knight captures it first."

"Hold there, varlet," says Sir Ronald irritably. "I have pledged my sacred word to serve the people of my beloved Golden State for four long years, here in the Tangled Thicket."

"But Sire," cries Sancho, "the fame, the fortune!"

"A pox on fame and fortune; I shall not seek the Treasure." Sir Ronald resumes hacking straight ahead, allowing only an occasional glance over his shoulder to the East. "Of course, you might keep an eye on it, Sancho," he adds, "in case it comes seeking me."

"Verily," says Sancho, "I think sometimes I serve the most clever of masters."

Corny as the plot may sound in Hoppe's parody, Reagan's men are dead serious about his national ambitions. In the interest of those ambitions, Reagan struck up a nonaggression pact with California's liberal Republican Senator, Tom Kuchel, who had endorsed George Christopher in the 1966 primary and pointedly refused to back Reagan in the general election. With Kuchel facing re-election in 1968, conservative Republicans were eager to settle the score, and Max Rafferty, the conservative state superintendent of public instruction, was eager to run. But Reagan wanted no destructive primary fight in his home state a month before the national convention. He met with Kuchel in the spring of 1967 and announced he would take no part in any primary contest. Rafferty complained that Salvatori and the other conservative money men were "saving their money for Reagan" and had shut their wallets on him. Meantime, Reagan himself approved the decision for Stu Spencer and Bill Roberts to handle Kuchel's campaign.

By May, 1967, Tom Reed, the wealthy young San Franciscan who had managed Reagan's northern California campaign and served briefly as his patronage secretary, was turning up around the country as a "traveling secretary" for the Governor. Reed, Roberts and others in the Reagan circle were in frequent contact with F. Clifton White, the Goldwater organizer who insisted publicly he would not affiliate himself with any candidate until the autumn of 1967. Reagan himself took to the road, visiting most of the western states, Nebraska, Wisconsin and Illinois, disclaiming all the while any intention of campaigning for the presidency. But the Reagan men are convinced that the 1968 convention will be one where there will be plenty of room for bargaining. If the presidency proves unattainable for Reagan, the vice presidency may not be out of reach; and, in any case, his will be a voice to be reckoned with.

Whatever the odds, Reagan's friends—and perhaps Reagan himself —think he can be, not Kingmaker, but King. "Romney's never going to get off the ground," one close associate said in early 1967. "Nixon is a loser. The only man in the whole Republican party who has stirred any excitement in the last six months is the guy in there," pointing at Reagan's office.

"There's plenty of support available to him around the country right now, if he gives the signal to let it move. If we come through this session of the legislature in one piece, we should be in good shape to go."

With his last words, his hand moved in an upward arc, the classic parabola of success. Like a jet taking off from California, carrying Sir Ronald and his Creative Society message across the mountains and the plains, toward Washington and the sunrise, the music swelling to crescendo.

GOVERNOR RONALD REAGAN

Levine, **The Atlantic,** April, 1966

III

The Regions

9 EAST

THE RCA 501 Computer had been programmed, checked, rechecked and pronounced ready. The returns from the indicator precincts in the Eastern states and a few Midwestern cities were fed into the machine. And at 10:30 P.M. on election night, as Theodore H. White recalls in *The Making of the President—1960,* the National Broadcasting Company projected John Kennedy's victory over Richard Nixon by a margin of 401 electoral votes to 134.

This epic misjudgment of what turned out to be the closest American election in this century resulted from oversimplifying the complex pattern of conflict in a presidential compaign, and forgetting that a presidential election is really fifty separate state elections (now fifty-one, counting the battle for the District of Columbia's three electoral votes).

All those acquainted with American history are familiar with the strife between the Tidewater and the Frontier, between the Eastern railroad owners and the Western shippers, between the slave-holding South and the free-labor North. Many supposed those sectional and regional conflicts had disappeared as an influence on national politics with the coming of the superhighway and the jet airplane, national radio and television broadcasts and mass-circulation national magazines. It was, now, they supposed, one nation, indivisible. . . .

And yet the Kennedy tide that the RCA computer accurately measured midway through the vote count broke at the Appalachians, spilling over just enough to give him Illinois and Michigan. Of twenty-four states west of the Mississippi, Kennedy carried only seven. In the Midwest and the West, the Boston-accented Roman Catholic was still, somehow, alien. Old prejudices and preferences, supposedly blended away in a single homogenized culture, resurfaced.

Nor was this really surprising considering the infinite variety of political customs and habits, of personalities and styles, that shape an American election. All elections in this country, even a presidential one, are ultimately local elections; the votes are cast and counted precinct by precinct, county by county, state by state. Afterward, men may speak of national trends and write of the broad significance of the results. But, in the first instance, it is what is happening in the precinct that counts.

Nowhere is the struggle for votes in fifty separate, sovereign states more visible than on the floor of a presidential nominating convention, in that climactic moment when the chairman calls the roll of states. "Aa-luh-baa-muh," a deep, rich Southern drawl replies, "casts twenty-six votes for the next President. . . ." "Uh-las-kuh," the next delegation chairman booms out, and so it goes, each response summarizing a struggle shaped by the personalities, the political climate of that particular state.

It is on the playing fields of the fifty states that the 1968 presidential aspirants must contrive their strategy for nomination. Moreover, it is ultimately in these states, grouped in four regions, that the future history of the Republican party will be determined.

For most of this century, the East has financed the Republican party, picked (if not provided) its presidential candidates and shaped its approach to public policy. Its dominance exists no longer.

The East is a declining force in American politics. Its monopoly on investment capital has been broken by the emergence of rival financial centers in the Midwest, the South and the West. The oldest part of a young nation, its growth has not kept pace with that of other sections. In the decade from 1950 to 1960, only four of its twelve states matched the national average of 18.5 percent population increase.

Within the region has developed America's largest megalopolis, a vast urban belt stretching, almost unbroken, from Boston to Norfolk, from New York to Pittsburgh. The old farms, no longer productive, are disappearing into suburbs, just as the old Yankee stock earlier was outnumbered by newer immigrants, the Irish, Italians, Poles, Jews, Southern Negroes, Puerto Ricans and French-Canadians. None of these trends helps the Republican party, rooted as it is in the Protestant, small-town or rural past—a past the East cannot recapture.

A few Yankee Republicans have survived in politics, like former Massachusetts Senators Leverett Saltonstall and Henry Cabot Lodge, by adapting their viewpoint to that of their new constituents, while preserving, as a piquant reminder of the past, their own personalities. In some few cases, the Eastern Republicans have recruited new leaders from the ranks of the immigrants. But by and large the Eastern Republicans remain what they have been—world-minded WASP's, internationalist in their foreign policy views, flexible in their domestic policy, occasionally innovative—and there are fewer of them all the time.

The decline is fairly dramatic. In 1952, eight of the twelve Eastern Governors were Republicans; now there are five. Of the twenty-four Senate seats, Republicans have dropped from fifteen to ten; in House seats, from seventy-four down to forty-eight. In the entire sweep from Maine to West Virginia, there is only one Republican of presidential stature, the twice-married, twice-vanquished Nelson A. Rockefeller, Governor of New York. And he has ruled out ever running again for President.

The decline of Republicanism in the East is reflected in the region's loss of power in the national convention; its share of delegates has dropped from 30.8 percent in 1952 to 26.1 percent in 1968. Yet any liberal hopeful of nomination has to—and probably can—count on winning as much as four-fifths of the East's 355 votes.

Even that support is not an unalloyed blessing. For to many Republicans in other regions, the East, debilitated as it is, still conjures up the image of a modern Goliath—a powerful Wall Street, internationalist bully, controlling the major media of mass communications, dictating to others what they should do. Barry Goldwater was not alone when he fantasied sawing off the Eastern Seaboard from the rest of the country, which is probably why George Lodge, when discussing Governor Romney in a 1965 interview, said with obvious relish, "At least the liberal candidate isn't from the East."

The old adage, "As Maine goes, so goes the nation" (because the state used to hold its elections in September, two months before the rest of the country), once pointed the way to Republican victories. But since Edmund Muskie taught Down Easters how to vote Democratic in 1952, the compass point has swung nearly a full 180 degrees. In 1966, potato grower John H. Reed, a lackluster liberal, was one of only two Republican Governors to be defeated for re-election. And capping this humiliation was the party's loss of its last House seat after 1st District incumbent Stanley Tupper accepted appointment from President Johnson as U.S. representative to Expo 67, the Canadian World's Fair, rather than face the hostility of his party's conservatives, who had not forgiven him for failing to support Goldwater in 1964.

The one bright spot was the re-election to a fourth term of Senator Margaret Chase Smith. But even this provided little comfort because the dauntless Mrs. Smith's triumphs are always highly personal. The barber's daughter from Skowhegan, who went to work in the five and dime at thirteen, and married the local political leader (whom she succeeded in Congress), has earned a reputation in Washington for independence and for never missing a roll-call vote. It was she who delivered a "declaration of conscience" in 1950, denouncing fellow Republican Senator Joseph R. McCarthy for his "witch-hunting" tactics. It is not true, as often reported, that when there was talk of her for Vice President in 1948 she replied to a newsman's question about what she would do if she woke up in the White House, "I'd apologize to Mrs. Truman and go home." But this did not mean that she was without ambition. In 1964 she entered the New Hampshire presidential primary, spent $250 of her own money, and lost. Then she entered the Illinois primary, spent $85, and also lost. "For $335 I didn't do badly," she said. At the San Francisco convention she was the "favorite daughter" of Maine and her name was placed in nomination by Senator George D. Aiken of Vermont. She would probably happily accept the designation again in 1968 to give her fellow Down Easters time to decide where finally to bestow their votes.

If Mrs. Smith is trying to prove something, George Aiken of Vermont, dean of all Senate Republicans, is not. He nominated Mrs. Smith because she was his friend and neighbor. The white-haired, gentle Aiken, a farmer and holder at various times of every position of importance in his native state—speaker of the House of Representatives, Lieutenant Governor, Governor—has now spent a third of his seventy-five years in the Senate. He never asserts himself, but other Senators often come to him. On most issues (except ones like reapportionment that directly affect the rural interests of his rural state), he advises the progressive stance. In a significant Senate speech

in May, 1967, Aiken said he had concluded the Johnson Administration "cannot achieve an honorable peace in Vietnam" and urged
Republicans to nominate a candidate who will "promise a new look
at United States policy in Asia." Vermont also has a second Republican Senator, middle-of-the-roader Winston L. Prouty, a modest,
colorless ex-lumber dealer, and a Republican as the state's one
Congressman, popular Robert Stafford, who has grown more liberal
since his arrival in Washington and is generally considered the heir-
apparent for the next Senate vacancy. While Vermont has an all-
Republican congressional delegation, it is a tradition for those in
Washington to stay out of state politics.

In the state since 1962, when a Democrat became the first of his
party to win the governorship since 1853, the revised adage has been,
"As Maine goes, so goes Vermont." The combination of an ossified
G.O.P. and Goldwater's candidacy in 1964 produced a complete
wipeout for the party. The Democrats had filled out their ticket in the
slapdash manner that minority parties often do and so on election
day no Vermonters were more surprised than the victorious eighty-one-
year-old Democratic candidate for state Treasurer or the seventy-two-
year-old Democratic dairy farmer who was elected Secretary of
State. However, the Republicans' 1964 disaster cleared out some political cobwebs and the party has now begun regrouping around some
energetic men in the middle thirties to early forties, including James
Oakes, forty-three, who returned the Attorney General's office to the
G.O.P. in 1966; Shelburne manufacturer Richard A. Snelling, forty;
Richard Mallory, thirty-eight, speaker of the House; House floor leader
Luther Hackett, a former state YR president; and Thomas L. Hayes, a
past national debating champion and aide to Senator Prouty. Vermont Republicans normally are counted in the liberal Republican
column and they are likely to be there again in 1968.

New Hampshire, a mountainous wedge between the calm hillsides
of Vermont and the wild forests of Maine, is more urban, more industrial, and a great deal more politically frisky than its upper New
England neighbors. Yet the tong war every fourth year over its
handful of presidential convention votes would be relatively mean-
ingless were it not that as Bert Teague, Nelson Rockefeller's 1964
manager in the Granite State, rightly noted, "The importance of the
New Hampshire primary is what the press makes it." And since it is

always the first election of the presidential year—falling on March 12 in 1968—the national press always makes a great deal of it.*

The New Hampshire primary has a lively, if overplayed, history. In 1952, led by then Governor Sherman Adams, the Eisenhower forces gained a psychologically impressive victory over Senator Taft; in 1956, at the height of the "dump Nixon" fervor, New Hampshire's senior Senator, Styles Bridges, quietly organized a write-in campaign that produced a phenomenal 82 percent vote for the Vice President and did much to convince G.O.P. leaders that his renomination would not be a drag on the national ticket; and in 1964 Henry Cabot Lodge from faraway Saigon temporarily scrambled the presidential sweepstakes with an amazing write-in performance over active campaigners Goldwater and Rockefeller.

The Republican party in New Hampshire has never recovered from the death in 1961 of Senator Bridges, posthumously called "the one authentic American Tory." Among the leaders who have tried unsuccessfully to fill his shoes are his widow Doloris; former Governor Wesley Powell, an unpredictable maverick; Senator Norris Cotton, leader of the Goldwater forces in 1964; Ex-Governor Hugh Gregg, leader of the Rockefeller forces in 1964; moderate Congressman James C. Cleveland; conservative Congressman Louis Wyman, the only New Englander to vote against the 1964 Civil Rights bill; viper-tongued publisher William Loeb of the Manchester *Union-Leader,* the only newspaper with a statewide circulation; and a Loeb protégé with the Dr. Strangelove name of General Thyng, who, as a Vietnam hawk, was defeated for Senate in 1966.

From this jumble of leaders in a leaderless party, with their competing ambitions and open wounds, George Romney and Richard Nixon must find their allies for 1968. Some gravitate toward one presidential contender for no better reason than that a long-standing enemy is in the camp of the other. Yet if the delegates to be won are few and the hazards many, there is still a rationale for the nation's first primary.

* The New Hampshire primary, in fact, is not one but two contests at the same time. There is the preferential, or "beauty contest," primary. Here the voter casts his ballot for a presidential candidate. This in no way binds the state's convention delegates. The prize to the candidate is strictly national publicity.

The second contest is the actual balloting for delegates to the national convention. Each candidate normally enters a slate of eight names who are voted for individually. Here the prize is not publicity but eight votes when the party convention chooses its presidential nominee.

For on those long, cold, dark winter's days, the shrewd New Hampshiremen have invented a grand entertainment. Ever since 1952, when the Eisenhower strategists imported Fred Waring and his Pennsylvanians, they have been assured of a good show.

Moreover, the candidates spend many thousands of dollars in the state (Nixon figures that it costs a quarter million dollars to run a campaign in New Hampshire), while the three television networks compete for the costly honor of being the first to tell the nation of New Hampshire's decision. In 1964 it was estimated that the broadcasters put out more than two dollars for each vote cast. Walter Cronkite's people at CBS were paying an average of twenty dollars apiece for election night workers; ABC got local college students at about fifteen dollars each to phone in the returns; and NBC hired the whole New Hampshire League of Women Voters. Then, of course, from early January on there are all those expense-account reporters slushing through Concord, Laconia and Lincoln. It probably is not true that there are more reporters than voters, but at times it certainly seems that way.

In this modest primary—with less than 100,000 Republican votes —New Hampshire has found an effective antipoverty program.

John H. Johnson, the founder of *Ebony* magazine, once predicted the possibility of a Negro Vice President by 1985 and Robert Kennedy has said the United States might have a Negro President by the year 2000. But such timetables could be outmoded by the election in 1966 of Edward W. Brooke, Jr., of Massachusetts to the U.S. Senate.

Although in 1888 Mississippi Senator Blanche Kelso Bruce, "the sable legislator," received eleven votes for the G.O.P. vice-presidential nomination, and Frederick Douglass got a vote for President at the same convention, the thought of a Negro on the national ticket was considered a very good joke in 1892, when columnist Eugene Field of the Chicago *Daily News* wrote that H. H. Kohlsaat, publisher of the rival *Inter-Ocean*, was going to the Republican convention intent on promoting a Negro for Vice President and would pay the expenses of anyone who wished to join him. The embarrassed publisher had to tell a line of eager colored applicants that it was all a hoax.

But Edward Brooke is like no other Negro politician in American history. He is really not a Negro politician at all, but a Negro in politics. For his race is in no way his political determinant. As Harvard professor James Q. Wilson has pointed out, "For decades, American ethnic groups have been producing two kinds of politicians: taciturn, supple, organizational leaders, and flamboyant, individualistic spellbinders." Yet Brooke is neither. He has nothing in common with Chicago Congressman William L. Dawson and as little in common with Adam Clayton Powell as John Fitzgerald Kennedy had with James Michael Curley.

If it is true that the American electorate is likely to give national recognition to a member of a minority group in inverse proportion to his ethnocentricity, then it might be argued that Brooke is a more acceptable candidate than Senator Jacob K. Javits of New York. As Milton Viorst has written, Javits is "such a Jewish Jew." But Brooke is a very un-Negro Negro. It is not just that Brooke—with his blue-green eyes, his finely-arched eyebrows, his slightly Nixonian nose, his thin, cupid lips, and his skin the color of an early summer sunburn—hardly looks Negro. It is not just that Brooke—articulate, well-modulated speaker; wearer of finely-cut, conservative suits; chancellor of the Old North Church (whose lantern started Paul Revere on his ride); member of Trinity (Episcopal) Church in Copley Square; president of the Opera Company of Boston (a Cabot is vice president and a Parker is treasurer)—hardly can be considered a threat to prevailing white middle-class standards.

It is more that in the racial tinder box that is mid-twentieth-century America, Edward Brooke appears to be one of the few men—white or black—who has made his peace with the race issue. It is probably this quality, even more than his fine record or the bendover-backwards effect of a Negro candidate on liberal white voters—that has won three elections for Brooke in a state with a 98 percent white electorate.

"I am not a civil-rights leader, and I don't profess to be," says Brooke. "I don't think all Negroes should or can be civil-rights leaders." Negroes agree, but some, such as former executive secretary of the moderate Boston NAACP, feel that Brooke is "overly neutral." And the militant chairman of the Boston Action Group said at a public meeting, "Brooke ain't nothing but an Uncle Tom, man. That cat can't help us. He's too involved with the white power structure." It was even a Massachusetts joke that Brooke was elected to the Senate in 1966 on the strength of the white backlash—his white opponent, Endicott Peabody, being the more outspoken liberal on civil rights. But this hardly means that Brooke is indifferent to the plight

of the Negro. He has argued civil-rights cases before the Supreme
Court and argued for a strong civil-rights plank in the 1964 Republican platform.

Rather, it is more a reflection of Brooke's basic approach to *all*
problems. He is a conservative. Not a reactionary. Not a believer in
no government, or even little government. But a man who moves with
deliberate caution, weighing all the evidence and alternatives carefully, and putting great emphasis on working through duly con-
stituted authorities. This is not a sudden adjustment to political ex-
pediencies, but a deeply ingrained attitude that goes back to childhood. When he was an undergraduate at Howard University in Washington, D.C., there was a protest demonstration against segregation
at a drugstore chain. Brooke did not join in. Recently he said, "I
have never participated in a riot in my life. I reject them. I deplore
them." It would be as difficult imagining Brooke rioting as the late
Lucius Beebe eating at the Automat.

In Massachusetts Brooke moved in an almost-totally white world.
As two-term Attorney General of the Comonwealth he presided over
an almost-totally white staff. When he made speeches he looked out
over an almost-totally white audience. He has a white wife. Brooke
has been called "color blind" and a Negro reporter has said that he
has achieved "absolute assimilation." Traveling with him, observing
him, interviewing him, talking to those who know him well, one
sees no reason to doubt these assessments.

What makes this all the more remarkable is that, as Brooke has
said, "Until I was twenty-six, when I entered B.U. [Boston Uni-
versity], my life has been spent almost totally among Negroes. My
home life, my boyhood friendships, my secondary schooling, my
undergraduate education, my military service—all these I lived
among my own people. The world of white men was something which
I observed from afar and which I felt no particular desire to be
part of."

Brooke is the grandson of a Pullman porter and the son of a
Veterans Administration lawyer. The Washington where he was born
in 1919 and where he grew up was a segregated, sleepy Southern
city. Within its Negro community, the family was definitely upper
class—father was a professional man, a sister is married to the director of medical affairs of a major pharmaceutical manufacturing
firm, a cousin teaches sociology at Boston University and is a member

of the National Council on the Humanities. His mother, in the traditional pattern of the Negro matriarchy, ran the house. There were no traumatic experiences. No one ever called him a nigger. Washington's concerts may have been Jim Crow, but Mrs. Brooke took her Eddie to Carnegie Hall and the Metropolitan Opera in New York. He graduated from Howard as a premed ("because of the social prestige. . . . Every girl I knew wanted to marry a doctor"). And he joined the Army in World War II as an officer with an all-Negro regiment. He fought bravely, won a Bronze Star, and married an Italian girl who he thought looked like his mother. After the war he moved to Boston, got a law degree, and became a Republican by accident. In 1950 he entered both the Democratic and Republican primaries for a seat in the state legislature, lost the Democratic primary, won the Republican primary, and has remained with the party that gave him his first break.

He came to prominence in the Bay State as the appointed chairman of the Boston Finance Commission, a watchdog agency, in which he built a reputation for ferreting out corruption, and which proved to be a natural avenue to election as Attorney General. Yet he never has been very comfortable in the role of society's avenger. "I would much rather prevent a man from committing a crime than punish him for it afterwards," he has said. "I don't enjoy sending men behind bars." This may have been one of the reasons why Brooke started in 1965 to put pressure on the Massachusetts G.O.P. to advance him to Senator, a job then held by that ancient Republican worthy Leverett Saltonstall.

Brooke's maneuvering showed him to be a consummate politician. On September 19, 1965, David Farrell, in an exclusive story in the Boston *Herald*, wrote: "Attorney General Edward W. Brooke is seriously considering retirement from office at the end of his current term." As reporter Farrell spelled out, "Unless an opening occurs at the top of the GOP ticket via retirement from office of Senator Saltonstall, Brooke in all probability will finish his present term and accept one of the many positions which are or will be available to him at that time." Just so Brooke would not look too pushy, he promptly and publicly wrote Saltonstall urging him "to continue your distinguished service. . . ." But, at the same time, Brooke's press secretary, Jerry Sadow, was distributing the Farrell article to leading Washington columnists. As Robert Healy, political editor of the Boston *Globe*, pointed out, "The effect of such circulation [of the retirement story] would be that the Republican party in Massachusetts was holding back one of its brightest stars and the highest elected Negro official in the country." Within twenty-four hours after Saltonstall announced that he would not seek another term in December, 1965, Brooke told a combined press conference and pep rally that he would be a candidate. His fast response pre-empted the field and caught completely off guard the Republican Governor, John A. Volpe, who had greater claim to the office and might have muscled Brooke aside if he had been as decisive.

The Governor is a proud man. And justly so. Around Boston political clubhouses they like to say, "Whatever happened to Horatio Alger?" To which the proper answer is, "He changed his name to John A. Volpe."

Son of an Italian laborer, Volpe had been christened "Gionne" in 1908 because his parents wanted him to have an American name like "Johnny," but there was no "J" in Italian. In the depth of the depression, Volpe cashed a $300 insurance policy, borrowed another $200, and started his own construction company. Having become a millionaire by 1951, he turned to other fields to conquer and chose politics. After serving as Massachusetts public-works director and first Federal Highway Administrator, he was elected in 1960 to the first of three nonconsecutive gubernatorial terms. A short man, not much over five feet, who goes to Mass every day (his idea of a vacation is to take noon Mass, "so I can sleep later"), Volpe has been described by *The Catholic Digest* as managing "to be humble and cocky at the same time." While his victory in 1966 was overshadowed in the news media by the first popular election of a Negro to the Senate, in fact, Volpe's performance was far more impressive than Brooke's—although he had a weaker opponent—and the Governor even captured the Democratic stronghold of Boston by 10,063 votes, whereas Brooke did exceedingly well to hold his loss in the city to 23,868.

Also in 1966 Lieutenant Governor Elliot L. Richardson was elected to succeed Brooke as Attorney General. In Massachusetts, a state of "balanced tickets," the forty-seven-year-old Richardson represents the bluest-blooded Yankee. He is the very wealthy son of a very distinguished surgeon, and a Harvard boxing champion, law clerk to Supreme Court Justice Frankfurter, assistant to Senator Saltonstall, as well as the U.S. Attorney who won conviction of Bernard Goldfine. In 1962 Richardson lost bitter convention and primary battles to Brooke for the Attorney General nomination, but came back to win election as Lieutenant Governor in 1964, and from that generally untaxing position was able to originate most of the Volpe

The GOP Goal Scorers

SENATOR-ELECT EDWARD BROOKE, ATTORNEY GENERAL-ELECT
ELLIOT RICHARDSON, GOVERNOR JOHN VOLPE

Szep, Boston **Globe,** Nov. 14, 1966

Administration's impressive programs in the fields of health, welfare and education.

It is hardly surprising that Volpe and Brooke behave more like rivals than allies—if only because of the teeter-totter effect of politics. At the moment both are up—a phenomenon that defies gravity—but since each secretly covets the vice-presidential nomination clearly one will have to fall for the other to rise. In 1966 relations between the two became frosty enough for them to avoid each other. The Democratic state chairman had a moment of radiant amusement during an otherwise gloomy fall when he issued a two-page press release chiding the two Republican leaders for their apparent disunity. Indeed, as Hearst columnist Marianne Means reported, their relations reached a point where "tempers flared over such a simple joint decision as when the two candidates should appear before a G.O.P. clambake."

In the unspoken contest between them for a place on the 1968 national ticket, Brooke has the Senator's advantage of dealing with the major national and international issues and being at the center of political attention in Washington. Less than three months after his election, Brooke captured headlines across the country, presidential praise and a fistful of laudatory editorials by returning from a trip to Vietnam and announcing candidly that he had changed his mind. Previously a critic of the bombing policy, Brooke now said, "It does not appear that suspension of the bombing in the North would, by itself, produce fruitful negotiations. . . . Since I believe that North Vietnam is not prepared to negotiate in a meaningful way at this time, I reluctantly conclude that the general direction of our present military efforts in Vietnam is necessary." His statement, coming at a time when Negro civil rights leaders like Martin Luther King were stepping up their criticism of the war, had major impact on public opinion.

In Boston, Volpe had no such dramatic news to make, but, as the state's Governor, he has the advantage of controlling the party organization. A new and untested Massachusetts primary law allows the state chairman to stage an open preference contest among all presidential contenders—a test that Romney might welcome, but which Volpe appears inclined to attempt to foreclose through a favorite-son candidacy of his own.

Brooke, like Javits and Romney, repudiated the national ticket in 1964; Volpe appeared once with Goldwater but stayed as far away from him thereafter as possible. But, where Goldwater has been unforgiving of other 1964 apostates, he sent Brooke a $100 contribution in 1966, which prompted Brooke to remark, "I only hope I would be as big under the same circumstances." Richard Fleming, a former research director of the Massachusetts Republican State Committee, thinks "conservatives feel Brooke as a Negro had to take liberal stands [in 1964], including not endorsing Goldwater—stands that they would not readily accept if they had been taken by a white candidate."

If the 1968 convention were to make a choice based merely on numbers, Brooke would have twice the chance of Italian Volpe and four times the chance of the Jewish Javits—although these odds should be scaled down because half the Negroes live in the South and a smaller percentage are registered voters. For the numbers counters, Grant Reynolds, director of the National Negro Republican Assembly, made a convincing case during a Houston speech in 1965 that more attention to the Negro voters would have elected Nixon in 1960.

But Brooke's trump as a potential running mate for Romney is that his selection would be the most dramatic step the Michigan Governor could take to prove his total commitment to equal rights, despite the second-class station of Negroes within his Mormon Church. By the same token, Brooke's nomination would be the best proof a Nixon or a Reagan could offer that his conservatism is untainted by any appeal to racial prejudice or "backlash." Brooke may not be the Negroes' ideal representative, yet as columnist Carl T. Rowan, himself a Negro, pointed out when Brooke was elected to the Senate: "It will renew the faith of millions of Negroes who in recent months were becoming inclined to believe the Stokely Carmichael line that he never knew a white man he could trust."

Nevertheless, all segments of the electorate would not greet a Brooke candidacy with equal enthusiasm. Although Senator Richard B. Russell, the Georgia patriarch and leader of the Southern Democrats, made a point of shaking Brooke's hand on the day he was sworn in as a Senator, perhaps a more typical response comes from South Carolina state Senator Earl E. Morris, Jr., who doubles as Democratic chairman. "I like this talk of a Romney-Brooke ticket," he said. "I just wonder if I could be that lucky."

Still, when Brooke entered the United States Senate in January, 1967, he was escorted down the aisle by the new senior Senator from Massachusetts, the youngest brother of President Kennedy. And when Edward M. Kennedy was a freshman legislator in 1963, he had been ceremonially presented to the Senate by his senior, the Yankee Protestant Brahmin, Leverett Saltonstall. It is a socio-political progression that may have further presidential overtones.

Just over the border in Rhode Island, the Republican party is not troubled by the type of jockeying for position that is taking place in Massachusetts. For the state's G.O.P. is, in fact, one man. When

"I try harder"

GOVERNOR JOHN CHAFEE, RHODE ISLAND

Fawcett, Providence **Evening Bulletin**, Dec. 13, 1966

John Hubbard Chafee, forty-four, accepted congratulations in January, 1967, at his third inauguration as Governor, the band played "On a Clear Day You Can See Forever." Some thought the tune auspicious.

At the 1968 convention the littlest state could have its first "favorite son" in the history of the Republican party. The votes would be complimentary, of course; but behind them would be the hope that some confluence of forces or collective recognition of talents might single out its Governor for a place on the national ticket.

For those who may be amused by the idea, Chafee supporters point out that their man is a Protestant in the most Catholic state in the nation, a blue-blood Yankee in the state with the nation's highest proportion of immigrants and their second- and third-generation progeny, and a Republican in the state that gave the greatest vote percentage to the Democrats in the last two presidential elections.

Chafee, whose official biography describes him as "a jut-jawed ex-Marine," was the Minority Leader of the Rhode Island House of Representatives when he first ran for Governor in 1962 against incumbent John A. Notte, Jr. During the campaign the tall, lean Republican with the boyish cowlick, the heavy black eyebrows and the great Saltonstall nose, shook hands with nearly every eighth person in his state's 860,000 population. Twenty-four days after the election, when all the mail ballots had been carefully counted, he was declared the winner by 398 votes. He has not stopped running since. When, as a typical example, there was a ribbon to be cut to commemorate the completion of a little temporary bridge over a small stream in Coventry, Chafee was right there with his scissors. Rhode Islanders obviously like his style, which a Providence reporter said conveys "the impression of the eager Boy Scout, shyly looking for old ladies to help across the street."

His greatest challenge came in 1964 when Goldwater was at the top of the G.O.P. ballot. In order to re-elect the Governor the party adopted a "Vote Chafee First" strategy. As Raffaele V. Delmonaco, Johnston Republican town chairman, recalled in March, 1966: "We wanted to win every office, yet we knew that the future of the Republican party in our state hung largely on our ability to retain the governorship." Rhode Island voters have been conditioned to pull one master lever to vote the straight Democratic ticket. In order to break this habit, a "Let's Re-elect Governor Chafee," comic book was widely distributed. It began, "Once upon a time, the Democratic State of Rhode Island had a very wise and dedicated Governor. He was Republican." Page two: "All the people liked him because he was fair and took care of everyone, not just one part of the people, or just one party." (The cartoon shows a smiling farmer Chafee feeding a carrot to the Democratic donkey with one hand while brushing the Republican elephant with the other.) The moral, of course, was that "a voter can split his ticket and vote for Chafee, Johnson, [Democratic Senator John] Pastore and any other candidates of his choice." Obviously "Little Rhode" got the message. Goldwater received 19 percent,

Chafee got 62 percent—Chafee had won re-election by a margin greater than Goldwater's total vote in Rhode Island! The Governor carried every community in the state except industrial, labor-oriented Woonsocket.

As if to vindicate his "Vote Chafee First" strategy, in 1966 the Governor campaigned with a "team" and succeeded in electing a Lieutenant Governor and an Attorney General—the first time since 1938 that the Republicans have won any statewide posts other than Governor. This time Chafee carried every town in Rhode Island, including Woonsocket.

Working with a legislature that has been more than two-to-one Democratic in both chambers, Chafee has nonetheless put through 75 percent of his program. Asked by reporter Paul A. Kelly of the Providence *Evening Bulletin* whether "the Republicans and you in particular are taking a more liberal side than the Democrats who traditionally are supposed to be the liberal party in Rhode Island," Chafee replied, "The answer to your question is yes." But the Governor is quick to add, "Sure I'm a spender, but I'm a taxer too for anything we're willing to spend, because that's the way you have to run."

With his election as vice chairman of the Republican Governors Association for 1967, a position that entitles him to membership on the high-level Republican Coordinating Committee, and his automatic elevation to the chairmanship of the G.O.P. Governors in 1968, Chafee is just beginning to get national recognition. Romney has patted him on the back—"John Chafee is a fighter and I like fighters" —just as he has found kind words for all other moderates who harbor vice-presidential ambitions; and Chafee has returned the compliment by announcing the formation in June, 1967, of a Romney-for-President Committee in his state, with a member of his staff as its chairman. Chafee's main drawback as a potential running mate, of course, is that his state casts such a modest shadow, yet a grand irony for the Rhode Island Governor may be that an Arizona Senator in 1964 shattered the big-state precedent.

Moreover, Rhode Island's motto is *"Hope."*

Connecticut Republicans in 1957 held both U.S. Senate seats, all six seats in the U.S. House of Representatives, and even G.O.P. National Chairman Alcorn was from the state. Nine years and four Congresses later, the Democrats held the two Senate seats, the six House seats, and even Democratic National Chairman Bailey was from Connecticut.

While Connecticut has become highly urbanized in recent years, social change alone cannot account for this incredible reversal of form in such a short period. The Connecticut Republicans have been victims of their opponents' strengths and their own clashing ambitions, modest talents, weakened party discipline and ideological divisions. The first cracks in the G.O.P. power structure began to appear during the 1951-55 administration of the state's last Republican Governor, John Davis Lodge of the distinguished Massachusetts dynasty, whose early career had been as a movie actor in such epics as *Bulldog Drummond at Bay* and *Queer Cargo*. Lodge upset enough Republicans to make the difference in his 3,115-vote-loss to Democrat Abraham A. Ribicoff in 1954. Since then, almost every major Republican nomination has been hotly contested and the losers' supporters have generally sulked through election day.

The personal petulance of the state's G.O.P. leaders was further aggravated by the presidential candidacy of Barry Goldwater, which accentuated the existing liberal-conservative split within the party and led to the creation of competing organizations. The regular state committee, liberal in outlook, was led by A. Searle Pinney, a Danbury lawyer, who was once described as carrying his "265 pounds on his six-foot frame as if he were a man whose feet hurt." The conservative organization, called the Connecticut Republican Citizens Committee, was led by John M. Lupton of Weston, a former New York advertising executive. The conservative faction took charge of the fall campaign, in which the Republican candidate for President received only 32 percent of the vote.

The size of the Goldwater defeat was the liberals' mandate to take over the 1966 gubernatorial contest. They rammed through the nomination of political novice E. Clayton Gengras, father of eleven, who had left high school in the 1920's to sell Stutz Bearcats and now controlled several large insurance companies. During the campaign the party finance chairman bitterly complained that many conservatives were starving the state effort while sending money in bushel baskets to Ronald Reagan in California. Democratic Governor John N. Dempsey, a genial native of Tipperary, Ireland, handed Gengras a mortifying defeat and the Republicans lost both houses of the legislature. Even the Fourth Congressional District, whose lower Fairfield

County towns of New Canaan, Darien, Greenwich and Westport made it one of the wealthiest areas in the United States, rejected the Republican candidate. Only in the largely rural northwest quadrant of the state did Republicans have any success. Tiny Thomas J. Meskill, a former Mayor of New Britain, narrowly captured a congressional seat. After the election, State Chairman Pinney, announcing that he was "exhausted physically and financially," resigned.

The liberals had blocked the conservatives in 1964 and the conservatives had blocked the liberals in 1966. Perhaps both sides were tired of losing. To replace Pinney, the party chose Howard E. Hausman, a sixty-year-old bachelor and Yale man, who, although backed by the conservatives, was not strongly identified with either wing of the party. "So far as I am concerned, from this moment forward," said the new party leader in March, 1967, "there are no factions."

Whether the new "factionless" Connecticut Republicans can stay united in 1968 is questionable; in 1964, they split twelve to four for Scranton over Goldwater, and early in 1967 appeared divided between Romney and Lodge's candidate, Nixon.

Ever since the convention system was invented, New York—along with Ohio—has shown great skill as a practitioner of presidential politics. Nonetheless, in 1968 when New York has three leaders of considerable ability—in some respects the three most vital figures in the G.O.P.—the men of the Empire State are relegated to the secondary roles of would-be kingmakers, "favorite sons," vice-presidential hopefuls, and "dark horses."

Probably the most remarkable sight in American politics during 1964 was the fifty-five-year-old Governor of New York running for the Republican presidential nomination. While it was commonplace for chief executives of major states to seek advancement, this one had every right to feel that he had written his political obituary. For he had just shed his wife of thirty-one years in order to marry a woman eighteen years his junior, who, in turn, had left her husband and four children to join him. And, as if to underline that he was thumbing his nose at the conventions of the puritanical electorate that he was asking to send him to the White House, his new wife gave birth to a son three days before the most crucial presidential primary. Still, there he was: barnstorming a nation that cherished a log-cabin tradition, spending an estimated $3 million or more of his own money as if his name was Rockefeller, which, of course, it was. Yet stranger things have happened, and if Nelson Aldrich Rockefeller had not consistently refused to recognize what other men regard as prevailing political realities he would not now be Governor of the Empire State.

Probably the most remarkable sight in American politics during 1965 was a forty-three-year-old Protestant, white, Anglo-Saxon Republican running at full speed for Mayor of New York, a city that is more than 75 percent Democratic, 48 percent Catholic, 30 percent Jewish, and 17 percent nonwhite. Still, there he was: marching down Fifth Avenue in the St. Patrick's Day parade, eating blintzes on the Lower East Side, making the scene in Harlem. Yet stranger things have happened, and if John Vliet Lindsay had not challenged great odds he would not now be Mayor of America's largest city.

Probably the most remarkable sight in American politics during 1966 was a short, bald sixty-two-year-old New Yorker chasing the Republican vice-presidential nomination with the intensity of Jason on the trail of the Golden Fleece. His timing, age, religion, home base, ideology, party-loyalty quotient and personality were wrong. Even his wife rubbed the wives of the G.O.P.'s kingmakers the wrong way. And besides, as the candidate admitted, "No one runs for the vice-presidency." Still, there he was: flying around the country, distributing copies of a campaign manifesto, and announcing, "I'm entitled to national consideration. . . ." Yet stranger things have happened and if Jacob Koppel Javits had not been running all his life he would not now be the Empire State's senior United States Senator.

Clearly, these three—Governor, Senator and Mayor—composed an uneasy, suspicious triumvirate, and, even if their ambitions had not been in conflict, they would not have liked each other much. They were as different as men can be in background and personality.

—Javits, the janitor's son from the ghetto, the scrappy, penetrating lawyer who made his million by specializing in business bankruptcies; first a Congressman in 1946 because no one else wanted a hopeless nomination, then a Senator in 1956 because they could not afford to keep him off the ticket. The man with the New York electoral *schtick:* upstaters voted for him because he was a Republican; liberals because he was a liberal; Jews because they had pride in one of their own; Democrats because it made them feel smugly independent. Here was a most unclubbable member of the nation's most exclusive club whose know-it-all abrasiveness stood in sharp contrast to the easy style set by the Senate's senior Southerners; yet here too was a highly disciplined, wide-ranging, creative mind that eventually earned the grudging respect of his colleagues.

—Rockefeller, son of a man who had devoted his life to giving away the money his father had amassed; grandson of two school dropouts, one of whom became the world's first billionaire, the other the wily boss of the U.S. Senate. Although without political experience, he turned on his paternal wealth and maternal charm in 1958 and plucked the gubernatorial nomination from the outstretched arms of a pride of old pros, then proved himself as the most engaging, ingratiating candidate that New York had experienced since Jimmy Walker. As Governor he gave the state a number of progressive programs and higher taxes, while his Gallup ratings dipped and peaked like the Coney Island rollercoaster. In part through skill, in part through the luck of having weak opponents, he survived to become the conservative Republicans' vision of the liberal incarnate.

—Lindsay, once called New York City's "golden *goy*," nearly as tall as Lincoln, with dirty-blond curls and a chiseled nose; a four-term Congressman who stood virtually alone for civil liberties, yet admitted that as a legislator he came "close to the edge of being ineffective"—not just a part of the minority of the minority, but on some issues, such as supporting Halleck over Ford for the House G.O.P. leadership, he was a minority of a minority of a minority. As Mayor he started with the great advantage of believing his city was governable, the capacity to attract first-rate technicians to his administration, and the cultivated good will of New York's most disadvantaged.

Here were three stubborn individuals—one with the stubbornness of the self-made man, one with the stubbornness of the supremely wealthy, the third with the stubbornness of one who has been often told that he is a child of destiny. If their relations were bound to be inherently difficult, they were made incredibly difficult because there was only one sense of humor among them, and even that one was not top drawer. The Governor made an attempt at being funny, but found he was more successful with shrugs, winks and occasional wisecracks than with his patiently memorized anecdotes, whose punch lines he frequently flubbed. The Mayor understood humor, but it often came out surprisingly coarse, and even reporters were known to blush at some of his efforts. The Senator did not even try.

"Lindsay, Javits and Rockefeller circle each other as warily as cats in a cage," wrote Tom Wicker, Washington bureau chief of the New York *Times*. Javits has been quoted as complaining that Lindsay is "ungrateful for the help I've given him. . . ." And Rockefeller could hardly not have noticed that during his struggle for re-election in 1966 Lindsay made not a speech or a gesture on his behalf. Yet, while Javits and Rockefeller may be less fond of Lindsay than of each other, they also view him as less of a threat. For, while he well may be pushy, he is of another generation.* But Javits will be sixty-four in 1968 and Rockefeller sixty. This then is likely to be their last national adventure.

The relationship between Rockefeller and Javits has never been that of exact equals. Part of the difference, of course, is the inherent political inequality of Senators and Governors—rarely does a Senator control state politics when the Governor is of the same party. But there is also the unspoken difference between anyone and a Rockefeller, for when one is so fantastically advantaged it is bound to affect his attitude toward others and theirs toward him. One of the great joys of politics for a Rockefeller is that he can actually be an underdog, and most Rockefellers go to considerable lengths to appear ordinary; yet, when it gets right down to the infighting, an anti-Rockefeller act is considered *lèse majesté*. This must be particularly galling to Javits, who takes his own dignity very seriously indeed.

It is therefore instructive to examine what has happened since the 1962 election, in which there was a reversal of roles and Javits in fact got the upper hand.

In 1962, when both Javits and Rockefeller stood for re-election, the voters gave the Governor a majority of a half million and the Senator one of nearly a million. For the divorced (but not yet remarried) Rockefeller, who was hoping to use a sizable victory as an object lesson for another presidential race, his margin over the most ineffectual campaigner the Democrats have ever put up can only be con-

---

* Two other promising New York Republican politicians of the younger generation are U.S. Representatives Charles E. Goodell, forty-one, and Ogden R. Reid, forty-two. The upstater, Goodell, as noted in Chapter 1, has made himself into a congressional power; Reid, from suburban Westchester County, is more in the Lindsay mold as a Congressman. He is a member of the prominent family that once owned the New York *Herald Tribune,* and was himself an Ambassador to Israel. If Reid is to rise in Republican ranks, it most likely will have to be as a future candidate for statewide office.

sidered a disappointment. But for Javits the results were phenomenal, his winning margin exceeding the total population in fifteen states.

Rockefeller's embarrassment, even coupled with his remarriage to Mrs. Margaretta ("Happy") Murphy, did not discourage him from seeking the G.O.P. nomination. Except for the Oregon primary, he hardly could have done worse; nonetheless he reaped considerable praise from the press for being the only moderate Republican to make a meaningful attempt to block Goldwater.

Javits, having again managed to be pushed out of the spotlight, held a background conference for Washington reporters in January, 1965, and announced, though not for direct quotation, that he did not plan to support Rockefeller for President in 1968. This was followed, in February, by considerable jockeying for position in the New York City mayoralty race. Both Javits and Lindsay indicated that they might run under certain conditions, one being that the state leaders must unite behind a candidate by March 1. Since Rockefeller then was in the midst of a legislative session in which he counted heavily on the support of Democratic Mayor Wagner, he was not likely to do anything as unfriendly as accept the Lindsay-Javits demands. So by March 1 Lindsay and Javits had formally withdrawn their potential candidacies, neither thinking any more kindly toward the Governor.

(After Lindsay reversed himself in May, a *Newsweek* article by Emmet Hughes, a former Rockefeller strategist, said it was a promise of $500,000 from the Governor that finally convinced Lindsay to enter the contest. Lindsay supporters promptly denied the story and called it a Rockefeller "plant." During the mayoralty campaign Lindsay rejected the help of "national" Republican figures, a category that he expanded to include Governor Rockefeller, but accepted the assistance of Senator Javits, who he classified as a "city" figure. On election night, Mayor-elect Lindsay bristled when Rockefeller greeted him with a cheerful "Well, *we* did it.")

On May 14, 1965, state Senator John H. Hughes of Syracuse wrote Javits to urge him to take the lead in opposing Rockefeller's renomination in 1966. "A campaign in which the Governor runs for reelection will bring nothing but disaster," wrote the conservative state Senator to the liberal U.S. Senator. The enterprising team of Evans and Novak printed the Hughes letter in July—Javits vigorously denying that he had "leaked" it—and Rockefeller sarcastically noted that Javits and Hughes made "strange pen pals."

But there was more than a germ of truth in the Hughes epistle. Indeed, some 1965 polls showed the Governor's standing with the voters as low as 21 percent. Clearly the time had come for Rockefeller to make a good-will gesture to the Senator. In fact, he made two. First, on July 25 at the National Governors' Conference in Minneapolis, he announced that he would not seek the presidency in 1968. When asked what prompted his decision, he replied, "Well, I think, frankly, that this last [1964] presidential campaign crystallized the party around two figures—an extreme position, from my point of view, that Senator Goldwater took, and a moderate position. I think in order to pull the party back together, to unite it, to make it possible to forget some of the scars of the past, that my withdrawing from the scene will be a real asset in accomplishing this." Second, in Ithaca on October 26, 1965, he announced that Javits "is our favorite son from New York for the vice presidential spot" on the Republican ticket in 1968. But Javits, at last being courted, soon made it abundantly clear that the Governor had not yet won his affection. A "favorite son," he told reporters, can only be a candidate for President, not Vice President. Thus Rockefeller had made "a self-contradictory statement."

Rockefeller's next ploy was to ask Javits to be his campaign manager. It was hardly a subtle move, since Javits's acceptance would have foreclosed the possibility of his running for Governor. While Rockefeller said he expected the Senator to accept the offer, he added, with a tinge of annoyance, "You never know with Jack Javits just what he's going to do." The role of courtier was obviously a strange and difficult one for Rockefeller.

What Javits did was to go fishing in troubled waters. In April, 1966, he toured upstate New York—"inventorying," he called it—to see if there was sufficient support for him to wrest the nomination from the Governor in the party convention.* The convention system, as he probably knew, virtually assures an incumbent Governor of renomination. Nor, of course, could he bluff a man who had recently felt himself capable of winning a presidential nomination out of going after a gubernatorial one. But there was another reason why Javits decided not to challenge Rockefeller. In the New York context, at least, the Senator has always been a strong party man. And ultimately he was not willing to put the Republicans through the blood bath that

---

* New York was then one of the rare states that did not pick candidates in open primaries. In 1967, the legislature passed and Rockefeller signed a bill providing primary elections for Governor and Senator. It takes effect in 1968.

a Javits-Rockefeller encounter would have been. Perhaps, as has been suggested, he was influenced by reminders of what happened to the G.O.P. in California when Governor Knight and Senator Knowland maneuvered into the same type of contest.

The whole issue finally was resolved with the Governor announcing his support for a Javits favorite-son candidacy for *President,* meaning, of course, in the strange double-talk of politics, that Javits now would be in a position to run for *Vice President.* And, to dramatize his new position, Rockefeller chose an appearance by Governor Romney in Garden City, Long Island, on May 23, 1966, to endorse the team of Romney and Javits. (He failed to give advance notice to a surprised Romney.) For Javits, this was his finest hour. And the beaming Senator committed himself wholeheartedly to the re-election of Rockefeller.

In the fall of 1966 Rockefeller waged what has been called "the almost-perfect political campaign."* It was brilliantly planned by William C. Pfeiffer, the salty campaign chairman; Republican National Committeeman George Hinman, a Binghamton lawyer; and the Governor's personal intellectual, Dr. William J. Ronan, a former dean of the New York University Graduate School of Public Administration. It was, of course, lavishly financed, with a paid staff of 307 and 27 million buttons, brochures, and broadsides—about 4½ items for every voter. There was some Rockefeller literature directly aimed at every special interest group—"except the Times Square prostitutes," said Pfeiffer. The total cost of the campaign was estimated at over $6 million.

But what made the campaign unique was the work of the Governor's advertising agency, Jack Tinker & Partners, a small firm that specializes in being different, and had been best known for its handling of Alka-Seltzer and Braniff Airways. Since Rockefeller was well known, and was not an effective TV performer anyway, his commercials concentrated on the record, not the man. For example, one sixty-second film, titled "Fish Interview," showed a hand wearing a press hat talking to a fish puppet, and went, in part:

REPORTER: You, sir.
FISH: Uh huh.
REPORTER: How do you feel about Governor Rockefeller's Pure Waters

* See James M. Perry, "Nelson Rockefeller's Last Hurrah," *National Observer,* January 9, 1967; also Tom Buckley, "The 3 Men Behind Rockefeller," *New York Times Magazine,* October 30, 1966.

Program?

FISH: His pure what?

REPORTER: Pure waters.

FISH: Oh, oh yeah.

REPORTER: This program, sir, is wiping out water pollution in New York within six years.

FISH: Well, it was pretty smelly down here.

Under the slogan "Governor Rockefeller for Governor," the agency also was creating a series of imaginative, eye-catching posters, such as "12,000 miles of better roads. Pothole-haters for Rockefeller." But, while the Governor's commercials may have been soft-sell, he was accusing his Democratic opponent, New York City Council President Frank D. O'Connor, of being soft on crime because he opposed Rockefeller's program for the compulsory commitment of narcotics addicts.

The election, in which, besides the two major parties, there also were two major minor parties and two minor minor parties, showed that New York was getting downright continental in its approach to politics. The final results were: Rockefeller, Republican, 2,690,626; O'Connor, Democrat, 2,298,363; Paul L. Adams, Conservative, 510,023; Franklin D. Roosevelt, Jr., Liberal, 507,234; and a scattering of votes for the candidates of the Socialist Labor party and the Socialist Workers party. Javits was defeated as part of the Republican slate of delegates to the 1967 state constitutional convention, though his name was not listed on the ballot; Lindsay's pet proposal for a Police Department Civilian Complaint Review Board was defeated despite active campaigning by the Mayor. Of the Republicans' big three, only Nelson Rockefeller, written off as a national candidate, was a winner.

As a contrast in the art of politicking, John Lindsay's strategy in his race for Mayor in 1965 was as successful as the Governor's in 1966, yet poles apart in basic approach. While Rockefeller had made his major impact through a television saturation campaign that began in early July, the photogenic Lindsay—of near-classic handsomeness—put almost none of his $2.5 million budget into TV, concentrating instead on a network of 117 neighborhood headquarters.

The architect of the Lindsay strategy was Robert Price, a thirty-two-year-old lawyer, who theorized that money spent on television is wasted because "commercial time is when you get up and go the kitchen whether they're selling Lux soap or John Lindsay." Price's view may have been formed, in part, by his experience as Lindsay's manager during four congressional campaigns, in which the considerable expense of TV commercials would have bought the attention of a great many metropolitan-area listeners who lived out-

"IT FOLLOWED ME HOME. CAN I KEEP IT?"

side Lindsay's district. Price first met his candidate through Young Republican activities, he being a student at New York University while Lindsay was president of the New York YR's. Like Nixon, Price was a grocer's son of modest means; like Javits, he was a Jew who became a Republican out of a distaste for the Democratic city machine. "One of the difficulties of growing up without money," his wife once said, "is that you don't learn how to relax, play tennis, that sort of thing." Relaxation for Price became politics. He had a genius for organization, a dry wit and the absolute confidence of a rising star. To friend Robert Blum it was obvious in 1965 that Price had been planning Lindsay's mayoral campaign for years. When Blum reported on opening a storefront headquarters in a distant corner of Brooklyn, the campaign manager promptly told him to move it to another location across from a pool hall at the intersection of heaviest traffic. The amazed aide concluded that Price knew New York City's 365 square miles almost block by block. Price's storefront operation was giving Lindsay an instant clubhouse organization —the G.O.P. having none of its own—while bringing the campaign to hundreds of thousands of New Yorkers who had never before been personally solicited for their votes.

Ironically, however, it was William Buckley at least as much as the storefront strategy that elected Lindsay. About ten days before the election, when all of Lindsay's carefully constructed position papers had failed to spark any voter enthusiasm, he dropped his studied indifference toward the Conservative party candidate and aimed his campaign against him. What Lindsay was saying, in effect, was that Buckley was the agent of Goldwater and the radical right, whose only purpose in the race was to defeat him: therefore, a vote against Lindsay is a vote for Goldwater. Enough liberal New Yorkers got the message to elect Lindsay over lackluster Democrat Abraham Beame by 136,144 votes out of more than 2.5 million. "Bill," said Goldwater to Buckley, "as a political kingmaker, you're a wrong-way Corrigan."

While Rockefeller and Javits may be a special breed of Republican, they have never denied their Republicanism; Lindsay ran for Mayor by running away from his party. He was part of a "fusion" ticket and made a point of saying that he was running "as Lindsay," not as a Republican. Two G.O.P. leaders, Bliss and Nixon, publicly acknowledged that this was the only way a Republican could get elected in New York City. Yet for most Republicans—the kind who become delegates to national conventions—Lindsay's performance was deeply offensive. "If you tie a lemon on an orange tree, it's still not an orange," was the way Nevada's National Committeeman Melvin Lundberg characterized Lindsay's Republicanism. When the Indianapolis *News* interviewed Indiana G.O.P. chairman Charles O. Hendricks on November 8, 1965, he remarked, "Lindsay is not really a Republican, he's an independent. He has said that himself. Since he does not consider himself a Republican, it's difficult really to measure his national stature in the party when he's not even on your team." Lindsay's dramatic victory, especially coming in an off-off year, put his picture on the cover of the national magazines, but it did not make him a hero to the party's wheelhorses around the country.

As the New York Republicans look to the 1968 convention, the delegation—according to an arrangement between Rockefeller and Javits in April of 1966—is committed to the favorite-son candidacy of Javits. How firm this commitment is remains to be seen. Rockefeller suggested in a June, 1967, interview that being favorite son might interfere with Javits' campaign for re-election to the Senate and said that "as a last resort" he might be willing to be favorite son himself. In the same interview, he ruled out running in any primaries. But pundits and politicians just cannot get it out of their minds that Nelson Rockefeller may yet have another go at the nomination. *Fortune* magazine said in June, 1967, that "Rockefeller's record puts him unquestionably at the top of the Republican list. . . . In the end, his emergence is inevitable." In the same week, the liberal *New Republic,* while decrying his hawkish Vietnam views, said, "Nelson Rockefeller may prove to be the man." His third inaugural address was based on his concept of a "Just Society"—the words were capitalized —which sounded suspiciously like a presidential slogan. On March 31, 1967, James Reston's column offered "to bet one (1) plugged nickel" that Rockefeller would be the G.O.P. nominee. But if so it would have to be via the same "compromise candidate" route that backfired for his arch-foe Nixon in 1964.

And Rockefeller is not really a "compromise." For, as Stewart Alsop wrote in the *Saturday Evening Post,* April 8, 1967, on the basis of a talk with Goldwater: "If Rockefeller again becomes a serious candidate, Goldwater will fight, bleed and die to prevent his nomination." Indeed, the circumstances that could produce a Rockefeller candidacy appear to be of the parlor-game variety. First, the Romney boom would have to collapse. (Rockefeller gave Romney his tacit endorsement early in 1966, and has entrusted to him the records of his 1964 candidacy and several veteran campaign aides.) Romney would then have to acknowledge his own incapacity to continue the campaign. Finally, something would have to happen to remove Percy from contention, because Percy has progressive credentials almost as good as Rockefeller's without any of the scars the New Yorker carries from 1960 and 1964. Then and only then could Rockefeller unify even the progressive wing of the party—and that would still leave all the other Republicans united against him.

Yet that fact did not keep a variety of people, some of them sincere and others, like White House aides and conservative Southern Republicans, obviously with ulterior motives, from suggesting repeatedly that Rockefeller ought to and would run. In 1967, Rockefeller appeared to understand as well as they that his entering the race would only split the progressive Republicans and pave the way for the nomination victory of Nixon or Reagan. But those who stirred his ambitions could hope—and Romney and Percy fear—that Rockefeller would find the temptation irresistible, open up his wallet again and deal himself into the White House game. Meantime enemies and friends agreed: *if* Nelson Rockefeller could ever win a Republican presidential nomination, he might well be the toughest opponent Lyndon Johnson could face.

After three campaigns for Governor, one-and-a-half for President, and a full decade in politics, Rockefeller still manages to give the impression of freshness and vigor. This talent for improving with age like a fine wine comes from a rare internal combination: a genuine fondness for people, at times almost overpowering, and a sense of personal mission, an attitude that whatever he seeks is both important and attainable. These are tools he brought to public life. To them he added a hard-earned ability as a political operator, so that when he was faced with a Democratic legislature in 1965, for example, he proved crafty enough to exploit the deep divisions within the opposition party to get most of his program enacted.

Rockefeller came into elective politics with a long and honorable record as an internationalist committed to both anti-Communism and to generous investment in underdeveloped countries, and a dedicated advocate of civil rights. In Albany, especially during his third term, he earned the reputation of being a free-wheeling and expansive Governor. Without the blink of an eye, Rockefeller proposed a transportation program of $2.5 *billion*. To the new breed of Republican Governors he was the practical sage who knew the answers almost before they asked the questions: medical assistance, air pollution, water pollution, higher education, land use—he had been through it all himself.

And the Rockefeller of those 1964 primaries, whose repeated BOMFOG's (speeches that dwelled on the "Brotherhood of Man, Fatherhood of God") made reporters wince, seemed to disappear the minute he lost the last glimmer of the presidential nomination. That spring at the National Governors' Conference in Cleveland he gave a scathingly funny display of aristocratic contempt for those who scorned to fight Goldwater early and who panicked when they discovered it was too late. Clearly it was this new Rockefeller, obviously relaxed, faintly amused, whom some prominent columnists and politicians hoped to glimpse again in 1968.

While some thought that Rockefeller was catching his second wind in national politics, Jacob Javits's position had eroded considerably since he stood beside Romney at Garden City in 1966. His frank campaigning for the vice-presidential nomination proved to be not only precedent-shattering, but also distasteful to most Republican politicians, and he abandoned it in early 1967, in part because he needed to give his undivided attention to his own re-election to the Senate. His effort to promote himself for the second place on the national ticket was directed ultimately at only one man—George Romney. "If the Governor needed a liberal running mate from the East," said Javits, "I could offer proven voter appeal, a strong base of support in the state with the most delegate and electoral votes, a progressive record, appeal to minority groups, and enlightened foreign policy record. And frankly," added the Senator, who did not list modesty as an attribute, "I'm a warm human being with great feeling for other human beings."

But, as a top New York Republican pointed out, Javits's description also fits Lindsay, who is "17 years younger, six inches taller and sexy." While New York's City Hall has always been considered a politician's graveyard, and it has not been a political springboard for anyone since DeWitt Clinton, as Javits himself commented to author Robert Bendiner in early 1965, "Precedent wouldn't apply. . . . A man who can capture New York City for the Republicans doesn't need the governorship [to be a national figure]." Lindsay is suspect to fellow Republicans as a liberal who has shunned the party label, but, as the nature of government changes—with Washington more and more by-passing the states to deal directly with the cities—the office of mayor is certain to take on additional political luster. Besides Lindsay, in recent years Congressmen have run for Mayor of Los

Angeles, San Francisco, Newark and Milwaukee. As Lindsay has said, "The action today is in the streets of the cities."*

What Javits does have that is unique is his religion. In 1924 there was a rumor that Supreme Court Justice Brandeis might be Senator La Follette's running mate on the Progressive party ticket, but that is as close as a Jew has come to being a major national candidate. (Barry Goldwater, whose father had been born a Jew, is a practicing Episcopalian.) Recently when a noted Yale professor was asked about the possibility of a Romney-Javits ticket, he jokingly replied, "Impossible, there wouldn't be a Gentile on it!" Jews make up a mere sliver of the population, only 5.6 million. But they are placed well politically. Half live in New York, with sizable concentrations in Los Angeles, Philadelphia and Chicago, and smaller numbers in Boston, Miami, Baltimore and Washington. In fact, there are almost exactly as many Jews in the electorate as there are farmers, a special-interest group that has always managed to be well represented.

When Democratic Governor Richard J. Hughes of New Jersey won a smashing re-election victory in 1965 and carried with him both houses of the legislature (for the first time in fifty-two years), it left whatever hopes the shattered Republicans had of making a comeback in the hands of imperturbable Clifford P. Case. The tall, spare Senator, with the reddish eyebrows, bushy hair and somewhat professorial ways, would be up for re-election to a third term in 1966. Once the conservatives in his party had spent vast sums to defeat him. But now they were either too dispirited or too wise to make the effort. Relieved of the usual pressure of defending himself from right-wing attack, he proceeded to gather in the expected union endorsements. The Republican Senator also was supported by the ADA and campaigned in a car provided by a Negro organization whose leader said, "We all want to see people here pull themselves up by their bootstraps, but Cliff Case understands that first they've got to have some boots."

The reason for such unusual support, as Arlen J. Large of the *Wall Street Journal* noted, was that "By almost any measurement the sixty-

* A "National Lindsay for President Committee" was organized by a Dartmouth College student shortly after the 1965 New York City election. Its leader says, "We hope to mobilize hundreds of college students to campaign for him wherever the Republican convention might be."

two-year-old Mr. Case is more liberal than most Democrats in the Senate. . . ." Yet, as reporter Large pointed out, it was not just that Case had outpromised the opposition in a highly industrialized state. There was also about him the "low-keyed projection of purity in a wicked world" and his electioneering stressed such reformist issues as the need for a set of ethical standards for Congressmen. Case was returned to office in 1966 with an impressive sixty percent of the vote, his twelfth successive general election victory. The week after the election, New Jersey's Republican leaders met in Trenton and State Chairman Webster B. Todd told the waiting newsmen, "We agreed to build the party around Senator Case." That building could take the form of making Case the favorite son of the forty-vote New Jersey delegation in the state's presidential primary. In 1964, the conservative faction in the state managed to split off half the delegates for Goldwater, but if Romney or Percy shows strength going into the 1968 convention, either should be able to command a healthy majority of the New Jersey votes.

Probably the most unaccountable fact when examining the East is that Pennsylvania, the great Keystone State, has never had a flair for national presidential politics. The third most populous state—and either the second or third in population ever since the first census was taken in 1790—Pennsylvania has managed to produce only one President, the mediocre James Buchanan, and has not even had a native-son nominee since General Hancock was the Democratic candidate in 1880.

Pennsylvanians again showed their ineptness in 1964 when Governor William Scranton made his futile eleventh-hour attempt to wrest the nomination from Goldwater. Once described as "a likeable fellow with the face of an intelligent and rather handsome frog," Scranton was the son of a retiring regional aristocrat and a flamboyant, aggressive mother, known as the "Duchess," who had been a Republican political power for many years and was considered something of a joke in her social set. There seemed to be a private tug of war within him between his mother's and father's genes. Being ambitious he seemed to feel was somewhat second rate. He was a reluctant congressional candidate in 1960 and a reluctant gubernatorial candidate in 1962, but once engaged in each race he turned into a dynamic performer, not even above exhibiting himself in silly costumes.

Unable by law to seek another term as Governor in 1966, Scranton played a major role in selecting a strong slate of candidates, which Republican leaders called "the dream ticket," and gave them a record to run on—"a record," said the Pittsburgh *Press,* "of few shortcomings and many accomplishments."

The G.O.P. standard-bearer was Lieutenant Governor Raymond P. Shafer, forty-nine, a brawny, ruggedly good-looking man with prominent blond eyebrows, a firm jaw and a cleft chin. He was a small-town lawyer, a former district attorney, and a genuine World War II hero, who had won the Bronze Star for saving seventeen paratroopers trapped on Corregidor, taking them off the island in a rubber dinghy while under sniper fire. He was capable and progressive without making any pretense to greatness. In the fall, Shafer and his running mates were easily elected.

Scranton gladly turned over the reins of state government to his understudy. "I think I have done my stint," he said. "I have taken seven years from a normal type of life, and I think that is all I have to give." Thus bidding farewell to politics as a sort of Community Chest obligation that he was pleased to be done with, the Governor issued a statement that clearly out-Shermaned Sherman's—"I am not going to run, ever again, for any public office, under any circumstances."

However, from retirement, Scranton continued to serve as cheerleader and counselor to his favored candidate, Romney. Also backing Romney is Pennsylvania's junior U.S. Senator Hugh D. Scott, sixty-six, an urbane and witty lawyer who combines an educated taste in Oriental art with an unfailing instinct for the political jugular. The leader of the traditionally uncommitteed favorite-son delegation will be Governor Shafer, whose prestige was heightened by his successful campaign in May, 1967, for a constitutional convention and who is ambitious for higher office himself.

Two other Keystone State Republicans also deserve watching. Wealthy Congressman Richard S. Schweiker, forty-one, of Philadelphia's Main Line, withdrew as a candidate for Governor in 1966, an act for which he was widely thought to have earned a crack at Democrat Joseph S. Clark's Senate seat in 1968; and Arlen Specter, thirty-seven, elected a reformist District Attorney of Philadelphia in 1965, son of poor Russian Jewish immigrants, the member of the Warren Commission staff who was primarily responsible for the controversial theory that one bullet struck President Kennedy and Texas

Governor Connally, and in 1967 the unanimous choice of his party to return Philadelphia's City Hall to G.O.P. rule for the first time since 1951.

Tiny Delaware—as represented in the U.S. Senate—carefully keeps one foot in each ideological camp. Of its two Methodist Republican Senators, John J. Williams is roughly twice as conservative as J. Caleb Boggs. And their personal styles differ about as markedly. "Cale" Boggs is folksy, a rememberer of birthdays, the type of politician who never forgets to go to the kitchen to thank the help. He is a lawyer and retired Air Force general. "I admire John Williams," said one Delaware Republican, "but I would never dare ask him for a favor, even for help in hastening a passport. I just call up Cale Boggs and it's done." John J. Williams (called "Whispering Will" by his peers, because he is so hard to hear on the Senate floor) is a stern moralist and a tireless exposer of Federal misfeasance, nonfeasance and malfeasance. Before getting elected to the Senate in 1946 he was a chickenfeed dealer in Millsboro (pop. 536). "Just an average feed store," he says. "Picture one in Kansas and one in Millsboro; they're no different." Williams has become a great favorite with Republican audiences because, as writer Frederic W. Collins says, he "has perhaps brought down more wrong-doers operating in the United States Government, or chiseling from it, than any other man." His most recent trophy was Bobby Baker, the powerful Senate Democratic aide. As in its choice of Senators, Delaware splits its presidential convention votes—twelve in 1968—between the liberal and conservative candidates.

Maryland, historically a stronghold of progressive Republicanism, is blessed in 1968 with the most effective G.O.P. leadership in its recent history. Governor Spiro T. (Ted) Agnew, elected in 1966 from his post as chief executive of suburban Baltimore County, has proved to be every bit as adept on the state level. Of Greek origin, the polished Agnew had the good fortune to take office with the first Maryland legislature since reapportionment; like all Maryland legislatures, it was Democratic, but its new suburban majorities rallied to Agnew's leadership and passed a program of tax reform, open-housing legislation and other liberal measures that left the old-timers in Annapolis awed.

Agnew's first choice for his party's 1968 presidential nominee is Nelson Rockefeller, who politely but firmly told the Marylander in a May 1st meeting to join him in supporting Romney. Backing Agnew in the drive to put the state's twenty-six delegates behind a progressive Republican nominee are two exceptionally able young Congressmen —Charles M. (Mac) Mathias of Western Maryland and the Eastern Shore's Rogers C. B. Morton, the younger but heftier brother of Kentucky Senator Thruston B. Morton—and Baltimore's aging and multi-accented Mayor Theodore Roosevelt McKeldin, the man who nominated President Eisenhower in 1952.*

If Maryland has both tradition and leadership in its Republican party, West Virginia is lacking in both. About all that remains of the G.O.P. in that state is Representative (and National Committeeman) Arch A. Moore, Jr., whose instincts, like those of the corporate interests that dominate the state's Republican party, tend toward Nixon and the conservative side of the ledger.†

* In late June, 1967, the sixty-six-year-old McKeldin announced that he would not be a candidate for re-election in November. "There is nothing I would rather be than Mayor of Baltimore," the twice mayor said, but, having fought for increased taxes and civil rights, he indicated that he was bowing out because he did not think that he could win. Commenting on his decision, the Baltimore *Sun* praised his "extraordinary enthusiasm, the skill and the zeal for right against wrong that have marked his years in public life. . . ." As the Republican candidate for mayor, McKeldin then endorsed Arthur W. Sherwood, forty, a lawyer who had been a reformist member of the Baltimore elections board.

† Also considered part of the East are Puerto Rico, the Virgin Islands, and the District of Columbia. They will again have seventeen votes at the Republican National Convention, and can probably again be expected to cast the overwhelming majority of them for the most liberal candidate. The three delegations are polled at the end of the roll call, and in 1964, although Goldwater had already been nominated, they still gave thirteen of their seventeen votes to Scranton. The Rockefellers, because of their extensive land holdings, have considerable influence over the G.O.P. in the American islands. In 1968 the Nixon forces in the District of Columbia will be led by wealthy E. Perkins McGuire, an Assistant Secretary of Defense during the Eisenhower Administration. However, capital Republicans will be strongly drawn toward Romney because of his long friendship with the powerful J. Willard Marriotts, she being the G.O.P. National Committeewoman.

10 SOUTH

THE starkly modernistic Lockheed Research Laboratory at Marietta is described by the company as a "multi-purpose complex designed to create an atmosphere that is functionally and aesthetically conducive to scientific inquiry." At its entrance, along the Georgia highway, is a large billboard: IMPEACH EARL WARREN. Scientists and technicians pass it every day on their way to carry on experiments in physical, aerospace, materials and systems sciences that will help develop the world's largest and most sophisticated aircraft, the C-5A. As they start home in the evening, back on the Georgia highway, they are exposed to the reverse side of the sign: GET THE U.S. OUT OF THE UN AND THE UN OUT OF THE U.S. The juxtaposed billboard and laboratory graphically illustrate the split personality of the South today—a region in transition—and of the Southern Republican party.

Before 1952, as political scientist Alexander Heard wrote in that year, "To many citizens of the South, a Republican is a curiosity."*

Not quite typical of this curious breed—but, in many ways, not so very atypical either—were Colonel Edward Howland Robinson Green and William Madison McDonald, to give them their full, if unused names. To most folks they were Ned Green and Gooseneck Bill McDonald. The former came to Texas from New York because he was the son of the world's richest and meanest woman, Hetty Green, who had organized the Texas Midland Railroad in 1892 and had sent her easygoing son down South to look after it. Out from under

---

* See Alexander Heard, *A Two-Party South?* (Chapel Hill: University of North Carolina, 1952), p. 37. Also see V. O. Key, Jr., *Southern Politics* (New York: Vintage Books, 1949) and John C. Topping, Jr., John R. Lazarek and William H. Linder, *Southern Republicanism and the New South* (Cambridge: The Ripon Society, 1966).

Mother's thumb for the first time in his twenty-five years, Ned decided he would like to make a splash in politics and he turned for guidance to Gooseneck Bill, a tall, gaunt Negro with hawklike features and an enormous Adam's apple. Spreading Ned's money lavishly, in 1896 Gooseneck Bill got his white protégé elected chairman of the Texas Republican Executive Committee, the highest party position in the state. Bill went on the payroll at the then handsome salary of $575 a month and kept Ned in office and out of trouble until he got the notion to run for Governor in 1906, at which time Hetty put an end to her prodigal son's adventure.

Gooseneck Bill and Ned represented two-thirds of the component parts of the pre-1952 G.O.P. in the South. There were the Negroes, the Northern carpetbaggers (more often looking for booty than for kicks) and the mountain men.

In the Deep South not all Negroes were Republicans but most Republicans were Negroes. As the great Frederick Douglass said: The Republican party was the ship, all else the sea. The party of Lincoln became in South Carolina the party of "Tieless Joe" Tolbert and in Mississippi of Republican National Committeewoman Mary Booze and her male counterpart, Perry Howard. Howard's long hold over the Magnolia State's G.O.P., which lasted until 1956, was especially remarkable because he lived in Washington, D.C. The Democrats, of course, were more than delighted to encourage a lily-black Republican party.

If the delta Democrats' political loyalties often appeared a prime example of heredity triumphing over self-interest, the same could be equally said of the generations of Republicans who seemed to be trapped by time and geography in the Blue Ridge Mountains stretching from western Virginia across western North Carolina, eastern Tennessee, northern Georgia, and similarly in the Ozarks of Arkansas and the German counties of south-central Texas. These present pockets of Republicanism—like "The Free State of Winston" (Winston County, Alabama)—are the direct descendants of the non-slave-holding small farmers who bitterly opposed the Civil War. That they still follow their tradition is evident from the vote in Gillespie County, Texas, in 1952—92 percent for Eisenhower—making it the Republicans' banner county in the nation. And Representative James H. (Jimmy) Quillen of eastern Tennessee consistently received the largest percentage of any Republican Congressman. (In 1966, he drew 87.1 percent of the vote.)

In 1952, the primary purpose of the Republican party in this thirteen-state region—the eleven states of the old Confederacy plus Oklahoma and Kentucky—was to gather in the Federal patronage in the event of a national Republican administration. It was in the interest of these "post-office Republicans" to keep the local parties small and controllable. Yet, only twelve years later, their successors were playing presidential politics of a very different kind, and for

Crockett, Washington **Star**, Nov. 11, 1966

vastly higher stakes. In 1964, the Southern Republicans nominated Barry Goldwater as the G.O.P. candidate for President and, as it turned out, provided virtually all the electoral votes he received.

The growth of the party is measured in clear statistics: there were no Republican Governors among the 13 from the South in 1952, in 1967 there were 3; there were no Republicans among the 26 Senators in 1952, now there are 5; the Republicans had only 6 of 122 Representatives in 1952, now they have 28 of 119.

The phenomenal growth recorded in these figures is, in fact, the greatest political revolution in the country. And it is a continuing revolution, for Republicanism in the South is still on the rise. What form that Republicanism will take is of major significance to the national party and indeed to the future of American politics. With growth comes power, and in the 1968 Republican convention the South will command more votes than any other section of the country. Its share of convention strength has risen from 19 percent in 1952 to 26.7 percent in 1968. Any Republican who can line up the South's 356 votes in 1968 will be more than half way home to nomination.

But the Southern Republican party is not a monolithic structure; it could not be. For its growth has not been a smooth, placid process, but rather has come in waves of bitter internal struggle. The first occurred in 1952, when the old-guard Republicans, predominantly pro-Taft, found themselves confronted in several states by insurgents who, using the popularity of the prospective Eisenhower candidacy, sought to broaden the party's base and, not so incidentally, to boost themselves into power. In Louisiana, Georgia and, most notably, Texas, thousands of new recruits, almost all of them nominal Democrats, were sent swarming into precinct, county and state conventions to vote for Eisenhower delegates. The uproar and the battle continued right onto the floor of the national convention in Chicago, where the contested delegations were finally resolved in Eisenhower's favor, thus sealing his nomination.

The "new-guard" Southern Republicans included some men of real ability, such as the professionally and socially successful New Orleans attorney John Minor Wisdom, now a Federal judge. As a group they were young, moderate, internationalist, urbane, racially tolerant, sophisticated and intrigued by the organizational side of politics. With the war hero as their candidate, they carried Florida, Oklahoma, Tennessee, Texas and Virgina in 1952, but failed to budge the strongly-segregationist Deep South. In 1956, despite the school desegregation decision written by Eisenhower-appointed Chief Justice Earl Warren, the President held all the Southern states he had won in 1952 and added Kentucky and Louisiana. In 1960, despite the use of Federal troops at Little Rock and Republican sponsorship of the first two civil-rights bills since Reconstruction, Nixon carried Florida, Kentucky, Oklahoma, Tennessee and Virginia, while Alabama was giving some of its electors and Mississippi all of them to third-party candidates.

Throughout the Eisenhower years, from 1952 through 1960, the growth of Southern Republicanism was largely an urban phenomenon; a special division in the Republican National Committee, called "Operation Dixie" and headed by Virginian I. Lee Potter (now the executive director of the Republican Congressional Campaign Committee), was set up in .1957 to speed the techniques of organization from the cities like Dallas and Atlanta, where they were first developed, to other Southern metropolitan areas.

There were several reasons for the metropolitan and cosmopolitan character of Southern Republicanism in the 1950's. The industrialization of the region was bringing many young business and professional families from other sections. Many of the new arrivals brought their Republicanism with them and spurred the growth of organizations where none existed before. As a North Carolina Democrat put it, "Every time we entice industry into the state, it brings a batch of Republicans." One recent Alabama chairman, Dr. Thomas Brigham, was a Vermont dentist; every single Republican elected to high office in Florida was born outside the state; and the Virginia chairman, Robert J. (Jack) Corber, is an attorney who came naturally by his political affiliation during a Topeka, Kansas, childhood.

Second, the Southern cities were the recipients, not only of expatriate Yankees, but of the tide of postwar migration from farm to city within the South. Young Southerners, uprooted from their farms by World War II, settled in the booming Florida cities and in the suburbs around Atlanta, and made metropolises of Dallas and Houston. Leaving the farm, they threw off the "brass collar" Democratic habits of their parents and began to think for themselves. A succession of student-body presidents at "Ole Miss" went straight from college into the fledgling Republican party of Mississippi. Across the South, the Republican party became the party of youth, and it remains so today. When thirty-two-year-old James C. Gardner resigned as Republican state chairman of North Carolina in 1966 to run successfully for Congress, he was replaced in the top party post by thirty-one-year-old James Holshouser. Twelve new Republican Congressmen were elected in 1966 from the Southern states and their average age was forty-two. In 1965, the average age of the G.O.P. statewide ticket in Virginia—for Governor, Lieutenant Governor and Attorney General—was thirty-seven.

By contrast, the Democratic party in the South is an old man's party. The hierarchs of the Senate, the committee chairmen who represent the epitome of Southern power in the Democratic party, are Lister Hill, seventy-two, and John Sparkman, sixty-seven, of Alabama; J. William Fulbright, sixty-two, and John McClellan, seventy-one, of Arkansas; Richard B. Russell, seventy, of Georgia; Allen J. Ellender, seventy-seven, of Louisiana; James O. Eastland, sixty-three, of Mississippi; A. S. Mike Monroney, sixty-five, of Oklahoma; and B. Everett Jordan, seventy-one, of North Carolina. The only Southern Democratic chairman under sixty is Russell B. Long of Louisiana, a sprightly forty-nine, who had the advantage of being his father's son.

The southern G.O.P. has played on the mobility and ambition of the young newcomers from the farms and from Yankeeland to build this metropolitan-area organization. Status conscious, but not always well connected with the established aristocracy of the Southern cities, the Republicans of the 1950's managed skillfully to enhance their politics with a certain degree of snob appeal, thus tapping the energies of young executives and their capable, pretty and highly competitive wives. Young couples in strange surroundings found the local Republican party a port of entry into the acceptable, indeed estimable, social structure of their new communities. Republicanism became chic; and the chic, savvy and dedicated young Republicans organized the precincts from Dallas to Daytona Beach as few Republican precincts anywhere in the United States have ever been organized.

To the extent that ideology was of consequence at all to the Southern Republican party of the 1950's, there was sufficient ammunition in the national party's pledges of fiscal conservatism, firm anti-Communism and a generalized dedication to limited government. The rapid economic growth of the South in the decades following World War II produced an attitude in the moneyed and middle-class voters not unlike that of the North during the Republican Era following the Civil War. The fruits of progress and industrialization were there for anyone to enjoy; from government, they asked no more than to be left alone.

But another strain of ideology, one much older and of much greater emotional intensity, was also part of Southern politics. The politics of race—the legal and extralegal suppression of the Negro—had shaped Southern politics from the end of Reconstruction, but for most of the period it worked within and was contained by the dominant Democratic party. However, in 1948, when the national Democratic party wrote a strong civil-rights section into its platform, Southern rebellion took the form of the "Dixiecrat" movement headed by Strom Thurmond of South Carolina; Thurmond carried four states—Alabama, Louisiana, Mississippi and South Carolina.

In 1960, the Southern Republicans were feeling enough heat on the race question so that their spokesman on the platform committee, John Tower of Texas, battled hard to soften the civil-rights pledges; but Nixon, committed by personal conviction and the record of the Eisenhower Administration, and hounded on his other flank by Nelson Rockefeller, gave the Southerners little comfort.

It was not until after his defeat that the riptide emotions of protest against liberal social programs and pro-civil-rights policies of the Federal government, now controlled by the Democrats and personified by the hated "brothers Kennedy," engulfed the Southern Republican party and unleashed a series of internal battles more violent than those of 1952. In isolated cases, the battle between the Goldwaterites and the "moderates" in 1964 was simply a replay of the 1952 script with a different ending. Spokesman for the losing Taft faction of the Georgia G.O.P. at the 1952 convention was Roscoe Pickett, Jr., from the party's mountain redoubt in the extreme northern part of the state. His father, of the same name, had been a Republican party dignitary in the state since 1908. The young Pickett, a red-hot segregationist, liked to recall the old days when the party had a largely docile Negro membership and sports writer Ralph McGill of the Atlanta *Constitution* described the Jim Crow bleachers at Crackers' baseball games as "the Roscoe Pickett grandstands." Except politically, things had gone well for Roscoe Pickett since 1952. His real-estate ventures enabled him to lose (almost cheerfully) $400,000 in the short-lived Atlanta *Times,* a right-wing attempt to counter the *Constitution*'s liberalism, and he rode around the capital city in a $23,000 Mercedes Benz.

But the party, from 1952 until 1964, was run by a moderate, G.O.P. National Committeeman Robert Snodgrass, scion of a famous baseball family whose "Uncle Freddy" was the New York Giant outfielder best remembered for a World Series muff. The Republican leader, now head of an Atlanta-based finance company with thirty-eight offices throughout the South, was born in Oklahoma City, where his father was managing the professional team; his childhood memories are of spring training camp in Mineral Wells, Texas, with his devoted friend Dummy Taylor, the deaf-mute pitcher. Under Snodgrass' influence the Georgia G.O.P. became the least-strident political voice below the Mason-Dixon Line. When Eisenhower sent troops to Little Rock to enforce school integration in 1957, the executive committee of the Georgia Republican party formally commended him.

However, in 1964, Robert Snodgrass was unceremoniously and decisively dumped from his job as national committeeman by the rampaging backers of Barry Goldwater, and the man who replaced him was Roscoe Pickett.

The emotional force that unseated Snodgrass and changed the face of Southern Republicanism was the politics of protest—at big government in general, and the Kennedy Administration's efforts to force integration in particular—that came to be known as the Goldwater "Southern strategy." John Kennedy had carried six Southern states in 1960, despite his Catholicism and his liberalism, because he was a Democrat, because he was identified no more strongly as a civil-rights advocate than Richard Nixon, and because he had a Southern Democrat, Lyndon Johnson, on the ticket with him. But as President, Kennedy and his brother, Attorney General Robert F. Kennedy, federalized troops to meet one school integration crisis in Alabama, sent regular Army forces to fight a pitched battle over the integration of the University of Mississippi, and in 1963 called on Congress to enact the most sweeping civil-rights legislation in history. They thereby made the Democratic party the party of integration—or as Southern Republicans were quick to tag it, "the party of [James] Meredith, [Martin Luther] King and Kennedy."

Barry Goldwater, on the other hand, at a celebrated news conference in Atlanta in November, 1961, had said that school integration was "the responsibility of the states. I would not like to see my party assume it is the role of the Federal government to enforce integration in the schools." Coincidentally or not, Republicans were on the upswing in the South; John Tower had won Lyndon Johnson's old Senate seat in Texas in a special election in 1961; in 1962, Southern Republicans elected five more Congressmen and a Governor of Oklahoma, and narrowly missed winning a Senate seat in Alabama, of all places.

By mid-1963, it was generally accepted that Kennedy would face a tough battle if Goldwater was the Republican nominee. A map distributed at the Independence Day "Draft Goldwater" rally in Washington's armory showed how electoral victory was possible by adding a Solid Republican South to a few traditionally Republican Midwestern states, like Ohio and Iowa, even if Kennedy carried all of the Eastern industrial states and California—normally the vital prizes in a presidential campaign.

Southern Republicans caught a kind of fever at this prospect. Tom Stagg, Jr., a bespectacled Shreveport attorney and Republican national committeeman for Louisiana, said after Goldwater's Atlanta press conference, "I just hope to God that for once my party has the guts to say the hell with carrying New York. I hope for once we have the guts to say to hell with those Eastern liberals."

Sane, pragmatic Southern Republicans were caught up in the emotion. Lee Potter, the architect and champion of a moderate, urban-based, economically-conservative but nonracist Southern Republican-ism posed happily in Charleston, South Carolina, in October, 1963, with three empty rocking chairs, representing John, Robert and Edward Kennedy. "That's our issue for 1964," he told reporters.

John Grenier of Alabama, an archetype of the "new Republican-ism," young (thirty-one when he became state chairman in 1962), bright, tough-minded, a superb organizer, a product of the raffishly elegant Dekes fraternity and with a master's degree from New York University law school, decided early in 1963 that Goldwaterism was the wave of the future and signed on as chief delegate-hunter in the southern states.

At about the same time that Grenier made his decision, Ralph de Toledano, the conservative publicist in Washington, sat down at his typewriter and wrote a book called *The Wining Side: The Case for Goldwater Republicanism*. He said: "Of the 13 southern states . . . only Arkansas remains precariously in the Kennedy column. . . . All the rest seem locked in the Goldwater embrace. . . . Only the tolerance of the South had sustained him [Kennedy] in 1960. Without the South, 1964 will be a bleak vista for the Democratic party."

De Toledano's book was published on November 12, 1963. Ten days later, Kennedy was dead, and so was the logic of the Goldwater "Southern strategy." But the latter fact was not to be proven until a year later, and in the meantime the Goldwater fever had remade the Southern Republican party so thoroughly that John Grenier was able to deliver 271 of the region's 278 votes to nominate the Senator in San Francisco.

The cause of Goldwater, the most prominent Republican to oppose the Civil Rights Bill of 1964, appealed to thousands of states' righters and segregationists. Most prominent of these was Strom Thurmond, the 1948 Dixiecrat presidential candidate, who bolted the Democratic party again in 1964, this time to join what he was careful to call "the Goldwater Republican party." Perhaps like John Quincy Adams

PO' ELIZA

Zschiesche, Greensboro **Daily News,** Sept. 15, 1964

he could say, "I have been styled a deserter from all parties because I truly never belonged to any party." But Thurmond was too big a catch to be ignored; his dominant personality and premier place in the political life of his state put the Republican party of South Carolina somewhat in the position of a minnow that has swallowed a whale.

In short order, Thurmond installed as state chairman his bright young administrative assistant, Harry Dent, and built a stable of candidates, who, like him, had held high office as Democrats and most of whom, including Albert Watson, the smooth and darkly handsome Congressman from the capital city of Columbia, were staunch segregationists. Relations between Thurmond and Dent and the pre-Goldwater South Carolina Republicans, like National Committeeman J. Drake Edens, Jr., were frequently tense.

The same kinds of politicians were pulled into the party by the Goldwater candidacy all across the South. In Mississippi, the genteel Republicans from "Ole Miss" and the Delta plantations found themselves with a newly-elected Republican U.S. Representative named Prentiss Walker, a heavy-set chicken farmer whose language was as down-to-earth as his vocation. In 1960, when Nixon ran, Walker had backed the movement for unpledged presidential electors in his district and, as he said, "found we had no place to go after we won." So, being a practical fellow, he signed up with the Republicans in 1964 after they had adopted a state platform saying that "segregation of the races is absolutely essential to harmonious racial relations and the continued progress of both races in the state of Mississippi."

In Georgia, the Goldwater cause attracted a segregationist from a different social class, Howard H. (Bo) Callaway, West Point graduate and heir to a textile fortune. As a fellow Georgian of less-exalted station put it: "The minute the doctor slapped Bo Callaway on the butt he was a millionaire." In 1962, Callaway was a Democrat, putting his money and effort behind segregationist ex-Governor Marvin Griffin against moderate Carl Sanders in the Democratic gubernatorial contest. Sanders won, and in 1964 Callaway turned up as the successful Republican candidate for Congress, charging Lyndon Johnson had "turned traitor" to the South.

The "Southern strategy" of the Goldwater campaign proved a national disaster for the Republican party; even within the South its effect was so uneven as to leave in question how durable its impact would be. On its face, it achieved considerable success: Goldwater carried all five of the Deep South states—South Carolina, Georgia, Alabama, Mississippi, Louisiana—and in those states alone Republicans gained seven seats in the U.S. House of Representatives. But even in Southern terms it was a failure. Goldwater's forty-seven Southern electoral votes were fewer than Eisenhower received in either of his campaigns and even fell short of Nixon's 1960 showing. Florida,

Oklahoma, Virginia and Tennessee—Republican since 1952—all reverted to the Democratic column. In Texas, where Goldwater's candidacy had its real base, every Republican on the ballot with him lost, save one lonely state legislator, and the gains of a decade were all but obliterated in a single day.

Close analysis showed that Goldwater had run worse, not better, than earlier candidates in the cities and metropolitan areas where Southern Republicanism had its start. The pattern of his vote was much closer to that of the 1948 Dixiecrat candidacy of Thurmond than to the Eisenhower and Nixon patterns of 1952, 1956 and 1960. Elections analyst Samuel Lubell noted that "of the 507 southern counties which Goldwater won, 233 had never gone Republican before. The five Deep South states he carried are a measure of the depth of support for a separatist racial policy." Democratic Congressman Charles Longstreet Weltner of Atlanta said it more succinctly: "Southern Republicans are simply Dixiecrats in button-down collars."

The problem, of course, was that Goldwater made no appeal to the Negro vote, a growing force in Southern politics. At his Atlanta news conference in 1961, he had said, "We're not going to get the Negro vote as a bloc in 1964 and 1968, so we ought to go hunting where the ducks are." His conduct of the 1964 campaign made this a self-fulfilling prophecy. Nixon got 58 percent of the Negro vote in Atlanta; four years later Goldwater received less than 1 percent.

It was a policy the party could not afford to continue, as Republicans were quick to recognize. A month after the election, Robert L. Gavin, the Republican moderate who had lost the North Carolina governorship to a segregationist Democrat because the Negroes voted a straight Democratic ticket against Goldwater, journeyed all the way to Denver to tell the Republican Governors that he was one Southern Republican who would "never again" go along with the so-called "Southern strategy."

That the Goldwater-Grenier approach would be short-lived was indicated by the statistics of Negro suffrage in the South. The five states Goldwater carried had from 62 to 93 percent of the voting-age Negroes unregistered in 1964. With the passage of the Voting Rights Act of 1965 and the concerted registration efforts that followed, it was doubtful the "Southern strategy" would make sense even for those five states in 1968, for in each the number of unregistered Negro voters is substantially larger than the size of Goldwater's margin.

At any rate, in 1965 the Southern Republicans themselves began to turn from the "Southern strategy." Virginia Republicans chose as their standard-bearer an outgoing forty-one-year-old Roanoke attorney, A. Linwood Holton, who had no tolerance for intolerance. Holton made perhaps the most wide-ranging appeal to the Negro electorate in the state's recent history. Besides strongly opposing the poll tax, he promised to appoint a qualified Negro to the state Board of Education and to put Negroes in white-collar positions and on the state police force. Yet the Negroes, gun-shy from the Goldwater campaign, not only failed to support the G.O.P. ticket, but probably gave the Democrats their winning margin. On the other hand, 1965 elections in Louisville and Atlanta indicated that the Negroes would vote for the Republican party despite Goldwater if properly cultivated. In the Kentucky city, where Lyndon Johnson received 95 percent of the Negro vote, within one year the G.O.P. municipal administration, which had opened more city jobs to Negroes than any of its Democratic predecessors, carried the Negro wards by a two-to-one margin; while in Atlanta liberal Republican alderman Rodney Cook, who had been discouraged from running for Congress in 1964 because of Goldwater's nomination, won a 1965 seat in the Georgia legislature with 48 percent of the Negro vote.

Negroes have voted overwhelmingly Democratic since New Deal days, and economically have been a natural segment of the old Democratic coalition, but on the overriding issue of civil rights they usually exhibit considerable sophistication, picking their friends across party lines. Today most registered Negro voters are Democrats, although most Negroes have not been in the habit of casting ballots long enough to have formed fixed ways. The Republicans, even before the Goldwater campaign, did not start on a par in the competition for Negro votes. Yet as Thruston Morton of Kentucky told the Republican National Committee in late 1962, "When a Republican gets 40 percent of this [Negro] vote, he can win anywhere."

Virginia-born novelist William Styron has written, "The racial misery is within inches of driving us mad." The Republican party in the South has not yet learned to live with or overcome this racial madness. In Strom Thurmond's South Carolina the all-white 1966 G.O.P. state convention was held beneath a Confederate flag, while in Tennessee G.O.P. senatorial candidate Howard Baker, Jr., probably made the most ardent appeal for Negro votes of any Southern candidate save Alabama Attorney General Richmond Flowers. Claude Kirk was elected the Republican Governor of Florida on the Jim Crow slogan, "Your home is your castle—protect it," while Winthrop Rockefeller was elected the Republican Governor of Arkansas by defeating the most blatant race baiter in any 1966 contest.

Two factors, however, are working to shove the Republicans of the South in the direction of racial moderation. Externally, they are under steady (if, to liberal Republicans, inadequate) pressure from the national party leaders to avoid racist appeals. House Minority Leader Ford canceled a Mississippi speech when he found that the audience would not be integrated; Charles Percy, also in Mississippi, addressed the integrated Council on Human Relations despite strong warnings from the local G.O.P.; and Richard Nixon in speeches throughout the states of the old Confederacy firmly advised Republicans "not to go prospecting for the fool's gold of racist votes."*

This external pressure strengthens the forces within the region pushing the Republicans toward moderation. Chief of these, of course, is the growing Negro vote, which reduces even the short-term advantages of an overtly racist appeal. The 1966 elections were, for the most part, an object lesson to Republicans in the futility of trying to "out-seg" the Democrats in the South. Prentiss Walker, the Mississippi chicken farmer, tried to paint Senator Eastland as some sort of crypto-integrationist and was soundly trounced. In Alabama, John Grenier, the architect of the 1964 "Southern strategy," tried to use it against Senator Sparkman and failed; also in Alabama, Representative James Martin, who had almost been elected to the Senate in 1962 with backstage help from George Wallace, had the bad judgment to run for Governor against George's wife, Lurleen, and was summarily retired to private life for his lack of chivalry to that symbol of Southern womanhood.† Their experiences prompted one Deep South Republican chairman to remark privately to Ray Bliss, "If we're going to get anywhere from now on, we've got to go after all the votes, not just the white ones."

* For Percy's comments on Southern Republicanism, see p. 178ff.; for a discussion of Nixon and the South, see p. 221.

† Barry Goldwater, the South's *beau sabreur* just two years before, campaigned with a conspicuous lack of success in Alabama and Mississippi in 1966. Senator Eastland attacked him as "a life-time member of the NAACP" and George Wallace said he "should stay in Arizona and take care of the civil rights of Indians."

There is perhaps a third factor moving the Southern Republicans toward moderation, and that is their status consciousness. They are unlike the Southern Democrats, who have come to accept their role in the national party, which gives them dominance in Congress but leaves them unable to nominate a President. The Southern Republicans desperately want to be accepted as full partners in their national party. It did not escape notice among them that Ray Bliss twice passed over the head of the Southern State Chairmen's Association—first Wirt Yerger, Jr., of Mississippi and then Peter O'Donnell, Jr., of Texas—for appointment as leader of the national Association of State Chairmen, even though both Yerger and O'Donnell had seniority over the men who were chosen.

Most Southern Republicans resent and reject the racist label. One veteran politician sought ministerial comfort in 1966 because, as he said, "I'm so shook up at being labeled a racist that I'm about ready to quit." Another, South Carolina's Drake Edens, took to carrying in his pocket reprints of a home-town newspaper editorial, "South Carolina Republicans Aren't Racists," which recited Edens' personal fight against Klansmen and other arch segregationists who attempted to invade the G.O.P.

For the most part, Republican gains in the South in 1966 came in the areas of pre-Goldwater growth—Texas, Tennessee, Florida, Virginia, North Carolina, Kentucky and Oklahoma. Georgia was the only one of the five Goldwater states where the party's record improved. There, in a bid to become Georgia's first Republican Governor Bo Callaway won an exceedingly narrow popular-vote plurality over Democrat Lester Maddox, who ran an overtly segregationist campaign. But a write-in vote for moderate Democrat Ellis Arnall denied either man a majority and threw the election into the overwhelmingly-Democratic Georgia legislature, which promptly chose Maddox. However, Republicans held Callaway's House seat and added another to strengthen their position in the state.

With the gains of 1966, Republicans emerged with attractive local leadership in most of the Southern states and two men—Texas' John Tower and Kentucky's Thruston Morton—with background and credentials as national Republican leaders and possible vice-presidential choices.

Morton is a man of irresistible charm, tall, courtly, born to the

Louisville aristocracy (the family owned the Ballard Mills) and polished at Yale. One of the great raconteurs of contemporary politics, Morton is a worthy Republican successor to the late Alben Barkley; and he is a true Kentuckian, too, in his appreciation of good bourbon whiskey, fine horses and beautiful women. Elected to the House three times from the enlightened and relatively liberal constituency of Louisville, he gave up his seat in 1952 to manage the Kentucky campaign for Dwight D. Eisenhower, then served the Eisenhower Administration as Assistant Secretary of State for Congressional Relations during the difficult time when Senator Joseph McCarthy was warring on his own party and Republicans in the Senate were trying to hamper the President's authority in foreign affairs by passing the Bricker Amendment.

In 1956, Morton latched onto the Eisenhower coattails and won a narrow, upset victory over Senator Earle Clements. In the Senate, he has been a consistent supporter of civil rights, a conservative on most other matters. He moved quickly to a place of influence on the Finance Committee, was tapped by Eisenhower and Nixon for the key post of Republican National Chairman during the 1960 campaign, and was one of those on Nixon's final list of vice-presidential prospects in 1960. Later, he served for two years as chairman of the Republican Senatorial Campaign Committee and presided fairly if unhappily as the permanent chairman of the cacophonous political aberration that was the Republican National Convention of 1964.

As a Senator and as a party official, Morton has come to represent an open-minded, live-and-let-live political philosophy. His popularity is great throughout the South, where his personal support of civil rights and steadfast opposition to racist Republican candidates is accepted tolerantly, in part, one suspects, because Morton never forgets that the first rule for a successful Southern politician is to be entertaining.

At sixty and facing a campaign for his own Senate seat in 1968, Morton would normally not be considered a front-rank possibility for a vice-presidential nomination. But he appears to have shaken off his somewhat casual attitude toward Senate and party leadership this past year, gotten a spiritual and intellectual second wind, and emerged much to everyone's astonishment as the leader and spokesman for the moderate Republicans challenging the long Dirksen-Hickenlooper dominance of Senate Republican foreign policy. It was Morton who organized Republican support for the Consular Treaty with the Soviet Union (an issue on which Dirksen finally and belatedly reversed himself); Morton who backed the Javits proposal for a restudy of the NATO alliance; and Morton who, with strong backing from Percy, espoused the cause of increased East-West trade, which Dirksen and the Old Guard Republicans in both Senate and House firmly opposed.

In so doing, Morton not only put himself in line to challenge strongly for the job of Dirksen's successor as Minority Leader; he also built a political alliance with the younger progressive Republicans like Brooke of Massachusetts, Griffin of Michigan and Hatfield of Oregon, which is an extremely useful extension to his already-established popularity in the South and among party leaders of the Eisenhower-Nixon era. He also has an increasingly-Republican political base in Kentucky. In 1966, Kentucky voters re-elected his respected and soft-voiced colleague, liberal internationalist John Sherman Cooper, and increased the number of Republicans in the House delegation from one to three. One of the freshmen, William O. Cowger, progressive former Mayor of Louisville and a man of tough mind, was promptly elected president of the 90th Congress Club of new House Republicans, and at forty-four is a bright prospect for future national leadership in the G.O.P.

Morton himself gave indications in 1967 that he would favor Romney, Percy or Rockefeller for the 1968 nomination over his old ally, Nixon. His geographical and ideological situation—a border-state moderate, with appeal to the South, to the organization Republicans and to the progressives—gives him the graceful option of balancing a ticket with any of the prospective nominees.

If Morton is not a typical Southerner, John Tower is about as far from the Texan of legend as one will ever meet. He is, for one thing, notably short in the saddle: five feet, four inches, by the perhaps-generous measurement of his official biographers. He is also a product of the London School of Economics (along with such closer-to-home institutions as Southwestern University and Southern Methodist University) and, in a state where the free-enterprise cult heaps scorn on the professor who has never met a payroll, he spent his entire pre-Senate career on the political-science faculty of Midwestern University in Wichita Falls, his home town.

Tower was a typical Texan in one way, however. A Methodist minister's son, he started out in politics as a Democrat, passing out handbills in one of the early, unsuccessful campaigns for attorney general of his present colleague, liberal Democratic Senator Ralph Yarborough. He switched to the Republican party in 1951, finding it closer to his own increasingly conservative political and economic philosophy, and in 1954 was thoroughly vanquished in his first race for the state legislature. But he stayed active in the fledgling Republican party, became a member of the state executive committee, and, in 1960—after two more prominent prospects had turned it down— was offered the nomination against Senator Lyndon B. Johnson. "I'll tell you honestly," Tower says, "there wasn't much of a struggle to get that nomination; the party felt a moral obligation to run a candidate against the Democratic Majority Leader, and after others had refused to run, they came to me and said, 'You can articulate the party philosophy; you do it.' "

As things developed, 1960 was the year in which Lyndon Johnson was on the Texas ballot twice: once for United States Senator and once for Vice President of the United States. Tower ran a creditable, if unspectacular, race, losing by 379,972 votes, while the Kennedy-Johnson ticket carried Texas by 46,233 votes. When Johnson resigned his Senate seat to become Vice President in January, 1961, Tower was the logical Republican candidate to be his successor. In the free-for-all special election, it was Tower, the lone Republican, against *seventy* Democrats. He finished as high man, with barely 31 percent of the vote, and went into a runoff against the top Democrat, the appointed interim Senator, William Blakley, principal stockholder in Braniff Airlines and other Texas enterprises. When they were faced with a choice between "Cowboy Bill" Blakley, a stiff and unbending conservative Democrat, and conservative Republican John Tower, the liberal Democrats of Texas (who have tried without success for years to realign their own party in reasonable approximation of the national Democratic party) saw no choice at all and stayed home. John Tower won by 10,343 votes (50.6 percent of the total) and became the first popularly-elected Republican Senator in Texas' history.

Tower's victory was a major impetus to the "Southern strategy" then developing. Goldwater had been in Texas to help his campaign, and the junior Senator soon became a Goldwater protégé on the Labor and Public Welfare Committee. He earned himself a 99 percent favorable rating by the Americans for Constitutional Action for his first four years in Washington and joined early and enthusiastically in assembling the Goldwater-for-President drive, whose real political base was John Tower's Texas.

But when Goldwater was defeated in 1964, taking down with him Texas' two Republican Representatives and all but one of the lesser G.O.P. office seekers on the state ballot, nobody understood the implications more clearly than his good friend John Tower. In 1965, Tower voted for the Johnson Administration farm bill, even leading the fight for an amendment to restore some reduced conservation payments. He left the Labor and Public Welfare Committee, where he had regularly opposed domestic spending programs, and moved onto the Armed Services Committee, a traditional Texas bailiwick, where, like Lyndon Johnson before him, he found great merit in the multi-billion-dollar aircraft procurement programs in which Texas has so sizable a stake.

When he was asked if he was deliberately changing his image, Tower replied, "I never have been what you could describe as an ultra-conservative. I'm not philosophically doctrinaire. The only thing now is I'm accentuating the more positive things, instead of constant opposition."

The Armed Services Committee assignment was Tower's ticket to three trips to Vietnam, where he filmed some startlingly effective campaign documentaries of himself and the Texas troops and also essayed a partial rapprochement with his old antagonist, Lyndon Johnson. From 1961 through 1964, John Tower would fly anywhere in the country a Republican audience could be assembled in order to deliver an assault on his fellow Texan, the Vice President and later President. But beginning in 1965 Tower's rule became, "I never mention the President except to praise his staunch leadership against the Communists in Vietnam." Tower wanted Lyndon Johnson to feel no personal grudge that would bring him dashing home at the last minute to purge the Republican upstart in his home state; and, in fact, Johnson never did throw his full weight into the Texas campaign.

There were other steps taken, too, to avoid stirring the latent power of the Texas Democratic establishment. The Republicans in 1964 had contested all twenty-three Texas congressional seats, the Senate and the governorship, but in 1966 they concentrated almost exclusively on saving Tower. The candidate against unbeatable Democratic Governor John Connally was told to make himself as unobtrusive as possible. The organization sanctioned congressional candidates in only three predominantly Republican areas and managed to keep self-starters from running in all but three of the others.*

The Democrats helped Tower, as they had in 1961, with their choice of a candidate, the bland and colorless conservative state Attorney General, Waggoner Carr. As in 1961, liberal Democrats and labor-union leaders found little to choose between the two candidates and refused to support either. Tower was the beneficiary. Carr chose to campaign for the conservative vote, but Tower met this tactic by stressing his seniority and his strategic Armed Services Committee spot and by talking endlessly about his part in the successful Senate filibuster to save Section 14(b) of the Taft-Hartley law, and with it the Texas right-to-work law.

When the votes were counted, Tower, the winner by 10,000 votes in 1961, had been re-elected by a resounding 198,646 votes. And he had won by himself this time, permitting virtually no outside speakers. Asked early in the 1966 campaign year if he would invite Barry Goldwater to help him, Tower replied with a smile, "Barry who?"

Once re-elected, the Senator lost little time in plunging back into Republican presidential politics. He flew to California on December 30, 1966, to share with Governor-elect Reagan his thought that the conservatives in the party ought to form a holding action, through favorite-son candidacies, to preserve their bargaining position until the Republican presidential picture began to clarify. Reagan was receptive; Ohio Governor James A. Rhodes was moving in the same direction; and Tower made plans to line up Texas behind his own favorite-son candidacy. "Our three states alone," he says, "will have two hundred votes. Add in the rest of the South and you have almost enough to nominate a man." The "loose coalition" that Tower envisages would appear to lean philosophically to Richard Nixon over George Romney, but Tower, while agreeing to that fact, always is careful to add, with a grin, "It depends on who else is available." He is not the least hesitant, however, about conceding that if the party does not choose a conservative-minded presidential candidate, he would be available for the second spot on the ticket. To give

---

* One man who was permitted to run for the House and who was elected in 1966 is forty-year-old George Bush of Houston, tall and handsome son of former U.S. Senator Prescott Bush (R., Conn.). Bush was the losing candidate for the Senate in 1964. A moderate by Texas standards, with a secure political base, he can be expected to play an increasingly important role in state and even national Republican politics.

the cause a boost, a Tower for President committee was formed in Los Angeles in June, 1967, and the Senator himself made speaking appearances in a score of states. As if to prepare himself for such a role with Romney or Percy, Tower is always insistent that, though he opposed the civil-rights bills of 1964 and 1965, which they both endorsed, "civil rights is no longer an issue in the South; the Southerners know they're whipped on that one in either party." Tower's statement is probably more applicable to his own Texas than to the South as a whole, but with Negro voter registration rising throughout Dixie, the number of Southern Republicans who agree with his pragmatic view is certain to rise.

For Tower's hopes to succeed, he would have to be able to deal not just with Texas' fifty-six votes, but with those of the whole South; for the political value of a Texas candidate in the Republican party is seriously discounted by the expectation that President Johnson will carry his own home state again in 1968.

One obstacle to Tower's self-designated role as spokesman for the South is the upsurge of Republican leaders in other Southern states in the 1966 election. While Georgia, Alabama, Louisiana and Mississippi might be willing to look to Tower as their spokesman, the rest of the Southern states have their own leaders, who, if not vice-presidential hopefuls like Tower and Morton, would not be likely to surrender their proxies to either of them.

In 1962, Oklahoma elected its first Republican Governor, Henry Bellmon, a forty-one-year-old farmer from Billings. Ineligible to run again in 1966, Bellmon temporarily retired from politics, while giving every indication that he would challenge Democrat Mike Monroney for his Senate seat in 1968. In the meantime, Oklahoma rewarded Bellmon for his above-average administration and the care with which he picked the G.O.P. slate by electing another Republican, Tulsa oil man Dewey F. Bartlett, forty-seven, to succeed him in the Governor's mansion. The second G.O.P. chief executive is a Catholic in a state where more than sixty percent of the population belong to fundamentalist churches and which supposedly voted against Alfred E. Smith and John F. Kennedy because of their membership in the Church of Rome.

Arkansas Republicanism came of age in 1966 with the election of Winthrop Rockefeller as the first G.O.P. Governor since 1874 and the election of John Paul Hammerschmidt, a forty-four-year-old former state chairman, as the first Republican member of the House delegation.

Rockefeller's victory in his second try for Governor (he lost to Orval Faubus in 1964) marked the end of a long climb for the man and the party he built and financed. Four years younger than brother Nelson, Rockefeller came to Arkansas at the age of forty-one in 1953 to start a new life after a stint as a playboy and a marriage that produced endless publicity and ended in divorce. With a new wife, Rockefeller literally carved a 24,597-acre empire out of the top of Petit Jean Mountain, sixty-five miles west of Little Rock, and began breeding Santa Gertrudis cattle. Soon after, he entered the public life of his adopted state as head of the Arkansas Industrial Development Commission, which encouraged the building of six hundred new plants during his nine-year chairmanship.

A breed apart from the other new Republicans in the South, and not just because of his name, Rockefeller is an emotional man, rather than a natural administrator. His attitude on social problems, including race relations, is akin to brother Nelson's, but he has moderated his views just enough to suit his Arkansas constituency, opposing, for example, certain provisions of recent Federal civil-rights legislation without damning the cause of civil rights. Rather than running on social-economic issues in 1966, he waged his successful campaign chiefly as a reformer, promising a clean-up of the highway department and the end to some of the other notorious patronage practices that grew up during Faubus's seven terms as Governor.

For a man who has spent a fortune to build a political party where none existed before, Rockefeller always has operated party affairs with a notably loose rein. In 1964, when Arkansas, like the rest of the South, caught Goldwater fever, he made no effort to deny the Arizonan nine of the state's twelve votes, but cast his own ballot for brother Nelson. In 1968, he probably will be his delegation's nominal "favorite son," but, facing his own campaign for re-election, he is again unlikely to seek to determine where the delegates go after they pay their compliment to him.

The most spectacular Southern winner of 1966, both in personality and in the surprise of his victory, was Claude R. Kirk, Jr., the first Republican governor of Florida since 1872. A handsome, fleshy man of forty, Kirk was born in San Bernardino, California, was raised near Chicago, served in the Marines in both World War II and Korea (a Marine Corps buddy is California's Lieutenant Governor Robert H. Finch), graduated from the University of Alabama Law School and came to Jacksonville, Florida, in 1956 to set up an insurance company, which became highly profitable and which he later translated into an investment-company partnership. Like most Southern Republicans, Kirk started as a Democrat, campaigned for Eisenhower and Nixon without bothering to switch his party registration, and took the whole plunge into Republicanism with Barry Goldwater. Like Tower of Texas and Rockefeller of Arkansas, it took him two statewide campaigns to produce his first victory. In 1964, he claimed the unwanted nomination against Senator Spessard L. Holland, a Democrat of unimpeachable conservatism, and lost by 435,373 votes, trailing far behind Goldwater and the G.O.P. gubernatorial candidate. But the first campaign made Kirk's name at least moderately well known and he bounced back in 1966 to run for Governor under far more favorable circumstances.

Haydon Burns, the Democratic incumbent, who had been combating charges of corruption for most of his two years in Tallahassee and in the Democratic primary and runoff election of 1966, was toppled by a coalition of opponents tenuously united behind the candidacy of Miami Mayor Robert King High. The Burns-High runoff was exceptionally bitter, even by Florida standards; the result close—High won by a 54-46 margin; and the wounds enduring. Burns refused to endorse High, saying that for him to support "High's ultra-liberal philosophies" would "be a complete breaking of faith with the 509,000 Floridians who voted for me and for conservative government." Many of Burns's major financial backers, including representatives of the vast Du Pont holdings, moved over behind Kirk.

Moreover, High was a far more tempting target for Kirk's campaigning than the conservative Senator Holland had been. A racial moderate, whose cosmopolitan Miami constituents were worlds apart politically from the conservatism of Democratic north Florida, High was probably the most liberal nominee ever to seek the Florida governorship. Kirk picked up the "ultra-liberal" charges Burns had already publicized, focusing particularly on the fact that three former campaign aides to Senator Robert F. Kennedy had helped High in the primary. In addition, he opened up two new themes: he attacked the crime syndicate operations he said High allowed to go unchecked in Miami and, in the final days of the campaign, bid openly for segregationist votes by adopting the "Your home is your castle—protect it" slogan that had worked wonders for a Democratic candidate in the 1966 Maryland gubernatorial primary.

Kirk's campaign was guided by Robert E. Lee, a shrewd political manager from Denver, who in 1962 had engineered the remarkable Colorado G.O.P. recovery. Under Lee's guidance Kirk managed to be elsewhere when Barry Goldwater came campaigning in Florida in 1966. On election day, he rolled up a 152,957-vote margin over High. Kirk's explanation of his victory, a classic single-sentence summary, was that "it demonstrates the new, bipartisan, cross-over morality that is as old as America itself."

Once elected, Kirk set out on a course of action that rivaled in fireworks what Reagan was doing at the other end of the country. Even before he was sworn in, he announced that he was launching a "war against crime" by the unorthodox method of hiring his own privately-financed detective service to investigate collusion between criminals and public officials. For this delicate task, he chose the firm of George R. Wackenhut, a former special agent for the Federal Bureau of Investigation, whose specialties ranged from "industrial security" task forces to the issuance of monthly bulletins on "Communist-front" organizations.

Then the new Governor, twice married and twice divorced from the mother of his four children, showed up at his inaugural ball with a spectacular blonde companion, whom he introduced as "Madame X." A week later, she was identified as Erika Mattfeld, native of Germany but newly-divorced from her Brazilian husband, and on February 18 she became the second (or third, depending on the method of computation) Mrs. Kirk, at a ceremony attended by the ubiquitous Richard M. Nixon.

Evidently Florida voters had been waiting all their lives for a Governor who was both crime fighter and swinger, for in a court-ordered special election of a newly-apportioned legislature in April, 1967, they gave Kirk the most Republican legislature in the South. The G.O.P. emerged with 20 of the 48 Senate seats (up from 11) and 39 of 119 house seats (up from 26). This victory appears to have insured Kirk's prospects as the favorite-son candidate in the Florida presidential primary and to have whetted his appetite for national politics. Shortly after the state election, it was revealed that the Florida Governor was being counseled by New York public-relations man William L. Safire, whose clients have included Nelson Rockefeller, Ex-Lax and Richard Nixon; while an associate of Kirk's in Tallahassee said that the Governor "has this theory that the Republicans will nominate a liberal or moderate for President and will want to balance the ticket with a conservative." Consequently, the aide reported, Kirk has decided to create an "ultra-conservative image" for himself.

The third bright new face in Southern Republican ranks to emerge from 1966 was Howard W. Baker, Jr., who became the first popularly-elected Republican Senator from Tennessee. The circumstances were strikingly similar to those that produced Kirk's victory in Florida and Rockefeller's in Arkansas: a bitter Democratic primary setting the stage for an upset by a Republican who had been beaten in 1964 when running against a different and stronger Democrat.

But Howard Baker, Jr., unlike Kirk and Rockefeller, was a native son, born and bred to the Republicanism of the state he now represents. His father served the staunchly-Republican eastern Tennessee 2nd District in the House from 1950 until he died in 1963; Mrs. Baker was then elected to complete her husband's term. Baker's wife, Joy, is the daughter of Senator Everett Dirksen; and his sister, Mary, is married to Virginia G.O.P. Congressman William C. Wampler.*

A wispy fellow, barely five foot, six inches tall, but possessed of great presence, Baker took over his father's Knoxville law practice and made his first try for public office in the unfortunate year of 1964. Despite the difficulty of running in Tennessee on a ticket headed by a man who wanted to sell the Tennessee Valley Authority, Baker managed to come within 51,575 votes of beating Democrat Ross Bass for the two years remaining in the term of the late Estes Kefauver.

In 1966, he came right back, winning the Republican nomination

---

* Baker has a favorite story about his father-in-law. In 1960, when Baker was visiting Illinois, he went out stumping with Dirksen, who used his son-in-law's military career to make a point about John F. Kennedy. "It happens," said Dirksen, "that my son-in-law was a PT boat commander, too, but I haven't heard anyone suggest that that qualifies him for public office." Baker says Dirksen dropped the story when he came to the Senate. Baker's congressional brother-in-law comes from just across the Tennessee border in the Southwestern Highland region of Virginia. The forty-year-old Wampler, known as "the bald eagle of the Cumberland," represents a mountainous area of small farmers and coal miners, who, historically, have been both Republican and radical.

from Goldwater's Tennessee campaign manager, while Bass was losing out in a rough Democratic primary to Frank G. Clement, the somewhat mercurial Governor. In the general election, both men bid openly for the Negro vote, and Baker managed to increase his share of it from the 2 percent he received in 1964 to 15-20 percent in 1966. Rolling up big margins in the traditionally Republican areas of East Tennessee, he also managed to carry every one of the nine major metropolitan areas except Nashville and defeated Clement by 99,200 votes. His platform emphasized strong support for Federal tax sharing with the states—a position that typifies the "positive conservatism" that Baker, like much of the new Southern Republicanism, claims to represent.

As top Republican officeholder, Baker was the likely favorite-son choice of the twenty-eight-man Tennessee delegation in the 1968 convention, but conservatives in the state G.O.P., led by Chattanooga Congressman William E. Brock, III (who also is the attractive scion of a well-to-do political family), were capable of pressing for an early commitment to Nixon.

As the maneuvering for the 1968 nomination began in the Southern states, most of Goldwater's ardent 1964 supporters still felt a far stronger affinity for those (Nixon and Reagan) who campaigned for their champion, than those (Romney and Percy) who either disowned him entirely or kept their distance from him.

A number of the Southerners gravitated early toward formal or informal alliances with Nixon. Among them were Peter O'Donnell, Jr., the Texas state chairman, and Fred LaRue, the Mississippi national committeeman, both early and fervent Goldwaterites. Linwood Holton, the unsuccessful Virginia gubernatorial candidate, announced his support as soon as the national Nixon-for-President headquarters opened; while James Gardner in North Carolina, John Paul Hammerschmidt in Arkansas and most of the other members of the Southern congressional delegations were also pro-Nixon.

Romney began sampling Southern attitudes toward his candidacy in the spring of 1967, dipping first into Williamsburg, Virginia, then into Little Rock and Atlanta—outposts of "moderation" in a generally-conservative region. His managers knew that with his 1964 apostasy and his strong civil-rights record, even the conservatism of his fiscal policies would glean him few more than a handful of the region's

356 convention votes. One Romney leader commented, "We'd settle right now for 50 of them, and count ourselves lucky."

But the candidate who most excited the South was the diminutive Democratic former Governor of Alabama, George C. Wallace. "If Wallace runs for President on a third-party ticket in 1968," said Nixon-backer Barry Goldwater early in 1967, "it would be a disaster for the Republican party." And Wallace showed every sign of doing just that.

The "Fighting Judge," as he likes to be called, is something special in American politics. Elected Governor in 1962 on a vow "never" to permit integration of Alabama's schools and public facilities, Wallace was forced to see his pledge broken a dozen times and more during his four years in office. But by elaborately-staged confrontations, Wallace managed, in the eyes of his constituents, to wrap himself in a martyr's mantle, as the man who "stands up for Alabama" against the Federal tyranny.

In 1964, Wallace, as vainglorious a publicity seeker and skillful a demagogue as contemporary politics affords, had the happy conceit of testing his anti-Federal-government thesis in several Northern Democratic presidential primaries. The results were enough to give the Democrats a bad case of jitters. Running against Governors and Senators named as "stand-in" candidates for President Johnson, Wallace received 29.8 percent of the votes in Indiana, 33.8 percent in Wisconsin and 42.8 percent in Maryland.

Wallace's showing also had dramatic impact on Republican leaders, who found in it evidence that there was a national "white backlash" against Negro civil-rights demands, which a Republican candidate might be able to exploit. Eager to capitalize on this hope, John Grenier and Jim Martin, Alabama Republicans then on cordial terms with Wallace, bustled around the country in the weeks before the 1964 convention, promising that if Goldwater was nominated Wallace would drop his publicized plan to run as a third-party candidate. Whether they had Wallace's promise or were simply guessing that his financial support would dry up if Goldwater was the G.O.P. nominee is unknown; but on the Sunday after Goldwater's nomination Wallace told a national television audience that he would not run for President.

The decision, in the view of Washington elections analyst Richard M. Scammon, saved Goldwater and the Republican party from the ignominy of finishing third in the electoral college vote. Scammon, in company with others, is convinced that had George Wallace stayed in the race he would have carried four of the six "Goldwater states" —Alabama, Mississippi, South Carolina and Louisiana; muddled the vote so thoroughly in Georgia that it might have ended in the Democratic column; and, likely, left Goldwater with only the five electoral votes of his home state of Arizona.

Thus, when Goldwater says, as he did in February, 1967, that "Wallace would seriously cut into Republican strength in the South. . . . I don't think he could possibly get elected, but I think he would assure the re-election of Lyndon Johnson," he is talking from personal experience.*

Wallace has been emboldened to pursue his third-party plans by developments since 1964. He confounded the skeptics by the ease with which he flouted Alabama's prohibition on a second consecutive term for its Governors by the simple device of nominating and electing his wife to succeed him in 1966. Mrs. Wallace, a pretty former dime-store clerk who had previously played a retiring role in her husband's public life, received a majority of all votes against nine other candidates, including two former Governors, in the first primary, winning nomination without even the expected necessity of a runoff. In the general election against Jim Martin, who realized too late the emotional force building up behind Lurleen and George, the Wallaces won by better than a two-to-one margin.

On January 16, 1967, Lurleen, wearing a black cashmere suit and a little pillbox hat, stood on the steps of the capitol in Montgomery and promised "as a wife and mother" to fight the Federal school desegregation orders, which she called "an effort to gain control of the hearts and minds of our children." Sworn in as Alabama's first and the nation's third woman Governor, Mrs. Wallace explained that she was taking over state duties "to permit my husband to take our fight to the final court of appeals—the people of the United States in whom rests the ultimate sovereign power of this Nation."

---

* Goldwater's judgment was supported two months later, in April, 1967, when the Gallup Poll showed that whereas Romney led Johnson in a two-man race, 52-43, with 5 percent undecided, if Wallace's name were added, the results became: Johnson 43, Romney 35, Wallace 13, and 9 percent undecided. In a similar pairing with Nixon, Johnson tied Nixon 48-48, with 4 percent undecided, but with Wallace added, it became: Johnson 46, Nixon 36, Wallace 12, and 6 percent undecided.

Governor George made it even more specific in his talk to the 100,000 Alabamians who had come out to cheer and to take home the souvenir programs entitled "Two Governors, One Cause." "Alabama," said George Wallace, "is where freedom lives and works. That is why the words 'Alabama' and 'freedom' have come to have the same meaning to peoples around the world. . . . We see no reason why a man from Alabama would not make just as good a President as a man from New York or California—or maybe even from Texas."

In April, 1967, Wallace made his first stumping tour of the North, talking of entering the presidential primaries and then going onto the ballot "in all fifty states" as a conservative protest candidate. Vowing he would not run as a segregationist, he told Robert E. Baker of the Washington *Post,* "There is no backlash against civil rights or the Negro. But there is a backlash against big government . . . and neither of the major parties are talking about preserving states' rights and the property ownership system."

Back home in the capitol office, where he continued to administer most of the affairs of Alabama as his wife's unpaid "No. 1 assistant," he bragged to Scripps-Howard's Ted Knap in April, 1967 that he had already received $1 million toward his $10-million campaign kitty, and that his eight-man national campaign staff, housed outside the capitol, would soon be expanded to a nationwide political organization.

What George Wallace could do in the North as a third-party candidate is conjectural. Since 1964, racial tensions have been aggravated in the great cities by riots, demonstrations and marches. Open housing, the first civil-rights goal that really affected the North, proved to be so controversial that in 1966 the Senate killed a civil-rights bill by filibuster for the first time since 1957.

Single-issue presidential campaigns—and Wallace, despite his talk, is still chiefly identified with the civil-rights issue—normally have only marginal appeal except in the area where that issue dominates all others.

But no politician questions the likelihood that Wallace could carry the Deep South states of South Carolina, Georgia, Mississippi, Alabama and Louisiana on a third-party ticket, and run strongly enough in Arkansas, Florida, North Carolina and Virginia to affect the outcome. The prospect's effect on the fledgling Republican party of the South is clear. It would, as nothing else could, separate out the segregationists and the states'-rights adventurers, who are using the G.O.P. for their own purposes, from those committed to the genuine development of a two-party system in the South. And in those terms, no matter what its short-term impact, it might help the Republican party become unequivocally, what it is not now, an effective agency for change and progress in the New South.

11 Middle West

LOOKING like a Park Avenue Buddha, John A. Wells pushed back from his period-piece desk and folded his hands across his ample belly. It was dusk of a late fall day in 1966; Christmas shoppers and office workers formed an elaborate ant colony fifty-two floors below his office in New York's Pan Am building. He was a member of one of those legal colossi whose senior partners always seem to include a former Democratic Secretary of War and a former Republican Attorney General. Wells himself had equally impressive credentials—he was a Rhodes Scholar with three Oxford degrees, author of one book and editor of another, and one of the elite handful of Republicans who have managed presidential nomination campaigns (Rockefeller, 1964). "The next Republican candidate for President," he said, pausing for emphasis, "will be a Midwesterner." Like any good delphic oracle, he had spoken and would say no more.

Did he mean George Romney, Governor of Michigan? Or Senator Charles H. Percy of Illinois? Did this exclude Richard M. Nixon, who had grown up in California and now lived in New York? No, Nixon's father had come from Ohio, his mother's family from Indiana, and in many ways he was the most Midwestern of them all. Even Ronald Reagan, newly elected Governor of California, was a native of Illinois with a Chicago wife.

If Wells's prediction, on closer scrutiny, looked safe, it was also appropriate. For if the South represented the growth area of recent Republicanism and the East represented the slow but unmistakable decline of yesterday's Republicanism, then the Midwest represented the stability of traditional Republicanism.

Indeed, two Midwestern towns—Ripon, Wisconsin, and Jackson, Michigan—vie for the title of birthplace of the Grand Old Party; the controversy that brought the party into being is symbolized by a piece of legislation bearing the names of two Midwestern states—the Kansas-Nebraska Bill; and Abraham Lincoln, the patron saint and enduring symbol of the Republican party, came out of the wilderness down in Illinois.

Oliphant, Denver **Post**, Nov. 10, 1966, © 1966, The Los Angeles Times Syndicate

The Midwest is stamped indelibly on the party of Lincoln. Of the 20 Republicans nominated for the presidency, 12 were Midwesterners. The Midwestern states have voted for Republican presidential candidates 215 times; for Democratic candidates 91 times. Of the 12 states, only Missouri has been in the Democratic column more often than in the Republican.

Midwestern Republicanism has many roots. The most important probably was the conflict that produced the Civil War. The "brave boys" recruited in Wisconsin and Ohio and other Midwestern states who were lucky enough to come home after Antietam and Chickamauga formed the Grand Army of the Republic; they nominated and elected their former commander, Ulysses S. Grant of Illinois, as President and effectively kept the war alive as a political issue right up to the turn of the century.

But there were other things besides "waving the bloody shirt" that sustained Republicanism in the Middle West. It was and is farm country—two out of every five farms in the United States are there. And farmers, even the mechanized, businesslike farmers of the rich Corn Belt, with a quarter-million dollars of capital in their land, their stock and their equipment, retain the values Thomas Jefferson associated with tillers of the soil—rugged individualism, voluntary cooperation, preference for government closest to the people. These are American values, but they are, perhaps, particularly Republican values.

Third, the Middle West is, as one writer said, "surrounded, shielded, insulated." It was, in part because of such stridently anti-British newspapers as the Chicago *Tribune*, the home of American isolationism between the wars.

In the minds of many Middle Westerners, especially those who inherited their politics from Civil War grandfathers, the Democratic party became identified not just with the South and slavery, but also with wars and with the "machine politics" that accompanied the waves of later migrants to the Midwestern cities. Most of the Midwest cities are of middle size—Green Bay, Grand Rapids, Canton and the like—and retain their middle-class Republican ways. But the giants— Chicago, Detroit, Cleveland and St. Louis, with their thousands of Poles, Italians and Negroes—spawned great Democratic machines. Thus, the pattern of contemporary Middle West politics has developed as a struggle between the major Democratic metropolis and the small-town Republican outstate, upstate or downstate rural sections.

The growth of the cities, partially offset in recent years by the movement from city to suburb, has weakened the hold of Midwestern Republicanism. It is far stronger still than it appeared to be in 1964, when Barry Goldwater lost all the Midwestern states and the G.O.P. lost nineteen seats in the House of Representatives. In 1966, Republicans recovered all of the lost House seats and two more besides, picked up an extra Senator and one more Governor. But, going into 1968, Republicans were still substantially weaker in the Midwest than they were on the eve of the 1952 election: six Governors instead of seven; 11 Senators instead of 19; 80 Representatives instead of 95.

The weakened position is measured, too, in the weakened influence of the Midwest delegations at the 1968 nominating convention. The 12 Midwest states' 352 delegates comprise 26.4 percent of the total, down from 30.8 percent in 1952. But influence is not measured by numbers alone, and in terms of power positions the Midwest exceeds any other region, by far.

The chairman of the Republican party is Ray C. Bliss of Ohio. The Republican leader of the U.S. Senate is Everett McKinley Dirksen of Illinois. The Republican leader of the U.S. House of Representatives is Gerald R. Ford of Michigan. The assistant leader or whip is Leslie M. Arends of Illinois. The chairman of the House Republican Conference is Melvin R. Laird of Wisconsin. The Midwest may be weaker in numbers than formerly, but with Romney and Percy, Dirksen and Bliss, Ford and Arends and Laird, its power and its policy influence are still second to none.

The Midwest also has six of the sixteen presidential primaries, including two—Wisconsin and Nebraska—which may be as influential as any in the country. But one state with a presidential primary, Ohio, expects no contest. Ohio expects no contest because James A. Rhodes wants none, and no potential candidate is likely to challenge the Governor on his own territory.

Ohio's Republican Governor is fifty-eight years old, with the face of a friendly but foxy pharmacist, which he is not, but rather a lifetime, career, working politician, and one of the most spectacularly successful in the history of a state that is renowned for the craftiness of its political leadership, Republican brand. Rhodes is a methodical man, and when the depression forced him to drop out of Ohio State University in order to help the family, he decided his first goal would be to become Mayor of Columbus. He made it in four steps: ward committeeman, school board member, city auditor and finally, when only thirty-four, Mayor. He stayed three terms as Mayor, where his sideline activities included such controversial projects as organizing the National Caddie Association and the All-American Newspaperboys Sports Scholarship. Sometime in that city-hall period, the pleasures of the state capitol began to beckon. In 1952 he was elected state auditor, remaining in that unglamorous post for ten years, while building good will among the capital correspondents by maintaining a daily free lunch in his back room, and among the citizens by swooping down on the occasional big spender whose bills came under his scrutiny. In 1962, when his chance came to run for Governor, James Rhodes showed he had put his time to good use; he defeated the incumbent Democrat, Michael V. DiSalle, by over half a million votes.

The keynote of his administration has been industrial development, pegged to a tax structure that critics contend is obsolete. (Ohio is one of the few states with neither a corporate nor a personal income tax.) Rhodes has floated more bond issues than any previous Governor, a policy that critics say is merely a postponement of the inevitable day of reckoning; yet Rhodes still has starved some state services. In May, 1967, Rhodes tried to escape the squeeze by creating an Ohio Bond Commission, authorized to borrow additional funds for capital expenditures, but suffered a politically humbling defeat when voters rejected it by a 2-1 margin. Earlier, in 1966, the Columbus *Citizen-Journal,* which supports him politically, noted that though Ohio is the sixth-wealthiest state, it ranked forty-third in state support of public education and dead-last in state support for child-welfare services.

Rhodes's defense is that economy brings industry and industry brings jobs and jobs are the only source of wealth. On the record, it is hard to fault him. The Ohio Development Department has won numerous national awards for its programs, and more tangible endorsement, too. The number of native industries expanding in Ohio and the number of new companies moving in were both more than five times larger in 1966 than in 1962. "I don't say we invented industrial development," says Rhodes modestly, "but we perfected it."

The emphasis of his administration suits Rhodes's personality, for he is more at home promoting Ohio than he is in administering it. The day-to-day operations of the state are largely in the hands of two capable assistants, Executive Secretary John M. McElroy and Finance Director Richard Krabach.

The Governor's contribution is the hustle and inventiveness of his promotional skills. A man whose formal oratory is occasionally betrayed by his battle with English grammar, Rhodes has no trouble reducing a message to its essential element. Soon after he became Governor, Ohio began buying big ads in the *Wall Street Journal* and other business organs, showing Rhodes's eminently common-sense face and the slogan: "Profit Is Not a Dirty Word in Ohio." Any businessman considered likely to locate a plant in Ohio can count on a call from the Governor pledging his personal assistance in settling the deal to the company's satisfaction. Nor does Rhodes sit by and wait. He led trade missions to Europe and the Orient, opened state-financed offices in Brussels and Tokyo to promote markets for Ohio products.

In Rhodes's hands, everything becomes a tool to promote "The Wonderful World of Ohio." The formerly somnolent state fair has had its budget boosted to a point that enables it to rival Las Vegas for a few weeks each summer in the quality of its attractions. All this activity leaves Rhodes open to criticism that he is not "minding the store." But when an opponent complained about the frequency with which the Governor was pictured at some fishing site or camping area, obviously having a fine time, Rhodes deflated him quite simply. "Tourist promotion brings us $1.8 billion a year," he said, "and I'm the entire Ohio tourist promotion department."

Whatever the accuracy of such boasts and the logic of Rhodes's approach to government, he has a method that seems to work wonders with the voters. In 1966, running for re-election, he defeated the nominee of the badly-divided Democratic party, state Senator Frazier Reams, Jr., by 703,223 votes. In doing so, he broke John Bricker's old record for the largest percentage vote won by any Ohio Governor. Paced by Rhodes's 62.2 percent margin, the Ohio Republicans came out of 1966 with every statehouse office, control of both houses of the legislature and nineteen of twenty-four Congressmen—five more than they had previously.*

Rhodes's Ohio record has given the party a dominance unmatched in any other major industrial state, and naturally has stirred some speculation that the methodical man was ready to move up one more step—to Vice President, say. Thus, the February 24, 1967, issue of the *Ohio Republican News* (the largest-circulation party newspaper in the nation) gave front-page prominence to this story:

Gov. James A. Rhodes this week tried to stop a "Draft Rhodes for President" meeting which was organized by a Warren County man.

The meeting, scheduled in Middletown on Friday, was promoted by Don Gingerich of Carlisle.

The governor's executive assistant, John M. McElroy, issued a statement that was sharply critical of the draft move. McElroy said he had talked with Gingerich last Friday and asked him to call off the meeting.

"I pointed out to him that his efforts are a disservice both to the Governor and to the Republican party inasmuch as such a promotion inti-

* In his 1966 landslide, Rhodes carried every one of Ohio's 88 counties except Pike (pop. 19,380), which he lost by 350 votes. Defeated Democrat Reams, surveying the results, told a reporter, "I guess we concentrated too much on Pike County."

mates that the Governor is seeking advancement for himself," McElroy said.

He added that Rhodes has repeatedly disclaimed interest in being considered for national office.

Indeed, Rhodes had been very busy disclaiming any such interest. He went to the Colorado Springs meeting of Republican Governors to disclaim his ambition. In New Orleans to receive a trade award, he "dropped in" on a meeting of the Republican National Committee to disclaim his interest. He plays host to Republicans from other states at special seminars on industrial development.

His most interesting missionary work was the special technical-assistance program he set up, through Finance Director Krabach, for newly-elected California Governor Reagan. Twice in the early months of the Reagan administration, Krabach journeyed to California to coach the fledgling conservatives around Reagan. Reagan's basic script—the budget-cutting exercise, working-on-holidays ploy, the reduction in numbers of state employees, the squeeze on higher-education funds, the enrollment of businessmen-experts to analyze the management of state agencies—follows the Rhodes scenario for his first year in Ohio. That the two governors also saw eye to eye on political strategy was evidenced when they declared, almost in unison, their intention to be their states' favorite-son candidates.

What use Rhodes will make of his fifty-eight-vote delegation, fourth-largest at the 1968 convention, is not to be guessed, for of all the major G.O.P. politicians none is more unpredictable than he. His relationships with his fellow-Republican Governors are, to put it gently, a bit strained. He makes no effort to hide his impatience when his sophisticated Ivy League colleagues try to settle the problems of the world at one of their conferences. "One I went to," he recalls, "they had about seventy-five resolutions on the United Nations and what-all, and I got disgusted and left; I told them their job was to do something for the people of their states and I figured the UN was here to stay no matter what we said, so what the hell."

Rhodes has skipped some Republican Governors' meetings, ducked out of what others considered key sessions for a round of golf, and generally gone out of his way to stress his independence. The high point came in early 1966, when the Governors were called to the White House for a briefing on Vietnam, a sensitive subject in a campaign year. At the end of the briefing, Rhodes rose in his place, and read out a resolution praising President Johnson and endorsing his policy as the "only logical course" to end the war on honorable terms. The resolution was a last-minute inspiration, concocted by the President and Rhodes during a morning session of Appalachian Governors, where Rhodes was the only Republican present, and drafted by White House staffers. When Rhodes disclosed it, in the presence of the President, his Republican colleagues had no choice but to go along. But many were furious at being trapped by Rhodes that way. A year later, in 1967, back at the White House again for another Vietnam briefing, they obtained a promise from him for no hanky-panky. Rhodes kept his pledge and introduced no resolution. But that night at a White House dinner he offered a toast to the President that managed to say the same thing, and went home with a scribbled message of appreciation from Lyndon Johnson on the back of his White House place card, another trophy for the Wonderful World of Ohio.

Among his fellow Governors, Rhodes is most noted for his stock of bawdy stories and his way of making his comments and suggestions on political strategy with the simple but eloquent force of the four-letter Anglo-Saxon verbs. Some suspect he enjoys the shock value of his vocabulary on Romney, for whom he entertains no great affection. The two men are polar opposites in personality: Romney frequently borders on the sanctimonious; Rhodes is always ready to operate on the premise that everybody's got an angle. As neighboring Governors, they are natural rivals, as are their states, and their geographic proximity, among other things, makes it almost impossible for them to be on a national ticket together. What really chilled the relationship, on Rhodes's side, was a Romney visit to Toledo, the Ohio city closest to Michigan, right in the area where the battle between the two states for industries is fiercest. In a speech there, Romney was foolhardy enough to suggest that Michigan's industrial-development plan was better than Ohio's—and that is something James Rhodes does not tolerate. Rhodes's friends suspect that he reveled in winning by a larger margin and bringing in more Republican victors than his Michigan neighbor in 1966. His antipathy toward Romney makes him a natural ally for 1968 of Nixon or perhaps of Reagan or Percy. But guessing where James Rhodes will end is hazardous, for in 1964 he tricked everyone, including his own state party leader, Ray Bliss, by pledging the Ohio delegation to Goldwater on the eve of the convention.*

Former Governor William W. Scranton of Pennsylvania, whose slim hopes of nomination were ended completely by Rhodes's action, says Rhodes came to him in San Francisco and urged him to take the vice-presidential nomination because the "backlash" was going to boom Goldwater to victory. If so, it was a curious argument for Rhodes to advance, for he has carefully cultivated Negro support for himself, and won it, more successfully than any other Ohio Republican in years. He signed, but did not lead the fight for, Ohio's first open-occupancy law. His chief appeal has been through appointments of Negroes to judgeships and state posts; W. O. Walker, publisher of several Negro newspapers, is in the Rhodes cabinet as director of industrial relations.

Most Ohio Republicans conclude Rhodes knew that Goldwater was a loser and handed him the delegation simply because opposition was futile and the gesture would placate Goldwater's large contributors in Ohio, whose support would later be useful to Rhodes himself. At any rate, once Goldwater was nominated, Rhodes lost all interest in him, shunning the Senator when the campaign brought him through Ohio. (Goldwater, however, remains a fan of Rhodes, frequently mentioning him as a dark-horse presidential possibility.)

Looking to 1968, Rhodes's hopes for a vice-presidential nomination seem to rest almost entirely on the idea that Ohio's fifty-eight delegates will become crucial to someone's victory in the presidential race. His public popularity, outside Ohio, at this point is about what William E. Miller's was when Goldwater tapped him for Vice President. As a friend said of Rhodes, "He's got to figure out a way to take the vice-presidential nomination if he wants it; nobody is going to hand it to him because he's a swell fellow."

If Rhodes moves onto the ticket, it is a safe prediction that the country will hear repeatedly that the Republican party means jobs. "What people really want," he says, "is security through a job. That's what this civil-rights agitation, crime, social problems all stem from— lack of jobs. Democrats every Labor Day stand up and say we'll get you jobs and the Republicans, like damn fools, stand up the next day and say 'It can't be done.' Well, we've shown in Ohio it can be done. I go to the union guys—the leaders—and I tell them, 'I know you

* See Chapter 2, p. 44.

guys don't like Republicans, but here's one Republican who gets you jobs; and you know as well as I do that guys who aren't working don't join unions. Guys on welfare don't pay dues to you. You guys get in trouble when people aren't working. Well, I'm in the business of getting jobs. We need one thousand new jobs a week in Ohio, and I can't put them on the state payroll; so I get the industry that hires them.' They cheer their heads off," says Rhodes.

There is, of course, a second Ohioan who might command consideration for Vice President for very different reasons. Robert Taft, Jr., having lost his Senate bid in 1964, barely won his way back into the House in 1966 in a supposedly-safe Republican district. But his is still a name to be reckoned with, and a not inconsiderable talent.

Young Bob, as he is always called, is now fifty. He is tall and powerfully built, and, unlike his late father, possesses a cheerful, outgoing personality. During his two nonconsecutive terms in Congress he has proved to be an internationalist and a strong advocate of civil rights. He was one of only eleven Republicans to vote against the expulsion of Adam Clayton Powell in the first House test. During his 1966 campaign he modeled his string of storefront headquarters after John Lindsay's, a project in which he received the willing cooperation of Robert Price, Lindsay's first Deputy Mayor. And when he returned to the House of Representatives in 1967 many were surprised to learn that he joined the liberal Wednesday Club. Yet the man who accepted defeat for a long-cherished Senate seat rather than repudiate Barry Goldwater still commands affection from the party's right wing. While he is no longer a power in the Ohio G.O.P. delegation, Robert Taft, Jr., with a moderate record and a conservative name, makes an interesting speculation for balancing a presidential ticket.

Next door to Ohio is a state of almost equally Republican tradition but one where decay and demoralization of Republican leadership have let the Democrats gain dominance. The decline in Indiana first was evidenced in 1958—that year of national Republican disaster— when the Democratic Mayor of Evansville, round-faced R. Vance Hartke, upset G.O.P. Governor Harold W. Handley for the Senate seat being vacated by the strident William E. Jenner. In 1960, despite Nixon's lopsided victory over Kennedy in the state, a handsome, courtly Vincennes lawyer, Matthew E. Welsh, won the governorship for the Democrats from Lieutenant Governor Crawford E. Parker.

In 1962, thirty-four-year-old Democratic state Representative Birch Bayh kept the string intact by upsetting aging Republican Senator Homer Capehart; and in 1964 Democrats reached their peak by re-electing Hartke, putting Roger D. Branigan, a florid-faced Lafayette lawyer, in as Governor to succeeed Welsh and carrying the state for President Johnson. Two years later, Republicans staged a mild recovery, winning back one of the two House seats lost in 1964 and regaining a majority in the state House of Representatives, but they are still far from restored to their normal health.

As happens so frequently, the party has become more conservative as its popular base has shrunk. In 1964, Goldwater won the Indiana presidential primary by a two-to-one margin over the token opposition of Harold Stassen. A move to repeal the primary law failed in the 1967 session of the legislature, so another primary is scheduled for 1968. Nixon has maintained his ties in the state with frequent campaign appearances since 1960 and is the prohibitive early favorite. Because Indiana law binds the delegates to support the primary winner on the first ballot, the Nixon camp has counted twenty-six Indiana votes, at least for one ballot.

Missouri presents much the same picture as Indiana: a long period of Republican decline (the last Republican Governor was in 1944) and increasing conservative influence in the party. In 1964, for example, Goldwater was backed by twenty-three of twenty-four Missouri delegates, but received only 36 percent of the vote against President Johnson. Missouri has no primary, but conservative forces are expected to dominate the delegate-selection process.

The only Missouri Republican of national stature is independent-minded Representative Thomas B. Curtis. The fifty-six-year-old Curtis, a Dartmouth man from St. Louis, has been in the House since 1950 and has won grudging respect from both parties for his work on the Ways and Means and Joint Economic Committees. He was a leader in the coup that led to the replacement of Charles Halleck by Gerald Ford in 1965. An argumentative, almost nagging man, Curtis loves House debates as do few other members and does not hesitate to challenge the accepted shibboleths of either party's leadership. In 1967 Curtis began to take soundings for a possible Senate race against incumbent Democrat Edward V. Long. Another Republican possibility for statewide office is Lawrence K. Roos, forty-nine, a banker who has made a commendable record during two terms as Supervisor of St. Louis County.

Neighboring Iowa and Kansas present a different picture. Though the two states have no front-rank national Republican leaders, both have active, relatively flourishing Republican parties, with a wide range of ideological representation.

Iowa is probably the more liberal of the two. Younger leaders of the state organization recognized the Goldwater nomination for what it was in 1964—a threat to the traditional G.O.P. dominance of the state—and swung ten of the twenty-four delegates to Scranton, in a futile bid to avert the inevitable.

Their apprehensions were thoroughly justified by the results. Goldwater received less than 38 percent of the votes in a state that Nixon had carried by 57 percent. Worse, the congressional delegation shifted from six Republicans and a Democrat to six Democrats and a Republican. The sole G.O.P. survivor was H. R. Gross, a conservative curmudgeon, who eked out a 419-vote margin in his normally-safe district. But instead of succumbing, the Iowa Republicans under the leadership of State Chairman Robert D. Ray and Senator Jack Miller, whose seat was at stake in 1966, strengthened their paid staff and set to work immediately on the rebuilding job. The results showed in 1966, when Miller won easy re-election to a second term and Republicans took back four of the five House seats lost in the previous election.

Ray's work was recognized by the national party when Bliss tapped him in 1967 as head of the Republican State Chairmen's Association. The young Iowa leader, who backed Scranton in 1964, is close to Romney's Michigan organization and Romney probably also has other allies in the state delegation. But Nixon, as one Iowan remarked, "has spent half his political life campaiging in our state," and has close ties to the state's senior Senator, Bourke B. Hickenlooper. There could be pulling and hauling for Iowa's twenty-four votes before it is over.

Kansas, with twenty delegates, was one of the states where the Goldwater forces organized early and well for the 1964 struggle, mustering such strength that they summarily dumped then-Governor John Anderson from the convention delegation when he refused to commit himself to Goldwater.

But Kansas has a progressive Republican tradition of long-standing: William Allen White, Arthur Capper, Alf Landon, the whole Eisenhower movement took root there. Landon welcomed Romney to Topeka on one of the Governor's early 1967 probings, and support for Romney was forthcoming early from junior Senator James B. Pearson and was thought likely from the elderly but still influential senior Senator, Frank Carlson. Romney lost one important ally when Governor William Avery was defeated for re-election in 1966 in a protest vote against his first-term tax increases.

The conservative wing of the party is led by National Committeeman McDill (Huck) Boyd, a skillful operator, and is represented in Washington by Representative Robert J. Dole, a smoothly-handsome and well-connected fourth-termer with ambitions to rise to the Senate, although he is from the "wrong" (i.e., thinly populated), Western part of the state. Former Kansas Congressman Robert F. Ellsworth, a liberal Republican who lost out to Pearson in a 1966 Senate primary, has joined forces with Nixon, thus adding weight to what may well be a close struggle for control of the delegation.

In the upper Midwest, North and South Dakota have eight and fourteen delegates respectively, and, for reasons of size and geography, usually are overlooked by presidential contenders. South Dakota has a presidential primary, but since it falls on the same day as California's (June 4 in 1968), it is normally overshadowed. That may not be the case in 1968, but the early wish of the state's Republican leaders— bachelor Governor Nils Boe and veteran Senator Karl E. Mundt—was for an uncommitted or favorite-son slate. The state is traditionally conservative (Taft beat Eisenhower there in 1952) and Mundt is one of the conservative pillars of the Senate. But Romney has been courting Boe with hopes of winning him to his side.

North Dakota Republicans, who are now purged of their long-time alliance with the Populist-tradition Non-Partisan League, take the party doctrine straight and conservative. They are not quite the force they once were, having failed to dislodge Democratic Governor William Guy or Democratic Senator Quentin Burdick, but they control the legislature by lopsided majorities, hold both House seats and have in seventy-year-old Milton R. Young the third-ranking Republican in the Senate.

Of greater influence than the Dakotas is Minnesota, with its twenty-six delegates and its tradition of leadership in the national party. It was the write-in vote in the since-abolished Minnesota presidential primary that gave General Eisenhower a long push toward the 1952 nomination; over the years, the exceptional men of Minnesota have played a larger-than-life role in the national G.O.P., just as they have in the Democratic party.

Six-foot-three-inch Albert Quie and six-foot-four-inch Clark Mac-Gregor, two of Minnesota's five Republican Congressmen, are among the most influential members of the House. Quie—whose Norwegian name means "pregnant heifer"—is a farmer, former hot-rod pilot, and perhaps the party's leading expert on Federal education and antipoverty programs. MacGregor, a forty-five-year-old lawyer, has a range of knowledge that extends from open-housing laws to problems of Western Hemisphere immigration.

In 1964, Quie, MacGregor and State Chairman Robert Forsythe, fought off the Goldwater forces in a series of bloody convention battles and delivered eighteen of Minnesota's twenty-six votes to the nominal favorite son, ex-Representative Walter H. Judd. That fall, though Goldwater lost the state by a 64-36 margin, the four incumbent Congressmen were saved from the fate that befell their brethren in neighboring Midwestern states. In 1966, all came back and a fifth seat was added to the Republican holdings.

Minnesota has been blessed with a succession of strong and able party chairmen—the late Ed Viehman, Forsythe, and currently George Thiss. If MacGregor and Quie can be faulted, it is for their lack of courage in tackling the Democratic organization of Vice-President Humphrey in a statewide race. Either of the two Congressmen could have had the gubernatorial nomination in 1966; instead, both declined, and, after a fifteen-ballot marathon, the state convention picked Harold E. LeVander, a bland fifty-seven-year-old South St. Paul attorney (a former partner in the firm was Harold E. Stassen) and prominent Lutheran layman who was making a belated debut in elective politics.

Muddled as the Republicans were, they were in good shape compared to Humphrey's Democrats. A party revolt against incumbent Governor Karl F. Rolvaag produced an endorsement on the twenty-second ballot for Lieutenant Governor A. M. (Sandy) Keith to replace him. But Rolvaag shook off this rebuke and gave Keith a decisive beating in the September primary. By that time, however, even the shreds of party unity were gone; LeVander and his running mate for Lieutenant Governor, thirty-year-old James Goetz, a radio station owner, were easily elected.

The new Governor, who bears a strong physical resemblance to actor-comedian Harold Lloyd, drew most of his early support from the rural, conservative (and, in 1964, pro-Goldwater) elements of the party, but since his nomination and election has moderated gradually toward the dominant progressivism of the Quie-MacGregor school. The dynamism of the Republican party in the state, however, comes not so much from LeVander as from a group of young state legislators from Hennepin County (suburban Minneapolis) and their allies in the party organization.

On the face of it, Minnesota should be prime territory for Romney's vote hunting, but his backers were slow to organize there. Nixon, as a campaigner and as director of the Minneapolis-based Investors Diversified Services Company, has been in the state frequently and is obviously prepared to contest for the support of a delegation whose influence exceeds even its not inconsiderable size.

What happens in the Midwest, and, indeed, across the country may well turn not so much on the outcome of the delegate battles in individual states as on the results of two key Midwestern primaries: Wisconsin and Nebraska.

Wisconsin's role as a president maker or a giant killer is historic. It finished off Wendell Willkie's comeback hopes in 1944, launched John F. Kennedy toward the White House in 1960. The peculiarity of the Wisconsin primary law that makes it particularly dangerous is the provision permitting Democrats to ask for Republican ballots, and vice versa.

In 1967, the legislature revised the primary law in an effort to assure Wisconsin voters the broadest possible choice of presidential aspirants and to reduce the likely impact of the crossover vote without eliminating it entirely. The new plan allows an eleven-member bipartisan commission to enter on the ballot the names of all prospective presidential candidates. To have his name removed, the politician in question would have to file a disclaimer of candidacy with the secretary of state. The commission lists its entries by February 9, 1968, and the final withdrawal date is February 29. The primary is on April 2. Delegates are chosen by the state and congressional district committees of the two parties after the primary, and are pledged to support the primary winner for at least one ballot. In addition, the list of delegates must be approved by the candidate who wins the primary.

The expectation of the sponsors is that the new law will assure a contest in both parties in 1968. On the Democratic side, the expected contestants are President Johnson and former Alabama Governor George Wallace, who ran in Wisconsin in 1964. Should the President be the only man entered, Wisconsin Democrats could still express their sentiments by voting for him or by voting "No" in a box provided for that purpose on the ballot. Or they could cross over and vote in the Republican primary.

The Republican field is certain to include Romney, Nixon and Reagan, with Percy a possible fourth starter. All four have ties to Wisconsin. Romney is not only a neighboring Governor but a former president of American Motors, whose main manufacturing plant is in Kenosha. Nixon has long-time political alliances in the state (which he carried in 1960) and more initial support among organization Republicans than anyone else. A Reagan-for-President committee was organized and functioning in the spring of 1967, even before Reagan scheduled his first appearance in the state. And Percy, as a neighbor (his home is less than twenty miles from the Wisconsin border), also has easy entrée with Wisconsin Republicans.

Under the circumstances, the leading Wisconsin Republicans were understandably grateful that they did not have to guess which candidate to support in the primary in order to assure themselves a place in the convention delegation. (Their anxiety to avoid being put on the spot was, in fact, a major motivation in the revision of the law.) Chief among them are Governor Warren P. Knowles and Representative Melvin R. Laird. Laird is anxious to make no misstep that could jeopardize his leadership position in the House; Knowles, weighing the odds on running for a third term against the possibility of challenging Democratic Senator Gaylord P. Nelson, also has one eye cocked for a possible vice-presidential bid from Nixon or Reagan, geography virtually ruling out a place on a ticket with neighbors Romney or Percy.

Despite his age, fifty-nine, Knowles has several things to commend him as a potential number-two man. He has a clean-cut face, curly silver hair and an attractive wife; more important, though not widely known nationally, he has a solid record as a progressive state Governor in a year in which Republicans are emphasizing their skill as administrators and their concern for improving Federal-state relations.

Moving up the Republican ladder in Wisconsin—fourteen years in the state Senate, three terms as Lieutenant Governor—he was elected Governor in 1964 over incumbent Democrat John W. Reynolds by 18,878 votes. (At the same time, Goldwater, whom Knowles shunned but did not repudiate, lost by over 400,000 votes.) As Governor, Knowles walked a skillful path between the Republican Senate and the Democratic House, coopting several Democratic proposals, then modifying them just enough to give them a Republican stamp. In this way, he achieved a degree of tax reform, an open-housing law, an overhaul of state government, improved educational programs and a model water pollution bill, without antagonizing anyone particularly in the process. His 1966 re-election margin over Democratic Lieutenant Governor Patrick J. Lucey was a healthy 86,783 votes. The party, ably led by his state chairman, Ody J. Fish, reclaimed the two House seats it had lost in 1964 and regained control of both houses of the legislature.

The other influential figure in the Wisconsin delegation will be Laird, the tough-minded conservative chairman of the House Republican Conference. Laird, who was a key figure in the platform fights of 1960 and 1964, thrives on the intrigue of national conventions. Not a potential vice-presidential candidate like the Governor, he will have influence among House colleagues at the convention. Personal preference and political calculation probably incline both Knowles and Laird to prefer Nixon over Romney, but with the excuse provided by the new primary law, both men were remaining conspicuously silent on their choice in 1967.*

In the early 1967 jockeying to line up prominent Wisconsin sup-

* For a more detailed discussion of Laird's role in the House of Representatives, see Chapter 4, especially pages 26-30.

porters, Nixon took a fast lead. While the Romney committee was being organized by Wilbur N. Renk, a well-to-do farmer-businessman from Sun Prairie, who had been twice defeated for statewide office (Governor, 1962; Senator, 1964), the Nixon steering committee included such Wisconsin G.O.P. stalwarts as Talbot Peterson, a former state chairman; William Kraus, Knowles's 1966 campaign chairman; and John MacIver, who directed the Governor's re-election bid in Milwaukee County.

Last of the Midwestern states, and in some ways the most vital, is Nebraska. In 1966, a hitherto-unknown banker from the tiny town of Wausa (pop. 700) named Norbert (Nobby) Tiemann won the governorship in his first race for public office.* The forty-two-year-old Tiemann shook the conservative-minded state government by asking and getting substantially increased expenditures for higher education, highways, recreation facilities and economic development, and combined sales-and-income taxes to finance the record budget.

While Tiemann may be altering the ideological balance of the state's G.O.P., by tradition Nebraska has been a conservative stronghold. Its 1952 primary favored Taft over Eisenhower in a battle of write-ins. In 1964, Goldwater, the only man on the ballot, received half the votes; Nixon, on a write-in campaign, took 31 percent, and Lodge, also on write-ins, only 15 percent.

However, not only the cast of characters but the rules of the game have been changed for the next Nebraska primary. In 1965, the unicameral and nonpartisan legislature, spurred by maverick Republicans who were angry at what they called "high-handed" tactics by the Goldwater managers in 1964, put through a new primary law modeled on Oregon's "all-star" system.

It empowers the Secretary of State (currently Republican Frank Marsh) to enter the names of all men "generally advocated or recognized as candidates in the national news media" and allows a man so entered to withdraw his name only by filing an affidavit that "he is not now and does not intend to become a candidate for the office of

---

* Tiemann flabbergasted an Eastern reporter who inquired, early in the campaign, for a phone number where Tiemann could be reached. "The business phone, at the bank," said Tiemann, "is one. My home phone is eleven." "Just one or eleven?" asked the reporter. "That's right," said Tiemann, and they stared at each other for a moment across the unbridgeable gap of the missing area codes and seven-digit numbers.

President of the United States at the forthcoming election." The preference poll is not binding, but delegates, elected the same day (May 14, 1968), may indicate on the ballot whether they are un-committed or prefer a particular candidate. A delegate who states his commitment is bound to support that man until released, or for two ballots, or until he receives less than 35 percent of the convention vote.

The new Nebraska law attracted little notice when it was passed, but belatedly some observers saw in it the handiwork of Fred Seaton, Nixon's political ally and a Hastings, Nebraska, publisher. Knowl-edgeable Nebraska Republicans, however, say this theory exaggerates Seaton's influence in the legislature; the only direct link is that the bill's chief sponsor was a Nixon supporter in 1960 and 1964. Whatever the design, the new system is said to serve Nixon's interests by forcing Romney to contest him in a state in which Nixon and con-servatism are reputedly strong and where Romney and liberalism are reputedly weak. The theory is plausible-sounding, but open to ques-tion. For the new law brought in not only Romney but also, by his own statement in early 1967, Reagan, who might well draw conservative votes from Nixon. (Percy on a visit to Nebraska in 1967 left open the question whether he would allow his name to stay on the ballot.)

Party leaders early began to feel the pressure to choose up sides. Lieutenant Governor John Everroad joined Seaton in the Nixon cam-paign in May, 1967. Governor Tiemann, damaged at least temporarily in the state by the heavy load of taxes he put through, was wooed by the Romney men but avoided an early commitment. Senator Carl Curtis, Goldwater's 1964 floor manager, passed the word to his friends that he wanted no part of the 1968 fight. Perhaps the most influential figure, Senator Roman L. Hruska, a moderate conservative with close ties to Senator Everett McKinley Dirksen, listened to all sides but made no promises. And Nebraska's national committeeman, Donald Ross, a power in national party affairs as well as in Nebraska, promised his friend, Ray Bliss, that he would stay publicly neutral right up to convention time.

Besides Romney, Nixon, Reagan and Percy, another name may be entered in the crucial primary. In early 1967 Harold E. Stassen hired the Washington-based public-relations firm Sorin-Hall, headed by genial, hefty Pat Gorman, who played the presidential game once before as director of the National Dick Nixon Clubs in 1960. It was Gorman's job to keep Stassen in the news while he measured the temperature of his chronic White House fever. Stassen, the former "boy Governor" of Minnesota, now past sixty, could claim that he too qualified under John Wells's prescription for success—that the next Republican presidential nominee would be a Midwesterner.

Out of the Midwest —
Burck, Chicago **Sun-Times,** Oct. 27, 1966

12 WEST

JOHN F. KENNEDY spent the first ten days of his presidential campaign in 1960 rattling through the West—from Anchorage to Pocatello (with a quick detour back to Detroit) to Seattle to Portland, down by train through California's Central Valley and then on airport hops across Texas from El Paso to Texarkana.

As he prepared to leave the Lone Star State—heading for St. Louis and then upstate New York, his schedule maker, Kenneth P. O'Donnell remarked, "That's the end of the scenic tour; now we're going where the votes are."

The problem of scale confuses everything in Western politics. So vast are the distances, so magnificent the landscape, so tonic the atmosphere and so breezy the personalities, that it is hard to remember what the West really amounts to in national politics. Take out California, which is an empire and a law unto itself (and which has been discussed in Chapter 8), and the rest of the West has only 55 electoral votes—barely 10 percent of the total, less than New York and Massachusetts alone.

California in 1968 has 86 votes at the Republican convention; the other 10 continental states, Alaska and Hawaii only 176 more. Yet the region has one potentially-serious contender for the presidential nomination, Ronald Reagan of California, three or four vice-presidential hopefuls and a boisterous confidence in its own role and destiny in the party.

"Barry Goldwater's nomination," says George W. Abbott, the Republican chairman of Nevada, "shifted the center of power in the Republican party about one thousand miles to the West. It's not moving back."

The assertiveness of the Western view—"too big for their damned britches," said a proper Eastern Republican, who overheard Ab-

379

bott's remark—is a fact of life and will color the Westerners' operations in the 1968 nomination struggle. Barry Goldwater's feat in proving that a Senator from a small Western state could whip the assembled power of the Eastern Establishment in a Republican convention stirred ambitions in other Republicans from the Rockies to the Pacific.

Thus, it was Tom McCall, the newly-elected Republican Governor of Oregon, who blithely circularized his fellow-Republican Governors in the spring of 1967 and announced that half of them endorsed his view that they should withhold all endorsements for a time and then act as a group to pick the presidential nominee. McCall, as it happens, regarded the Goldwater nomination as a disaster, but he is swayed, as other Westerners are, by the notion that the West's day is dawning in national politics.

Just how realistic this notion is depends, in part, on the chances for cohesion within the region. The states have certain common problems and therefore common political concerns. The West is, as Professor John W. Caughey wrote in *The Utah Historical Quarterly,* "a land of distances, of remoteness," where "the problem of transportation has always been uppermost." It is a land of geographic and climatic extremes, predominantly arid, so reclamation and conservation are of great concern. It is a region that has been dependent on the Federal government for development capital. Though its own wealth is impressive, the dependence continues, whether through airplane contracts in California and Washington, hydroelectric dams on the Columbia and the Colorado, shipping subsidies in Hawaii or military payrolls in Alaska. The West is also the region of most rapid population growth, and therefore an area with special concern for programs for aiding the elderly and educating the young.

But if the West has common features and common problems, it also has its divisive forces. Geography and distance are barriers to overcome. Jealousy over the precious commodity of water is another. Water quarrels divide the Upper Colorado Basin states from those of the Lower Colorado, the Northwest from California and the Southwest, Arizona from California.

There is natural resentment from smaller states of giant California, one factor that makes it unlikely that Reagan will be able to assemble a solid Western bloc behind his favorite-son candidacy. There are also sharp ideological differences between the liberal-leaning Republicans of Washington, Oregon and Hawaii, and the conservative Republicans of the Mountain States, a prime target area in recent years of the John Birch Society and other right-wing groups. Moreover, the political habits of the Westerners almost preclude regional solidarity,

"Then Agreed! We're Against LBJ and Each Other!
Anybody Happen to Know What We're FOR?"

Haynie, Louisville **Courier-Journal**, Nov. 16, 1966, © 1966, The Los Angeles Times Syndicate

for they are the most ticket-splitting, independent-minded voters of the nation; their attachment, said Frank H. Jonas in *Western Politics*, "is clearly to personalities rather than to political labels." As a sample of what he means, consider what the voters of Washington's 1st Congressional District (part of Seattle and King County) did in 1964:

moving down the ballot, they gave pluralities of 28,613 votes to President Johnson, Democrat; 48,336 to Governor Daniel J. Evans, Republican; 90,043 to Senator Henry M. Jackson, Democrat; and 38,975 to Representative Thomas M. Pelly, Republican.

Rather than talking about the West, even the West excusive of California, as a monolithic if minor convention bloc, one must look at the region state by state.

A good place to start is Washington, for if there is any one man who represents the "new breed" Western Republican (and particularly the Republican Governors who now occupy eleven of the thirteen Western capitals) it is Governor Daniel J. Evans. "The people these days are problem-oriented, not philosophy-oriented," Evans told the New York *Times*'s Tom Wicker in a 1966 interview, making a distinction that is crucial to the whole school of Republicanism he represents. "If they have any philosophy, it is probably pragmatism. And if they have any crystal-clear goal, it would be to solve the problems of society and the economy and of government, in a logical, factual manner." The "New Breed" are recognizably Republican in their anti-Federal-government bias and in their belief that problems are best dealt with close to home, at the level of state government. But they are a departure from the past generation of Republicans in their recognition that problems exist, that voters will demand action on them from *some* level of government, and that political leadership, indeed political survival, depends not so much on opposing the Democrats' solutions as on moving faster to provide solutions of their own.

Evans is particularly at home in this philosophy, for his professional career is not as a politician or even a lawyer, but as a civil engineer, a notably non-ideological profession. A native of Seattle, a Navy ensign at nineteen, Evans received his engineering degrees from the University of Washington, then was recalled to active duty in Korean waters. He went to the legislature in 1957, served two terms as Republican floor leader and in 1963 decided to take a run for the governorship. It looked hopeless. The first survey showed him the least-known and the least-preferred of six prospective candidates. But Evans assembled a young organization from among his legislative colleagues, campaigned nonstop for almost a year on a detailed, thirty-five-point "Blueprint for Progress," and, in the September primary, defeated a conservative Republican rival by more than 100,000 votes. Then in the general election, Evans beat two-term Democratic incumbent

Albert D. Rosellini by 148,564 votes, while Goldwater was losing the state by 309,333 votes and four Republican Congressmen were going down to defeat. (Evans gave nominal support to Goldwater but ran a wholly separate campaign.) At thirty-nine, he became the youngest Governor in Washington's history.

In his first three years in office, Evans fought pitched battles on tax reform, increased financing for education, modernization of state government, and long-range economic planning. He also outmaneuvered the Democratic legislature by putting through a reapportionment bill that permitted Republicans to recapture control of the state House of Representatives in 1966.

Evans has emerged as a major advocate of Federal tax sharing with the states and as one of the Republican party's most articulate spokesmen on the subject of Federal-state relations. In a New York speech in 1966, for example, he said:

Six weeks ago, President Johnson presented his third State of the Union address to the nation. It was a document of magnificent proportions, a manifesto of both war and peace, an extension of the Great Society within the shadows of an even greater war . . . [that] not even the Republican leaders could find much to quibble with.

But I can. Not because I reject the goals, or the programs . . . but because I believe that, in more than one measure, the State of the Union should be more deeply concerned with its constitutional corollary—the Union of the States.

Because I believe in a strategy of government which permits competition and innovation, a strategy which produces alternatives instead of consensus. Because I believe that "flexible response" should apply not only to defense policy but to domestic policy as well. And because I believe that, regardless of the nobility of purpose, Federal largesse historically has been, is now and will be followed by increased Federal leverage.

Evans has been an activist, not only in government, but also in party affairs. Backed by the elected Secretary of State, A. L. (Lud) Kramer, a rising political power in his own right, and by rotund state Republican chairman (and former lumber lobbyist) C. Montgomery (Gummie) Johnson, Evans set out in 1965 to crack the power of the far-right elements that fastened onto the G.O.P. in the year preceding Goldwater's nomination.* At a meeting of the Republican State Com-

---

* The Goldwaterites' takeover of Washington state, a classic operation, is fully described by Theodore H. White, *The Making of the President 1964* (New York: Atheneum, 1965), pp. 132-35.

mittee in September, 1965, Evans, Kramer and Johnson put their full political muscle and prestige behind a resolution, approved 43-15, which said:

> The Republican party did not achieve greatness nor will it regain greatness by being the party of radicalism or of the lunatic fringe. Extremists of neither the Right nor the Left contribute to the strength of America or her political institutions. Both feed on fear, frustration, hate and hopelessness. Both have lost faith in themselves and the American Dream and both quite openly predict an American Disaster.
>
> Such groups as the John Birch Society demonstrate by their methods, their leadership and their policies that they fail to meet the tests and follow the traditions of the Republican party. They do not contribute to its victory but to its defeat; they do not strengthen it but weaken it; they do not effectively promote conservative principles, they subvert them.

This resolution has been used by the Governor and his party chairman as a hunting license to weed out the extremist elements in the county and state organizations. They have had some local successes, but over all have failed to dislodge the conservatives from many of the key power posts. In mid-1967, Evans conceded that his opponents, including National Committeewoman Fran Cooper and King County (Seattle) Chairman Ken Rogstad, still controlled the five largest counties and had strength in several others.

Thus, the solidity of Evans's control of the twenty-four-member Washington delegation, largest in the West outside California, is in great doubt. If the Governor can command his own forces and maneuver them to support the presidential nominee, he could be a strong contender for the vice-presidential nomination—particularly on a ticket headed by Midwesterners Romney or Percy.

Daniel Jackson Evans, just forty-two now, slim, handsome, athletic, with an attractive wife, three young sons and a sincere, effective speaking and television style, is almost everything an up-and-coming young Republican should be. If he wins a second term as Governor, as he is favored to do in 1968, Evans could be right in the middle of the 1972 or 1976 race.

In neighboring Oregon, there is a presidential primary of national renown, a Republican Senator who is perhaps the party's most durable bright young man and a Republican Governor who is just beginning to weigh in the national scales.

Oregon, which passed the first preference-poll presidential primary law, pioneered the "all-star" system in 1959, now virtually duplicated in Nebraska and Wisconsin. Under it, the Secretary of State (currently Republican Clay Myers) enters the names of all prospective presidential candidates; a name may be removed only by a sworn statement that the supposed candidate is not and will not become a contender for nomination. So, in 1968, as in every year it has been in operation, the Oregon ballot will include the names of all prospective rivals, both active and inactive.

Coming only two weeks after the similar test in Nebraska, and with no major open contests to follow it, the 1968 Oregon primary on May 28 promises to be the most important single contest of them all. Eighteen delegates are directly at stake (Oregon, unlike Nebraska, binds the delegates to support the preference-poll winner), but even more important is the prestige of winning the last test likely to include the names of all possibilities.

The Oregon Republicans, though as unpredictable as their counterparts throughout the West, have a tradition of liberalism. In 1948, they gave Thomas E. Dewey a narrow (but vital) 10,000-vote victory over Harold E. Stassen, after a celebrated debate in which Stassen advocated, and Dewey opposed, outlawing the Communist party. In 1952, Eisenhower was a landslide winner there, and in 1964 it was the only state where Rockefeller was able to win. Rockefeller and Lodge polled 173,359 votes between them, compared to 98,379 for the more-conservative Goldwater and Nixon.

Conditions in Oregon seem as favorable to Romney and/or Percy as conditions in Nebraska do to Nixon and/or Reagan. Nor is there likelihood of a favorite-son move that would pre-empt the field. Oregon voters traditionally are hostile to spurious favorite sons. The last home-bred to win an Oregon primary was Senator Charles L. McNary in 1940, and he was powerful enough nationally to wind up as Wendell Willkie's running mate. When Senator Wayne Morse tried to duplicate McNary's feat in the 1960 Democratic primary, Kennedy gave him a humiliating licking.

The best-known Oregon Republican is not likely to be on the Oregon presidential primary ballot. That, of course, is freshman Senator Mark O. Hatfield, at forty-five still almost as youthful looking as he was in 1950, when he began his string of seven unbroken election victories by winning a seat in the Oregon House of Representatives. Hatfield has been the bright young man of the Republican party for so long now that he faces the danger of being overlooked. Named by *Life* magazine, no less, as "one of the hundred most important young men and women in the United States" in 1962, nominated for Vice President by fourteen collegiate mock conventions in 1964, Hatfield found himself in 1967, somewhat embarrassingly, hundredth in Senate seniority, occupying a former committee hearing room as an office and isolated from virtually every other leader of the party on the crucial issue of the day, Vietnam.

Hatfield's political career was laid out in bull sessions at Stanford University in 1947-48 with Travis Cross, the fellow student who became his press secretary and top assistant in all his campaigns (and who is now working for Romney). Hatfield had gone to Stanford for a master's degree after graduating from Willamette University and serving as a Navy amphibious officer at Iwo Jima and Okinawa. He returned to Willamette in 1949 as political-science professor and, later, dean of students, while beginning his career in the legislature. His political progress moved straight on the Stanford timetable: two terms in the state House of Representatives, one in the state Senate; then statewide victory in 1956 for Secretary of State, and in 1958, at age thirty-six, the first of two four-year terms as Governor. In all that period, Hatfield proved an unbeatable vote getter in an increasingly-Democratic state (even winning AFL-CIO endorsement for re-election) and an able Governor, with a record of exceptional leadership in education, civil rights, transportation and welfare areas. He also developed the reputation of being an accommodating, eager fellow, polished, tactful, never one to offend, equally at home with management and labor groups, with Democrats and Republicans; and always ready with the right sentiment for the occasion. To the Western Conference of Teamsters in 1961, Hatfield said, "One of the greatest needs of organized labor today is to again inculcate into the minds and the hearts of its membership the real benefits of the trade union movement in this country." For the *Salesman's Opportunity Magazine,* in 1962, he wrote, "America's future progress, and the fate of the world, rests in the hands of the salesman."

So it was wholly logical that Richard M. Nixon should tap Hatfield to nominate him for President in 1960, which Hatfield did in just 288 well-chosen words (". . . a fighter for freedom, a pilgrim for peace, the Vice President of the United States . . ."), the shortest such speech since Norman B. Judd used 27 words to nominate Lincoln in 1860.

And it was logical, too, that William E. Miller, Barry Goldwater's runningmate-to-be, arranged for Hatfield to keynote the 1964 Republican convention. Hatfield assailed extremist organizations and named the Birch Society as one of them, something the platform writers declined to do, but, unlike other liberal Republicans, he did not reject Goldwater as a candidate, a fact which Goldwater remembers and praises. "Hatfield," he has said, "is a man Republicans can buy. Hatfield didn't agree with me. He didn't agree with the platform completely, but, by God, he got out and worked."

This talent for pleasing all sides was serving Hatfield so well that when he announced in 1966 for the Senate seat being vacated by Democrat Maurine Neuberger he seemed a cinch for victory. His undoing—almost—was Vietnam. Hatfield had been on record as early as 1965, at National Governors' Conferences, as opposing the U.S. military commitment there. In 1966, he was the only Governor of the fifty in Los Angeles to vote against a vaguely-worded resolution of support for American policy in Vietnam.

Why Hatfield took up the issue so strongly is a matter of conjecture among his friends, but many think the roots of his attitude are found in his strong religious convictions. A Baptist, Hatfield neither smokes nor drinks and, unlike George Romney, does not serve liquor in his home. As a young man, he belonged to the Youth for Christ, as an adult served three terms as moderator of the First Baptist Church in Salem. His marriage in 1958 to Antoinette Kuzmanich, daughter of a Yugoslav immigrant longshoreman, who converted from Catholicism to Hatfield's Baptist faith, seems, if anything, to have deepened his religious impulses. The New York *Herald Tribune*'s Don Ross asked Mrs. Hatfield in 1963 if she would like her husband to be President. "Only if the Lord wants him to be," she said. "Whatever Mark Hatfield does is for the Lord."

There are, of course, millions of devoted Baptists who disagree with Hatfield's views on Vietnam, but friends say it is conscience that dictated his opposition to the war and religious conviction that holds Hatfield to a course of obvious political risk. In a question-and-answer session with George Fox College students in 1963, Hatfield said:

The office of Governor is not a Christian office in the sense that it is to be used in any way to further any particular faith. But this does not mean that I haven't the right as a Christian, as any other Christian has, to live a life that is a witness in whatever position I'm in, whatever day of the week. . . . I believe that a Governor or legislator is elected to a public office to carry out certain basic philosophies or basic programs, but at the same time he is charged with helping to lead and establish opinion—public opinion and public positions.

For Hatfield the sternest test of this view came in 1966, when Representative Robert B. Duncan, an able and attractive Democrat, challenged him for the Senate and sought to convert the campaign into a referendum on Hatfield's Vietnam views. Hatfield promptly and wisely decided he would not let it become a single-issue campaign. He talked about his record, about inflation, about the problems of Oregon's lumber industry. But in every question period, he was led right back to the issue of Vietnam. When his opponent pressed the attack, Hatfield became evasive enough for the Portland *Oregon Journal,* normally a backer of his, to publish a stinging editorial, "Hatfield: The Dove Who Ducks," which said he was "acting as if his strategy is to win by being vaguely remembered by the voters as that nice young man who is so worried about Vietnam."

Republican strategists who had counted Hatfield a sure winner in the spring were privately writing him off in late September. The turn-about came when President Johnson announced his plans for the Manila conference. Hatfield quickly took to statewide television with a half-hour program called "Prelude to Manila." Ending his self-imposed exile from the Johnsonian consensus, Hatfield said, "The President's going to Manila could become the cornerstone of a great foundation being built for the cause of peace. . . ." Johnson, he said, "is doing the same things for which I was criticized as un-patriotic when I advocated them eighteen months ago."

A week before election, the influential Portland *Oregonian,* con-ceding the "dilemma" of finding itself "in closer agreement" with Duncan on the overriding issue, nonetheless endorsed Hatfield with the argument that "the loyal opposition must be strengthened if the United States is to be saved from one-party, one-man government." By a narrow, 24,017-vote margin, Hatfield kept his career alive, and came to Washington, where he soon resumed open disagreement with what he termed "the war party, the war administration."

In a widely-reported speech to the Harvard Young Republican Club, Hatfield, the new campus hero, said that "nationalism and not Communism is the predominant thrust of Ho Chi Minh" and that "the conflict in South Vietnam is clearly a civil war among the Vietnamese people and not a war of aggression initiated by a foreign power."

From these assumptions, he argued:

> On the basis of a misrepresentation by the Administration, the American public allowed the President to send American boys to fight a war he had said should be fought by Asians, to falsely redefine the conflict as primarily a war of aggression, and to seek a military solution to this political problem. . . . Thus is created the tyranny of the big lie—a tyranny of no alternatives, a tyranny that does not allow Americans the liberty of choice and that does not allow us effective voice in directing our nation's course.

His call for a halt in the bombing of North Vietnam and substitution of Asian troops for Americans won the support of only one prominent Republican, Mayor John Lindsay of New York. Thus, Hatfield appeared in 1967 to have cut himself off from any real possibility of a place on the 1968 ticket, unless a shift in the war or in public opinion shows him to have been a prophet of rare perspicacity. If the Oregon Senator has any influence among the party rank-and-file, his personal preference would probably lie with Nelson Rockefeller (though Rockefeller wholly disagreed with him on Vietnam), for whose losing cause in 1964 Hatfield did all that a supposedly-neutral Governor could do. But, barring a dramatic reversal of Vietnam opinion, Hatfield appeared to have isolated himself from the bulk of Republican leadership to such an extent that only time could restore him to a contending position again. His consolation, perhaps, is that he is only forty-five.

Hatfield's successor as Governor, fifty-three-year-old Tom McCall, is of a very different species, as emotional in his manner as Hatfield is detached. The two men maintain a correct, but barely friendly relationship. McCall, the tallest Governor in the nation (a towering six feet five inches), is as much a product of television as is neighboring Governor Reagan. For twenty years he came into Oregon homes as the state's leading news commentator, taking time out only for a stint as administrative assistant to Governor Douglas McKay from 1949 to 1952. A leader in campaigns against pollution of Oregon's streams and rivers, McCall ran for Secretary of State in 1964 as an avowedly anti-Goldwater Republican and won handsomely, moving up to the governorship in 1966 by a margin three times the size of Hatfield's. Outspokenly liberal in domestic policy and hard-line anti-Communist abroad, McCall, whose speech still shows clear evidence of his Massachusetts birth, is blunt and impulsive. Of comparisons between himself and Reagan, he says, "In all my years as a broadcaster, I never smiled at anyone. You can't say I beguiled them."

While Hatfield was dissenting on Vietnam, McCall told the Oregon Young Republicans, "I would caution you, as you sit here in the lap of euphoria amid the comforts of a secure and prosperous society, to have the decency if you plan to blame someone, to take a hard cut at Communist aggression and, if you plan to commend someone, to make a special point of stressing your appreciation of your brothers' courage and sacrifice in southeast Asia."

In typical fashion, McCall came to his first meeting of Republican Governors, a month after his election, pronouncing himself ready to endorse Romney if asked, which he was not. Three months later, he condemned Romney's vague position on Vietnam and pronounced him "finished." He said in the spring of 1967 that he favored Percy "as of now," then wrote Rockefeller a letter asking him to run. Where he will end is anyone's guess, but he will not be shy about expressing himself as he goes.

Of all the Western states, none showed greater resurgence of Republican strength in 1966 than Alaska, where the G.O.P. elected its first Governor since statehood, and also took the lone seat in the U.S. House of Representatives, the Secretary of State's job and control of both houses of the legislature from the Democrats.

Pacesetter of this near sweep (only Democratic Senator E. L. (Bob) Bartlett, opposed by a Birch Society dentist, Lee McKinley, bucked the tide) and key figure in the rejuvenated Alaska Republican party is Governor Walter J. Hickel, a pleasant, forty-eight-old middle-road Republican who defeated Alaska's first (and only previous) Governor, Democrat William A. Egan. The oldest of ten children of a Kansas tenant farmer, Hickel landed in Alaska in 1940, twenty years old and with just thirty-seven cents in his pocket. After earning a modest stake, he plunged into the wartime building boom, later branching out into hotels and shopping centers, and, in the process, made himself a millionaire.

The party he heads has a number of bright young men, including Representative Howard W. Pollock, state Senator Lowell Thomas, Jr., son of the famous newscaster, and state Representative Ted Stevens, one of Fred Seaton's political protégés during the Eisenhower Administration. It also has a yawning split between its moderate-liberal majority and its vociferous far-right minority, a gap Hickel is laboring hard to overcome, in hopes that someone can defeat aging Democratic Senator Ernest Gruening in 1968.

Nixon was thought to be certain of Alaska's twelve delegates because he was active in the drive for statehood in 1958, carried the state in his presidential campaign of 1960 and flew all the way up there in 1966 to help Hickel and Pollock. But when Romney went to Anchorage in early 1967, Hickel greeted him with a virtual endorsement, telling the Alaska Republicans they had a "duty" to convince Romney he should run. When Romney remarked that Hickel's campaign slogan, "There Is a Better Way," was almost identical to the words chiseled in stone over the entrance to the American Motors headquarters, there seemed to be a communion between the two men that was almost beyond utterance. But Hickel conceded that Nixon would still be the favorite to win the delegation if Alaska's convention had been held then, instead of in 1968. It was a situation he seemed determined to change.*

Ironically, Hawaii which was brought into the Union in 1959 on the supposition that its Republicanism would balance Alaska's Democratic bias, has remained almost solidly in the Democratic column. The only notable Republican officeholders in the fiftieth state are Senator Hiram L. Fong, sixty-year-old multi-millionaire descendant of Chinese contract laborers, and Honolulu Mayor Neal Blaisdell, sixty-five. The party leadership is divided between liberal Republicans like Fong and Blaisdell, who win with the help of Harry Bridges' International Longshoremen's and Warehousemen's Union (ILWU), and conservatives who prefer to sacrifice their chances for victory rather than make what they regard as such dubious alliances. In 1964, the Hawaii delegation split down the middle between Goldwater supporters and opponents. Goldwater received only 21.2 percent of the vote (his lowest percentage anywhere except the District of Columbia), but in 1966 Republican gubernatorial candidate Randolph A. Crossley came within 4,516 votes of upsetting the incumbent,

* For a fuller account of Romney's Alaska visit, see p. 91.

ILWU-endorsed John A. Burns. In 1968, Hawaii's fourteen delegates are likely to favor a liberal-leaning Republican.

The conversion of Western Republicans from Goldwater conservatism to pragmatism is neatly illustrated by the evolution of Paul Laxalt, who moved up from Lieutenant Governor to Governor of Nevada in 1966. A good-looking, forty-four-year-old lawyer and son of an immigrant Basque sheepherder, Laxalt was an all-out Goldwater enthusiast and card-carrying conservative when he ran against Democratic Senator Howard Cannon in 1964 and lost by a microscopic forty-eight votes. He immediately began his campaign to deny Democratic Governor Grant Sawyer a third term, but with a different approach. Teaming with Republican State Chairman George Abbott, Laxalt staged a dramatic fight on the Birch Society at the 1966 state convention, charging in a fiery speech that it had smeared his brother and "turned white against Negro, Gentile against Jew." He won a resolution barring Birchers from leadership in the party and followed up this appeal to Nevada's small but vital minority groups by slating a Negro candidate (named Woodrow Wilson) for the legislature, and switched his campaign emphasis from denunciation of the Federal government to calls for improved education in Nevada. "It's all right to criticize," Laxalt told an interviewer, "but I learned we have to present alternatives. The truth is, we've been sitting around in our country clubs spouting theories about what the people need while the Democrats have been down in the beer parlors asking the people what they want." By getting down in the beer parlor and presenting alternatives, Laxalt beat Sawyer by 5,937 votes (and Woodrow Wilson became Nevada's first Negro legislator).

In 1967, Laxalt played host to contenders Nixon, Romney and Reagan and bestowed his compliments impartially among them, while conspicuously withholding his blessing. "I am a victim of 1964," he would say. "We learned some very valuable lessons in that campaign, and one of them was that too-early commitments aren't too wise." Smart politician Laxalt would not make the same mistake twice.

Next door, in Utah, there is no question who the favorite is. Romney, the almost-native son, the first Mormon in the history of the Utah-headquartered church to be a serious presidential prospect, has the delegation lined up as long as he is even remotely a contender.

Regrettably for him, there are only eight delegates there, the most prominent of them likely to be Senator Wallace F. Bennett, author of *Why I Am a Mormon,* and a staunch conservative, who, like many others whose views diverge from Romney's, is more than willing to overlook the ideological differences in his indescribable pleasure at the prospect of having a Latter-day Saint at the head of the ticket. (Bennett's joy is particularly acute because he is up for re-election in 1968.)

The same factor provides fuel for the Romney cause in other Mountain States—Idaho, Wyoming, Arizona and New Mexico—where varying-sized Mormon populations are a force in politics. But the effectiveness of this vote varies from state to state, depending on other factors.*

In Idaho, for example, the tone of the state G.O.P. has been increasingly conservative—so much so that much of the party leadership, including the sharp-tongued and influential national committeewoman, Mrs. Gwen Barnett, probably prefers Reagan to Nixon and certainly prefers Nixon to Romney.

Moderate Republican Governor Robert E. Smylie was defeated for renomination to a fourth term in 1966 by state Senator Don Samuelson, a hulking sporting-goods store owner from Sandpoint who is without serious challenge as the least-articulate officeholder in the Republican party today. Samuelson went on to win the governorship in November, after the original Democratic nominee was killed in an airplane crash. With him in the capitol, conservatives have a leg up on the fight for the fourteen-man delegation, but moderate Republicans like Smylie and National Committeeman Harley Markham make Idaho a battleground.

Wyoming, with twelve votes, is perhaps more solidly in the conservative column, with Governor Stanley Hathaway (the former state chairman), Senator Clifford P. Hansen (the former Governor) and ancient Congressman-at-large William Henry Harrison, the three top Republican officeholders, all leaning in that direction. Their simultaneous wins in 1966 seem to have confirmed Wyoming's reputation as the most conservative of the Mountain States.

* See pp. 103-04 for a discussion of the size of the Mormon vote in the Western states.

Arizona's sixteen votes will almost certainly follow its hero, former Senator Barry Goldwater, wherever he goes—which in all likelihood means to Nixon. Republicans had their greatest victory in history in 1966, defeating the Democratic Governor, winning a majority of the House delegation and control of both houses of the legislature for the first time since statehood. The party hierarchy—Governor Jack Williams, a fifty-eight-year-old former radio broadcaster, newspaper columnist, and Mayor of Phoenix, Senator Paul Fannin and Representative John J. Rhodes—are all in line with Goldwater's thinking. Goldwater, planning to run for the Senate in 1968, has protected his flank with the sometimes-vital 10 percent of the voters who are Mormons by announcing well in advance that he will support whomever the convention nominates, even if it is his old foe Romney.*

The fourteen votes of New Mexico look far more promising for Romney, thanks to one of the major upsets of 1966, the election of thirty-seven-year-old state Representative David F. Cargo as the state's youngest and possibly most liberal Governor. Cargo, a native of Michigan who came to Albuquerque to practice law and married a strikingly-beautiful Spanish-American girl, whipped the conservative Republican organization for nomination and then a conservative Democratic opponent to gain election. His platform was as unconventional as his candidacy: he campaigned for urban-oriented reapportionment and expanded welfare benefits, won the endorsement of most of organized labor and a great hunk of the normally-Democratic Spanish-American vote, and was elected with the total expenditure of $14,000, none of which, he delights in reminding Ray Bliss, came from Republican National Committee, which believed right through election day that he was a sure loser. Cargo, up for re-election in 1968, gave Romney a virtual endorsement early in 1967, despite the fact that Nixon had campaigned for him and Romney had not.

Cargo is personally comfortable with Romney's relative liberalism on civil rights and social issues, and as a Catholic Governor in a state with a substantial Mormon population he felt he might be helped by Romney's presence on the ticket. Also, Cargo may have been mindful of the fact that New Mexico was one of the few Western states Nixon failed to carry in 1960. But Nixon retains many friends in the

* For background on the Romney-Goldwater and Nixon-Goldwater relationship see Chapters 2, 5 and 6.

predominantly-conservative state organization, notably former Governor and National Committeeman Edwin L. (Big Ed) Mechem.

The last two Western states, Montana and Colorado, continue the pattern of contrasts so notable in the whole region. Montana's Governor (defeated in a bid for the Senate in 1966) is conservative trucker Tim Babcock, one of the few Republican Governors in 1964 who was genuinely enthusiastic about the Goldwater nomination and one of the few who counseled against the dump–Dean Burch move at the Denver meeting of Republican Governors in December, 1964.

A measure of the depth of his conservatism was his refusal to designate United Nations Day in Montana, insisting instead that the state mark United Nations Improvement Day as a symbol of its discontent with the organization's current ways. Babcock and fellow conservative U.S. Representative James F. Battin likely will steer the fourteen Montana delegates to Nixon, though Reagan backers count the Governor a potential ally if the Californian plunges into the race.

Colorado Governor John A. Love, though elected to his first term in 1962 as a conservative, has been moving steadily toward a leadership role in the moderate wing of the party nationally, while his running mate of 1962, Senator Peter H. Dominick, has remained one of the hopefuls of the conservative wing. Both men—Love is fifty-one, Dominick, fifty-two—are ambitious for higher office, specifically the vice-presidency. But proximity and the political timetable give Love the advantage this year in influencing the eighteen-man Colorado delegation.

Love and Dominick were the handsome twin stars of the 1962 Republican revival in Colorado. Love, an Illinois-born Colorado Springs attorney, making his first race for public office, defeated Governor Stephen L. R. McNichols by 86,452 votes. Dominick, wealthy son of a New York stockbroker (Dominick & Dominick), graduate of St. Mark's School, Yale and Yale Law School, moved to Colorado after World War II with the idea of entering politics, served two terms in the state House of Representatives, one term in the U.S. House of Representatives and, in 1962, defeated Senator John A. Carroll by 49,069 votes.

Settling in under Colorado's senior Republican Senator, the respected but relatively unambitious Gordon L. Allott, Dominick quickly became part of Goldwater's Senate clique and a popular speaker on the conservative banquet circuit. The 1964 convention was his moment. While Love was sitting unhappily on the floor, one of only three members in the eighteen-man delegation supporting William Scranton, Dominick was on the platform, helping defeat the Rockefeller-backed platform amendment on extremism. Dominick quoted from what he later acknowledged to be a spurious eighteenth-century New York *Times* article, accusing Patrick Henry of extremism, and explained afterward that he thought everyone would know he was kidding.

The 1964 results somewhat altered the power relationship between Colorado's bright young men. Goldwater's old conservative cronies in the Senate tried to install Dominick in Goldwater's former post as chairman of the Republican Senate Campaign Committee, thinking he could use it as a buildup for a 1968 national race. But the plan was blocked by Dirksen and Morton, and Dominick retired to relative obscurity. Now facing his own re-election fight in 1968, the Colorado Senator has had to soft-pedal and probably postpone his ambitions for higher office.

Meantime, Governor Love became a leader of the successful dump–Dean Burch movement and won a second term by a comfortable 69,598 votes in 1966. A month after his re-election he was named head of the Republican Governors' Association for 1967, at which time he told his fellow Governors that the next G.O.P. presidential nominee would be from their ranks, a remark apparently intended to rule out Nixon and endear himself to Romney. To further underscore his national aspirations, Love went on an eight-day "fact-finding" trip to Vietnam. He also waded into a fight with some of his home-state conservative county chairmen in an effort to keep from being outnumbered at the 1968 convention as he had been in 1964. However, the 1964 state chairman of the Goldwater organization, Herb Koether, and a number of other prominent right-wing activists had already set up a Reagan-for-President Committee by mid-1967, and it was far from certain that Governor Love would be able to unite the Colorado delegation for anything other than a nominal favorite-son candidacy.

CONCLUSION:

LOOKING FOR A WINNER,

1968 AND BEYOND

ONLY seven years have elapsed since a Republican Administration last governed this nation. But so rapid is the pace of our politics, so accelerated the rate of change in the personalities and the issues, that already it is difficult to retrace the connection of the Eisenhower Era to the electoral contest of 1968. Only one of the four front-rank possibilities for the 1968 nomination—the durable Richard M. Nixon—held public office at any level when General Eisenhower came to the end of his White House tenure. And Nixon, of course, stepped back into private life himself the same day Eisenhower turned over his office to John F. Kennedy.

Since that cold January morning, the Republican party has gone down to the second-worst defeat in its history, and rebounded to such seeming vigor that it can challenge seriously for the presidency again.

What we have been recording is the recovery of the Republican party—its return to politics, its return to government, its return to reason. These are the recurring threads of our story.

A Return to Politics. During the long exile from power in the 1930's and 1940's, the Republicans came perilously close to forgetting that the object of a party is to win elections—not to place itself athwart the process of political change, but to serve that process and, if possible, to guide it. Even in the Eisenhower Administration, when power and policy were in Republican hands, simple politics was neglected. The man who became the first Republican President in twenty years was a professional soldier, not a professional politician. He was a man who, not surprisingly, was to tell his Cabinet that he was "sick and tired" of discussing patronage—patronage, the glue that helps to hold a party organization together. Whatever he might owe his party, the already ailing G.O.P. owed a debt of greater value to the hero who brought it two national victories. Yet this did not change the fact that under Eisenhower the Grand Old Party continued to wither at ite roots. The sources of future leadership dried up. In 1950, the pre-Eisenhower Republican party elected 199 Representatives, 47 Senators, 25 Governors. In 1960, at the end of the Eisenhower years, the same party elected only 174 Representatives, 36 Senators and 16 Governors.

A measure of the Eisenhower Administration's isolation from politics was its conspicuous failure to produce a new generation of political leaders from its own ranks. Of the nineteen men and one woman who served in the Eisenhower Cabinet, for example, only three—Fred Seaton, the late Douglas McKay and the late James P. Mitchell—ran for office after serving in Washington, and all three were defeated. Since McKay and Seaton, when appointed to the Cabinet, were that rare exception—professional politicians—it can be said that the President's Cabinet, an ideal proving ground for political leadership, produced in eight years for the Republican party a net gain of one unsuccessful politician.

The other Cabinet members went back to their law firms, their businesses or their pleasures and let the party fall into the hands of the doctrinaire ideologues who gave the Goldwater movement its characteristic and disastrous tone. "The nature of this movement," writes Karl Hess, Goldwater's favorite intellectual companion, "was not organizational. It was ideological." Goldwater, says Hess, did not "even want to run the race if it had to be run according to the advice of the so-called 'professional politician.' " The contempt in that phrase is unmistakable. Within a political party there must be a place of respect for the unalloyed egghead, the man of pure ideas. But the dangers of turning over the party to him while excluding the man whose talents are to translate those ideas into votes is bound to spell defeat, as it did for the Republican party in 1964.

The choice of Ray Bliss to succeed Goldwater's man, Dean Burch, as party chairman signaled the return to organizational politics, for Bliss is the party's most professional "nuts and bolts" organization builder. His program was the exact opposite of an ideological approach. As paraphrased by the New York *Times*'s Tom Wicker, the chairman's advice to Republicans was to "stop worrying about [ideological] position, collect a lot of money, put up as many attractive new faces as [you] can find, advise them all to adapt themselves . . . to the conditions of the local electorates, and run like hell, shouting 'me too' if necessary. That way the Republicans might win back enough offices to make a position mean something."

The advice has been followed, with results that constitute a sort of Republican "revolution of rising expectations." So successful did it prove in 1965, 1966 and 1967 that all elements of the party—from left to right, from East to West, from North to South, from the leaders of the House and Senate to the newest precinct captains—now agree that the criterion for picking the 1968 nominee should be *Can he win?* Even Barry Goldwater's Free Society Association got the message. "Both parties have to offer a candidate who strikes people as electable," it said. "Any challenger, if he's to succeed, has to begin by casting his appeal widely. He has to stick pretty close to the middle of the spectrum. He has to convince, first his own party and then the electorate, that he really is a potential President."

The 1968 aspirants—however much they may dislike it—are going to be judged by their party peers as *politicians,* not as moralists or movie actors, not as men of vast experience or as men of infinite promise, but simply and solely for their capacity to draw votes. The Republicans are looking for a winner, and the scales they are using to weigh the contenders are political.

A Return to Government. The Republicans have been given a direct responsibility for meeting public problems. Republicans are *governing* states where more than half the Americans live, are *running* major cities from New York to Honolulu. As a result, the semipermanent cadre of Republican Congressmen and old-guard state legislators has been forced to yield at least a portion of its monopoly control of party policy. The Republican Governors have acquired a greater sense of identity and of purpose. Their influence, in turn, is beginning to work some changes on the congressional wing of the party. In the 90th Congress, elected in 1966, 116 of 187 Republican Representatives come from states with Republican Governors. House Republicans offered proposals for rehabilitating slums, combating poverty and improving education, some of them more costly than those of the

Democrats, and mounted a major drive for tax-sharing with the states. In the Senate, where the five new Republican Senators included two former Governors and one former state Attorney General, Minority Leader Dirksen has found his flock less submissive to his direction than it had been in the years of Republican decline.

A Return to Reason. The bitter and futile ideological quarrels that racked the Republican party before and during the 1964 campaign have been stilled to a remarkable degree considering how recent was the blood letting. Tempers have cooled; the old antagonists, Goldwater and Rockefeller, have retired to the sidelines of the 1968 struggle, taking with them their angry and unproductive debate about social security, nuclear weapons control and other settled issues. The efforts of the extremist organizations to infiltrate the Republican party are being met, and for the most part successfully, at state and local levels. The issue of "extremism" is unlikely to erupt again.

Not Birchers but intellectuals have been quietly increasing their influence in the Republican party in recent years. Academics have found places on staffs of Republican Governors from Alaska to Florida and in the offices of Republican Senators and Representatives. From outside, the Ripon Society pamphleteers and William Buckley's *National Review* shower the party with programs, criticisms and suggestions. Gradually Republicans are learning to stop shouting and to start reasoning with each other.

Thus, a party that was on the brink of breaking up in dissension, of being discarded by the voters as an irrelevant, quarrelsome nuisance, has been hauled back from the precipice and set on its feet. The real heroes of this rescue operation, in all likelihood, are not the party chairmen, the office holders, the office seekers, but the thousands of *committed* Republican workers in the states, the counties and the cities who would not let their party dissolve. Once again, the genius of America's political system has asserted itself; the historical and institutional forces of party loyalty have proved themselves strong enough to withstand the riptides of emotion, of rigid ideology, and of sectionalism. The Republican elephant has survived its doctors. Perhaps, as someone said, it was "just too dumb to die."

All this is not to say that Republicans have reached the political millennium. Quite obviously, they have not. Not all of them are moving in the same direction; some are still facing determinedly to the rear. Everett McKinley Dirksen, perhaps the most influential man in the party, was still devoting himself in 1967 to calling a constitutional convention for the purpose of overthrowing the principle of equality of representation in state legislatures. The same Dirksen the previous year helped a Senate filibuster kill off the open-housing bill that young House Republicans, led by Maryland's Representative Charles Mathias, had written, thus negating as brillant and constructive a piece of legislative craftsmanship as any American minority party ever performed.

On a whole range of major issues, foreign and domestic, the Republican party remains divided: How far should the United States go in fostering trade with the Soviet Union and the Communist countries of Eastern Europe? What combination of military and diplomatic tactics is most likely to produce peace with honor in the agonizing struggle in Vietnam? How can the United States best contribute to the economic development of the poor nations of the world? What should be our relationship to the Europe governed by the successors of Winston Churchill, Konrad Adenauer and, someday, Charles de Gaulle? Through what mechanisms and under whose direction can the rehabilitation of America's cities be accomplished? How can we close the gap between the "two nations" within our own country—the prosperous predominantly white majority and the poverty-crippled predominantly Negro minority? How can the economy continue to grow without the price of inflation? What equitable method can be found to ease the uncertainties of the draft? These are issues on which the public needs information and discussion. The electorate in our country does not require of the opposition party that it provide answers to every problem, but only that it address itself to the real questions.

The Grand Old Party is quite obviously headed in this direction. Yet there is still a danger that the Republican revival could be overthrown by a candidate who made an emotional and dogmatic appeal to the public's latent anti-politics, anti-government bias.

There is danger, too, though perhaps a less serious one, that Republicans might return to the discredited "Southern strategy" of 1964. What 1964 showed, of course, is that civil rights is not just another issue for Republicans; in the party of Lincoln, it is *the* moral issue, and even a hint of appeasement of racists will quickly provoke a crisis of conscience which the Republican party, with its tradition, cannot compromise. There is room for debate and difference among Republicans about the content of specific measures required to speed desegregation; such differences exist among Romney, Percy and Nixon

LBJ POLL

BURCK

I go pogo

Burck, Chicago **Sun-Times,** Jan. 22, 1967

on open-housing legislation. Reagan, like Goldwater before him, carries the disagreement one step closer to the danger point; he has opposed Federal legislation on civil rights and even sought repeal of a state open-housing law without making it clear how local or voluntary action will meet the demands for racial justice. Most Republicans realize that identification with racist extremism would clearly produce convulsions within the party. The real hazard for both parties is that a more gentlemanly form of racial prejudice will take its place, responding to the anxieties of the white middle-class and upper-class suburbs, North and South, where many of the new generation of voters live.

Moral considerations aside, there is compelling political reason for Republicans to disdain the segregationist vote in 1968; the reason is George Corley Wallace and his intended third-party candidacy. Though Goldwater suggested in a February, 1967, interview that Wallace is less likely to run if the Republicans nominate Nixon than Romney, Wallace's own words offer no evidence that he can be "bought off" again by the character of the Republican nominee, as he was in 1964. "None of the Republicans—Nixon, Reagan, Romney or Percy," he said in 1967, is "talking about reverting back" to his kind of state's rights doctrine, and neither, of course, is Lyndon B. Johnson. "There are plenty of possible candidates that would satisfy me," said Wallace, mentioning "the Alabama Congressmen," Senator Richard B. Russell of Georgia and some other conservative Southern Democrats, "but they're not considered and won't be considered candidates. I just don't have any illusions that one of the national parties will come up with a satisfactory man."

If the Wallace candidacy has the effect of taking several Deep South states out of the arena of two-party competition, as most observers think it would, then Republicans have all the more reason to concentrate their appeal on the constituency that remains—the East; the Midwest; the West; and the "new South" of Florida, Tennessee, Kentucky, Texas, Oklahoma, North Carolina and Virginia, where the party made notable gains in 1966; the farm areas, bubbling with discontent at Democratic policies in 1967; the suburbs; and even the big cities, where Negroes have shown an increasing independence in their voting habits.

What does the Republican party stand for, what does it have to offer the voters of those areas? The answer, of course, is that its detailed program is unformed. The Republican Coordinating Committee has issued white papers on two dozen topics; the platform will contain the usual mass of specific promises; but history shows that, while it may be possible to talk about the program and policy of a government, it is rarely safe to talk about a party's platform as a guarantee of what it will perform in office.

Franklin Roosevelt was elected in 1932 on a vow to reduce Federal spending, but built the Federal bureaucracy to hitherto-unimagined size. Dwight Eisenhower went into office in 1953 pledged by his platform to "repudiate all commitments . . . which aid Communist enslavements" and to end "the negative, futile and immoral policy of 'containment,' " yet settled the Korean War on terms that left the Communists installed where they were when it began, and refrained from aiding the rebellions against Communism in East Germany and Hungary. John Kennedy was elected in 1960 talking about a totally nonexistent "missile gap," and largely unschooled in economics. No one could have predicted that the major accomplishments of his brief service would be the installation of the "new economics" or the long-sought mastery by a civilian management system of that military maze known as the Pentagon.

So one should approach the content of the Republicans' alternative for 1968 with caution, knowing their program—if they are elected—will differ from what they promise. Certain main thrusts or biases are identifiable, however. There is a clear Republican preference for decentralizing the administration of government programs, chiefly by turning back to the states a share of the revenues and authority that now accrue to Washington. The tax-sharing plan, developed by Walter Heller when he was President Johnson's economic adviser but never implemented by the Democrats, now bears a Republican stamp and is the keystone of the G.O.P. approach to domestic problems.

Similarly, there is a bias for expanding the role of business and other private institutions in programs from the reconstruction of the slums (as in Percy's housing bill) to the distribution of foreign aid. All four of the Republican presidential prospects agree that they would propose new Federal programs only as a last resort, preferring private, volunteer, local or state initiative on unsolved problems.

Third, Republicans have (along with many Democrats) an abhorrence of an American ground war on the continent of Asia. Their solutions to the Vietnam conflict, as offered in 1967, were far from uniform; some talked of intensified air and sea attacks, some of new approaches to negotiated settlement, and some of both. But Romney, Reagan, Nixon and Percy—like Eisenhower and Taft on Korea—start from the principle that the United States finds itself in its worst position when an American army is fighting an Asian army in a conventional or guerrilla war on the frontier of Communist Asia. Just how a Republican President would escape the Vietnam "bind" is unpredictable; that he would seek some new course of action to end the long, grinding land war is certain.

Beyond their approach to specific problems, the Republicans offer leadership of two kinds in the presidency. They call themselves "problem solvers," which probably means no more than a willingness to re-examine the processes of government itself, as Reagan is doing with his businessman task forces in California and as Romney did in the Michigan constitutional convention. The Republicans' criticism of the Johnson Administration programs for combating poverty and urban blight are not so much that they are wrong as that they do not get the desired results. Republicans sense correctly an unwillingness on the part of the public to assume that programs formulated in the pattern of the 1930's are necessarily the most effective programs for the 1970's, and thus they talk the language of political pragmatism.

Republicans also talk more often than the Democrats of providing moral leadership. They sense, and again correctly, that the country approaches the decade of the seventies sorely tried, its younger generation experimenting with the "new morality" and the exotic but dangerous delights of drugs, its cities bearing the scars of riots and disorder and crime, its conscience deeply troubled by the contrasts of affluence and poverty in the world, its participation in Vietnam resulting in mounting casualties and sticky questions about our "right" to be there in the first place.

But the task of problem solving, the task of moral leadership is not the task of the platform drafters; it is the responsibility of the men who would be President. For what the impending American election comes down to, ultimately, is not a choice of philosophies but a choice of men.

When the Republican national convention meets in the summer of 1968 there will be 200 million people in the United States, one of whom will become the party's presidential nominee. But the job of narrowing the field to that 1/200,000,000 of the population is not as breath-taking as it may at first seem. For there are constitutional, traditional and political considerations that vastly limit the choice.

The constitution states the President must have reached thirty-five years of age—thus over half the population is immediately ruled out. Now the delegates need only consider 100 million potential applicants. But half of these are women—to date excluded by tradition. Now there are 50 million. Since only 30 percent of the remainder are probably Republicans—and it is rather unlikely that the party would turn to a nonmember—the list has shrunk to 15 million.

Then it is possible to weed out most members of the following groups: Negroes, Jews, people who do not wear a coat and tie to work, Orientals, radicals, people who never went to college, the poor, the old, people whose annual salary is less than $10,000 (the sum Arkansas pays Winthrop Rockefeller, the lowest-paid Governor in the United States).

The list becomes more manageable. Realistically, by category, there remain 25 Republican Governors, 36 Senators (seven excluded because they were born in the nineteenth century), 187 members of the House of Representatives (46 of 47 first termers excluded because of their freshman status), 3 of the 5 ex-presidential nominees, the four Republicans on the Supreme Court (two overage), a big-city Mayor, and a handful of top industrialists, bankers, military men, educators and publishers. Now there are about 200 possibilities of varying degrees of availability, and only modest political sophistication is necessary to further cut the prospects to 25.

Still there are certain fine points in the game that are difficult to grasp, and are, in fact, almost inexplicable. Thomas H. Kuchel has the exact characteristics to be a front-ranked prospect. He is the senior Senator from the most populous state, holds a responsible position in the party's congressional hierarchy, and is of the right age, intelligence and personal attractiveness. Yet, when lists are drawn, he is never on them. The main reason is probably that the list drawers—party activists and newsmen—sense a lack of high ambition in his makeup. Although it has always been fashionable for candidates to pretend that the office seeks the man, the truth is a man has to want to be President. Kuchel does not.

Clearly there are four other Republicans, despite the usual protestations of their profession, who do. And because in the scenario of the politician's "winter book" one of them is likely to be the G.O.P. contender for the office—although it will be many months before his identity becomes known—we have paid special attention to the political chemistry of George Romney, Richard M. Nixon, Ronald Reagan and Charles H. Percy.

For the sake of politicians and journalists—and all others who like to tidy the political scene—the four are pigeonholed into neat, if somewhat inaccurate categories: Romney, left-of-center front runner; Nixon, right-of-center front runner; Reagan, right-of-center backup; Percy, left-of-center backup. Although we have tried to picture them wearing a somewhat fuller plumage of ideology, it is also important in explanation and prediction to recognize that the politicians (who will select the nominee) and the newsmen (who will describe and influence the process) choose to use this convenient shorthand. The perception really may be more significant than the actual fact. If Romney is *thought* a liberal by the delegates to the 1968 Republican convention, this is of more importance in the selection process than the fact that he holds some very conservative views.

The four chief G.O.P. hopefuls are remarkable men. Yet we have dwelled at some length on their flaws. For as aspirants for the nomination they are also flawed men. Indeed, it would be rather surprising if, only four years after the party absorbed a monumental defeat, this was not the case.

In July, 1965, Walter Lippmann ventured the guess that "the Republican recovery will, perforce, have to be led by a new political generation. It will have to be led by men who are modern in their minds and in their spirits and have not burned their fingers with Goldwaterism." In a sense, all four of the 1968 prospects "burned their fingers" in the Goldwater year; yet they have recovered and are trying again.

George Romney, a superb campaigner in his three successful races for public office and an outstanding Governor of a large industrial state, has a limited knowledge of world affairs and difficulty in clarifying his views. His rhetoric is reminiscent of an earlier Republicanism, moralistic, vague and somehow negative.

Richard M. Nixon, the most widely experienced in world affairs of any candidate the G.O.P. could offer, with a quick, logical mind, and the gift of articulation, has a threadbare political image from an overexposure to the electorate and has not measured up to the major challenges of his life—the presidential campaign of 1960 and the gubernatorial campaign of 1962.

Yet Romney and Nixon have an advantage over Percy and Reagan; the former are in the race, their positions as front runners clearly established, their organizations going. Percy and Reagan did not enter public office until January, 1967, which barely gives them time to compile a record to run on. More important, they must contrive to shove the front runners aside before their chance can come. Reagan finds Goldwater, a natural ally, already committed to Nixon; Percy can court Rockefeller, but Rockefeller is publicly pledged to Romney.

The history of recent conventions shows that the prize usually goes to those who get started earliest. Not since 1940 has a late-bloomer won a Republican nomination, and Adlai Stevenson's "draft" by the Democrats in 1952 was more a designation by an outgoing President who had kept the situation fluid until a few months before the convention by silence on his own willingness to seek renomination. Percy may, as his backers say, be a perfect candidate for a "stampede operation," and so may Reagan if either of them can defeat the active contenders, Romney and Nixon, in the wide-open presidential primaries of Wisconsin, Nebraska and Oregon. Reagan, however, has the special disadvantage of being the most conservative of the quartet at a time when the party is still trying to recover from its adventure with Goldwater. As Senator Morton said in an early 1965 interview, the last presidential election "doesn't rule out taking a man from either extreme of the party in the future—but he will have to be someone with more finesse than Barry."

The obstacle course that the American party system has constructed for those who quest after its national nominations makes prediction from a distance of anything greater than ground zero about as unreliable as a television weather forecast. The factors of chance are so formidable: the assassination of a President, the divorce-remarriage of a Governor turned the early outlook on the 1964 nomination struggle upside down. The variables are almost infinite: Will it rain or snow on a major primary election day? Will a candidate have a good night's sleep before a debate? Will he label the wrong person an "opportunist" or blow up in anger at a press conference?

Still, there will be 1,333 delegates to the national convention, the magic number for nomination is 667, and certain general descriptions of the battlefield in the 1968 struggle can be made.

Starting with the front runners, Romney's strategy is to unite the traditional liberal bloc of the East, the power base of his own industrial state, and sizable support from the Mormon West, with the backing of the party's gubernatorial wing, greatly bolstered in numbers and prestige by the 1966 elections. In the summer of 1967, his strategists counted on a base strength of about 270 votes, derived from some or all of the delegates of Alaska, Connecticut, Hawaii,

Idaho, Iowa, Kansas, Michigan, Minnesota, Nevada, New Jersey, New Mexico, Rhode Island, Utah, Vermont, Washington, the District of Columbia, Puerto Rico and the Virgin Islands.

Nixon's strategy is to expand his impressive strength in the South through his allies in Congress and the party organization into the Midwest and West. In mid-1967, his managers counted his base strength as being larger than Romney's, perhaps in the vicinity of 350-360 votes. They were expected to come from Alabama, Arizona, Delaware, Georgia, Louisiana, Mississippi, Missouri, Montana, Nebraska, North Carolina, North Dakota, Oklahoma, South Carolina, Virginia, West Virginia and Wyoming.

Confronting both Romney and Nixon was the possibility that more than 600 delegates—perhaps enough to deny anyone the nomination—might be tied up on the first ballot by favorite-son candidates. Major states with possible favorite sons include California, Florida, Massachusetts, New York, Ohio, Pennsylvania, Tennessee and Texas. At least that many more small states are also contemplating favorite sons.

To budge the favorite-son states into their own column, to captivate a party oriented to "looking for a winner," both Nixon and Romney aim for a sweep of the primaries in New Hampshire, Wisconsin, Nebraska and Oregon. A sweep by either man would, in all likelihood, give him the nomination. It would also bar the door to fall-back candidates Reagan and Percy. In midsummer of 1967, Nixon knew that Reagan would be on the ballot at least in Wisconsin, Nebraska and Oregon; what he did not know was whether he would have an active challenge from the right. Romney kept an equally wary eye on Percy, but Percy gave no hint through July whether he would let his name go into the primaries or not.

Normally, there is some primary contest that proves decisive in settling the nomination for the party out of power. But 1968 may be the exception, and the candidates may arrive at the convention with the issue still in doubt.

Among the possible favorite-son states, New York (with 92 votes), Pennsylvania (64), Massachusetts (34), Maryland (26), Maine (14) and Colorado (18) are inclined to prefer a liberal-to-moderate candidate. Texas (56 votes), Tennessee (28), Florida (34), California (86) and perhaps Arkansas (18) will be inclined to come down on the moderate-to-conservative side.

But if a bargaining situation develops, there is literally no telling what may emerge. James Rhodes of Ohio (58 votes), Everett Dirksen of Illinois (also 58 votes) and Thruston Morton of Kentucky (24 votes) are centrists who will hold high cards when and if the dealing starts. Add in John Tower of Texas, Nelson Rockefeller, Raymond Shafer, Clifford Case and John Volpe, and there are dozens of possible combinations and permutations.

More pertinent probably is an assessment of the early odds on any Republican's beating President Johnson. Romney, according to the 1966 and early 1967 polls, would have the best chance; he was the only one of the four Republican hopefuls in that period who held a lead over the President; Nixon was at or near the break-even point; the lesser-known Percy and Reagan trailed Johnson.

But the polls obviously would change—not only with the public reaction to the President's own performance, but with the ups and downs of the Republican hopefuls as they battled through the primaries and the state conventions.

In terms of "image" contrast, Romney and Percy offer perhaps the best appeal to voters disillusioned with Johnson "the wheeler-dealer." Both have the clean-cut, strong-jawed visages that one associates with the "presidential look." Romney, with white streaks in his hair, fits as the "father figure," if that is what voters want; Percy has the appeal of youth, the only one of the Republican prospects who is identified with the Kennedy generation. Reagan has a Western sort of glamour; like Goldwater, he stirs a partisan audience to greater storms of enthusiasm than either Percy or Romney. But Reagan, like Goldwater, is burdened with a load of ideological positions that might enable Johnson to wage the same sort of "fright" campaign he put on so successfully in 1964.

When it comes to a mastery of the range of issues that are likely to dominate 1968, none of the three men can match Nixon. Percy and Reagan, judging by their state campaigns, have the capacity for intensive homework, skillful speaking and artful handling of press conferences that could enable them to close the headstart Nixon has in this regard. Romney's verbal skills are in doubt; he is the kind of candidate who is likely to be in trouble when he gets away from a prepared text or into a press conference.

Nixon's problem, of course, is that he is not starting fresh but with the visible scars of twenty-some years of partisan warfare. Johnson knows how to campaign against Nixon; he knows, too, that no Republican is so likely to persuade grumbling Democrats that they had better stick with their own man rather than switch to the one they call "Tricky Dick."

In sum, the Republicans do not have an "ideal" candidate for 1968, nor is 1968 necessarily the ideal year in which to be the Republican nominee. A comparable situation, perhaps, existed in 1940—four years after the last previous Republican débacle which resembled that of 1964. In 1940, just as now, the country was nervous and discontented; Europe was at war and it seemed unlikely the United States could avoid being dragged ever deeper into the conflict. The depression lingered, despite the vast increases in Federal spending designed to end it. Franklin D. Roosevelt had lost the support of some of his original Democratic backers—men of power and influence like James A. Farley and Vice-President John Nance Garner. Publicists and intellectuals like Raymond Moley and Stanley High, once with him, now denounced him. Moreover, the Republicans found a ready-made issue in his violation of the two-terms-only tradition. The Republican party, bolstered by the 1938 midterm election gains of eighty seats in the House and six in the Senate (twice as large as those in 1966), mounted a vigorous campaign behind an exciting, attractive new face—Wendell L. Willkie. Willkie drew more votes than any previous Republican candidate for President and still was swamped in the electoral college—449 to 82.

The sobering fact is that only once in its history—in 1888 when Benjamin Harrison opposed Grover Cleveland—has the Republican party been able to defeat an incumbent Democratic President. True, 1968 may be another 1888, but it might also be another 1940.

In another perspective, 1968 is a year of great opportunity for the Republican party, whether it wins the White House or not. The timetable of American politics in both parties was thrown askew by the murder of President Kennedy. Kennedy was the forerunner of a new generation of political leadership. The first President born in the twentieth century, he came to office in 1961 as the youngest elected President, succeeding the oldest man to hold that office. Had Kennedy lived out his likely two terms through 1968, it is probable that both parties would have been forced to put forward men of his own age or younger.

In these terms, Lyndon Johnson is more the representative of a previous political generation, the last of the original New Dealers in politics. Three of the four Republican presidential prospects—all but Percy—are older than Kennedy would be if he had lived. With roots in the small-town Middle West or West, with their rhetoric flavored by an unmistakable nostalgia for the simpler, less sophisticated nation that America will probably never be again, Richard Nixon, George Romney and Ronald Reagan may well be less pivotal figures than part of a transitional period in Republican politics.

It is not without significance that the 1968 Republican vice-presidential prospects—the younger men in the governorships, the Senate and the leadership ranks of the House who have not yet achieved sufficient national stature to run for Pesident—are probably more exciting as a group than the four presidential prospects. And the "third-generation" Republicans—some freshmen and sophomore representatives, the lieutenant governors, attorneys general, secretaries of state and mayors—may have even more appeal.

The Republicans have survived the disaster of 1964. That fact is an achievement worth noting for what it tells of the durability of our two-party system. The Republicans will also survive 1968, no matter what happens in the presidential election. Their real reservoir of talent is well protected. Only nine of their twenty-five Governors face re-election campaigns in 1968; the other sixteen are safe until 1970. There are eight Republican Senators under fifty; not one of them must run again in 1968; in all likelihood, their number will be doubled by the 1968 elections.

The Republicans have a future; they have also been given a clue how to use it, if they will heed it.

When Lyndon Johnson won his landslide victory in 1964, most analysts predicted that the nation was entering another "Era of Good Feeling." The President was the master of consensus politics and he had just been given whopping majorities in both houses of Congress on which to cast his spell. But one writer did not agree. Peter F. Drucker, the brilliant management consultant from New York University, saw the future of domestic politics as dominated by unfamiliar issues, centering on the metropolis and the school, and a new power group. "Whatever the President may want," wrote Drucker in *Harper's,* "the educated young people who make up the professional, technical, and managerial middle classes will force on us new political alignments."

Following Drucker's thesis, the Senate Republican Policy Committee pulled together an impressive compilation of data: By the 1968 presidential election, the average age of our population will have dropped from 33 years to 27 years or less. . . . More than half of our

Peb, Philadelphia **Inquirer,** Nov. 10, 1966

190 million population is now 28 years old or less. . . . This is a young country and growing younger. . . . There are 32 million Americans between 21 and 35. That is more than the number of people who voted for the Republican presidential candidate in 1964.

The nation is not only becoming younger, it is also becoming more urban. . . . Today over 58 million Americans live in the suburbs, a gain of almost 50 percent in the last census decade . . . an 11 percent rise in the central cities and a drop in rural areas and small towns. . . . By 1960, only 11 states had more rural than urban population. . . . America's metropolitan complexes are where three-fourths of all U.S. citizens live today.

The nation is not only becoming younger and more urban, it

is also becoming more educated and more concerned with education. . . . Teachers have become the largest single occupational group in the United States. . . . Fully one half of the young men now reaching adulthood have education beyond high school.

Recorded in these dry statements of fact is a revolution so great that few who are part of it can even comprehend it. Drucker comes closest to a definition when he writes:

> In the decades just ahead, our domestic politics will be dominated by unfamiliar issues—not only new, but different in kind from the things we have been arguing about since 1932. They will be concerned, not primarily with economic matters, but with basic values—moral, aesthetic and philosophical. Moreover, the center of our political stage is now being taken over by a new power group: a professional, technical and managerial middle class—very young, affluent, used to great job security, and highly educated.

In 1968, for the first time, there will be voters in a presidential election who were born *after* World War II, who know Pearl Harbor, Bastogne and Iwo Jima only as musty names in history. In every election from now on, the proportion of voters who have any memory of the Great Depression will be smaller.

The coalitions and the issues of the New Deal that Lyndon Johnson knew and that he still talks of are being displaced. "The politics of distribution," in the useful phrase of Robert Wood, MIT political scientist, is giving way to "the politics of innovation." Instead of "satisfying needs for goods and services, allocating scarce resources, mediating between conflicting classes or ideologies (business and labor, farm and city)," as in the "politics of distribution," the focus of concern in the "politics of innovation" becomes nothing less than "the quality of our national life." Raising minimum wage levels and providing farm price supports are the staples of the old politics; combating pollution, building community colleges and art centers are the staples of the new politics. Gerald Ford, the House Republican leader, was on the right track in his 1967 "Republican State of the Union message," when he kept repeating that "this Administration has revived tired theories of the Thirties," and sees solutions through the "rear-view mirror of the Thirties."

But the question of which party will mobilize the new generation of voters is as yet unsettled. The Democrats are hardly dunderheads, and not all of them are eighty years old either. The same Robert

Wood who was prescient enough to distinguish the "politics of distribution" from the "politics of innovation" came to Washington in 1966 to join Lyndon Johnson's sub-cabinet as Undersecretary of Housing and Urban Development.

Yet there is obvious comfort for the minority party in Samuel Lubell's analysis of "how much easier it has become to shift the party allegiance of the American voter." A major ingredient in the Republicans' battle for the huge new generation of voters will be the appeal of the new faces they can choose to show them. For the "politics of innovation" is also the "politics of identification," a politics in which party labels mean far less than the "integrity" and attractiveness of the individual candidate.

In 1964, while the nation was knocking down the two-party system to one and a half, a little-known Republican engineer Daniel J. Evans was defeating an incumbent Democrat to become the youngest Governor in the history of Washington State. After the election, he was invited to tell the nation's Republican leaders how he did it. (His speech probably earned a place in American political annals by opening, "Oscar Wilde once observed . . .") The Evans prescription was hardly profound: get good candidates, build a sound organization, campaign on meaningful issues, unite. The clue to victory was not in his words but in Evans himself. Thirty-nine years old, handsome, smoothly articulate, Evans did not have the answer; he was the answer.

So was Robert Finch, Nixon's young professional, running for Lieutenant Governor of California with one-tenth of Reagan's money, but outpolling him, perhaps because Finch keyed his campaign to the problems of the "urban environment."

Howard Baker was the answer in Tennessee, John Chafee in Rhode Island, Spiro T. Agnew in Maryland, George Bush in Houston and John Lindsay in New York, and many others around the country. Not just because they were young and handsome. But, more important, because—even though their programs were often fuzzy around the edges—they were directing their attention, in a concerned and compassionate fashion, to the things that really troubled the people.

As the electorate looks to the seventies and beyond, change is the rule and access to power—even the summit of power that is the presidency—will be more wide open than ever before. Ray Bliss caught the cue to this "new politics," showing again what a canny old pro he is. In a speech on the University of Wisconsin campus late in

1966 urging students to join the G.O.P., he said, "We do not demand that you submit to policies already established by leaders of preceding generations. . . . Because the Republican party is the minority," its National Chairman continued, "it has fewer people seeking to advance to positions of leadership. Hence your chances of rising rapidly to a leadership role are not only excellent but certain, if you are qualified."

A party as open to innovation as the party Bliss described; a party as pragmatic in its approach as Nelson Rockefeller or Melvin Laird; a party as tolerant in its dissent as young Mark Hatfield or old George Aiken; a party broad-based enough to elect Edward Brooke and Claude Kirk, John Tower and John Volpe on the same day; such a party can serve the national interest by giving to the American people, not just in 1968 but for years to come, "the luxury of choice."

Appendix A:

REPUBLICAN CONVENTION DELEGATE STRENGTH

1. BY STATE

State	Delegate Appor- tionment 1960	Delegate Appor- tionment 1964	1964 Convention Vote			Delegate Appor- tionment 1968	Current Electoral Votes
			Goldwater	Scranton	Other		
Ala.	22	20	20			26	10
Alaska	6	12		8	4	12	3
Ariz.	14	16	16			16	5
Ark.	16	12	9	2	1	18	6
Calif.	70	86	86			86	40
Colo.	18	18	15	3		18	6
Conn.	22	16	4	12		16	8
Del.	12	12	7	5		12	3
Fla.	26	34	32	2		34	14
Ga.	26	24	22	2		30	12
Hawaii	12	8	4		4	14	4
Idaho	14	14	14			14	4
Ill.	60	58	56		2	58	26
Ind.	32	32	32			26	13
Iowa	26	24	14	10		24	8
Kan.	22	20	18	1	1	20	7
Ky.	26	24	21	3		24	9
La.	26	20	20			26	10
Maine	16	14			14	14	4
Md.	24	20	6	13	1	26	10
Mass.	38	34	5	26	3	34	14
Mich.	46	48	8		40	48	21
Minn.	28	26	8		18	26	10
Miss.	12	13	13			20	7
Mo.	26	24	23	1		24	12
Mont.	14	14	14			14	4
Neb.	18	16	16			16	5
Nev.	12	6	6			12	3
N. H.	14	14		14		8	4
N. J.	38	40	20	20		40	17
N. M.	14	14	14			14	4
N. Y.	96	92	5		87	92	43
N. C.	28	26	26			26	13
N. D.	14	14	7		7	8	4
Ohio	56	58	57		1	58	26
Okla.	22	22	22			22	8
Ore.	18	18			18	18	6
Pa.	70	64	4	60		64	29
R. I.	14	14	3	11		14	4
S. C.	13	16	16			22	8
S. D.	14	14	12	2		14	4
Tenn.	28	28	28			28	11

REPUBLICAN CONVENTION DELEGATE STRENGTH
(*Continued*)

State	Delegate Appor-tionment 1960	Delegate Appor-tionment 1964	1964 Convention Vote			Delegate Appor-tionment 1968	Current Electoral Votes
			Goldwater	Scranton	Other		
Texas	54	56	56	..	..	56	25
Utah	14	14	14	..	..	8	4
Vt.	12	12	3	2	7	12	3
Va.	30	30	29	1	..	24	12
Wash.	24	24	22	1	1	24	9
W. Va.	22	14	10	2	2	14	7
Wisc.	30	30	30	..	..	30	12
Wyo.	12	12	12	..	..	12	3
D. C.	8	9	4	5	..	9	3
P. R.	3	5	..	5	..	5	..
V. I.	1	3	..	3	..	3	..
Totals	1,331	1,308	883	214	211	1,333	538

2. BY REGION

	1952		1960		1964		1968	
East	372*	(30.8%)	386*	(29.0%)	355*	(27.1%)	355*	(26.6%)
South	229	(19.0)	329	(24.7)	325	(24.8)	356	(26.7)
Midwest	372	(30.8)	372	(28.0)	364	(27.8)	352	(26.4)
West	229†	(19.0)	242	(18.2)	256	(19.6)	262	(19.7)
§Totals	1,206		1,331		1,308		1,333	

* Includes Washington, D.C., delegation.
† Includes Alaska and Hawaii, which were not yet states.
§ Adds in Puerto Rico and Virgin Islands to regional totals.

Reprinted by Permission of *Congressional Quarterly*.

Appendix B:

1968 PRESIDENTIAL PRIMARIES SCHEDULE

State*	Primary Date	Filing Deadline	Consent of Presidential Candidate	Type of Primary	Voter Quali-fications†	1964 Republican Results
New Hampshire	March 12	Feb. 1	Not required but may withdraw in 10 days.	Non-binding preference poll; election of delegates who may be pledged to a candidate.	Closed	Lodge (write-in) won 35.5% of vote. Goldwater 22.3%, Rockefeller 21%, Nixon (write-in) 16.8%.
Wisconsin	April 2	Feb. 29	Not required, but may withdraw by Feb. 29.	Preference poll is binding on delegates (chosen by party) for at least one ballot.	Open	Rep. John W. Byrnes ran unopposed as a "favorite son." All delegates supported Goldwater.
Pennsylvania	April 23	Feb. 13	Not required	Non-binding preference poll; election of district delegates who may state willingness to be bound by preference poll; at-large delegates chosen by party committee.	Closed	In write-in preference poll, Scranton won 58.3%, Lodge 21.1%, Nixon 9.7% and Goldwater 8.5%. Of 54 delegates, 52 supported Scranton, 2 were for Goldwater.
Massachusetts	April 30	March 5 (tentative)	New law has yet to be clarified.	Binding preference poll; election of delegates who may express preference on ballot. Delegates are bound to winner of preference poll for one ballot.	Closed	Lodge won 79.3%, Goldwater 10.5% in write-in contest. All delegates supported Lodge except three who favored Goldwater.
District of Columbia	May 7	April 6	Not required	Election of officially unpledged delegate slate.	Closed	9 unpledged delegates elected; on 1st ballot, 4 voted for Goldwater, 5 for Scranton.
Indiana	May 7	March 28	Required	Preference poll which is binding on delegates (chosen by state convention) for one ballot.	Closed	Goldwater won 67%, Stassen 26.8% of preference vote.
Ohio	May 7	Feb. 7	Required	Election of delegates who must be pledged to first and second choice candidates.	Closed	Gov. James A. Rhodes ran as a "favorite son" with no substantial opposition.
Nebraska	May 14	March 15	Not required but may withdraw by March 15	Non-binding preference poll; election of delegates who may be pledged to candidate.	Closed	Goldwater won 49.5%, Nixon (write-in) 31.5%, Lodge (write-in) 16.2%, and Rockefeller (write-in) 1.7%.

1968 PRESIDENTIAL PRIMARIES SCHEDULE
(*Continued*)

State*	Primary Date	Filing Deadline	Consent of Presidential Candidate	Type of Primary	Voter Quali-fications†	1964 Republican Results
West Virginia	May 14	Feb. 3	Required	Non-binding preference poll; election of unpledged delegates. Write-in votes are not permitted.	Closed	Rockefeller ran unopposed. 9 delegates were uncommitted, 3 favored Goldwater, 2 supported Rockefeller.
Oregon	May 28	Mar. 19	Not required; may withdraw.	Binding preference poll; election of delegates who may state preference for candidate on ballot.	Closed	Rockefeller won 33%, Lodge 27.7%, Goldwater 17.6%, Nixon 16.8%, Smith 2.9% and Scranton 2.0%.
Florida	May 28	March 6	Not required	Election of slate of delegates which may be pledged to candidate.	Closed	Goldwater slate won 41.9%, unpledged slate 58.1%. 32 of the 34 unpledged delegates voted for Goldwater on the 1st ballot.
California	June 4	April 5	Required	Election of slate of delegates either pledged to a Presidential candidate or unpledged.	Closed	Goldwater slate won 51.4%, Rockefeller slate 48.6%.
New Jersey	June 4	April 25	Not required but may withdraw.	Non-binding preference poll; election of delegates who may be pledged to candidate.	Closed	In write-in preference poll, Lodge won 40%, Goldwater 24.8%, Nixon 23.2%.
South Dakota	June 4	April 20	Not required	Election of slate of delegates which may be pledged to a candidate.	Closed	Unpledged slate won won 68.1%, Goldwater slate 31.9%.
Illinois	June 11	March 18	Required and may withdraw.	Non-binding preference poll. Election of unpledged district delegates; at-large delegates chosen by state convention.	Closed	Goldwater won 62.0% of preference vote, Sen. Margaret Chase Smith 25.3%.

* In addition, Alabama and New York hold primaries to vote for unpledged convention delegates. Texas election law does not provide for Presidential primaries, but nothing in the law prohibits a political party from distributing an extra primary ballot sheet on which voters could indicate their Presidential preference. Republican state committee has not yet determined whether it will conduct such a preference poll in 1968.

† An open primary is one in which any voter may participate. A closed primary is limited to voters who have established membership in or connection with the party in whose primary they wish to vote.

Reprinted by Permission of *Congressional Quarterly*.

ACKNOWLEDGMENTS

This book is the product of the authors' observations and interviews in all fifty states and the District of Columbia. Many hundreds of people have given to us generously of their time and insights—from our friends in the press to the nation's political leaders and their staffs. While it would be unfair to imply that they are responsible for the judgments we have made, it would be equally misleading to leave the impression that we could have written about so wide-ranging an institution as the Republican party without their help.

No authors with collectively (though not jointly!) two wives and six sons could write a book without the complete cooperation of their families. To Elena Shayne Hess and Ann Collar Broder go our deepest gratitude for encouragement, suggestions, typing, chauffeuring, and arranging our homes in such a way as to make this book possible; while to Charles and James Hess and George, Joshua, Matthew and Michael Broder we owe a very great debt for putting up with fathers who spent so much time behind typewriters—time that by right belonged to them.

Stephen Hess wishes to acknowledge his continuing gratitude to his mentors in Republicanism: Malcolm C. Moos, Bernard L. Lamb and Bryce N. Harlow.

David S. Broder wishes to acknowledge the help and generosity of the four news organizations for whom he has covered American politics: *Congressional Quarterly,* its founders, Nelson and Henrietta Poynter, and its executive editor, Thomas N. Schroth; the Washington *Star,* its editor, Newbold Noyes, Jr., and its assistant managing editor, Charles B. Seib, Jr.; the New York *Times* and its Washington bureau chief, Tom Wicker; the Washington *Post* and publisher Katharine Graham, managing editor Benjamin C. Bradlee and national editor Laurence M. Stern.

We should like to thank, too, Neal R. Peirce, political editor of *Congressional Quarterly,* and his colleagues for regularly providing the most accurate and useful compilation of data on every phase of contemporary politics; Mark Hanna and the library staff of the Washington *Post,* as well as the libraries of the Los Angeles *Times* and the Grand Rapids *Press;* and special thanks to Jan K. Krause, chief political researcher for the national desk of the Washington *Post.*

We gratefully acknowledge having had the benefit of unpublished material from the files of Robert Bendiner, John T. Dempsey, Walter De Vries, Paul S. Green, Thomas Houser, Earl Mazo, Ed Plaut, Duff Reed and Taft B. Schreiber.

Among our personal friends around the country who have generously and systematically provided us with material on politics in their area have been: Audra Carter (Los Angeles), Alan Epstein (Philadelphia), Charles L. Frankel (San Francisco), David Shayne (Chicago), Lawrence Sirovitch (Providence), Sherman Unger (Cincinnati), Clyde Wheeler (Tulsa) and John C. Whitaker (Washington).

The final manuscript was typed with speed and care by Joyce Gray.

And, finally, our deepest thanks to our friend and editor at Harper & Row, Jeannette Hopkins, who has given us unstintingly of her knowledge and perception, a gift of inestimable richness.

STEPHEN HESS
DAVID S. BRODER

Washington, D.C.
July 20, 1967

Bibliography

REPUBLICANS—GENERAL

Broder, David S. "The Struggle for Power," *The Atlantic*, April, 1966.
De Toledano, Ralph. *The Winning Side*. New York: Putnam, 1963.
Donovan, Robert J. *The Future of the Republican Party*. New York: New American Library, 1964.
Gilder, George F., and Bruce K. Chapman. *The Party That Lost Its Head*. New York: Knopf, 1966.
Hess, Karl. *In a Cause That Will Triumph*. Garden City, N.Y.: Doubleday, 1967.
Lubell, Samuel. "Are the Republicans Through?" *Saturday Evening Post*, February 14, 1959.
Moos, Malcolm. *The Republicans*. New York: Random House, 1956.
Novak, Robert D. *The Agony of the G.O.P. 1964*. New York: Macmillan, 1965.
Ripon Society. *From Disaster to Distinction*. New York: Pocket Books, 1966.
Roberts, Steven V. "The Best Republican for '68," *Esquire*, March, 1966.
Schlafly, Phyllis. *A Choice, Not an Echo*. Alton, Ill.: Pere Marquette Press, 1964.
White, F. Clifton, with William J. Gill. *Suite 3505: The Story of the Draft Goldwater Movement*. New Rochelle, N. Y.: Arlington House, 1967.
White, Theodore H. *The Making of the President 1960*. New York: Atheneum, 1961.
———. *The Making of the President 1964*. New York: Atheneum, 1965.

PRESIDENTIAL CONVENTION POLITICS

Bendiner, Robert. *White House Fever*. New York: Harcourt, Brace & World, 1960.
David, Paul T., Ralph M. Goldman and Richard C. Bain. *The Politics of National Party Conventions*. Washington: Brookings, 1960.
David, Paul T., Malcolm Moos and Ralph M. Goldman, editors. *Presidential Nominating Politics in 1952*. 5 vols. Baltimore: Johns Hopkins, 1954.

Moos, Malcolm, and Stephen Hess. *Hats in the Ring.* New York: Random House, 1960.

Wells, John A. *The Voter's Presidential Handbook.* New York: McDowell, Obolensky, 1960.

REGIONAL POLITICS

Broder, David S. "California's Political Free-For-All," *Look,* June 13, 1965.

Ellis, William S. "As New Hampshire Goes, So Goes Who?" *New York Times Magazine,* February 2, 1964.

Heard, Alexander. *A Two-Party South?* Chapel Hill: University of North Carolina, 1952.

Jonas, Frank H., editor. *Western Politics.* Salt Lake City: University of Utah, 1961.

Key, V. O., Jr. *Southern Politics.* New York: Knopf, 1949.

Knebel, Fletcher. "The Changing Face of Southern Politics," *Look,* November 16, 1965.

Lockard, Duane. *New England State Politics.* Princeton: Princeton University, 1959.

Reichley, James. *States in Crisis.* Chapel Hill: University of North Carolina, 1964.

Shannon, William V. "Lindsay, Kennedy, and the Power Struggle in New York," *Harper's,* January, 1966.

RAY C. BLISS

Broder, David S. "Bliss Rides the Elephant," *New York Times Magazine,* March 21, 1965.

Otten, Alan L., and Charles B. Seib. "The Minor Masterpiece of Ray C. Bliss," *The Reporter,* February 10, 1966.

Perry, James M. "For Ray Bliss, The Real Test Now Begins," *National Observer,* February 13, 1967.

EDWARD W. BROOKE

Brooke, Edward W. *The Challenge of Change.* Boston: Little, Brown, 1966.

Sheehan, Edward R. F. "Brooke of Massachusetts," *Harper's,* June, 1964.

Time, February 17, 1967.

EVERETT McKINLEY DIRKSEN

Bagdikian, Ben H. " 'The Oil Can Is Mightier Than the Sword,' " *New York Times Magazine,* March 14, 1965.

O'Neil, Paul. "Grand Old King of the Senate," *Life,* March 26, 1965.
Viorst, Milton. "Honk, Honk, The Marigold," *Esquire,* October, 1966.

GERALD R. FORD, JR.

Oberdorfer, Don. "He Wants to be Speaker of the House," *New York Times Magazine,* April 30, 1967.
West, Virginia. "GOP Congressman Gerald Ford: The Hawk who Ruffles Some Feathers," *Coronet,* June, 1966.

BARRY M. GOLDWATER

Broder, David S. "There's No Radical Change in Goldwater," *New York Times Magazine,* June 19, 1966.
Edwards, Lee. "Barry Goldwater Revisited," *The New Guard,* May, 1966.
Goldwater, Barry. *Where I Stand.* New York: McGraw-Hill, 1964.
Rovere, Richard H. *The Goldwater Caper.* New York: Harcourt, Brace & World, 1965.
Shadegg, Stephen. *What Happened to Goldwater?* New York: Holt, Rinehart & Winston, 1965.

JACOB K. JAVITS

Javits, Jacob K., with James C. G. Conniff. "A Jew in the White House," *Pageant,* December, 1966.
Javits, Jacob K. *Order of Battle.* New York: Atheneum, 1964.
Time, June 24, 1966.
Viorst, Milton. "Could This Jew Be President?" *Esquire,* April, 1966.

JOHN V. LINDSAY

Ajemian, Robert. "He Stirred the Hope That He could Make Things Better," *Life,* November 12, 1965.
Astor, Gerald. "John Lindsay: New GOP Hope," *Look,* April 6, 1965.
Button, Daniel E. *Lindsay, A Man for Tomorrow.* New York: Random House, 1965.
Cabot, Edward S. "John V. Lindsay: A Republican Wins in the City," *Advance,* February, 1961.
Citron, Casper. *John V. Lindsay and the Silk Stocking Story.* New York: Fleet, 1965.
Meehan, Thomas. "A 16-Hour Day with His Honor," *New York Times Magazine,* July 3, 1966.
Parmentel, Noel E. "John V. Lindsay: Less Than Meets the Eye," *Esquire,* October, 1965.

Reeves, Richard. "'A Great Mayor' 'That Bum?'" *New York Times Magazine,* January 1, 1967.

Shannon, William V. "Lindsay—The First Six Months," *New Republic,* July 16, 1966.

Weaver, Warren, Jr. "Big Gamble of John Vliet Lindsay," *New York Times Magazine,* May 23, 1965.

RICHARD M. NIXON

Alsop, Stewart. *Nixon and Rockefeller.* Garden City, N.Y.: Doubleday, 1960.

Bird, John. "Will He or Won't He?" *Saturday Evening Post,* March 17, 1964.

De Toledano, Ralph. *Nixon.* New York: Duell, Sloan & Pearce, 1960.

Donovan, Robert J. "Over-Nominated, Under-Elected, Still a Promising Candidate," *New York Times Magazine,* April 25, 1965.

Evans, Rowland, and Robert Novak. "The Unmaking of a President," *Esquire,* November, 1964.

Harris, Mark. *Mark the Glove Boy or The Last Days of Richard Nixon.* New York: Macmillan, 1964.

Kornitzer, Bela. *The Real Nixon.* Chicago: Rand McNally, 1960.

Mazo, Earl. *Richard Nixon.* Harper, 1959.

Nixon, Richard M. *Six Crises.* Garden City, N.Y.: Doubleday, 1962.

Witcover, Jules. "Nixon for President in '68?" *Saturday Evening Post,* February 25, 1967.

CHARLES H. PERCY

Furlong, William Barry. "How Faith Helped Charles Percy's Family Face Tragedy," *Good Housekeeping,* February, 1967.

Goldwin, Robert A., editor. *Percy of Illinois.* Chicago: Robinson Associates, 1964.

Higdon, Hal. "The Boy Wonder of Illinois Politics," *The Reporter,* May 7, 1964.

Mandino, Og. "The Chuck Percy Story: A Promise Is a Promise," *Success Unlimited,* October, 1966.

Percy, Charles H. "The Republican Future," *Saturday Review,* October 29, 1966.

Perry, James M. "Percy Declares . . ." *National Observer,* December 20, 1965.

Time, September 18, 1964.

Trombley, William. "New Challenger to the Kennedy Clan," *Saturday Evening Post,* September 28, 1963.

U.S. News & World Report, March 6, 1967.

RONALD REAGAN

Edwards, Lee. "The Republican More Like JFK Than Any Other," *The New Guard,* February, 1966.

————. "Why Californians Look to Ronald Reagan," *Human Events,* February 19, 1966.

Langguth, Jack. "Political Fun and Games in California," *New York Times Magazine,* October 16, 1966.

Litwak, Leo E. "The Ronald Reagan Story; Or, Tom Sawyer Enters Politics," *New York Times Magazine,* November 14, 1965.

Mitford, Jessica. "Ronald Reagan: Will the Man Who's Right Be Left Behind?" *Coronet,* June, 1966.

Murray, Jim. "Ronald Reagan to the Rescue!" *Esquire,* February, 1966.

Newsweek, May 22, 1967.

Oulahan, Richard, and William Lambert. "The Real Ronald Reagan Stands Up," *Life,* January 21, 1966.

Phelan, James. "Can Reagan Win California?" *Saturday Evening Post,* June 4, 1966.

Reagan, Ronald, with Richard G. Hubler. *Where's the Rest of Me?* New York: Duell, Sloan & Pearce, 1965.

Shearer, Harry. "Brown vs. Reagan: Into the Stretch," *Los Angeles Times West Magazine,* October 23, 1966.

Time, October 7, 1966.

NELSON A. ROCKEFELLER

Alsop, Stewart. "The Rockefeller Nobody Knows," *Saturday Evening Post,* July 25, 1959.

Astor, Gerald. "Rocky's Roughest Round," *Look,* October 18, 1966.

Gervasi, Frank. *The Real Rockefeller.* New York: Atheneum, 1964.

Morris, Joe Alex. *Nelson Rockefeller.* New York: Harper, 1960.

Perry, James M. "Nelson Rockefeller's Last Hurrah," *National Observer,* January 9, 1967.

Weaver, Warren, Jr. "Political Evolution of Nelson Rockefeller," *New York Times Magazine,* February 16, 1964.

GEORGE ROMNEY

Ferry, C. A. "George Romney Gone Bust," *New Republic,* January 25, 1964.

Fischer, John. "George Romney: Brightest Horse in the Stable," *Harper's,* March, 1962.

Fuller, Richard C. *George Romney and Michigan.* New York: Vantage, 1966.

Harrison, Selig S. "Romney and the Republicans," *New Republic,* March 5, 1962.

Havemann, Ernest. "The George Romney Family: All Aboard for the White House!" *Ladies' Home Journal,* October, 1966.

Hessler, William H. "New Face in American Politics," *The Reporter,* March 1, 1962.

Jones, David R. "This Republican for 1968?" *New York Times Magazine,* February 28, 1965.

Knebel, Fletcher. "George Romney: Why the Republican Pros Distrust Him," *Look,* March 10, 1964.

Mahoney, Tom. *The Story of George Romney.* New York: Harper, 1960.

Romney, Lenore, as told to Earl Mazo. "My Husband, George Romney," *Good Housekeeping,* June, 1962.

Shannon, William V. "George Romney: Holy and Hopeful," *Harper's,* February, 1967.

WILLIAM W. SCRANTON

Bird, John. "Bill Scranton, A Reluctant Candidate," *Saturday Evening Post,* January 18, 1964.

Ehrich, Henry. "Governor Scranton: Is He Really Reluctant?" *Look,* March 10, 1964.

Kraft, Joseph. "Interview with Governor Scranton," *Harper's,* July, 1964.

Welsh, James. "Portrait of a Not-So-Dark Horse," *New York Times Magazine,* January 12, 1964.

ROBERT TAFT, JR.

Armstrong, Richard. "A New Taft and a Young Kennedy Go to Washington," *Saturday Evening Post,* January 19, 1963.

Broder, David S. "48 Freshmen Build Their Fences," *New York Times Magazine,* December 12, 1965.

Hessler, William H. "Taft vs. Kennedy in Ohio," *The Reporter,* October 25, 1962.

Index

429